AF654179

Social Movements in Tribal India

Social Movements in Tribal India

Editor

S.N. CHAUDHARY

RAWAT PUBLICATIONS

Jaipur • New Delhi • Bangalore • Guwahati • Kolkata

ISBN 978-81-316-0763-3

© Contributors, 2016

No part of this book may be reproduced or transmitted in any form or by any means, electronic or mechanical, including photocopying, recording or by any information storage and retrieval system, without permission in writing from the publishers.

Published by
Prem Rawat for **Rawat Publications**
Satyam Apts, Sector 3, Jawahar Nagar, Jaipur 302 004 (India)
Phone: 0141 265 1748 / 7006 Fax: 0141 265 1748
E-mail: info@rawatbooks.com
Website: www.rawatbooks.com

New Delhi Office
4858/24, Ansari Road, Daryaganj, New Delhi 110 002
Phone: 011 2326 3290

Also at *Bangalore, Guwahati* and *Kolkata*

Typeset by Rawat Computers, Jaipur
Printed at Chaman Enterprises, New Delhi

Contents

Preface

The history of social movements in tribal areas of the country in general and in the states of Central India in particular is very old. Historical records reveal that during British and even during pre-British days number of social movements in tribal inhabited areas took place. Most of these movements were local and largely reformative in character. These movements had interaction with and support of outside forces in an insignificant manner. But as interaction of tribals with outside forces, culture and tradition increased, the nature, magnitude and intensity of social movements also increased. In contrary to the past, gradually these movements shifted from the issue of social transformation in their culture and lifestyle to their dignity, honour, human rights and so on. In the due course of time again with the increasing amount of interaction with unequal forces the nature and roots of social movements became diverse. Environment, displacement, poor rehabilitation package, erosion of human rights particularly by the state and its machinery alongwith market forces and investors, since the beginning of globalization in 1991, became very common. As a result, the local movements are now no more local in terms of its organization, style of functioning and issues raised. Some of these movements are violent and some are non-violent. Some are temporal and issue specific and some are, since long, diverse in nature. Electronic media and civil society organizations are providing significant space to these movements, both at the local level and at national and international level. Hence, the support base, either passive or active, of these movements have substantially increased during last couple of decades. In many cases these movements have either halted, slowed or forced the change agents to rethink on the model of development introduced in tribal areas as well as interests of tribal masses particularly with reference to *jal, jungle* and *zamin.* But in many cases these movements are incapable to influence policies relating to an introduction of mega projects in tribal areas and its implementation. All these development projects as well as various social movements have impacted tribal culture and tradition in multiple ways.

What are the historical roots and methods of these social movements? How these movements are seeking strength from outside forces? How these movements have impacted culture and quality of life of local people and societies? How state and other change agents are responding to these social movements? What shall be the nature of interface between ongoing model of development and human rights and identity of tribal masses? These are some of the pertinent issues and to discuss all these issues, a two-day (21–22 March 2014) national seminar was organized by Rajiv Gandhi Chair in Contemporary Studies, Barkatullah University, Bhopal. Scholars and activists from across the country participated in the seminar. In order to hold the seminar in a successful manner, ICSSR, New Delhi, was kind enough to sanction partial grant. I am extremely thankful to ICSSR, New Delhi, and its concerned officials for their gesture.

We received active support and cooperation from different persons. Vice-Chancellor of Barkatullah University was kind enough to provide all logistic support. Prof. K.L. Sharma, Ex-Vice Chancellor, Rajasthan University, Jaipur, delivered keynote address. Prof. R.S. Kureel, Director General, Dr B.R. Ambedkar National Institute of Social Sciences, Mhow graced the inaugural function as the chief guest. Prof. M.N. Karna, Ex-Director, A.N. Sinha Institute of Social Studies, Patna, and Prof. K. Gopal Iyer, Chandigarh, delivered Rajiv Gandhi Memorial Lecture. I am personally obliged and thankful to all of them for their help and cooperation.

Many scholars presented research articles in the technical sessions of the seminar. Important among them are Prof. Y.S. Sisodia, Prof. D.K. Verma, Mr Rahul Banerjee, Prof. S. Maiti, Dr R. Rajesh, Dr Sudhir Singh, Prof. R.D. Singh, Dr D. Debnath, Dr T.K. Dalapati, Prof. Parmanand Singh, Prof. Ravi P. Bhatia, Dr Tapan Mohanty, Dr R.S. Shrivastava, Dr Krishna Gopal, Prof. D.C. Sah, Dr S. Prabhakar and others. I am extremely thankful to all of them. Although many articles were submitted for publication in the present volume but it was not possible to include all these articles. This book covers only 15 articles. I am thankful to all contributors.

Last but not the least, I am thankful to research scholars and other staff working in Rajiv Gandhi Chair in Contemporary Studies not only for their continuous support to hold the seminar and also for their direct and indirect cooperation and support in editing this volume.

S.N. Chaudhary

Contributors

D.C. Sah, Emeritus Professor, Madhya Pradesh Institute of Social Science Research, Ujjain, Email: dc_sah@yahoo.co.uk

Debashis Debnath, Faculty of Sociology and Community Development, Indian Institute of Forest Management, Bhopal, Madhya Pradesh, Email: ddebnathster@gmail.com

Jaya Phookan, Research Officer, Women Studies Department, Barkatullah University, Bhopal, Email: jayakav78@yahoo.co.in

K. Gopal Iyer, Professor (Retd.), Panjab University, Chandigarh, Email: iyergopal1942@gmail.com

M.N. Karna, Professor (Retd.) & Ex-Director, A.N. Sinha Institute of Social Studies, Patna, Email: mahendrakarna@gmail.com

Mita Sarkar (Das), Visva-Bharati, Shantiniketan (WB), Email: mitasarkardas@gmail.com

R.K. Mohanty, Reader in Sociology, BPSPA, Bhubaneswar, Odisha, Email: rabisir@gmail.com

Rahul Banerjee, Social Activists, Dhas Gramin Vikas Kendra, 74, Krishnodayanagar, Khandwa Naka, Indore, Email: rahul.indauri@gmail.com

Ravi P. Bhatia, Independent Educationist and Peace Researcher, Retired Professor, Delhi University, Delhi, Email: ravipbhatia@gmail.com

S.N. Chaudhary, Rajiv Gandhi Chair Professor, Rajiv Gandhi Chair in Contemporary Studies, Barkatullah University, Bhopal, Email: rajivchairbpl@rediffmail.com

S.N. Tripathy, Professor, Ghokle Institute of Economic and Politics, Pune, Email: sn_tripathy2004@yahoo.com

Subhrendu Maiti, Activist, Howrah, West Bengal.

Swapan Kumar Kolay, Associate Professor & Head, School of Anthropology & Tribal Studies, Bastar University, Jagdalpur, Chhattisgarh, Email: kolay.swapan@gmail.com

Tapas Kumar Dalapati, Assistant Professor, Madhya Pradesh Institute of Social Science Research, Ujjian, Email: tapas273@gmail.com

Y.G. Joshi, Emeritus Professor, Madhya Pradesh Institute of Social Science Research, Ujjain, Email: ygjoshi15@yahoo.co.in

1

Introduction

S.N. CHAUDHARY

Once upon a time local ecology and environment played a crucial role in the construction and sustainance of indigenous knowledge, cultural practices, traits, attributes of civilization and so on among the relatively geographically isolated tribes of the country. Self-constructed local culture which was based on day-to-day practical experience was indispensable in their life. It solved their problems and sustained their lives for centuries. Role of youth organization, totem, taboos, shifting cultivation, local gods and goddess, festivals and many other social institutions and cultural practices were vital in their life. Most of the tribes were economically self-sustaining, non-monetized and culturally homogeneous. According to Dungdung (2013: 3) 'In the ancient period the Adivasis had ownership rights on the natural resources and they judiciously used these resources for their survival. Consequently, the Adivasis were living with autonomy, peace and prosperity. They were freely practicing their identity, tradition, culture, religion and language'. But on different heredity and environment based attributes tribes were also heterogeneous. In spite of spacial isolation there were a number of tribal kings and rulers who had linkage with the outside world. Hence, sociologically tribal society was not completely closed and isolated. The amount of interaction between tribes and non-tribal culture and tradition was limited up to the establishment of the Hindu rule in tribal areas, and as the frequency of interaction between tribes and non-tribal rule and culture increased, the amount of autonomy enjoyed by tribes gradually began decreasing. For instance, with the establishment of the Maratha rule in Madhya Pradesh the situation changed in a significant manner in the life of tribes. They were neither in need of nor habituated to farm work. But the Maratha rule was in need of revenue in the form of foodgrain. When they realized that local tribals were not interested in settled farm work they invited agricultural castes like Jats and Patidars from neighbouring states to promote deforestation and initiate farm work. And with this the practice of shifting cultivation was discouraged. Number of examples of similar nature may be cited from states like present Jharkhand and Odisha (Das Gupta, 2013). This development led to serious conflict between tribes and the alien forces in different pockets in Central India (Manohar, 2001). It had its serious negative impact on health status of forests, tribal culture and other components of environment which in turn negatively affected quality of life of tribal masses.

British administration perceived forest and other resources available in forest in a commodified manner. They believed in the prevalent dominant thinking that maximum exploitation of natural resources, with the help of modern technology, can lead to progress in human society. Material advancement became dominant sign of development. No attempts were made to underline social and cultural cost of technological modernization particularly on host societies and communities. British administration and its agenda of action perceived natural objects like forest, mountain, river, etc. as natural resources. This thinking led to enactment of different forest related laws which benefitted the British administration and fastened the ongoing process of ruinization of natural resources, and thereby pauperization among tribal masses, which was originally initiated by the Hindu kings like the Maratha rule in tribal areas of Madhya Pradesh. Accordingly, different forest related Acts and policies were passed by the British administration. Important among these are Forest Act of 1865, Forest Act of 1878, Forest Policy of 1894 and Forest Act of 1927. All these efforts increased deforestation and minimized tribal access to and control over forest and related resources. Their rights were changed into concession. This development negatively affected tribes in multiple ways.[1] Immediately after Independence the first National Forest Policy was enacted in 1952 but it was simply the replica of the acts and policies passed during the British period. With the help of all these acts and policies, including the Forest Policy of 1952, the state attempted to establish its hegemony on natural resources which in turn weakened symbiotic relations between tribes and natural resources particularly *jal, jungle* and *zamin*. These initiatives made every effort to promote timber rush at the cost of minimum basic needs and requirements of tribes. This development was dysfunctional for tribals in multiple ways which forced Elwin (1943) to coin a term 'Loss of Nerve' for them in order to refer to the pitiable social and economic condition of tribes. This phrase clearly depicts that once upon a time tribals had nerve but due to acculturation with outsiders they lost their nerve or what may be called identity and heritage. There are different articles in this volume which cover all these issues.

After realizing pitiable and decreasing socio-economic status of tribes, efforts have been made to restore their human rights by different change agents since Independence. Number of constitutional provisions have been made,[2] National Commission for SCs and STs was established and from time to time a number of welfare schemes have been formulated by the state; however, it is observed that most of these efforts were formulated without taking serious note of the grass-roots level tribal social reality. Most of these efforts lacked depth, direction, sensitivity and connectivity. Schemes were formulated like unconnected railway compartments. The same situation prevailed at the implementation level. The implementing agencies were accountable to their boss but they were not at all accountable to the unorganized and unassertive tribal masses. Formality prevailed over the tribal social reality which is informal and tradition ridden. The result was insignificant relief to tribes. Geographical isolation, absence of social capital and near absence of transportation and communication network encouraged tribes to remain excluded and isolated. Insignificant presence of push and pull factors and slow population growth also encouraged them to remain confined to their native places. However, over the time as per the desire of and in the wider interest of alien forces, tribal interaction with non-tribal world increased. And with this, pauperization and marginalization of tribes became fast and it continued increasing which in turn made them victims of acculturation. Tribes could not regulate ongoing acculturation with unequal partners, particularly Hindu culture, as per their cultural heritage.

Number of NGOs, addressing tribal concerns, have increased since Independence. Some of these organizations are located in tribal areas and some are found outside the tribal areas. Some NGOs are stationed in big cities and they claim that they are engaged in tribal development. Many of these NGOs are engaged in so-called capacity building work and some are putting question mark on the functioning of the state particularly in the tribal areas. Some are issue specific and some are working in the holistic manner. If we examine achievements of these institutions, particularly from human rights and development of tribes, the picture is largely frustrating. These efforts could not arrest marginalization. Only few tribes belonging to dominant categories and living around growth centres could achieve some relief. But how and to what extent these success stories are sustainable?

Literature on tribal studies reveal that local reputational leaders have played crucial role in the mitigation of problems faced by tribes since long. Tribals used to share problems and opportunities among themselves. The notion of 'we feeling' or 'live and let live' regulated their life. Village headman was the custodian of custom and tradition responsible for the peaceful functioning of socio-cultural institutions. But, with the introduction of institutional leadership and political institutions, the situation began changing in the opposite direction. The formal tribal leaders became accountable not to tribes but to their boss. They imitated alien ways of life. They became agents of change and development as per the wishes of the state. Many of them popularized corruption and red-tapism in tribal areas. Gradually some of them became powerful with having distinct ways of life which culturally made them outsider in their homeland. They promoted assimilation rather than integration and inclusion. There are examples to prove that in spite of innovative character of number of tribal development schemes the result is not upto the mark and in many cases frustrating primarily because all the implementing agents, including, Panchayat and Block level tribal elites and tribal dominated institutions are insensitive to tribal concerns. Many of these leaders are individualistic. Many emerging tribal leaders have imitated the culture of non-tribal established elites. The delivery mechanism is full of errors. Hence, inclusion of tribes in the development process remained at the distant place.

So far as tribal culture is concerned, whether it is material or non-material, it is rapidly losing its relevance today. Culture worked as crisis management mechanism till the establishment of Hindu rule.[3] Nobody can undermine role and importance of indigenous knowledge system in tribal areas.[4] But gradually tribal culture lost its problem solving character. Today, tribes are living in between their own and alien culture. Their dependence on alien culture is increasing day-by-day. Tribal youths are the immediate victim of cultural disintegration. Many elements of their indigenous culture is today almost dead. Many new opportunities have been created by the state and development projects have been initiated within and around tribal areas. But for want of essential requirements alien culture is still not their own culture and therefore all the alien culture based benefits, say for example, English language, modern medicine, modern education, modern money management mechanisms, modern means of transportation and communication systems, modern ways to interact with police, court and change and welfare agents etc. are far away from them. They have largely failed to avail benefits of modernization and development. Rather, in many cases, many of them are the victims of modernization and development (Chaudhary et al., 2013).

Globalization formally came to India in July 1991. Immediately after its introduction, tribal areas were logistically identified as proper places for investment and establishment of mega-development projects. Over the time, hundreds of such projects have been established in these areas. Thousands of tribes have been displaced from their native place without any proper rehabilitation. Rehabilitation policies and schemes are faulty. It is neither just nor humanistic from tribals' point of view. Due to near absence of voice against displacement and near silence on various uncalled for issues, including exploitation, industrial houses prefer to install their projects in tribal areas.

Because locals, particularly tribals, are not critical on environmental issues, displacement and rehabilitation package, the investment agencies seldom hesitate to violate environment and rehabilitation laws. It has a lot of negative social, economic, psychological and environmental consequences. And the immediate victims of this process are local tribals. It is true that hundreds of jobs of various types have been created in tribal areas by investors but in most of the cases only non-tribal specialists and workers are recruited. It has its serious demographic and cultural consequences. Tribes are becoming numerically inferior in their own homeland. And the state is either silent or siding with the investors in the so-called national interest. Under the given situation one can simply imagine about the state of human rights, culture and dignity of tribes (Chaudhary, 2013).

In the recent past, the concept of Corporate Social Responsibility (CSR) has become popular in the country. State has made it mandatory for factories, mines etc. to practice the guidelines of CSR. But how CSR can address the question of environmental degradation and poverty created by corporate houses themselves? How it can properly deal with different components of environmental degradation such as loss of bio-diversity, climate change, unregulated population growth, water pollution, deforestation, land degradation, desertification and so on? Critically speaking the notion of CSR is a myth. It is anti-tribal and anti-tribal ecological setting. It has miserably failed to address even those problems for the emergence of which these organizations are largely responsible.

In many pockets, particularly in the states of Jharkhand, Odisha, Chhattisgarh and Madhya Pradesh, the cases of seasonal out-migration have rapidly increased during the last couple of decades. In most of the cases, migration is informal and to urban areas, without any capacity building for the migrants in the formal and structured manner as per requirements of new occupations and new destinations. Push and pull factors created by modernization and capitalistic mode of production are responsible for seasonal migration. Expansion of consumer culture is now contributing to migration. However, studies reveal that this mechanism is also not capable enough to free tribals from the trauma of poverty and deprivation. Contrary to this, these migrants are now the victims of consumerism. As a result, whatever they earn they are incapable to save and invest. Studies prove that if income is increasing the cases of indebtedness is also increasing (Chaudhary, 2014). Their expenditure pattern is now highly influenced by alien culture. The increasing number of modern household assets in many tribal households support this argument (Chaudhary, 2012). The culture of imitation has increased the amount of tension and frustration in the life of many tribals.

During last few decades tribes of Central India, particularly in the states of Jharkhand, Odisha, Chhattisgarh and Madhya Pradesh, where large number of tribes are found, are experiencing different social movements. A number of articles included in this volume cover different issues relating to such movements. Primarily these movements are in favour of their human rights. Narmada Bachao Andolan and related ecological movements are addressing environmental question. Naxalite movement is also going on. It is also for proper rehabilitation of the victims of what Padel (2013) called 'investment induced displacement'. It is directed to the question of human rights and dignity of tribes. Neither of these two set of movements are separatist in nature. Both are primarily addressing the fundamental question that tribes should be allowed to lead a peaceful and dignified life. Their human rights must be restored. They are the original custodian of *jal, jungle* and *zamin* (Water, Forest and Land) and they should be handed over these things. But the alien forces, including the state, are completely against this proposition. Rather, efforts are being made to keep them far away from natural resources. But these movements are incapable of providing any relief to the tribes. In principle, naxalism stands for justice but it is massively engaged in retaliation. There are examples to prove that many tribes are equally tortured by the police and the so-called naxalites. In many pockets tribals cannot lead a natural and peaceful life. They have either to side with the police and administration and in this situation they are tortured by naxalites and their supporters or they have to live with the naxalites and in this case they are humiliated by the police and other agencies.

Partly in response to these movements and partly due to globalization, a number of experiments have been made by the state for the so-called welfare of tribes during the last two decades. These are the provisions of the Panchayats (Extension to the Scheduled Areas) Act-1996 (PESA), the Scheduled Tribes and Other Traditional Forest Dweller (Recognition of Forests Rights) Act-2006, New Panchayat Raj System, Mahatma Gandhi National Rural Employment Guarantee Scheme, Rehabilitation Policy, Land Acquisition Act, Food Security Act, etc. All these initiatives have miserably failed to restore their human rights and dignity. High illiteracy rate, increasing sex ratio, high dropout rate, poor quality of education, high mortality rate, maximum dependence on primary sources for their livelihood, decreasing number of agricultural farmers and increasing number of wage earners, their near absence in technical education, increasing cases of indebtedness, increasing seasonal migration, trafficking, land alienation, availability of primitive tribal groups even after several decades of their declaration and number of interventions etc. are sufficient enough to draw a conclusion that like the state, initiative made by civil societies, local culture, migration and CSR are not upto the mark.

According to the Annual Report of Ministry of Tribal Affairs (2007–08: 118) some of the factors and conditions responsible for the pitiable condition of Scheduled Tribes are 'the low capacity of the tribal economy, poor infrastructure in tribal and scheduled areas, lack of private enterprise and public-private partnership in tribal areas which can create employment, faulty processes of declaring forest leading to insecurity of tenure, and fear of eviction, gradual extinguishment of traditional rights and ownership of uplands going out of tribal possession, developmental activities leading to displacement, forced eviction from their lands and natural habitats, and reluctance of most state governments to make laws and rules that confirm to the spirit of the PESA Act'.

One of the important reasons not underlined by the Ministry is near absence of regulated voice of protest against the processes and agencies responsible for breaking down of symbiotic relationship between tribes and the local environment.[5] There are historical evidences to prove that local tribals and local environment have been regulated by the alien forces i.e. ideology, culture and governance mechanism. However, chapters of this book are mainly devoted to collective voice of protest or social movements going on in some of the tribal areas of the country in the historical perspective. The important questions addressed in the book are: Why all these movements have arisen? What are the historical and contemporary roots of these movements? How nation-state and its different institutions have responded to these movements? What is the nature and type of interface between civil societies and social movements in tribal areas? How these movements have been able to shape and re-shape the ongoing model and process of development? What are the perceptions of locals and non-locals about these movements? What are the gains and pains of these movements from the point of view of social justice, human rights and development of tribes? How these movements have addressed environment related questions? What is the future of these movements in an era of globalization and expansion of market forces and individualism? What are the perceptions and reactions of the ever increasing and expanding middle class of this country in relation to tribes, their plights and the status of natural resources? How these movements have operated and legitimized its presence at both local and macro level in an era of globalization? How these movements obtain, spread and retain its support base? How a meaningful dialogue is possible between the state, local tribes, civil societies and industrial houses in the wider interest of nation, locals, particularly tribals, industrial houses as well as components of ecology and environment under the existing socio-political context which are both functional and dysfunctional from democracy, social justice, ecological balance and human rights point of view?

II

The volume covers 15 articles. Most of the articles are empirical and field based. These articles are inter-disciplinary in nature. However, some articles are by and large conceptual and theoretical in orientation. Some articles are historical and cross-cultural and some are based on contemporary facts and statistics. Some are highly local and regional in nature and some depicts national scenario.

M.N. Karna, based on his rich experience of the north-eastern region, presented the brief profile of the north-eastern region and then moved to the structure, bases, causes, process and consequences of social movements in North-East India. He opined that crisis in the North-East is one of the conflicts between ethnicity and nationalism, a matter ultimately of identities and allegiances. He emphasized that the North-East has a culture of movement as aspirations of the people of the North-East region have not been seriously addressed by the state and other change agents.

K. Gopal Iyer, in his paper, dealt with the conceptual dimension of social movements. He underlined reasons behind the origin and continuity of forest based movements of Adivasis during colonial and post colonial period, especially in the context of present Jharkhand state, which have deep environmental and identity concerns. These movements resisted structural changes and its militant character has also been instrumental in promoting structural changes. He further highlighted the characteristics and conditions for successful forest based movements in India during colonial period and factors that sustained forest based movements during post colonial period. He emphasized that forest based movements, as a tribal movement, are still continuing which have influenced policy related to forest and one of the outcomes is Forest Right Act-2006.

D.C. Sah, in his paper, traced the historical as well as contemporary processes that marginalized the Barela tribe living in the hilly tracks of South-Western zone of Madhya Pradesh. He analysed the contemporary tribal struggles which are taking place in the region and the process of continuity and change in the tribal South-Western Madhya Pradesh. He emphasized that how political insurgency and alien intervention during the British rule marginalized people of these areas and how government intervention, in the name of development, displaced and deprived tribals from their habitation and resources which resulted into unrest and upsurge in most part of tribal areas. He also highlighted that control and encroachment over forest has brought civil society institutions in front to play role in movement like Adivasi Mukti Sangathan and Narmada Bachao Andolan.

S.N. Tripathy, in his paper, highlighted factors responsible for the emergence and continuation of tribal movements in India with special reference to Odisha and the policy measures required for the development of tribes and their economy. He delineated the nature and consequences of early tribal movements and contemporary tribal movements in Odisha and raised the issues of plight of displaced tribals as a result of industrialization. He urged that intensity of problems in tribal areas calls for an urgency in reviewing the causes of tribal unrest and movements, the need to reorganize our policies with regard to indigenous communities.

Y.G. Joshi analysed the issue of contradiction between natural resources and development which is a key issue for contemporary unrest in tribal areas of Madhya Pradesh. The resource rich Fifth Schedule Areas have not been able to link themselves to mainstream economy to take real advantage of their natural resources, but on the contrary, they are being pushed to disadvantaged position due to this linkage. Thus, on one hand there is a process of draining off resources of tribal areas to already rich and prosperous areas and, on the other hand, the resultant fall out of the negative impact of the development process in terms of environmental degradation and impoverishment. The paper highlighted dimensions of inverse relationship of resources and development which is the root of the discontent of local population.

S.N. Chaudhary, in his paper, delineates the history of dispossession, emergence of protest movements and institutional mechanisms to question the degeneration as well as to repair the fractured state of affair with reference to tribal masses of Central India. In his paper, he described the richness of tribal culture and their cordial relationship with local ecology and environment and the impact of environmental degradation. He also examined the process and consequences of the establishment of mega-development projects on tribal economy, livelihood and their culture. Against this backdrop, he examined some of the social and ecological movements going on in tribal regions to address plights and miseries of tribes and regions resided by tribes. He discussed various movements in his paper like Narmada Bachao Andolan, Kalinganagar Movement (Odisha), Lanjigarh Movement, etc. Some of the institutional steps taken during the era of globalization, particularly for the restoration of human rights and dignity of tribes have also been examined.

Ravi P. Bhatia, in his paper on 'Sustaining the Environment: The Adivasi Way', emphasized that development paradigm has to be tailored in such a fashion that it should not result in large scale destruction of the environment and dislocation of millions of Adivasis from their natural habitats. The Adivasis have been living in harmony and in close relationship with nature. For them, environment was a living entity that provided them with sustenance and livelihood and in turn that needed to be protected from pollution and degradation. The construction of dams, mining in tribal areas and encroachment in forest leads to resentment and protests by tribals. He pointed out how methods used by Adivasis can be used to improve their condition without affecting the environment.

R.K. Mohanty, in his paper, highlighted that how contemporary movements in Odisha are the outcome of 4Ds that is – discrimination, deprivation, dispossession and of late development induced displacement. His paper looked into the four Ds suffered by the tribals due to the historic conditions. He gave the brief overview of the five mining and industrial projects in Odisha which have severely threatened their community, life and living. Different movements emerged in the state because of these 4Ds like Kalinganagar Movement, Anti-POSCO Movement, Narayanpatna Movement, Kashipur Movement and their core issues have been discussed.

Rahul Banerjee, in his paper, highlighted how Bhil Adivasi mass organization in Western India under the ageis of Adivasi Ekta Parishad (AEP) have developed an innovative new tool of development in the form of cultural rejuvenation. The Bhil Adivasis along with AEP conserved and rejuvenated their traditionally rich cultural heritage to forge a new assertive identity for themselves to help them negotiate the complex social, economic and political milieu of modern liberal democracy and have, in the process, developed an equitable and sustainable development.

Debashis Debnath, in his paper, highlighted that in historical records violent protest against British invasion and intrusion of outside exploiters were reported among tribals where they claimed on their rights on their own land and also worked on the protection of bio-resources. He explored that how the persistence of conversation ethos and sub-nationalistic ethnicity among tribal converted into self-initiated forest protection since 1960s which led to several environmental movements at micro and macro levels and the new pro-poor and pro-people forest policy in 1988 in response to which participatory forestry also commenced.

Swapan Kumar Kolay highlighted the issue of left-wing extremist in PESA area, its causes and consequences where he pointed out that although PESA has been implemented in tribal areas but these regions where Maoism existed are under the grip of security forces. The local administration is unable to discharge their duties for welfare and development of the tribal communities. Tribes are struggling between the left extremists and the government, especially by militarization of PESA areas which is affecting the development of the area and tribes inhabiting the area.

Tapas Kumar Dalapati, in his paper, attempted to understand the structure of marginalization in tribal areas operating at the socio-cultural, economic and political level over the ages. The paper tried to understand the root cause of various tribal assertions in South-Western region of Odisha where he analysed the assertions of Kondh, save Indravati Movement, No-Tea Movement in Thuamul-Rampur, save Niyamgiri Movement from pre-colonial days to the ongoing neo liberal phase of development. He highlighted that whenever ruler/state tried to disturb the existing social relations of the people in the process of production, distribution, and consumption of the material resources in Kondh dominated area, they have resented incursions of unwanted exploiters in their territory but Kondhs have been still struggling hard for ensuring their livelihood because of the state laws.

Subhrendu Maiti, in his paper which is based on the cases of three police station namely Naxalbari in Darjeeling, Debra and Gopiballavpur of Midnapur in West Bengal, highlighted various stages of Naxalite Movements in West Bengal and agrarian unrest and clashes in these areas in which the Naxalite Movement of 1967–71 took almost a revolutionary shape, and by its impact, compelled both central and the state governments to take certain basic land reforms measures to pacify the agitated peasantry including tribals.

Mita Sarkar (Das) looked into the history of tribal struggle in the context of Surguja District of Chhattisgarh and highlighted tribal movements which have been launched in the region. To her these struggles have always revolved around the issue of autonomy specially with regard to access to natural resources–*jal* (water), *jungle* (forest) and *zamin* (land). After reviewing the history of the region in brief, she discussed the origin of forest *satyagraha*, post-Independence struggle for autonomy, Naxalite Movement in Chhattisgarh, role of industrial houses and development projects.

Jaya Phookan, in her paper, explored the emergence of forest conflicts in India, related movements and impact of these movements in bringing about changes in the forest policies. She highlighted that the history of forest governance in India is replete with the conflicts between traditional forest users and decades of colonial legacy of command and control forestry. When we speak of contemporary social movements, then environment based conflicts which revolve around competing claim for forests have increased in frequency and intensity in India since 1970s. These conflicts generated movement struggling for rights of the victim of ecological degradation which not only challenged the meaning, notion and patterns of development but also forced some notable changes in forest policy and Acts.

Notes

1. According to Hutton (1931) 'Far from being of immediate benefit to the primitive tribes, the establishment of British Rule in India did most of them much more harm than good .... It may be said that the early days of British Administration did very great detriment to the economic position of tribes through ignorance and neglect of their rights and customs ... . Many changes have been caused incidentally by the penetration of the tribal country, the opening up of communications, the protection of forests and the establishments of the school, to say nothing of the openings given in this way to Christian Missions. Many of the results of these changes have caused acute discomfort to the tribes.' According to Ghurye (1999) also, 'The acuteness of discomfort was very often so great that it led to apathy, indifference, moral deterioration and even a decline in population.'
2. These are protective provisions (Article, 15, 16, 19, 23, 29, 46, 164, 330, 332, 335, 338, 339, 342 and 371), development related provisions (Article, 15, 16, 19, 46, 275 and 399), administrative provisions in the 6th schedule (NE States) areas (Article, 344, 338 and 339) and reservation facility (Article, 330, 332, 334, 335 and 340).
3. According to Srivastava (2008), 'Tribes have themselves done a lot for their own improvement, they have led movements for environment protection,

saving their cultural and human rights, throwing the exploiters out of their territories, regaining rights over their lost land and other resources, closing liquor shops in their area, curbing practices of conspicuous consumption and putting a full stop to all those practices that reduce their respect in the eyes of others.'

4. In the tribal societies of Central India in particular, through their unwritten indigenous knowledge, tribals use medicinal plants, roots and herbs, etc. to cure the disease. They have their traditional mechanisms of collection of non-wood forest products, its processing, storage and marketing. They have their traditional mechanism to overcome the problem of snake bite and cleaning and ploughing, harvesting, house-making, well-digging, accident, unwanted pregnancy and so on. The two fundamental components of civilization, i.e. religion and language, have made their culture powerful in historical perspective. The tribals with natural objects as their totems have preserved natural balance over the time (Chaudhary and Singh, 2006).
5. According to Guha (2011), in spite of intervention by the state and civil societies condition of tribal masses could not improve. Rather, many of them became chronically poor due to following reasons: (1) They are historically residing in the resource rich areas which have drawn attention of investors and industrialists to establish mega-development projects as per their choice and condition, (2) tribals failed to produce a fighter like Dr B.R. Ambedkar for their cause, (3) they are geographically scattered here and there and they are not the solid vote-bank for the political parties, (4) tribal students of non-North-East areas largely failed to join high level bureaucracy to work as role models and effective change agents, (5) their indigenous knowledge system is not used in the complex domain to ensure their say in the formal sector, (6) except Santhali language, no other tribal language is recognized. Hence, tribal languages are not a medium of instructions in the schools and colleges, (7) many parts of tribal areas are conflict prone since the last few decades. It has a negative impact on development projects, and (8) modern media is neither fair nor friendly to their cause. Until and unless these issues are honestly addressed by all the stakeholders, the protection, development and empowerment of tribals is not possible.

References

Chaudhary, S.N. (2012), *In Search of Sustainable Development: Scenario in a Tribal Village of Madhya Pradesh*, New Delhi: Serials.

——(2014), *Tribal Indebtedness*, New Delhi: Serials.

Chaudhary, S.N. (ed.) (2010), *Tribal Economy at Crossroads*, Jaipur: Rawat Publications.

——(2013), *Globalisation, National Development and Tribal Identity*, Jaipur: Rawat Publications.

Chaudhary, S.N., M. Mishra and M. Sharma (2013), *Adivasi Gramo Me Tikau Vikas Ka Yathartha*, New Delhi: Concept.

Chaudhary, S.N. and R.P. Singh (2006), *Tribes of Panchmarhi Biosphere Reserve and Their Indigenous Knowledge*, Bhopal: Indira Gandhi Rashtriya Manav Sangrahalaya.

Das Gupta, Sanjukta (2013), *Adivasis and the Raj: Socio-economic Transition of the Hos, 1820–1932*, New Delhi: Orient Blackswan.

Dungdung, G. (2013), *Whose Country is it Anyway?: Untold Stories of the Indigenous Peoples of India*, Kolkata: Adivaani.

Elwin, V. (1943), *The Aboriginals*, Bombay: Oxford University Press.

Ghurye, G.S. (1999), *The Scheduled Tribes*, Bombay: Popular (Second Edition).

Government of India (2007–08), *Annual Report*, New Delhi: Ministry of Tribal Affairs.

Guha, R. (2011), 'Apni Trasdion Se Azadi Ke Intezar Me Adivasi', *Dainik Bhaskar*, Daily Newspaper, Bhopal, 15 August.

Hutton, J.H. (1931), *Census of India*, Delhi: Gain.

Manohar, D. (2001), *Bagh Ke Bacche Hai Ham (We are the Children of the Tiger)*, Hosangabad: Disha Samvad.

Padel, Felix (2013), 'Tribal Identity and Real Development in a Rapidly Globalising World', in S.N. Chaudhary (ed.), *Globalisation, National Development and Tribal Identity*, Jaipur: Rawat Publications, pp. 23–36.

Srivastava, V.K. (2008), 'Concept of "Tribe" in the Draft National Tribal Policy', *Economic and Political Weekly*, Vol. XLIII, No. 50, December 13, p. 35.

2

Socio-Economic Bases of Social Movements in the Tribal Areas of North-East India

M.N. KARNA

I am doubly honoured to have been invited to speak in the series of Rajiv Gandhi Memorial Lectures organized by the Rajiv Gandhi Chair in Contemporary Studies, Barktullah University. First, very eminent people have participated in the series before me and second, it is an honour to give a lecture in the memory of one of the most distinguished contemporary political leaders of the country. The very choice of the subject that I have selected for the occasion – Socio-Economic Bases of Social Movements in the Tribal Areas of North-East India (Seminar, 1990; Aggarwal, 1999; Karna, 1998; Karna, 2006; Bose, 1990) – gives me an opportunity not only to pay tribute to the great leader we are honouring today who sacrificed his life for sensitizing the contemporary globalized world to respect human rights and for modernizing national ethos for social justice but it also allows me to revisit the issues of movements in the context of the increasing crisis being faced by the tribal communities in India today. However, my focus primarily will be on the north-eastern region, the area dominated by a large number of tribal communities and it is one area on which I am able to talk more confidently.

I have divided my paper broadly into two parts. While the first section is devoted to the ethnographic profile of the region, the causes, processes and consequences of social movements have been discussed in the second part.

Change is a social fact, and so is conflict. Conflict is a universal and general process located in every society be it a highly integrated community or a pluralistic group. As such, every social system develops its own mechanism to resolve conflicts. Nonetheless, the structural contradictions in these social groups often become so much controlling and the available mechanisms so deficient in accommodating change and transformation in resolving tension and conflicts that a strong longing is felt for remodelling the system among those who become conscious and sensitive to such contradictions. Under the condition, the conscious and enlightened groups embark on organizing themselves around certain ideals and ideas with a programme of action for effecting change in the existing system. Such a process of organization gives rise to a movement.

Movements assume different character and may endorse different strategy to fulfil their aims and objectives. It is because of this several types of movements have been identified by the sociologists in India. Rao (1984) classifies movements into three broader types – reform, transformation and revolution. Reform movements may be identified with partial changes in the value system and consequential changes in the quality of relationships. In contrast, transformative movements aim at bringing about middle-level structural changes in the traditional distribution of power. Revolution, on the other hand, is associated with radical changes in the totality of the social and cultural systems. The need to classify movements by changes they intend to bring about has been advocated by Mukherjee. Based on this criterion Mukherjee (1984) suggests three divisions – social movements, revolutionary movements and quasi movements. Any collective mobilization for action directed explicitly towards ... transformation of the structure of a system can be properly understood as a social movement. When the collective mobilization aims at effecting wide-ranging and far reaching changes in the major institutional changes comprising the whole society, we can rightly term it a revolutionary movement. Collective mobilizations aimed at changes within a system are quasi-movements. T.K. Oommen's (1977) typology is based on the process of movement crystallization, the life-cycle and the phases of social movements. For him, movements are charismatic, ideological and organizational.

It is apparent from the above that there is a considerable agreement among sociologists on two basic elements of social movements – collective mobilization and change orientation. However, if sustainability as a process is taken as a crucial factor in a movement, two other distinct elements, ideology and organization, become equally significant. An appropriate and mannerly understanding of social movement, thus, must incorporate and assimilate all these crucial components.

Before I come to discuss the basic issues and elements embedded in the origin, processes and strategy of social movements in the tribal areas of the north-eastern region, it is appropriate here to briefly present profiles of various sub regions of our concern.

The North-East India stands out for its unique ethnic, cultural, linguistic and religious diversity not to be found in any other region of the country. A large number of Scheduled Tribes with different religions, with one-fourth of all languages and dialects spoken in the country and the strong impact of the topographical features on identity formation have multiplied the heterogeneous composition of this region. The ethnic heterogeneity of the region unfolds a complexity based on distinctive historical experiences. Out of the Seven sisters states, as many as four – Arunachal Pradesh, Meghalaya, Mizoram and Nagaland – are not only tribal majority states, but their culture and economy have features remarkably different from the tribal pockets elsewhere in the country. The three other units – Assam, Manipur and Tripura – have a majority of non-tribal plains population but even in these states the tribal population is substantially more than the national average. However, the similarity among the seven states in terms of numerical strength of ethnic groups does not reflect uniformity with regard to their socio-economic settings and the levels of economic development.

Compared to other parts of the country the colonial incorporation of the North-East started much later. While Manipur and Tripura were independent principalities maintaining relations with the British since the late eighteenth century, the colonial ruler annexed Assam in 1826 and subsequently the Naga, Mizo, Khasi, Jaintia and Garo Hills. The North-East frontier area came under its control in the second half of the nineteenth century. Thus, under the colonial dispensation certain areas were either ‘excluded’ or ‘partially excluded’ from the purview of the then prevailing administrative and statutory controls, allowing the people to maintain their customary control over land and forests. However, an attempt was simultaneously made to utilize the natural resources by establishing links with the process operating outside the region. Further, the extension of the market links, introduction of money, entry of government officials, traders, moneylenders and shopkeepers created a situation under which vested interest from the outside could grab land through alienation and control. The plains, primarily inhabited by non-tribals, were brought under revenue arrangements that were prevailing in other parts of the British India, while the tribal dominated hill areas remained under the customary land systems.

Thus, by the middle of the nineteenth century, a substantial area of the North-East came under the overall control of the colonial authority but no strong linkages were established with the outside market, except in the case of tea plantation. That being the case, the regional economy remained out of the orbit of the capitalist path and the people continued to lead a life of relative independence, the problem of poverty and destitution notwithstanding. Thus, given the context of agrarian social structure and localized traditional political authority and administration, it is not difficult to ascertain why a vast majority of tribals in the North-East could substantially protect their control over land, preserve their dialects, sustain their democratic character of social and political organization unlike tribal communities elsewhere in the country.

My contention is that the phenomena of identity and consciousness, apprehension about the impending crisis and awareness and mindfulness with regard to the nature of their solution are rooted in the history of the social structural reality and the nature of the socio-economic development of the area. The nature and extent of mobilization among the various communities for achieving certain aims and objectives has not only been articulated in the context of emerging factors and forces emanating from outside but it is also strengthened and consolidated by the complexion and disposition of the community concerned. It is essentially because the dominant mode of agricultural practice in tribal areas, characterized by swidden cultivation coupled with a feeble link with the emerging capitalist penetration, as indicated earlier, restricted the transformation of the internal dynamics of tribal social settings. The robust ties of kinship, the communitarian control of land and the associated social networks provided a solid base for building ethnic identity, political unity, economic independence and emotional bond among the people. The relative absence of differentiation within the community has historically been the foundation on which cohesion and group identity could survive making self-help and community sentiment functional to the community.

Thus, it is not difficult to suggest that multiplicity of culture, material existence, economic life, historical experiences along with the phenomenal intra-spatial variation in the form of dense forest, high hills and narrow valleys have contributed in keeping people confined to their territorial, local and parochial imperatives. This context provided a congenial and sympathetic locale for mobilizing people at the level of individual community and launching movements across the group.

My attempt so far has been to present the context and historical background of the region of our concern. Now, it is appropriate to talk about the nature and essence, issues and aims and strategy and design of the movements.

In course of the foregoing discussion, I have already indicated the multiethnic nature of the region. Interestingly, the people outside the North-East are hardly aware of the complex nature of ethnic and cultural moorings of this area. By now it is apparent that this situation has given rise to various shades of movements often popularized by different names in different areas of the region. Broadly speaking, the north-eastern region has a culture of movement and almost every unit (state) has experienced one or the other type of movement. Although the various movements witnessed in the region have maintained strong discernible differences in their forms, timings, areas of influence, ideological orientation and mass base, yet these have maintained a strong underlying unity in their content and socio-economic roots. In the process, both the analysts and researchers from outside the region as well as several critical insiders have labelled them differently. While some are known as nationality movements, the same have also been called as insurgency. Similarly, some mobilizations are described in terms of ethnic and identity movements and others as revivalist. What is being highlighted here is that interpretations of the situation of social, cultural, economic and political reality suffer in their use of theoretical and conceptual models. While some social scientists, particularly from the academia, tend and use formal and explicit models, many others, primarily historians, have structured their descriptions of the groups and the communities in the region in terms of the categories popularly used in the Indian nation-building discourse. Others use Gramscian concepts of historic bloc and hegemony, whereas some Marxian scholars analyse the awakening in terms of explanatory narratives around the notion of modes of production and class struggle. However, my attempt here has been to undertake the exercise empirically and intuitively empathizing with their issues and concerns leaving my analytical models implicit.

As the time and space do not permit me to talk in some more detail about the movement scenario found in all the different states of the North-East, I just present the context and factors succinctly which have facilitated the growth and enlargement of various movements which I have taken the liberty to include under the umbrella of social movement.

Most part of the present day North-East was included in the province of Assam. The North Eastern Frontier Agency (NEFA) was also there which is the present state of Arunachal Pradesh but for the purpose of defence it was under the control of the Foreign Ministry of the Government of India. Assam was first reorganized into autonomous units of Nagaland, Meghalaya and Mizoram, and in course of time North-East incorporated within its nomenclature Tripura, Manipur and Arunachal Pradesh (The state of Sikkim has also been included in the region recently but for historical reasons we have not talked about it in the present discussion). Just to refresh our memory, the Naga Hills and the Tuensang Tracts became Nagaland, the United Khasi and Jaintia Hills along with Garo Hills districts were included in the state of Meghalaya, and the Lushai Hills district became Mizoram. Although these states have geographical continuity but even a casual look at these societies distinctly reveal their differences in terms of economic advancement, cultural attainments, social and occupational mobility and most importantly in terms of their perception of *Indianness*. However, most of the tribal dominated areas have negative perception about the Indian 'nation' not to the same degree about the Indian 'state'. This is clearly manifested in various nationality movements, most of the time expressed as secessionism. The articulation of the Naga issue in terms of nation and the demand for Naga sovereignty is the oldest movement which has taken different turns at various stages of the north-eastern history. It was the Naga National Council formed in 1946 which has been spearheading the demand for a separate sovereign Naga nation. Our objective here is not to dwell upon the Naga tangle in detail but it is just to indicate how ethnic identity is also used as a political resource. Similarly, in Mizoram, the Mizo-National Famine Front formed on 2 October 1961 under the leadership of Pu (Late) Laldenga gave birth to the Mizo National Front (MNF) on 12 October 1962. The MNF spearheaded the demand for a sovereign Greater Mizoram. It was supposed to be organized on ethnic lines. Another model of secessionist demand was, of late, witnessed in Assam when the United Liberation Front of Assam (ULFA), a by-product of the Assam movement launched in 1979, propagated the idea of Assamese nation outside India. In fact, the All Assam Students Union (AASU), the Asom Gan Parishad (AGP) and the ULFA are manifestations of the single political ideology representing Assamese sub-nationalism. However, there is no real threat to the Indian state from the Assamese secessionism. Its primary purpose is to put pressure to snatch more concessions from the Centre.

Besides these three different models of movements, the contemporary designs of people's mobilization for change have commonly assumed shapes of movements found in other parts of the country. Women's movement, youth movement, educational movement and the religious movement are some such movements which have attracted the attention of the social scientists from the region and so also from outside the North-East.

It is now apt to identify and examine the forces and factors giving rise to these movements and processes and strategy adopted to achieve their objectives. My frame of analysis mainly includes three dimensions – political, economic and cultural.

The problems and crisis witnessed in the North-East in the wake of extra-constitutional movements which I include under political domain should be defined in terms of identity and/or ideology. It is suggested that the crises in the North-East is one of conflict between ethnicity and nationalism, a matter ultimately of identities and allegiances. It is a common knowledge that whenever problems of the North-East are brought in the debate with regard to the political aspirations of the people, the bounds of the debate are determined by the concepts such as national integration, national unity and the Indian Constitution. Mrinal Miri (1999) captures this situation very appropriately in these words: 'As very little debate is possible outside these bounds, movements for 'Independence' very quickly turn into armed struggles or insurgencies. The official Indian response to this is an armed solution, whether in the shape of considerable army operation … and police action of various degrees of intensity. A factor which, perhaps, contributes towards a violent expression of aspirations for political independence is the absence of a language native to a community in terms of which to generate a complex, nuanced, authentic imagination of the idea of freedom … . The official stance on these movements has, more often than not, been reactive rather than responsive – more like reflex actions than something informed by intelligence, sensitivity, care and concern.'

The economy of the North-East is another dimension which requires our attention. One does not require to be an economist to say that the economy of the region is stagnant. The nature of the developmental strategy adopted in the tribal areas of the North-East has to be brought into the debate to anslyse the various movements of the region. In fact, problems such as tribal and non-tribal conflicts, direct secessionist demands based on the assertion of ethnic identity and demands for further reorganization of the states, are all intertwined in the continuing backwardness and under development of the region. Dominance of non-tribals in trade and commerce, preponderance of non-tribals in modern occupations and professions and continuing influx of people from outside the country continue to be central issue frequently assuming the form of communal tension. It should not be missed that the never ending danger of inflow from the neighbouring countries has perpetually caused tremendous fear. Naturally, the demand for deportation of infiltrators that started with the foreign nationals was subsequently applied even to those who came to this area from other parts of the country.

Another explanation for the problem of the North-East concerns burgeoning employment situation in the region to which agricultural stagnation also is to have a contribution.

About cultural issues, the idea of mainstream is no longer very popular. Pluralism and not 'unity-in-diversity' seems now to be the central theoretical idea in terms of which we are to try and make sense of the cultural predicament of the North-East. How is the inter-cultural contact at all possible? Is cultural solipsism the necessary consequence of the serious acceptance of the idea of pluralism? What really constitutes the integrity and identity of a culture? What does it really mean to respect, to be generous to, or love another culture? These are deep philosophical and sociological questions to which there are no easy answers.

The occasion does not permit me to go into the subject further in greater detail. However, I would like to emphasize that disparities in the socio-economic development inevitably result in political fragmentation. Emerging regional elites and newly formed middle class tend to utilize the existing conflict potential for more share in power. Under the circumstances, dividing rather than compromising elements become the primary means of agitation towards this goal. Regional political parties and groups emerge to mobilize large sections of population on issues appropriate to common cultural, linguistic, ethnic and economic interests in their states. They add to the bargaining power to the states and communities which provide more strength to the periphery in bringing about a balance between the Union and the states. Prevailing situation in the northeast corresponds to this pattern. The growing social tension generated by various movements alone does not essentially endanger the stability of the society. So long the state is capable of balancing the disparities by arranging a socially durable distribution of national wealth and adopts democratic ethos in its policy formulation, conflict and militancy can be contained.

References

Karna, M.N. (1999), 'Ethnic Identity and Socio-Economic Processes in North-East India', in Kailash S. Aggarwal (ed.), *Dynamics of Identity and Intergroup Relations in North East India,* Simla: Indian Institute of Advances Study, pp. 29–38.

——(1990), 'Aspects of Tribal Development in North-Eastern India', in Ashish Bose et al. (ed.), *Tribal Democracy and Development in North-East India,* Delhi: B.R. Publishing Corporation, pp. 7–23.

——(1998), 'Perspectives in the Study of Social Movements', in M.N. Karan (ed.) *Social Movements in North-East India,* New Delhi: Indus Publishing Company, pp. 17–24.

——(2006), 'Introduction', in M.N. Karna (ed.) *Democracy, Pluralism and Conflict,* Jaipur: Rawat Publications, pp. 1–16.

——(1990), 'The Agrarian Scene', *Seminar No. 366,* (The North (East), pp. 30–38.

Miri, Mirinal (1999), 'India's North-East and North-East's India', in Kailash S. Aggarwal (ed.), *Dyanamics of Identity and Intergroup Relations in North-East India,* Simla: Indian Institute of Advanced Study, p. 15.

Mukherjee, P.N. (1984), 'Naxalbari Movement and the Peasant Revolt in North Bengal', in M.S.A. Rao (ed.), *Social Movements in India,* Delhi: Monohar Publications, p. 18.

Oommen, T.K. (1977), 'Sociological Issues in the Analysis of Social Movements in Independent India', *Sociological Bulletin,* vol. 26, No. 1, p. 16.

Rao, M.S.A. (ed.) (1984), *Social Movement in India,* Delhi: Manohar Publication.

3

Forest Based Movement in India During the Colonial and Post Colonial Period

K. GOPAL IYER

This paper is an attempt to understand the reasons behind the origin and continuity of Forest Based Movements of Adivasis during colonial and post colonial period, which have deep environmental and identity concerns. Some of the relevant questions in this regard are:

1. What are the characteristics and conditions for successful Forest Based Movements in India, during colonial period?
2. What are the factors that sustained Forest Based Movements during the post colonial period and continue to persist today?

The total forest area in India consists of 7,74,740 (sq km) which is 23.57 per cent of the entire geographical area. The mandate is to have one-third of the total geographical area under forest cover but we are at least short by 10 per cent. However, there are some states which have more than one-third area under forest, prominent among them being Arunachal Pradesh, Chhattisgarh, Himachal Pradesh, Odisha, etc. The states like Jharkhand (29.51%) and Madhya Pradesh (30.01%) have also substantial area under forest (State of Forest Report, 2003). Most of the area covered under forest is habited by Adivasis and this is also the area bestowed with mineral deposits. The states with majority Scheduled Tribe population (more that 80%) are Meghalaya, Mizoram, Lakshadweep and Nagaland; there are some states in

Central India where the ST population is between 20 per cent to over 30 per cent of the total population of their respective states – these are Chhattisgarh, Jharkhand, Madhya Pradesh and Odisha; some of the north eastern states like Manipur, Sikkim and Tripura have over one-third of the total population as scheduled tribe (Census of India, 2011). The overall literacy rate of the Scheduled Tribe at all India level is 61.60 per cent but there is a gender gap of nearly 18 per cent between male (70.70%) and female (52.10%) literacy. The literacy rate of tribals in Chhattisgarh, Jharkhand, Madhya Pradesh and Odisha are 66.9 per cent, 54.6 per cent, 56.9 per cent and 52.2 per cent. In all the four states, the gender gap in male/female literacy are 16.5 per cent, 21.4 per cent, 17.8 per cent and 19.8 per cent, respectively. They are one of the poorest sections in the country with 47.10 per cent population below poverty line in rural area and 28.80 per cent in urban area. The percentage of people below poverty line in the four states of Chhattisgarh, Jharkhand, Madhya Pradesh and Odisha are 39.93 per cent, 36.96 per cent, 31.65 per cent and 32.59 per cent respectively. As per the latest Agriculture Census data for 2005–06, around 3.6 per cent of them are land less, 67 per cent are marginal farmers, 14 per cent are small farmers and 5 per cent are medium and large farmers. It may be stated that most of the agriculture lands are hilly and hence less productive.

Social Movement Defined

Charles Tilly (1984) defines social movements as a series of contentious performances, displays and campaigns by which ordinary people make collective claims on others. For Tilly, social movements are a major vehicle for ordinary people's participation in public politics. Sidney Tarrow (1998) defines a social movement as collective challenges to elites, authorities, other groups or cultural codes by people with common purposes and solidarity in sustained interactions with elites, opponents and authorities.

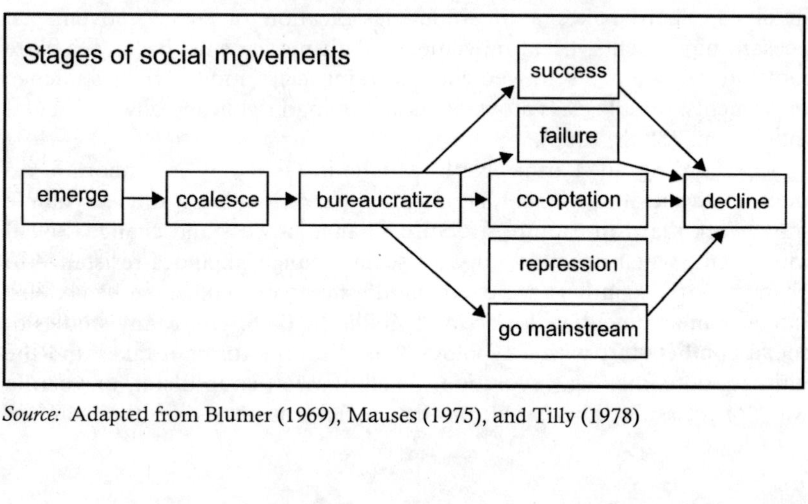

Source: Adapted from Blumer (1969), Mauses (1975), and Tilly (1978)

Social movements can be aimed at change on an individual level or change on a broader, group or even societal level. Social movements can also advocate for minor changes.

Social movements can be viewed as collective enterprises to establish a new order of life. They have their inception in the condition of unrest, and derive their motive power on one hand from dissatisfaction with the current form of life, and on the other hand, from wishes and hopes for a new scheme or system of living. One reason for the diversity of feminism is the fact that the women's movement is a potentially transformational social movement and, thus, draws supporters with a range of different agendas. The movement is transformational in the sense that it engages both a broad range of issues and a set of issues that can deeply affect the daily experiences of an individual's life. What this 'agenda' entails is nothing less than the reformulation of public life, the educational sphere, the workplace, and the home – that is, a total transformation of society (Kornhauser, 1959).

Mass movements mobilize people who are alienated from the ongoing system, who, do not believe in the legitimacy of the established order, and who therefore, are ready to engage in efforts to destroy it. (Turner and Killian, 1972). The greatest number of people available to mass movement will be found in those sections of society that have the fewest ties to the social order. Rather than seeing social movements as expressions of extremism, violence, and deprivation, they are better defined as collective challenges, based on common purposes and social solidarities, in sustained interaction with elites, opponents, and authorities.

Social movements primarily take the form of non-institutionalized collective political action which strive for political and/or social change. While India has witnessed many such movements over the centuries, it is only recently that scholars have begun to study them in depth. On the basis of the socio-economic characteristics of participants and the issues involved, Shah makes a nine-fold classification of social movements: peasant movements, tribal movements, dalit movements, backward caste movements, women's movements, working class movements, students' movements, middle class movements and human rights and environmental movements (Shah, 2004).

According to Partha Nath Mukherji (1988) it is important to inter-relate social movement, conflict and change within a single dynamic framework that can capture structure, change process and change. Social movement, when it has to do with social change, includes resistance to change. Social conflicts are overt manifestations of collective behaviour, rather than as potentials for action (Mukherji, 1986: 26). Many studies of social conflict start with a typology 'based on the forms it takes and the ultimate outcome, e.g. revolution, rebellion, riot, coup d'etat, or guerilla war, or classification based on the social categories of the war, or classification based on the social categories of the participants and social institutions primarily affected, e.g. peasant rebellion, political conflict or economic conflict' (Oberschall, 1973: 32; emphasis added). Tilly's conceptualization of social movements; or movements fall within the categories 'old' and 'new'; even revolutionary movements. *Only when social/collective movement's/mobilizations* emanate from sources of perceived, real or imagined, antagonistic relationships embedded in the contradictions within the social system would they qualify as social movements. Contradiction and conflict are the key concepts in this scheme of analysis.

Social movements that seek to or are instrumental in bringing about alternative changes in the social system by creation of additional structure/s or elimination of structure/s are structural-alternative social movements. The addition or elimination of structure/s in some way alters the social system. For example, a feudal agrarian system based almost entirely on a landlord-tenant-attached labour undergoes alterative changes as wage labour becomes another structural component of the system, or when share-cropping tenancy gets eliminated and basically a landlord-tenant-attached labour undergoes alternative changes as wage labour becomes another structural component of the system, or when share-cropping tenancy gets eliminated and a basically landowner wage labour agrarian system emerges.

Social Movement, Change and Praxis

Means/praxis	*Change promoting/resisting movement*	
	Intra-systemic	*Systemic*
Institutional	Quasi-structural movement e.g. strikes, lockouts, protest marches for legitimate demands and redressal of grievances. Stable state (A)	Quasi-structural tending towards structural alternative. e.g. Union claims for decision-making powers. Unstable state (B')
Non-institutional	Quasi-structural tending towards structural e.g. peasant revolt for 2/3rd crop share from existing ½ Unstable state (B'') Unstable state (B'')	Tending towards revolutionary movements e.g. Naxalite movement Charu Mazumdar underground phase. Unstable state: Flux. (C')
Institutional – Non-institutional	Quasi-social movement tending towards structural social movement. Unstable state e.g. riots, rebellions peasant revolts against oppression, exploitation. Unstable state (B''')	Situation of flux. Social transformatory and revolutionary movements e.g. structural towards changes associated with rebellion, revolution, terrorism, civil disobedience, satyagraha, etc. Unstable state: Flux. (C)

Source: Adapted and revised from Mukherji (1987: 1608)

Structural-transformative social movements occur when replacement of one or more or all structures take place bringing about transformative changes in the system. Naxalism or the Mao-inspired social movements for structural-transformative revolutionary changes that have taken place almost exclusively in remote, backward, mostly tribal, less-communicable areas of the country, where the responsible role of the democratic state has least penetrated, leaving feudal enclaves to persist and prosper outside the ambit of governance of the state. The demolition of these feudal vestiges may be transformatory with respect to the backward region, but not so for the environment external to it, where feudal structures are getting dismantled through market and other social forces.

How much change?

How much change?	Limited	Radical
Specific individuals	Alternative social movements	Redemptive social movements
Everyone	Reformative social movements	Revolutionary social movements

Based on Aberle (1966)

From the early 1970s, new forms of social mobilization began in India. They gained a variety of names such as social movement, people's movement, popular movements, etc. These movements emerged and highlighted some of the major issues. Movements of landless, unorganized labour in rural and urban areas, Adivasis, Dalits, displaced people, peasants, urban poor, small entrepreneurs and unemployed youth took up the issues of livelihood, opportunities, dignity and development. And also the issues of gender and environment.

Oommen (2010) makes a pertinent point that 'equity rather than equality is the motive force behind contemporary social movements'. He says that even 'radical groups are not arguing for equality of rewards these days' but ensuring 'distributive justice'. In defining social movements, Oommen counts in all mobilizations with ideology and organizational framework, irrespective of goals (change or stability) or means (violent or non-violent). He says that one of the aspects – ideology, organization, leadership – acquires primacy at different phases of all movements Oommen considers mobilization and institutionalization as a dialectical process. One of the four processes – repression, discredit, co-optation and institutionalization – will herald the death-knell of a movement. Movements will survive if they have the required legitimacy and appropriate resources'. Another significant point made by Oommen is that there is no hierarchy of identities, but only conceptuality of identities. He classifies social movements on grounds of the structural bases and the transformative agencies into four rubrics as class struggles, anti-colonial and national liberation movements, social liberation movements and other ethnic minorities and general democratic movements. He includes Dalits and Adivasis movements among the liberation movements. Another significant observation made by him is that Telangana, Naxalbari and Maoist movements are interrelating class with other social categories such as nationality, caste and gender.

Most well known movements in India during the second half of the twentieth century are Chipko Movement, Save Silent Valley, Narmada Bachao Andolan, Koel Karo, Chhattisgarh Mukti Morcha, Jhola Andolan (fighting polythene), Appiko movement, Save Kudremukh, Lok Satta Movement, Swadhyay Movement, Farmers Movements (Sharad Joshi, Karnataka Rajya Raitha Sangha), Adivasi Movement and Forest Based Movements. These movements largely distanced themselves from political parties, or tried to cut across the ideologies of the political parties. Yet many of them rooted themselves or drew from ideologies of Mahatma Gandhi, various shades of environmentalisms or gender politics, or socialism. Social movements are also 'campaign against corruption', led by a group of social activists-Anna Hazare, Arvind Kejriwal, Swami Agnivesh, Kiran Bedi and Baba Ramdev. Anna Hazare, a Gandhian, sat at Jantar Mantar during April 2011 on fast unto death, demanding enactment of the long pending Jan Lokpal Bill. This movement got support of general masses and media. This created a buzz when political leaders were denied sharing of dias with the social activists. This movement is a landmark in the constitutional history of Independent India, which has forced government to include five non-official members in the Jan Lokpal Bill drafting committee. This movement has certainly made corruption a major social issue in India.

On the basis of the definitions of social movements by distinguished scholars, it would be possible to conceptualize 'social movements' for the present study. In this paper, the focus will be on the Forest Based Movements primarily led by Adivasis and the Naxalite/Maoist movements. The Adivasi Movement in the country has a long stretch of social mobilizations and social movements for which there are very few parallels in the country. It has persisted both during the colonial and post-colonial period. The major issues of the Adivasi struggle have been on land, forest and identity issues. In this sense, they are structural, transformative, liberation and ethnicity based movements. They have exhibited tremendous autonomy, persistence and continuity in their movements. On the other hand, the Maoist Movements are based on the issues of the deprived classes, structural transformation and social equity consideration. Both Partha Mukherji and T.K. Oommen have emphasized on the transformational and structural changes as the essential ingredients of social change. The present paper would also emphasize on these two dimensions of Adivasi and the Maoist Social Movements in Central India.

Origin and Continuity of Forest Based Movement in Jharkhand

In this paper, we would use the term 'Adivasi' to characterize the autochthons/aboriginals who are otherwise referred to in the Indian Anthropological and Sociological literature as 'Tribes' or called as 'Scheduled Tribes'. In Sanskrit, Adivasi means 'original inhabitants' (Karlsson, 2003: 407). In 1987, the first delegation of Adivasis travelled to Geneva to claim solidarity with the global indigenous movement (Karlsson, 2003: 407). At the time they were appealing to the UN Working Group on Indigenous Peoples on Indigenous Issues (WGIP) (Karlsson, 2003: 407). The Indian State had refused to recognize the Adivasis as indigenous people, claiming that no category of people in India could be described as indigenous (Karlsson, 2003: 407). The newly formed Indian Council of Indigenous and Tribal Peoples (ICITP) was advancing the Cobo definition of indigenity, which places less emphasis on 'firstness', and more on a history of colonial subjugation and continued marginalization from dominant ruling groups (Karlsson, 2003: 407).

In Jharkhand, the Adivasis are the earliest settlers who cleared the forest to settle their habitation and agriculture land. The Adivasis attach significant religious and cultural values to their land and forest. They call it as 'Mother Earth' (Areeparampil, 2002: 6). According to B.K. Roy Burman, the Adivasis 'represent a different principle of organizing individuals into collectivities based on moral relations rather than coercive power, and on expansion of self into surrounding, as well as on reciprocity, mutuality and equity' (1994: 19). The identity of Adivasis is intimately linked to the National Resources and the surrounding environment in which they live. According to Areeparampil, 'The land (*zamin*), water (*jal*) and Forest (*jungle*) that their habitat belongs to them. They have developed various norms, values, beliefs and practices which regulate the use of the natural resources around them in such a way that nature always remained bountiful to them' (2002). The term Jharkhand means 'forest tract' which signifies forest upland known as Chhota Nagpur Plateau. Jharkhand has been the homeland of some of the major Adivasi community such as Santals, Oraons, Mundas, Hos, Kharias, Bhumij, Juangs, Birhors, etc. Besides the Adivasis, there are also other groups like the Kurmis, Tantis, Kumhars, Tamarias, etc. who have been residing in this region for ages and so form part of the indigenous communities. According to Areeparampil (2002: 18–19), there has been a sharing of space, material traits and cultural norms among these various communities-tribal and non-tribal-living in Jharkhand. The Mundas and their ethnic brother like the Santals, Hos, etc. through the extensive migration process finally settle themselves in the valley and *jungle* of Jharkhand which was a virgin forest. Each family of early settlers cleared the virgin land and constituted a *Hatu* of village and the boundaries of the village well recognized. Each village invariably had its own *Sarna* (secret grove) where the village gods were lodged. After the original founder of the village died, his tomb was built side by side in the same village. This original founded village came to be known as the *Khuntkutti Huttu* (village of the descendants of the original founder). After the death of the original founder, the eldest son became the head of the village for both secular and spiritual matters; the ownership of the land was held commonly by the *Khuntkattidars*. The community was made as the trustee of the village land and forest. The social structure of the Adivasis was basically egalitarian and democratic. There were initial threats to *Khuntkatti* system when the Chhotanagpur Raja encouraged Brahmins, traders, service castes and others to settle in the Adivasi territory; due to this there was marginal subversion of Khuntkatti System.

The British severely encroached on the Forest Rights of the Adivasis by introducing Private Property Rights to Land and Forest including the imposition of Zamindari system of Land Rights. According to Victor Das (1992: 177), the commercial logic of the British imperialism and the burgeoning restrictions on the rights of the tribals by the present government have alienated the forest-dwellers from their own milieu. The Adivasis strongly resisted the introduction of the Permanent Settlement and Private Property Rights in Land and Forest as the Adivasis started feeling the pernicious effect of Permanent Settlement. On the top of it, the traders, moneylenders, administrators and new settlers were allowed to encroach upon the Traditional Land and Forest Rights of Adivasis. As a result, there were a series of revolts launched by Adivasis. One of the most sever revolt was the first Kol insurrection of 1819–1820. In this insurrection many Larkakols lost their lives but they also destroyed the British troops. However, due to superior fire power of the British, by the end of May 1821, the HOs surrendered themselves under the threat of total annihilation. The British repression continued unabated which led to the great Kol Insurrection of 1831–32 which is also called as the First War of Independence. The spirit of revolt and insurrection spread like wild fire in the Chhotanagpur region inhabited by Adivasis, particularly in Chhotanagpur, Singhbhum, Manbhum and Palamau. Different Adivasi groups consisting of Hols, Mundas and Oraons had united together to suppress the British colonial onslaught.

The British realized their folly and introduced significant administrative changes particularly through Regulation XIII of 1833. Captain Thomas Wilkinson was appointed as the first agent to the Governor General. A code of simple rules was instituted by Captain Wilkinson for the restoration of civil justice. Another significant element was the prevention of transfer of land in lieu of rent and debt. It was intended to prevent alienation of Adivasi lands. Another significant innovation was the institutionalization of traditional Village Panchayat System in conformity with the existing Adivasi system of resolving conflicts. This was a paternalistic move of the British to replace a coercive system of administration to a legitimized democratic Adivasi system. This ensured immense satisfaction among Adivasis to which they are steadfastly committed even today. According to Areeparampil (2002: 120), 'The main features of the administrative set up proposed by Wilkinson were the preservation of the indigenous form of government, direct contact between the Assistant and the people without the intervention of subordinate officials or pleaders, the settlement of all disputes as far as possible through Village Panchayats on the spot and exclusion of foreigners (*dikus*) from the area. The general principles which were laid down by Capt Wilkinson in his letter were subsequently embodied in a set of statutory rules under Regulation XIII of 1833. These rules came to be known as 'Wilkinson's Rules'. The administration of civil justice in the Kolhan area is still carried on under these rules'.

The first evidence of a pan-Adivasi identity can be traced back to 1915 (Damodaran, 2006: 184). By 1930, the term 'Adivasi' was used by tribal groups as a unifying identity wielded for political gain, and by 1937 it was used to articulate an interest in creating a separate Adivasi State (Damodaran, 2006: 184). This was eventually realized in the creation of Jharkhand in 2000 (Basu, 2006: 134). Another conception of Adivasi identity has to do with considering those who are not Adivasi but outsiders, or Diku, while tribal people are insiders (Basu, 2006: 138). This does not always have to do with common ancestry but with a history of suffering and connection to the land (Karlsson, 2003: 523). The important features of Adivasi identity in this context have to do with connection to the land through cultivation, community and collective values, and religious ties to sacred areas of the forest (Ghosh, 2006: 523). Adivasi identity is worn with pride, and works to confound the influences of the state as they try to lure tribal populations into modernization projects (Ghosh, 2006: 524).

The Adivasis and forest dwelling people did not take colonial and post colonial oppression meekly. *They fought back within their own cultural context, traditions and identity*. Adivasi movement was galore during the colonial period on forest rights in which the traditional chiefs played a vital role. There have been major Adivasi and peasant movements against colonial oppression on forest rights issues as indicated below:

- Martyrdom of Tikha Majhi at the Bhaglpur Collectorate in 1784
- Kharwar or Sapha Hor movement of the Santhals of Jharkhand in the 1870s led by Bhaggirath.
- Ulugan (great tumult) of Birsa Munda 1899–1900 against erosion of *khuntakatti* joint tenures in Jharkhand.
- Tana Bhagat movement of the Oraons of Jharkhand 1914–1918.
- Dharmaraj movement of the Naikdas of Panchmahals, Gujarat in 1868 led by Roop Singh Gobar and Joria.
- Bhil Raj Movement of the Bhils of Banswara, Sunth, and Dungarpur, Rajasthan in 1913, led by Govind Guru.
- Revolt by Kacha Nagas of Cachar district, Assam in 1882, led by Shambhudan.
- Thadoe Kuki revolt in Manipur, during 1917–1919 against indentured labour.
- Gudem-Rampa Fituri (risings) of region comprising Godavari-Vishakhapatnam, Andhra Pradesh, Bastar, Madhya Pradesh, Malkangiri and Koraput, Orissa, in 1840, 1845, 1858, 1861, 1862, 1979–1980, 1986 led by Suria Raamanna and Rajana Anatayya and their Rama Dandu (Rma's Army), 1900 led by Korra Mallaya.
- Bastar rising in 1910 against ban on shifting cultivation and free use of forest produce.
- Khond rebellion in Daspalia Princely State, Orissa in 1914.
- Revolt against indentured labour in Mayurbhanj, Orissa in 1916.
- Mappila agrarian rebellions of Malabar, Kerala (32 Outbreaks) between 1836–1919, culminating in 1921 against increasing control of upper caste Namboodris and Nayar Jenmis.

Forest as State Property under British Colonial Rule

The British rule introduced scientific forestry and its narrow agenda was commercial timber production. It was developed to provide sustained profits to the colonial empire. The basic colonial approach was to declare forest as state property. Clear falling of forest from vast areas was the method followed to impose complete closure to grazing and collection of firewood, fodder, bamboo, etc. The Forest Department was established in 1868 to regulate and exploit the natural resources of the country for the profit of the empire. The Adivasis and forest dwellers were denied access to forest area for grazing the cattle and procure firewood, fodder and other forest produce.

The legal framework for forest policy was initiated during the colonial period as the Indian Forest Act-1865. This legislation declared forest as state property. It notified all lands covered with trees, Jungle and bushes as government forest. This was followed by The Indian Forest Act-1878 which accepted some of the traditional rights of forest people. Later on the Forest Policy of 1894 specified the objectives of scientific forestry. It gave primacy to economic interest and justified the curtailment of peoples traditional rights in the name of conservation. Subsequently, during the first quarter of the twentieth century, The Indian Forest Act-1927 was promulgated which divided the forests as Reserve Forest and Protected Forest. This Act severely curtailed the traditional rights and called them as concessions. Apart from this another category of Village Forest (VF) was also provided to meet the basic needs of village communities.

The land records and the *khatiyan* in the Kolhan area were with the tribal Munda, but in 1955 the Forest Department demarcated its own boundary in this very area without going for verification of rights and demarcation of the Adivasis. The Revenue Department notification dated 1 July 1955 read that '*The forest and the waste lands comprised in this notification shall be called Protected Forests. The nature of extent of rights and government and of private person in and over the forest and waste lands comprised in this notification has not been enquired and recorded as laid down in sec 29 of the IFA 1927, but as the State Government thinks that such enquiry and recording will occupy such length of time as in the mean time to endanger the rights of the Government and as the enquiry and record-of-rights will hereafter be made this notification is issued subject to all existing rights of individuals or communities.*' This happened in the area where communities were already in possession and CNT Act was powerful but even then by applying IFA 1927 the land was acquired without settling the claims.

After Independence, the Wildlife (Protection) Act-1972 created two types of protected areas i.e. National Parks and Wildlife Sanctuaries. It introduced blanket ban on all human activities leading to considerable suffering of local people by depriving them access to the forest. It has led to the alienation of local communities who continue to depend on forest resources for their survival but, on the other hand, it is not proving strong enough to fight pressure from commercial and industrial interest. Forest Conservation Act 1980 seeks to prohibit the diversion of forest land for non-forest purposes. This legislation has caused and continues to cause immense deprivation and suffering to millions of forest people all over the country. Forest and Taungya Villages are the worst legacy of the colonial forest management. Forest settlement known as 'forest villages' were established in the country after 1880. These were created for semi bonded forest labourers. They were provided with a piece of land to live on and, at the same time, they were forced to provide free labour in the forest for fire-fighting, timber harvesting and raising plantations. Traditional forest communities or migrant labourers brought from outside were settled in these forest villages. The villagers were not granted any land rights. Approximately, 7,000 forest/Taungya villages exist in the country today, in the states of Uttaranchal, UP, Bihar, Assam, West Bengal, MP, Chhattisgarh, Karnataka and Tamil Nadu. After more than 60 years of Independence, over 10 million people in more than 7,000 forest/Taungya villages have no rights over the land they are cultivating. It is a denial of their basic human rights.

Present Challenges

Forest Andolan (Jungle Kato Andolan) in Singhbhum District in Jharkhand

The historical injustice committed on forest villages are of more serious nature. These villages were settled by the Forest Department in order to plant and regenerate the forest in 1920s. Many of the existing revenue villages situated in deep forests were converted into forest villages by the British. These villages somewhere are also known as 'Taungiya villages', fixed demand or any other type of village were settled in UP, Uttarakhand, MP, West Bengal, TN, Maharashtra, Tripura, Assam, Gujarat, Jharkhand, etc. Official record put them as 2,474 villages but they are around 7,000. In the case of Odisha, the episode of Vedanta in Niyamagiri hills and Posco in Jagatsinghapur, where the state has been conspiring with the international companies in loot of nation's natural wealth and biodiversity is now well known to all of us. The loot of these companies could only be exposed by a strong and sustained movements by the local community and supported by other people's movements, which forced the central government to take some positive steps. Two committees formed for evaluation of these projects, Saxena Committee and Meena Gupta Committee, brought forth the facts that in both the cases Forest Rights Act, Forest Conservation Act and Environment Protection Act were grossly violated. Though these facts are in front of the nation today, even then the land of the law is allowed to be violated by the State Government in Odisha to favour these big multinational companies. This issue of forest land is the most critical issue of dispute inside the forest areas between people and the Indian State.

To say more precisely, today the forest areas are witnessing political struggles basically exposing the myth of nation-states created during the colonial regime on false grounds without taking into consideration people's culture and their livelihood practices. The government is in a dilemma whether to promote corporate interest or to implement political programme to ensure their vote banks. This was the reason that forced UPA 1 to enact this law after a big defeat of NDA and its core slogan 'India Shining' in 2004. The collective political consciousness generated due to forest rights is the logical culmination of 250 years of struggles and is not dependent on any political party or Maoists. If they are challenging the State then they are also entering into debates with Maoists challenging their methodology. For example, in Adhoura block of Kaimur district of Bihar, the villagers were very agitated when Maoists bombed the schools. Villagers announced that no one will feed Maoists in the village. Villagers claimed that they had an inalienable right over our forest land, we will collect all those documents from government records where our rights have been registered, we will fight to stop all those companies that have attacked our forests.

The tribals of Jharkhand have a long culture and tradition of living in harmony with the environment and safeguarding their dense forest. Jharkhand was deforested intensely in the name of development, urbanization and industrialization. Due to the policy of commercial exploitation of forest both during the colonial and post colonial period, the Adivasis in the Singhbhum district of Jharkhand took a violent protest (Jungle Kato Andolan) as opposed to the *Chipko Movement* launched by Sunderlal Bahuguna in Uttarakhand around the same period. One can raise the question as to why the Adivasis in Singhbhum took to the deforestation of one of the densest forest in the country. The rational has to be systematically explored in the background of the British declaring forest as a state property, apportioning it as reserve forest and protective forest and also using forest as a resource for timber. The Adivasis of Jharkhand were also dispossessed and uprooted from their villages in the process of conversion of reserve forest. They could identify cemeteries of their dead ancestors inside the reserve forest which led to their anger and annoyance. As revenge they fell large number of trees from the dense forest from 1978 onwards. In this context it would be appropriate to quote Victor Das (1992: 177), 'The growing alienation of the Adivasis from their own environment as a result of the restriction of their traditional rights on the forests is also to be examined with a view to suggest constructive alternatives'. Another precipitant factor was that the Porahat Forest Division in Singhbhum district was converted to the Porahat Forest Corporation. Further, a deliberate afford was made to promote Scientific Management of the forest. Instead of the traditional sal trees, teak trees were planted with profit motive. The Adivasis were also denied job opportunities in the forest. Victor Das (1992: 179), characteristically observe 'Thus, while the nationalization of the forests transformed the timber contractors into transport contractors, it made the forest-dwellers-forest destroyers'. Another reason for such a provocation of Adivasis illegal filling of forest because of the presence of Jamshedpur industrial belt and the emergence of timber mafia with the connivance of bureaucracy instrumental for Adivasis to take such a drastic step. The increase in the population of the Adivasis also prompted such a step.

The government had a limited success in felling of trees by introducing the Porahat Forest Corporation, it failed in providing the tribals with welfare schemes and employment. In the enthusiasm to promote commercial exploitation of forest, the government imposed oppressive laws on the tribals and let loose a blatant violent oppressive measures. The Adivasis were also emotionally surcharged because in the protective forest areas, there were evidence of their ancestors death abode, including the community operated *khuntkatti* system which was also recognized under Chhotanagpur Tenancy Act 1908. Adivasis claimed that the Forest Department had usurped their ancestral land in the name of Reserve and Protected Forest. The forests were also felled for industrial exploitation by

TATA Steel Company and by the industries located in the adjacent states of West Bengal and Odisha. Around the same time, the state government also started Subarnrekha Multipurpose Project which also contributed to deforestation. The opening of Bokaro Steel Industry also led to the Wanton destruction of forest. The Adivasis of Singhbhum district participated in a militant spirit in jungle kato andolan. The state government also reacted violently by undertaking police firing in several places between 1979 and 1981. A brief description of such police firing has been indicated below:

1. Chandil Firing – (30.04.1978) On 26 March 1978, there was a huge rally at Chandil in protest against the Subarnrekha Multipurpose Project which threatened to displace 75,000 people from 90 villages. A fast unto death programme began on 23 April 1978 and on 27 April 1978 the Satyagrahis were attacked and many of them were arrested. Two young men and two elderly people were killed.
2. Ichahatu Firing – (6.11.1978) On 6 November 1978, the Adivasis called a meeting at Ichahatu village against the plantation of sagwan trees in place of sal trees. The police force and the bureaucracy fired at them without any warning. In this process one of them died.
3. Serengda Firing – (25.11.1978) On 25 November 1978, police fired 12 rounds at the Adivasis who had collected at Serengda village. As a result three people died.
4. Gua Firing – (8.9.1980) On 8 September 1980, the Adivasis had assembled to protest and to submit a memorandum to the local Magistrate. They were suddenly attacked by the police in which three Adivasis died. In the local hospital another nine Adivasis were killed.
5. Kasijoa Firing – (7.10.1980) On 7 October 1980, the police attacked the Adivasis of Kasijoa village near Goelkera police station and arrested some people who were involved in forest felling.

Similarly few other incidence of police firing took place in the following places:

1. Baipi Firing (24–11–1980)
2. Tonto Firing (25–5–1981)
3. Kuira Firing (26–10–1980)
4. Kumbia Firing (5–11–1981)
5. Jojhatu Firing (14–11–1981)
6. Sarjomhatu Firing (25–11–1981)
7. Iligara Firing and killing of Gangaram Kalundia 24–4–1982)
8. Tonto Firing (22–5–1982)
9. Tiruldih Firing (21–10–1982)
10. Killing of Bidar Nag (1–6–1983)
11. Jhinkpani Firing (7–10–1983)
12. Bharbharia Firing (9–7–1984)
13. Goelkera Firing (27–3–1985)

In spite of police firing and brutal oppression, the Adivasis did not obtained the felled forest trees and cleared them for agriculture purpose. In spite of the severe state repression, the Adivasis converted the forest area into agriculture area and started cultivating different agriculture croups. The author happened to visit this area during 2012 and found that the entire deforested area was converted into agriculture. The Adivasis had claimed those areas under the Forest Rights Act 2006. The District Collector of Chaibasa distributed *pattas* to each household in several villages and joint *pattas* in the name of male and female members as also individual *pattas* in the name of widows and women headed households were distributed. This case study of Jungle Kato Andolan is an exemplary instance of the Adivasis taking revenge against the anti trible policy of the state were British colonial policy and subsequently the post colonial policy of The Indian Government had converted the traditional community forest into reserve forest.

The Contemporary Environmental Movements and its Interface with Forest Based Movements

In the absence of ground level awareness and concern, environmental aspects have remained more or less peripheral to the contemporary social movements in India. Some of the contemporary movements, however, acquired the status of ecological or environmental movements in retrospect as these movements have widened their focus from basic survival needs to ecological concerns (Sethi, 1993; Gadgil and Guha, 1994). In general, these movements are often grouped under tribal or peasant movements (Shah, 1990) and also under new social movements (Omvedt, 1993; Wignaraja, 1993). Some even characterize them as middle class or elitist movements (Shah, 1990; Sethi, 1993). The reason is that ecological aspects are linked with the problems associated with peasants and tribals whose survival is attached to the status of natural resources. The problems or demands of tribal as well as non-tribal poor are often articulated by urban middle class and elite. In the context of a coalition between affected people and the middle class spokespersons, the real issues tend to get clouded as the debate is drawn into different forums in order to attract national and international attention (Sethi, 1993). Environmental movements in India, therefore, are not necessarily for the 'green' or 'clean' earth or for saving mankinds' heritage and endangered species as in the West, *but for the very survival of the local poor.* Even among these ecological movements, only a few can claim success in achieving some of their objectives. On the other hand, the overwhelming popularity or coverage received by some of these movements overshadows the importance of other environmental problems. The success of the movement is often linked with its popularity rather than the importance of the issue.

The origin of modern environmentalism and environmental movements in India can be ascribed to the Chipko Movement in the central Himalayan region in the early 1970s. Chipko Movement, launched to protect the Himalayan forests from destruction, has its roots in the pre-Independence days. Many struggles were organized to protest against the colonial forest policy during the early decades of twentieth century. Peoples' main demand in these protests was that the benefits of the forest, especially the right to fodder, should go to local people (Bahuguna, 1990). These struggles have continued in the post-Independent era as the forest policies of Independent India are no different from that of colonial ones. However, the origin of Chipko has taken place during the year 1973. In early 1973, the Forest Department refused to allot ash trees to the Dashauli Gram Swarajya Sangha (DGSS), a local cooperative organization based in Chamoli districts, for making agricultural implements. On the other hand, the Forest Department allotted ash trees to a private company, i.e. Symonds Co. This incident provoked the DGSS to fight against this injustice by lying down in front of timber trucks and burning resin and timber depots as was done in Quit India Movement. When these methods were found unsatisfactory, Chandi Prasad Bhat, one of the leaders, suggested of embracing the trees and thus 'Chipko' was born (Bahuguna, 1990; Guha, 1989). This form of protest was instrumental in driving away the private company from felling the ash trees. With its success, the movement has spread to other neighbouring areas and then on the movement is popularly known as Chipko Movement internationally. Only during 1970s, this movement started tending toward concentrating on ecological issues such as depletion of forest cover and soil erosion.

Chipko Movement, with its wide following and success, though modest in achieving some of its objectives, can be termed as a watershed in environmental movements in India. This, in fact, kindled the environmental aspects of development and gave rise to numerous conflicts and protests over natural resources and ecological issues. However, despite numerous forest based movements during the last two decades in India, none of them had attracted (as much as Chipko did) public support or influenced the state policies. This may be attributed to three important aspects of Chipko Movement. First, the close links between the livelihoods of the local people and the nature of the movement. The local people consider Chipko as a fight for basic subsistence denied to them by the institutions and policies of the State (Guha, 1989). In addition, the specificity of the region where involvement of women in the contribution to households' subsistence and the anti-alcohol campaign has led to the overwhelming support of women which is unique to the Chipko Movement. Moreover, as aptly described by Guha (1989: 178), 'the 'private' face of Chipko is more a peasant movement, while its public profile is seen as an environmental movement'. Further, it has a face of a womens' movement as well (Omvedt, 1993). It is interesting to note that in the later stages when Chipko ceased to go beyond environmental concerns, i.e. limiting itself to protecting and conservation of trees, the problems started surfacing. The second aspect is with regard to the nature of agitation, for unlike other environmental movements, Chipko strictly adhered to the Gandhian tradition of freedom struggle, i.e. nonviolence. To quote Guha, 'There is the veneer of Gandhianism with which Chipko is cloaked, a matter of some embarrassment for a state claiming to be the rightful successor of the freedom struggle and upholding Gandhi as the Father of Nation. In this manner Chipko had, knowingly or unknowingly, successfully exploited the ambiguities in the dominant ideology of the Indian state' (Guha, 1989: 177). Thirdly, the simplicity and sincerity of the leaders like Sunderlal Bahuguna and their access to national leaders like Indira Gandhi and other politicians and officials also helped in the success of the movement to a large extent.

Despite its popularity and success, Chipko Movement is still considered to be incomplete and modest as it limited itself to ecological aspects (in the later stages) of protecting trees to the neglect of local people's requirements. In fact, to start with, Chipko Movement has had six demands – only one of which is complete stoppage of commercial cutting of trees. The other demands include: (i) on the basis of minimum needs of the people, a reorganization of traditional rights should take place; (ii) arid forest should be made green with peoples participation and increased tree cultivation; (iii) village committees should be formed to manage forests; (iv) forest related home-based industries should be developed and the raw materials, money and technique for it should be made available; and (v) based on local conditions and requirements, local varieties should be given priority in aforestation (Mukul, 1993). The recent evidence shows that due to the neglect of eco-development linkages (markets, techniques, forest based industries), the objective of ameliorating the conditions of local people in these regions remains a distinct dream. If the situation continues, i.e. increasing threats to the livelihoods of local people, it may jeopardize the achievements of the Chipko Movement and lose the peoples, support.

The other notable environmental movements relate to Tehri Dam, Silent Valley Project and Narmada Valley Projects. One of the early and complete successes of environmental movements was the abandonment of the Silent Valley hydro electric project in Kerala. The major concerns of this movement were the adverse environmental impact on Silent Valley, one of the last surviving natural tropical forests in India and protecting a rare breed of monkey, lion-tailed macaque. With the active support from the International organizations like World Wildlife Fund and the International Union for the Conservation of Nature and Natural Resources, the movement assumed International importance (Sethi, 1993). Though it gained popularity and coverage, the ultimate success of the movement was attributed to the then Prime Minister Indira Gandhi's desire to enhance her image among the International Conservation Community (D'Monte, 1985 as quoted in Gadgil and Guha, 1994). The longest struggle among the anti-big dam protests was the opposition to Tehri Dam, being constructed on the river Bhageerathi in the Garhwal region. The Tehri Baandh Virodhi Sangarshan Samiti, a committee for the struggle against the Tehri Dam founded by veteran freedom fighter Veerendra Datta Saklani, has been opposing the construction for more than a decade. The major objections include seismic sensitivity of the region, submergence of forest areas along with Tehri town, etc. Despite the support from other prominent leaders like Sunderlal Bahuguna, the movement has failed to gather enough popular support at national as well as international levels and the government is determined to complete the project.

The most popular movement in the environmental history of India is the movement against the Narmada River Valley Project. Though the movement started as early as late 1970s, along with the clearance of the project, it received momentum only during late 1980s. To start with, this movement was centred around the issue of human rights. In fact, some of the main leaders of the movement at present like Medha Patkar were working toward proper rehabilitation programmes for the dam displaced. Due to improper implementation of the rehabilitation programmes by the State, the human rights activists have become the articulators of anti-dam protests. Their demands included complete stopping of the dam, resettlement and rehabilitation benefits to the oustees (Wood, 1993). These demands were aptly supported by environmentalists who opposed construction of large dams for ecological reasons. The movement, however, gained wider public attention with mobilization and organization of oustees (mostly tribals) and the joining of the eminent social workers like Baba Amte, Sunderlal Bahuguna and Medha Patkar. Though its wider public attention is due to its coverage (impact) in three states, the most notable feature of this movement is the international support it has received. In fact, the main reason behind the World Bank's withdrawal of funding to the project was due to international pressures. To list a few instances: Japanese environmentalists persuaded their government in blocking the money advanced for the project. Similarly, the US environmental groups have worked hard to stop World Bank funding (Gadgil and Guha, 1994: 173). With this international support, the leaders of the movement received a sympathetic hearing from the US Congressional Sub-Committee. In the wake of the World Bank's independent review committee report, the European Parliament urged its member countries to instruct their World Bank directors to suspend all further aid to Sardar Sarovar and in the final voting all the donor countries voted against funding while poor recipient countries voted for continuation (Wood, 1993). This kind of international support is something unprecedented in Indian environmental history. The completion of Narmada Valley Project is not directly linked with World Bank funding and hence the success of the movement. Without international pressures it would have been very difficult for the leaders of Narmada Bacho Andolan (Save Narmada Agitation) to stop World Bank funding on their own.

Globalization and Violation of Forest Rights

The tribals in Goa trace their origin to Khunti region of present day Jharkhand. They identified their homelands to Munda Adivasi region and are designated as Gowda tribe, they settled in dense forest of Western Ghat. Arrival of Portuguese was a major setback to the status of tribes in Goa, particularly the Gowdas. Land of Goa was very fertile for both agriculture as well as horticulture. Most of the lands belonging to indigenous people were wrested by the dominant and owning community Bhatcars, who also had the patronage of Portuguese colonial rulers; they conferred legal ownership to land occupied by the dominant caste Bhatcars. In course of time, even the Brahmins became politically and economically dominant over the indigenous people. The church also alienated the Adivasi Land. The traditional socio-political institution of the indigenous people is known as *Mand* which had community ownership of land. Mining was opened up in Goa in 1945 and since then iron ore is being exported to Japan. Tribal people were drafted to work in the mines. Liberation of Goa largely meant land alienation to tribals' communities. Mass of tribal community in Goa has not only been alienated from their lands but also alienated from state structures. State agencies such as police provided security to mining companies, helping in destruction of forest cover and displacement of tribal forest land further bled the tribals white. The continued exploitation of the tribals Land and Forest Rights compelled them to initiate seeds of movements for getting status of Scheduled Tribes particularly by the Dhangar Community and their struggle still continues. Most of the mining leases is located in the forest area which has been the abode of the tribals (Rodrigues, 2007).

These forests have also been declared as Wildlife Sanctuary. The tribals living inside the sanctuary jurisdictions are subjected to various kinds of restrictions by the Forest Department. One tribal person was even shot dead by the forest guards while collecting firewood in the forest inside Khotigo Wildlife Sanctuary. In spite of tyranny of the Forest Department tribes are continuing inhabit the forest lands in most of the cases. It is only in the Bhagwan Mahavir Wildlife Sanctuary that the Forest Department has displaced few villages by paying compensation and not any land or cultivation spaces. While the Forest Department is severe with tribes inhabiting forest; they prevent them from catching forest crabs and harvesting mushrooms, it is largely relaxed when mining is carried on inside sanctuary jurisdictions. Large scale mining is going on since 2006 and 2007 in

Netravali wildlife sanctuary with active collusion of the Forest Department. Besides mining most of the industrial estates that came up all over Goa were on traditional tribal lands. Tribals were not empowered to protest instead they meekly surrendered their lands to industrial estates and also to megaprojects such as chemical plant of Swiss multinational Ciba-Geigy at Corlim, Tiswadi.

The Contemporary Forest Land Issue in Maharashtra can be traced to 2002 when following the infamous 3.5.2002 letter of the Inspector General of Forests, the Maharashtra Government initially issued a circular on 4.9.2002 regarding the formation of a 'time-bound Action Plan to remove unauthorized encroachments from Forest lands.' Eviction notice were issued to large number of cultivators in the district of Amravati and several other districts. However, due to sustained pressure from various quarters, the Maharashtra government was forced to reconsider its stand. On 17 September 2002, the Government of Maharashtra issued a temporary stay on the eviction of encroachment by Adivasis. In Amravati district, the district collector had issued 872 land certificates in 2001 for regularization of the claims. The state government had reported that about 73,000 hectares of land were under encroachment (Lobo, unpublished manuscripts).

Infringement of Forest Rights in the Post Colonial Era in Karnataka – Nagarhole National Park/Rajiv Gandhi National Park

The present area of the Nagarhole National Park or Rajiv Gandhi National Park is 64,339.26 hectares (643.39 sq km). The Park got its name from the Nagarhole (Snake River in Kannada). This park is connected to Bandipur National Park of Karnataka close to Kabini Reservoir. It is adjacent to Wynad Sanctuary of Kerala and this entire block forms the part of 4,500 sq kms of the Nilgiri Biosphere Reserve. It was declared as a Sanctuary in July 1955 with an area of 28,416 hectares which was increased to 64,339 hectares during December 1988. This park was renamed as Rajiv Gandhi National Park in May 1992. The tribals inhabiting the park were Jenu Kurbas (honey gatherers), Betta Kurubas (hill kurubas), Hakki Pikki (bird trappers), Yaravas and Soligas. In all, about 32,000 Adivasis were residing in and around the National Park. There was a serious concern among the tribal and voluntary organizations in Nagarhole area that the $ 68 million Eco Development Facility (GEF) and International Development Agency (IDA) of the World Bank was not formulated taking into account the plans already prepared by the tribals. They were prevented from having any access to Non Timber Forest Produce (NTFP) for their livelihood. This forced the tribals of Nagarhole to become wage labourer on the coffee plantation and affected their indigenous culture adversely.

The Government of Karnataka had invited the Taj Group of Hotels to set up a three-star hotel at Murakal within the Nagarhole National Park to cater to eco tourists. The local forest dwellers most notably the Nagarhole Kakarnakote Budakattu Janara Hakku Sthapana Samiti (NKBJHSS) had been protesting against the construction of the hotel complex, but the government did not take any action against the Taj Resort. On 28 August 1994 the Forest Department, the Principal Chief Conservator of Forest (PCCF) and the Chief Wildlife Warden entered into a lease agreement with the Taj Group of Hotels for 18 years to lease an area of 24 acres of land in Murkal. On 15 August 1996, a memorandum was submitted against the project by the Local Voluntary Organizations, to the President and the Prime Minister. A protest procession started from Murkal Haadi and culminated into a dharna at the Taj Project Site for 4 Hours. The pressure exerted by NGOs was followed by an interesting development. On 20 January 1997, the Karnataka High Court declared the lease to be illegal as it was in violation of section 20 of the Indian Forest Act 1926 and Section 35(3) of the Wildlife Protection Act-1972 which prohibits the acquisition of any land within a National Park. In August 1998, the National Human Rights Commission (NHRC), in its recommendations noted that 108 tribal families displaced during the construction of the reservoir are yet to be rehabilitated. The Hon'ble High Court of Karnataka had appointed a committee under the chairmanship of Dr Muzaffar Azadi which submitted its Interim Report in January 2006. As per the Interim Report, out of total 1,429 families in Hansur Taluk 1,106 families have been displaced and in H.D. Kote Taluk out of a total of 3,244 families, 1,801 families have been displaced due to National Park, between 1970s and 1990s. Until then 250 families were relocated in Nagapura. There were several problems for Scheduled Tribes living in new settlement; first was the lack of fair price shop; the Karnataka Forest Department has not given them the possession certificate (Patta or Pani) over the land and house. This had caused unhappiness among the relocated members of the Scheduled tribes. The Report of Dr Muzafar Azadi stated clearly that landlessness is the basic cause of poverty of tribals. Hence, the Government of Karnataka should evolve measures to distribute land to landless tribals. The tribals in Karnataka were being gradually deprived of minor forest produce (Iyer, 2007).

Odisha has been one of the thrust areas of exploitation of forest sources during the globalization era particularly by POSCO in Jagat Singh pur district, by Tatas and other groups of industries in Kalinganagar (Jajpur district), in the case of Vedanta in Niyamagiri hills. State has been conspiring with the international companies in loot of nation's natural wealth and biodiversity. The loot of these companies could only be exposed by strong and sustained movements by the local community and supported by other people's movements, which forced the central government to take some positive steps. Two committees formed for evaluation of these projects for Environmental clearance e.g. Saxena Committee and Meena

Gupta Committee brought forth the facts that in both the cases Forest Rights Act, Forest Conservation Act and Environment Protection Act were grossly violated. Today the forest areas are witnessing political struggles basically exposing the myth of nation-states created during the colonial regime on false grounds without taking into consideration of people's culture and their livelihood practices. The collective political consciousness is the logical culmination of 250 years of struggles not dependent on any political party or Maoists.

Organized mafia activities became common in many forest areas, including protected areas. Mafia activities take many forms, e.g. felling of commercially valuable timber trees, extraction and smuggling of precious medicinal and dye plants, poaching of wild animals, etc. Forest legislations in the country have not been able to make even a dent in the activities of the mafia-political groups-forests staff nexus. Instead, this nexus is the most pressing danger to Indian forests which gets stronger every day. In MP the involvement of Forest Minister and senior forest officers involvement in large-scale illegal timber trade came to light in 1999; when it was found that prime sal forests were being illegally felled under the guise of pest control. Most important Protected Areas like Rajaji National Park in UP (now in Uttarakhand), Nagarhole National Park in Karnataka, Betla Tiger Reserve in Palamau (Jharkhand) and many other forest areas of the country reported similar incidents. Within a period of 13 years between 1986–1999, poachers in various forest areas slaughtered 473 elephants. In the next three years, approximately 300 elephants were poached. Again, this was clearly done in complete connivance with officials supposed to be protecting wildlife. Most poaching cases remain undetected or unreported at source, and forest officials are seldom eager to report poaching. Villagers who oppose illegal felling of trees and poaching in Protected Areas, and oppose corrupt practices of the forest staff, are harassed by the Forest Department, and had court cases filed against them. The best example of this was the notorious 2001 Bandhabgarh cases; in which three Baiga tribal youth were arrested, tortured and made to 'confess' their involvement in the 'poaching' of a tigress. The Bandhabgarh incident is one of many, where the mafia terrorizes the villagers and force them to keep their mouths shut. They are the only ones who continue to speak out against poaching.

The Land Acquisition Act of 1894 introduced the concept of *eminent domain* of state ownership of land resources based on land acquisition measures. Involuntary displacement has become a human right issue. Impoverishment leads to landlessness, houselessness and marginalization. Liberal economic policy has led to much more land acquisition and displacement than was practiced in the past. This Act was promulgated during the colonial period and continues to be used during liberalization era as well which smacks of 'internal colonialism'. There was strong resistance to land acquisition for various developmental projects like Swaran Rekha project and Koel Karo project during post-Independence period. It also led to resistance by people in which one person was killed in the Bahra Gora (Singhbhum district) on 6 November 1978. It also led to large scale arrest, beatings and molestation of women (report of the Delhi Unit of PUCL, March 1979).

The Jharkhand Government has signed well over 100 MoUs with corporate sectors during the globalization era notable among them are international and Indian corporate giants, namely, Arcelor Mittals, Jindal, Essar, Tata, Hindulco, Abhijit Group, etc. Among the MoUs signed by the state government, 74 are for setting up steel plants and 24 for power plants with the estimated investment of ₹ 4,67,240 crores requiring approximately 2 lakh acres of land. Arcelor Mittal and Jharkhand government signed an MoU on 8 October 2005 for setting up an integrated steel manufacturing operation. The project encompassing 10,000 hectares in Gumla and Khunti districts comprises a steel mill of 12 million tonnes per annum capacity iron ore and coal mines – a captive power plant of 2500 MW. The total investment is ₹ 47,000 crores. The 10,000 hectares are spread out in four blocks covering 54 villages. Arcelor Mittal has been unable to acquire land from the villagers and has been fraudulently getting them to sign agreements on bond paper pledging their land to the company. These *ikrarnamas* (agreement) were conspicuously introduced in several villages by the company middlemen who coerced the villagers to sign them. On getting news of the some, people's organizations and village samitis confronted the middlemen and the innocent villagers understood the evil intentions of the company behind the *ikrarnama.* It was rejected and the malicious campaign was withdrawn by the company's middlemen. As per the MoU, the Government of Jharkhand will endeavour to provide the required land. It will endeavour to facilitate grant of all statutory clearances for withdrawal of water, power diversion off forestland, etc. There was turmoil when displacement was initiated by the state during October 2008; the villagers attacked the Kohinoor Steel Plant near Jamshedpur, seized 70 trucks and stopped the work. As a result, the Jindal Steel, Essar, and CESE were forced to leave the areas; the Government is not able to execute even a single MoU at the grass roots, due to strong resistance by the tribals. The land acquisition in the liberalization era has made land acquisition difficult in Jharkhand. In the state of Jharkhand forcible acquisition of land for mining and developmental purpose has became a very sensitive issue.

Impetus to Forest Based Movements in the Globalization Era

In India 23 per cent of the land is recorded as 'forest' which is under the control of the Indian State. Most of the countries' biodiversity, wildlife and country minerals are located in the forest which is inhabited by the Adivasis. The rights of most of the Adivasi communities were not recorded. Thousands of forest dwellers Adivasis have been residing in these forests. The Forest Guards exploit the forest dwellers and Adivasis. Several kinds of atrocities are perpetrated against them in the form of bonded labour, forced labour and sexual violence. Thousands of acres have been deforested due to the commercial purpose. The degradation of forest has destroyed the livelihood resources like minor forest produce, water and soil regeneration. This has also led to distressed migration of Adivasis to distance places resulting in trafficking, labour exploitation and sexual exploitation. Adivasis have a long tradition of fighting for their homeland. The community consciousness and community solidarity have remained very strong among the Adivasis. The impetus of globalization coincided with the threat to Adivasis and forest dwellers to evict them from over 12 lakhs acres of forest lands from the various states like Jharkhand, Chhattisgarh, Odisha, Andhra Pradesh, Maharashtra, Rajasthan, Gujarat and other states. The Adivasis responded to such threads with protest and mobilization from the different states of India.

The Scheduled Tribes and Other Traditional Forest Dwellers (Recognition of Forest Rights) Act-2006, is a key piece of forest legislation passed on 18 December 2006. It has also been called the Forest Rights Act, the Tribal Rights Act, the Tribal Bill, and the Tribal Land Act. This law confers the rights of forest-dwelling communities to land and other resources, denied to them over decades due to the continuance of colonial forest laws in India. Supporters of the Act claim that this Act will redress the 'historical injustice' committed against Adivasis and forest dwellers, and also make conservation more effective and more transparent. The law has been the result of massive protest, demonstrations, mobilization and movement involving hundreds of thousands of people. Opponents of the law claim that it will lead to massive forest destruction and should be repealed. The Act was notified on 31 December 2007 and on 1 January 2008, this was followed by the notification of the Rules framed by the Ministry of Tribal Affairs. India's forests are governed by two main laws, the Indian Forest Act-1927 and the Wildlife (Protection) Act-1972. Nearly 82.9 per cent of the forest blocks in undivided Madhya Pradesh had not been settled as of December 2003, while all the hilly tracts of Odisha were declared government forests without any survey. In Odisha, around 40 per cent of the government forests are 'deemed reserved forests' which have not been surveyed. The Statement of Objects and Reasons of the Forest Rights Act describes it as a law intended to correct the 'historical injustice' done to forest dwellers by the failure to recognize their rights.

The rights which are included in section 3(1) of the Act are:

1. Right to hold and live in the forest land under the individual or common occupation for habitation or for self-cultivation for livelihood by a member or members of a forest dwelling Scheduled Tribe or other traditional forest dwellers;
2. Community rights such as nistar, by whatever name called, including those used in erstwhile Princely states, Zamindari or such intermediary regimes;

3. Right of ownership, access to collect, use, and dispose of minor forest produce (includes all non-timber forest produce of plant origin) which has been traditionally collected within or outside village boundaries;
4. Other community rights of uses or entitlements such as fish and other products of water bodies, grazing (both settled or transhumant) and traditional seasonal resource access of nomadic or pastoralist communities;
5. Rights including community tenures of habitat and habitation for primitive tribal groups and pre-agriculture communities;
6. Rights in or over disputed lands under any nomenclature in any state where claims are disputed;
7. Rights for conversion of *pattas* or leases or grants issued by any local council or any state government on forest lands to titles;
8. Rights of settlement and conversion of all forest villages, old habitation, unsurveyed villages and other villages in forest, whether recorded, notified or not into revenue villages;
9. Right to protect, regenerate or conserve or manage any community forest resource which they have been traditionally protecting and conserving for sustainable use;
10. Rights which are recognized under any State law or laws of any Autonomous District Council or Autonomous Regional Council or which are accepted as rights of tribals under any traditional or customary law of the concerned tribes of any state;
11. Right of access to biodiversity and community right to intellectual property and traditional knowledge related to biodiversity and cultural diversity;
12. Any other traditional right customarily enjoyed by the forest dwelling Scheduled Tribes or other traditional forest dwellers.
    - 12.1 *Title rights* – i.e. ownership to land that is being framed by tribals or forest dwellers as on 13 December 2005, subject to a maximum of 4 hectares; ownership is only for land that is actually being cultivated by the concerned family as on that date, meaning that no new lands are granted
    - 12.2 *Use rights* – to minor forest produce (also including ownership), to grazing areas, to pastoralist routes, etc.
    - 12.3 *Relief and development rights* – to rehabilitation in case of illegal eviction or forced displacement; and to basic amenities, subject to restrictions for forest protection
    - 12.4 *Forest management rights* – to protect forests and wildlife.

Eligibility to get rights under the Act is confined to those who 'primarily reside in forests' and who depend on forests and forest land for a livelihood. Further, either the claimant must be a member of the Scheduled Tribes (scheduled in that area) or must have been residing in the forest for 75 years. Section 6(1) of the Act provides that the gram sabha, or village assembly, will initially pass a resolution recommending whose rights to which resources should be recognized (i.e. which lands belong to whom, how much land was under the cultivation of each person as on 13 December 2005, etc.). This resolution is then screened and approved at the level of the sub-division (or taluka) and subsequently at the district level. The screening committees consist of three government officials (Forest, Revenue and Tribal Welfare departments) and three elected members of the local body at that level. These committees also hear appeals. Section 4(2) of the Act lays out a procedure by which people can be resettled from areas if it is found to be necessary for wildlife conservation. A great deal of the debate is fuelled by misunderstanding of the purpose of the Act. The most common is that the purpose of the law is to distribute forest land to forest dwellers or tribals, often claimed to be at the rate of four hectares per family. The Act is intended to recognize lands that are already under cultivation as on 13 December 2005, not to grant title to any new lands. The Act has met with much opposition from environmentalists and wildlife conservationists. Some of this opposition has been motivated by those who see the law as a land distribution scheme that will lead to the handing over of forests to tribals and forest dwellers. But the strongest opposition to the Act has come from wildlife conservationists who fear that the law will make it impossible to create 'inviolate spaces', or areas free of human presence, for the purposes of Wildlife Conservation. Tiger Conservation in particular has been an object of concern. Supporters of the Act take the position that the Act is not a land distribution measure, and further that the Act is more transparent than existing law and so can help stop land grabbing. The Campaign for Survival and Dignity described the final form of the law as 'both a victory and a betrayal' in their official statement on the occasion.

There have been numerous complaints regarding the manner in which the Act has been implemented after its notification. For instance, in September 2010, the Council for Social Development, a New Delhi based think tank, released a 'Summary Report on Implementation of the Forest Rights Act' which stated that:

'All of the key features of this legislation have been undermined by a combination of apathy and sabotage during the process of implementation. In the current situation the rights of the majority of tribals and other traditional forest dwellers are being denied and the purpose of the legislation is being defeated. Unless immediate remedial measures are taken, instead of undoing the historical injustice to tribal and other traditional forest dwellers, the Act will have the opposite outcome of making them even more vulnerable to eviction and denial of their customary access to forests … . Both the Central and the State governments have actively pursued policies that are in direct violation of the spirit and letter of the Act.'

Table 1

Details of claims received, titles and the forest land distributed as on 28.02.2014, in major states

States	*No. of claims received*	*No. of titles distributed*	*Extent of forest land for which titles distributed (in acres)*
Andhra Pradesh	4,11,012	1,69,370	14,56,542
Assam	1,31,911	36,267	77,609.17
Bihar	2,930	28	Not Available
Chhattisgarh	7,56,062	3,06,184	6,15,652.18
Gujarat	1,91,592	42,752	51,570.79
Himachal Pradesh	5,692	346	0.3548
Jharkhand	42,003	15,296	37,678.93
Karnataka	2,53,573	6,702	35,054.87
Kerala	37,535	24,599	33,018.12
Madhya Pradesh	4,98,378	1,83,719	10,81,677.98
Maharashtra	3,46,230	1,03,797	7,98,630.70
Odisha	5,46,547	3,29,381	6,67,566.96
Rajasthan	69,769	34,040	51,720.07
Tripura	1,82,617	1,20,473	4,16,555.58
Uttar Pradesh	92,433	17,705	1,39,778.04
West Bengal	1,38,640	31,809	16,891.556

Source: Government of India, Ministry of Tribal Affairs Status report on implementation of the Scheduled Tribes and Other Traditional Forest Dwellers (Recognition of Forest Rights) Act-2006 (for the period ending 28 February 2014).

Table 2

Gist of Titles and Area for which Forest Rights Given

Name of the States	*Individual + Community*		
	Titles	*Area in Hectare*	*Area in Acres*
Chhattisgarh, Maharashtra, Odisha, Rajasthan and West Bengal	**8,05,211** (7,99,649+ 5,562*)	**8,70,270.24** (5,81,490.07+ 2,88,780.17)	**21,50,461.46** (14,36,877.80+ 7,13,583.66)
Andhra Pradesh, Assam, Gujarat, Jharkhand, Karnataka, Kerala, Madhya Pradesh, Tripura and Uttar Pradesh	**6,09,117****	**13,47,411.13**	**33,29,489.56**
Grand Total	**14,14,328**	**22,17,681.37**	**54,79,951.02**

*Community titles ** Individual + Community titles

Source: Government of India, Ministry of Tribal Affairs Status report on implementation of the Scheduled Tribes and Other Traditional Forest Dwellers (Recognition of Forest Rights) Act-2006 (for the period ending 28 February 2014).

The response of People's Movements to the implementation of Forest Rights Act 2006 can be analyzed from four angles:

1. *States with a long history of Mobilization* – Gram Sabhas and elected Forest Rights Committees were constituted in the states of Gujarat, Madhya Pradesh, Odisha and Rajasthan.
2. *State driven moves along with hegemonic intentions* – There was a rush to convert a land title distribution in the states of Chhattisgarh, Andhra Pradesh, West Bengal and Tripura – it was more a bureaucratic initiative and the role of Gram Sabhas were largely by past.
3. *Slow pace initiatives* which include the states of Maharashtra and Kerala.
4. *Apathetic attitude*-negligible initiative by the state was taken up in states, such as Karnataka, Tamil Nadu and Jharkhand.

There was also conflict in the process of implementation due to interference of the Forest Department in large scale, holding illegal gram sabhas and dilution of Community Rights. Some of the states insisted that the claimants need to be either listed on the forest records as encroaches or they should produce the fine receipt of the Forest Department. Similar attitude was also demonstrated by the government and the Forest Department towards the recognition of forest villages. The states of Andhra Pradesh, Chhattisgarh. Madhya Pradesh, Maharashtra and Tamil Nadu were in this category. The gram sabhas in several states were called at Panchayat level instead of at hamlet level. One of the important radical measures included under Forest Rights Act-2006 is the recognition of community rights and powers over forest. Most of the state governments consistently tried to dilute this. It is astonishing to note that until May 2010 only two villages of entire country were conferred community rights. The mass forest based movements pressurized the government for the declaration of community rights across the country. In some parts of the country, the Adivasis and forest based communities have tried to use the Forest Rights Act as a legal instrument to confront the hight handedness of the forest authorities. There were several court cases in Uttarakhand which forced Van Gujjar communities to displace them from Rajaji National Park. Similarly, in Madhya Pradesh, the Jabbalpur High Court barred the eviction of the forest community. The Forest Rights Act became an intense democratic process for promoting powerful grass-roots struggle.

Simultaneously, the Ministry of Environment and Forest was also trying to provide forest land for the industries in violation of the Forest Act. This was amply clear when 2500 acres of forest lands which was utilized by local people for the livelihood in Jagat Singh Pur District, was granted to be felled by POSCO industries in Odisha in spite of the reports of two high powered committees (N.C. Sexena and Meena Gupta); it was volatile of the Forest Rights Act and the PESA Act. Similarly, forest dwellers were being forcefully displaced and uprooted from the wildlife sanctuaries. One of the notable examples is Madumalai Tiger reserve in Tamil Nadu where forest dweller was uprooted from the protective areas but the mass organizations resisted tooth and nail. The Forest Rights Act was not mere welfare legislation but it was struggle against exploitation and socio-political dominance. In spite of bureaucratic and political hurdles, the Forest Act has been a silver lining in providing Forest Rights and Land Rights to the Adivasis and forest dwellers. According to the data of the Tribal Ministry, Government of India, in 14 states 14,09,938 individual and community titles were conferred and 54.78 lakh acres Land Rights were entrusted to the Adivasis and forest dwellers. This has an achievement of the activist organizations against the historical injustice, committed against the vulnerable sections.

Maoist Movements: Formidable Challenge to the Indian State

Presently, the struggles in the forest areas are posing a big challenge to the rulers of modern Indian state. In Indian forests and in the interior fields hundreds of militant mass struggles are going on against the eminent domain of the State. But all these popular struggles, which are essentially democratic and led by local organizations and its leaders, are being branded as 'Maoists' struggles. According to the government, number of districts showing Maoist influence has increased (from 56 in 2003 to 200 today). On the other hand, there is equal number of growth of independent mass struggles, which is much larger than the Maoist struggle in various parts of the country. Unfortunately, such struggles don't catch the attention of media, researchers and academicians. Generally speaking, mainstream national and regional political parties and its affiliated trade unions are not interested in these democratic struggles as their politics is rooted around power in a centralized form. The reality is that these independent democratic struggles are spreading like fire in many areas and becoming a major threat to the State. These struggles today are not merely giving petitions but challenging the development paradigm of the State, which is focusing growth rate as development index. In some areas such popular struggles are becoming the main opposition to neo liberal regime. The struggles carried out in a democratic framework whose leaders are ordinary Adivasi, women and youth are challenging the State with their heightened mass political consciousness. Instead of starting a serious negotiation process with such activist organizations, the State is trying to crush all the democratic movements in the name of Maoist. Today, Forest Right Movements have two fundamental challenges. One is its direct contradiction with the Indian State and its resolution within a democratic framework and secondly to maintain its identity independent of the Maoist movement.

It also needs to be emphasized here that the Naxalite Movement (now termed a Maoist Movement) has been growing in Jharkhand since 1967 with the active involvement of MCC which has now spread to 16 out of 22 districts in the state. The Maoist Movement is not limited to armed operation but it has also established parallel system of governance that includes Jan Adalts and People's court. Denial of justice is emerging as one of the important reasons for the spread of the Maoist Movement and the tribals faith in the Maoist Movement. Economic blockades and bandh caused by the Maoist are some of the examples indicating the helplessness of the state. The penetration of left extremism in Jharkhand is minimizing the space for autonomous Jharkhandi Movement and also of other civil society organizations.

Conclusion

The paper has attempted to make a distinction between the concepts of 'Tribe' and 'Adivasi'. It has highlighted that the concept of Adivasis should be used as synonymous to 'Indigenous'/'Autochthones'. It has also emphasized that 'Forest' is an important ingredient of land, culture and identity of Adivasis. In the present study, the concept of social movements has been characterized as structural change, transformative, liberation and based on ethnic identity. This characterization of social imovements is particularly indicative of Adivasi Movements. The Adivasi Movements in India have been initiated during the colonial period and is continuing in the post colonial period as well. During its chequered career the Adivasi Movements have resisted structural changes and its militant character has also been instrumental in promoting structural changes. It has strong ingredient of transformative character. It has strong autonomous character. The main thrust of this paper has been to emphasize that the Adivasis have been involved in militant struggle on forest issues during colonial and post colonial period. The struggle during the globalization era against land acquisition involving community forest rights for mining, industrial and development purpose throughout India compelled the central government to promulgate the Forest Rights Act 2006. The various activist organizations including the Adivasi Organizations also further continued their protest for the implementation of the Forest Rights Act. One of the major anomalies in the implementation of the Act was that the Forest Department tried to create obstacles in conferring the Community Forest Rights to the Adivasis and forest dwellers. This is in spite of the fact that the Forest Rights Act in its preliminary statement accepted that they have committed historical injustice by denying the genuine rights of the forest people and the Adivasis. The Forest Department has rejected several legitimate claims of the forest people including their community rights. Still throughout the country, Adivsis and forest dwellers have been conferred title to over 54.80 lakhs acres which is indeed a significant achievement. This has to be recognized that there has been a significant contribution of the autonomous Adivasis and other activist democratic organizations in this achievement. Another point which needs to be acknowledged is that the Naxalite Movement also called as Maoist Movement also strongly resisted the anti-peoples' forest policy and anti-land acquisition policy of the Central Government during the globalization era inspired by new liberal policy. The strength of the Adivasis Movement is a strong bulwark against the anti-Adivasi policy and anti-people policy of the Central Government.

References

Aberle, David F. (1966), 'New Social Movements', Knowledge Center, Built on the Thematic Theme Framework.

Areeparampil, M.S.J. (2002), *Struggle for Swaraj*, Chaibasa, Jharkhand: Tribal Research and Training Centre (TRTC).

Bahuguna, Vimala (1990), 'The Chipko Movement', in Ilina Sen (ed.), *A Space within Struggle: Womens Participation in Peoples Movements*, New Delhi: Kali for Women, pp. 110–124.

Basu, S. (2006), 'Ethno-regionalism and Tribal Development: Problems and Challenges in Jharkhand', in G.C. Rath (ed.), *Tribal Development in India*, New Delhi: Sage Publications, pp. 133–52.

Blumer, Herbert (1939), 'Collective Behavior', in Robert E. Park (ed.), *An Outline of the Principles of Sociology*, New York: Barnes & Noble, p. 199.

Chowdhury, Ashok (2002), *Report on the First National Conference of National Forum of Forest People and Forest Workers (NFFPFW)*, Rashtriya Van Shramjeevi Manch, 30 September to 2 October, Nagpur.

Damodaran, V. (2006), 'The Politics of Marginality and the Construction of Indigeneity in Chotanagpur', *Postcolonial Studies*, Vol. 9, No. 2, pp. 179–196.

Das, Victor (1992), *Jharkhand Castle Over the Graves*, New Delhi: Inter-India Publications.

Gadgil, Madhav and Ramachandra Guha (1994), 'Ecological Conflicts and Environmental Movement in India', *Development and Change*, Vol. 25, No. 1, January, pp. 101–136.

Ghosh, K. (2006), 'Between Global Flows and Local Dams: Indigenousness, Locality, and the Transnational Sphere in Jharkhand, India', *Cultural Anthropology*, Vol. 21, No. 4, pp. 501–534.

Gopalkrishanan, Shankar (2010), 'The Forests Rights Act, the Adivasis, and the State', *India Social Development Report 2010*, New Delhi: Council for Social Development.

Guha, Ramachandra (1989), *The Unquiet Woods: Ecological Change and Peasant Resistance in the Himalaya*, New Delhi: Oxford University Press.

Hiremath, S.R. et al. (1997), *Report of Study Team on Nagarahole National Park and Tribals* (Mimeo), Dharwad: Janapara Vignana-Tantragnana Samsthe (JVS).

Iyer, K. Gopal (2007), 'Preliminary Draft Report: Study on Land and Forest Rights of Adivasis in Karnataka', *Other Media*, Delhi: SAIP., pp. 25–27.

Karlsson, B. (2003), 'Anthropology and the Indigenous Slot', *Critique of Anthropology*, Vol. 23, No. 4, pp. 403–423.

Kornhauser, William (1959), *The Politics of Mass Society*, New York: The Free Press, p. 212.

Lobo, Brian (unpublished manuscripts), *Status of Adivasi Lands in Maharashtra.*

Mukherji, Partha Nath (1988), *Social Movement, Conflict and Change: Towards a Theoretical Orientation*, New Delhi: Institute of Social Sciences.

Mukul (1993), 'Villages of Chipko Movement', *Economic and Political Weekly*, Vol. XXVIII, 10 April, pp. 617–622.

Oberschall, A. (1973), *Social Conflict and Social Movement*, Englewood Cliffs, N.J.: Prentice Hall Inc.

Omvedt, Gail (1993), *Reinventing Revolution: New Social Movements and the Socialist Tradition in India*, London: East Gate Book.

Oommen, T.K. (2010), 'Social Movements, Issues of Identity and Social Movements: Concerns of Equity and Security', in T.K. Oommen (ed.), *Readings in Sociology and Social Anthropology*, New Delhi: Oxford University Press, pp. 39–40.

Pagare, Ganesh and Vasudha Pagare (1994), 'A Village Like Ralegan', *Economic Times*, 6 June (The World Report on the Environment).

Patkar, Medha (1992), 'The Strength of a Peoples' Movement: Interview with Medha Patkar', *India International Centre Quarterly*, Spring-Summer, pp. 244–250.

Rao, M.S.A. (ed.) (1978), *Social Movements in India*, Delhi: Manohar Publications.

Rodrigues, Sebastian (2007), *A SAIP Study Project: Land, Mining and Indigenous People in Goa: An Overview* (Mimeo), Tiswadi (Goa), Mand-an Adivasi Rights Resource Centre.

Roy Burman, B.K. (1994), *Tribes in Perspective*, New Delhi: Mittal Publications.

Sethi, Harsh (1993), 'Survival and Democracy: Ecological Struggles in India', in Ponna Wignaraja (ed.), *New Social Movements in the South: Empowering the People*, New Delhi: Vistaar Publications, pp. 121–148.

Shah, Ghanshyam (2004), *Social Movements in India: A Review of Literature*, New Delhi: Sage Publications.

Shanley, P., F.C. Da Silva and T. Macdonald (2011), 'Brazil's Social Movement, Women and Forests: A Case Study', *International Forestry Review*, Vol. 13, No. 2, p. 233.

Tarrow, Sidney (1998), *Power in Movement: Social Movements and Contentious Politics*, Cambridge: Cambridge University Press.

Tilly, C. (1984), 'Social Movements and National Politics', in C. Bright and S. Harding (eds), *Statemaking and Social Movements*, Ann Arbor, MI: University of Michigan Press, pp. 297–317.

Turner, Ralph H. and Lewis M. Killian (1987), *Collective Behavior*, Englewood Cliffs, N.J.: Prentice Hall, p. 223.

Wignaraja, Ponna (1993), *New Social Movements in the South: Empowering the People*, New Delhi: Vistaar Publications.

Wood, John R. (1993), 'India's Narmada River Dams: Sardar Sarovar Under Siege', *Asian Survey*, Vol. XXXIII, No. 10, October, pp. 968–984.

Annexure 1
State-Wise Area under Forest

(sq km)

States/UT's	*Geographic Area*	*Reserved Forest*	*Protected Forest*	*Unclassed Forest*	*Total Forest area*	*% of Forest to Geographic, area*
Andhra Pradesh	2,75,069	50,479	12,366	977	63,821	23.20
Arunachal Pradesh	83,743	10,178	9,536	31,826	51,540	61.55
Assam	78,438	18,060	0	8,958	27,018	34.45
Bihar	94,163	693	5,779	1	6,473	6.87
Chhattisgarh	1,35,191	25,782	24,036	9,954	59,772	44.21
Delhi	1,483	78	7	0	86	5.73
Goa	3,702	237	822	165	1,224	33.05
Gujarat	1,96,022	14,156	395	4,663	19,113	9.75
Haryana	44,212	249	1,158	151	1,568	3.52
Himachal Pradesh	55,673	1,896	33,043	2,094	37,033	66.52
Jammu & Kashmir	2,22,236	2,551	17,643	36	20,230	9.10
Jharkhand	79,714	4,387	19,185	0	23,605	29.51
Karnataka	1,91,791	29,550	3,585	9,949	43,084	22.46
Kerala	38,863	11,098	170	0	11,268	28.99
Madhya Pradesh	3,08,245	58,734	35,587	900	95,221	30.89
Maharashtra	3,07,713	49,217	8,196	4,526	61,939	20.13
Manipur	22,327	1,467	4,171	11,780	17,418	78.01
Meghalaya	22,429	1,112	12	8,372	9,496	42.34
Mizoram	21,081	7,909	3,568	5,240	16,717	79.30
Nagaland	16,579	308	508	7,813	8,629	52.05
Odisha	1,55,707	26,329	15,525	16,282	58,136	37.34
Punjab	50,362	44	1,137	1,903	3,084	6.12
Rajasthan	3,42,239	11,950	17,862	2,975	32,488	9.49
Sikkim	706	5,452	389	0	5,841	82.31
Tamil Nadu	1,30,058	19,388	2,183	1,305	22,877	17.59
Tripura	10,486	3,688	664	2,041	6,293	60.01
Uttar Pradesh	2,40,928	11,078	22,425	3,323	16,826	6.98
Uttarakhand	53,483	23,827	10,673	162	34,662	54.81
West Bengal	88,752	7,054	3,772	1,053	11,879	13.38
Union Territories	9,478	3,159	4,248	3	7,410	78.18
Total	32,87,263	3,99,919 (51.62)	2,38,434 (30.78)	1,36,387 (17.60)	7,74,740 (100.00)	23.57

Source: 1. State of Forest Report, 2003.
2. Compendium of Environment Statistics India, 2006, Central Statistical Organization, Ministry of Statistics and Programme Implementation, Government of India.

Annexure 2
Encroachment on Forest Land in India

S. No.	*Name of States*	*Area Under Encroachment (in ha)*	*As on (Date)*
1	Andhra Pradesh	2,56,000.00	11.03.2011
2	Chhattisgarh	1,18,494.60	07.03.2011
3	Gujarat	34,791.00	31.03.2010
4	Haryana	184.63	24.11.2011
5	H.P	1,832.1403	21.03.2011
6	Karnataka	96,014.349	14.03.2011
7	Kerala	42,420.5085	16.05.2011
8	M.P	8,077.72	27.08.2011
9	Maharashtra	85,388	31.12.2010
10	Odisha	78,505.077	01.01.2004
11	Punjab	7,404	23.11.2011
12	Tamil Nadu	14,352.16	07.03.2011
13	Uttaranchal	9,676	31.03.2010
14	West Bengal	12,660.972	31.03.2010
15	Arunachal Pradesh	58,553.07	04.03.2011
16	Assam	2,59,700.00	18.03.2011
17	Manipur	1,918.37	02.08.2011
18	Meghalaya	9,378.00	21.03.2011
19	Mizoram	12,057.90	01.10.2010
20	Nagaland	2,671.86	22.11.2010
21	Sikkim	3,300.96	27.05.2011
22	Tripura	47,758.14	16.03.2011
23	A & N Islands	3,326.63	10.03.2011
24	Chandigarh	14.00	11.03.2011
25	D & N Haveli	613.30	22.12.2010
26	Daman & Diu	87.83	28.09.2010
	Total (All India)	6,65,186.22 (16,62,965.55 Acres)	

This Information was given by the Minister of State for Environment and Forests (I/C) Smt Jayanthi Natarajan in a written reply to a question By Shri Kanjibhai Patel in Rajya Sabha.

Annexure 3
State wise Percentage of Scheduled Tribes to Total Population: 2001–2011

State/ UT Code	*India/State/ Union Territory*	*Percentage of Scheduled Tribes 2001*			*Percentage of Scheduled Tribes 2011*		
		Total	*Rural*	*Urban*	*Total*	*Rural*	*Urban*
1	*2*	*3*	*4*	*5*	*6*	*7*	*8*
	INDIA	8.2	10.4	2.4	8.6	11.3	2.8
01	Jammu & Kashmir	10.9	13.8	2	11.9	15.4	2.5
02	Himachal Pradesh	4	4.3	1.3	5.7	6.1	2.6
03	Punjab	NST	NST	NST	NST	NST	NST
04	Chandigarh #	NST	NST	NST	NST	NST	NST
05	Uttarakhand	3	3.8	0.7	2.9	3.8	0.9
06	Haryana	NST	NST	NST	NST	NST	NST
07	NCT of Delhi	NST	NST	NST	NST	NST	NST
08	Rajasthan	12.6	15.5	2.9	13.5	16.9	3.2
09	Uttar Pradesh	0.1	0.1	0	0.6	0.7	0.2
10	Bihar	0.9	1	0.5	1.3	1.4	0.6
11	Sikkim	20.6	21.2	15.9	33.8	36.6	25.5
12	Arunachal Pradesh	64.2	69.7	43.4	68.8	74.1	51
13	Nagaland	89.1	93.7	67.1	86.5	92.8	70.8
14	Manipur	34.2	44.4	6.1	35.1	45.6	13.4
15	Mizoram	94.5	96.3	92.6	94.4	96.6	92.5
16	Tripura	31.1	36.5	4.7	31.8	41.2	5.1
17	Meghalaya	85.9	90.2	68.3	86.1	90.1	70.4
18	Assam	12.4	13.6	4.5	12.4	13.7	5
19	West Bengal	5.5	7.2	1.2	5.8	7.8	1.5
20	Jharkhand	26.3	31	9.8	26.2	31.4	9.8
21	Odisha	22.1	24.6	8.1	22.8	25.7	8.5
22	Chhattisgarh	31.8	37.6	8.4	30.6	36.9	10
23	Madhya Pradesh	20.3	25.8	4.9	21.1	27.2	5.2
24	Gujarat	14.8	21.6	3.2	14.8	23.1	3.5
25	Daman & Diu	8.8	11.1	4.9	6.3	12.6	4.2
26	D & N Haveli	62.2	74.9	19.4	52	82.4	17.2
27	Maharashtra	8.9	13.4	2.7	9.4	14.6	3
28	Andhra Pradesh	6.6	8.4	1.8	7	9.3	2.4
29	Karnataka	6.6	8.4	2.9	7	9.2	3.5
30	Goa	0	0	0.1	10.2	15.9	6.8
31	Lakshadweep	94.5	95.6	93.1	94.8	95.2	94.7
32	Kerala	1.1	1.5	0.2	1.5	2.5	0.3
33	Tamil Nadu	1	1.6	0.4	1.1	1.8	0.4
34	Puducherry	NST	NST	NST	NST	NST	NST
35	A & N Islands	8.3	11.9	0.9	7.5	11.3	1.3

Source: Demographic Status of Scheduled Tribe Population of India.

4

Marginalization and Dissent

Contemporary Movements in South-Western Tribal Belt of Madhya Pradesh

D.C. SAH

This paper after tracing the historical as well as contemporary processes that marginalized the tribes of South-Western Madhya Pradesh, analyses the contemporary tribal struggles taking place in the region and the process of continuity and change in the tribal South-Western Madhya Pradesh. Tribals have their own ways of life, cultural identities and customary modes of living. For centuries, they have lived in isolation, far away from the national mainstream. They have worshipped their deity whom they identified with their landscape and nature. Their isolation has kept them socially, economically and politically isolated with accompanying impediments of poverty, malnutrition, ignorance and exploitation. The colonial rulers looked to these social groups from the point of view of maintenance of law and order whereas the social scientists as objects of social antiquities to be preserved in isolation. Tribal population in India is about 8.2 per cent. Seventy per cent of these Scheduled Tribes are concentrated in Madhya Pradesh as also in Chhattisgarh, Bihar including Jharkhand, Maharashtra, Gujarat, Rajasthan, and Odisha. Amongst the Indian states, Madhya Pradesh mirrors forest, tribal and poverty. A third of its geographical area is under forest cover that is a rich treasure house of tribal communities. According to 1991 Census the tribal population of Madhya Pradesh is 15.4 million. This is nearly a fourth of the total tribal population of India. Out of 425 scheduled tribes of India, Madhya Pradesh alone has a share of 46 tribes, divided into nearly 161 ethnic groups.[1] Every fourth person in Madhya Pradesh belongs to a Scheduled Tribe. Anthropologists and sociologists are of the view that tribal population is not evenly distributed in all the districts of the state.

One finds *Barela* living in the hilly tracks of South-Western tribal zone of Madhya Pradesh. *Barela*, a relatively civilized and peaceful community, is engaged mainly in agriculture and farm or non-farm labouring. They are one of the three main tribal groups of the belt along with *Bhilala* and *Bhil*. In social hierarchy, *Barela* fall in middle between *Bhilala*, a *sanskritized* tribe high up in the hierarchy,[2] and the *Bhil* are relatively primitive groups. These three major tribes of South-Western Madhya Pradesh follow strict social relations where *Bhilala* would not marry with *Barela* and *Bhil*, and *Barela* would not have marriage relations with *Bhil.*[3]

Tribal Marginalization: A Historical Sketch

For a considerable period in history Madhya Pradesh had remained uninhabited and sparsely populated region. It is difficult to establish who the first settlers of the area are but *Kumar* tribe of Raipur were among the earliest inhabitants (Dubey, 1998). The tribal belt of the South-Western Madhya Pradesh, also known as *Nimar,*[4] comprises Khandawa, Khargone and Badwani districts, and is flanked by two-hill ranges, the *Vindhya* on its north and the *Satpura* on the south. At that time small tribal communities, Bhil and Meena who lived in the forest and cultivated small patches of land that they cleared by burning, populated Nimar. The tribal influx also started during the time, mainly from Rajasthan and Gujarat. This was the time when *Parmar* dynasty in the region was disintegrating. The state was in anarchy and tribal chiefs emerged as landowners, recognized *Garasiay* or unrecognized *Bhumihar*. Muslim invaders, unfamiliar with the region, could not control the tribal and encouraged Rajputs to settle and control them.

The *Badwani* state was established around thirteenth century and over time this small state with its barren soil and hilly surface escaped the coveted eyes of the Mughals, Marathas and the British Agents.[5] Although there are no known evidences about Badwani dynasty, what is known, however, is that Sisodia Rajputs from Udaipur were the rulers of the state (Shrivastav, 1970). As a result of the Muslim invasion of Rajasthan, Gujarat and Malwa that occurred around 1200 AD, many Rajput warriors fled and came to settle in the Narmada Valley. *Bhils* who had ruled this entire region till the eleventh century came to be gradually displaced, and could retain their rule only in the hills of Vindhyas and Satpura. The Rajput take-over reached its great heights in the fifteenth century. In order to establish their control on land, the *Sisodia* rulers hired *Bhil* warriors in their army. And, thus, the local *Bhil* came under the protection and patronage of *Sisodia* rulers. Many of these Rajput rulers married *Bhil* women and the result of the union is said to be the origin of *Bhilala* tribe. The *Bhil* polity that existed before the Rajput influx was not centralized. Territory was divided into a large number of localities each under a hereditary chief called *patel.* But there was no taxation, no system of surplus extraction to make the chief richer than his band. Later, as the *Bhil* were forced to accede to their subjugation, the Rajput selected some tribal chiefs to act as representatives of their authority in the villages, such that the chiefs came to be the link between their ruling political system and the traditional tribal polity. By the end of the eighteenth century, the tribal societies lived under the overarching authority of the Rajputs who were relatively more centralized in their kinship-based political organization. But this area remained untouched by the claims of *Mughals* and their armies. Perhaps, the area was perceived as being too poor to exploit (Shrivastav, 1970).

While *Mughal* supremacy eclipsed by the growing power of *Marathas,* the latter ruthlessly suppressed all resistance, including of the tribals. However, the *Marathas* did not remain united for long. The Peshwa, Holkars and Scindias fought with each other for supremacy in Malwa and Khandesh. During early nineteenth century, when the rains failed and famine stalked the land, Bhil took to the hills and from their stronghold descended down periodically to loot. These guerrilla raids of the *Bhil* upon rich plains were a thorn in the flesh of the *Maratha*. The bloodthirstiness of the *Maratha* against the *Bhils* indicates that the exploitation of tribals had started long before the colonial period.[6] A series of wars between the British and the *Maratha* – with *British* playing off one *Maratha* faction against another – culminated in November 1817 when the Peshwa, the Nagpur chief and Holkar rallied to form a united front against British. This alliance of the *Maratha* failed when Holkar's army was defeated in December 1817. After this defeat, Holkar ceded to the British all his territory south of Satpura. In 1918, the whole region south of Satpura hills came under direct British rule. But *Badwani state* with its chequered history kept moving in and out of British rule. In a sense, the state neither accepted British dominance nor did it come under any other rulers, Holker or Sindhia. Till 1947, the *Sisodias* could manage personal powers and hereditary perpetuity to rule Badwani.[7]

Between 1820s and 1860s, there were widespread Bhil disorders all over Khandesh, Satpura and *Nimar*. When military action failed to quell the *Bhils*, the British chose to investigate *Bhil* disorders, in order to understand what caused them, through that knowledge, control them, and prevent their recurrence. Thus, a policy of pacification came to be implemented (Shrivastav, 1970). Despite British co-optation of some *Bhils* into an indigenous force like the *Bhil corps*, and their deployment against other *Bhils,* resistance continued unabated throughout the region even after 1860s. Economically, the things were a lot worse off for the Bhils.

There are other reasons for Bhil insurgency. First, the *bania*, the trader moneylender, became ever present in tribal life, both as financier of agricultural operations and as a local agent for the collection of land tax (Baviskar, 1995). The *bania* became the instrument of the worst process of tribal exploitation, in nexus with state, to extract surplus.[8] Second, with the colonial rule, the authority of the headman, *Patel,* to permit fresh clearings in the forest came to be abrogated and was instead vested in state officials. In the process, property rights were sharply redefined. Tribals were increasingly excluded from the forest and their customary use rights restricted. Land was leased to contractors whose activities turned vast tracts of forest into semi-barren land. The expansion of the railways (1870–1910) also resulted in the widespread destruction of forests and the beginning of the process of tribal land alienation.[9] Third, the British had tightened the system of taxation; both where they ruled directly as well as in areas managed through the Rajput rulers. This surplus extraction had added to the miseries of tribals. And lastly, collection of excise duties was given out on contract to the *bania* who would advance loans to the *Bhil* in exchange for first rights to their produce. The *bania* who were intermediaries between the administration and the people, encouraged taxpayers to grow market oriented cash crops that were more risk prone during scarcity.[10] The increasing burden of taxation, depletion of natural resources and land alienation, and extraction of *bania* made survival even more precarious than usual, necessitating seasonal migration to the far off places during the bad agricultural years.

Bhil insurgencies consisted of looting and plunder of non-tribal villages in the plains. The *Bhil* had been pushed from the agriculturally more productive plains to the poorer hills because of British policy of encouraging immigrant *Patidar* settlement on fertile Narmada plains. From that position, the non-tribal plains below were plump and prosperous targets. This resistance, however, was not directed against the British, but against the rich villages that could be attacked more easily and profitably (Baviskar, 1995). This is also an indicator of the distance and suspicion, born out of experience of the *Bhil*, for the non-tribals.

The nationalist struggle for Independence, which mobilized people all over the country in the first half of this century, received little support from tribals (Baviskar, 1995). For the *Bhils*, people who were fighting the British – the traders – had an ideology emanating from groups whose interests were antagonistic to those of the *Bhils*. The *Bhil* who formed the bulk of the cultivating population had come out firmly in opposition to the local *bania* who favoured non co-operation despite the fact that a number of other movements in the region were successful.[11] When India became free tribal dominated districts of Madhya Pradesh including *Nimar* tribal belt were declared scheduled areas. *Bhil, Barela* and *Bhilala* were classified as

Scheduled Tribes. A number of programmes such as ashrams-shalas, IRDP, soil and water conservation schemes, and minor-irrigation schemes were initiated. But the process of modern development did not touch the tribal heartland.

Social Order and Institutions

The way of life among *Barela,* like any other society, is passed from one generation to the other through social institutions. These institutions help them not only preserve their culture but also preserve their social order. Unlike *Bhilala*, and despite their *sanskritization*, the *Barela* have not yet entered in *varn-jati* system.[12] Nevertheless, *Barelas* have their own culture that is being preserved and have a distinct identity among the other tribes of South-Western Madhya Pradesh. *Barela* are simple, peace loving and hard working people. Modernity has introduced a changed outlook between generations; both in appearance and more substantially in thinking. Older men wear traditional dhoti, *angarkha* and a shawl while the younger generation wears shirt and pant. The women wear *lugadi, kanchuli* and *lahanga*. The traditional staple diet of the region is maize, jowar, wheat and pulses. Among the poor, *rab* is very popular which is made out of cereals, water and curds. Use of oil or ghee is limited in their food. Non-vegetarian food is also common and is accompanied by home-brewed or purchased liquor, especially during festivals like *holi, diwali, idal, diwasa etc. Barela*, like other tribes of the region, are very fond of ornaments, especially of silver. They live in small houses made out of mud walls covered on top with baked tiles (*khaprail*). Well to do among the *Barela* use hand-made brick and wooden roof structure covered on top with home-baked tiles. The village is scattered in to five-seven *falia* with some 20–30 houses in each *falia*. Houses even in a *falia* are not at one place but located on the agricultural fields of the individuals. Brothers with agricultural land at one place though live separately but have houses near each other. *Sanskritized Barela* also display Hindu god, picture of Christ along with framed photographs of the family members.

Barela villages have three major social institutions that govern social interaction within and outside community. *Village Jati Panchayat* governs matters related to social justice and social interaction between communities. Each village has a traditional leader called *Patel* with a dynastic origin. He is the most influential person of the village and is treated with regard among the villagers. Often he is supported by three-four *falia wise-men* chosen by elders of the village. The main function of the *Patel* is to settle social and financial disputes among villages – like marriage and divorce, land disputes originating from lease of agricultural land, etc. The other main job of this institution is to (a) manage the social and religious functions of the community and (b) settle disputes resulting from clash of interests between villages. *Patel* has a high social rank within the community and justice done by him along with the members of village security committee (of Panchayati Raj) is generally accepted by the parties as well as the community. Disputes that remain unresolved, because one of the parties does not accept the judgement, are referred to civil institutions like court and police. The *Jati Panchayat* also levy monetary penalty on the offending party. This institution is an important forum where actions that have a bearing on community like displacement, forest Mafia, outsiders in village, etc. are discussed and decided.

The second important social institution of *Barela* tribe is *'gotra'* organizations. These institutions govern the actions relating to social networking and marriage. '*Gotra*' organizations are federation of households from similar *'gotra'*. Like the caste system of non-tribal society, the '*gotra*' panchayat of *Barela* is a process of production and reproduction of a set of norms that distinguish different groups. But unlike non-tribal caste system that creates social hierarchy positioning groups to have advantages in economic exchange, the *Gotra* Panchayats produce gradation without any hierarchy. The institution mainly helps to recognise legitimate groups for giving daughters and getting brides for their sons. Marriage between *Barela* from same *gotra* is discouraged and has no social sanction. Apart from this, *gotra* organizations also arrange caste feasts, festivals, meetings, etc. These organizations are fair source of creating social capital within a closely-knit network of individuals for coping with shocks and crises.

The third important social institution of the *Barelas* is family. In *Barela* terminology, family is defined as a group of sexually interacting individuals with an aim of progeny. Since progeny, child rearing and their education is the meaning of the family, bulk of the households are nuclear; joint family concept is rare in *Barela* tribe. Family as an institution is oriented towards establishing the division of labour within family that starts from age five onwards and is a process to train individuals for their livelihood struggles based on gender and age.[13] Family, the basic institution among the *Barela* in general, also rests on monogamy relationship. But one can find cases of polygamy especially having more than one wife in the region. Over years, polygamy, however, has become a costly affair amongst *Barela*. Majority of marriages take place through mutual agreement between families.[14] The newly married couples live separately as nuclear family.

Bride price among *Barela* is an important institution that recognizes the contribution of female to family income. *Barela* women are very hard working and contribute to family income substantially from early age. As a result, loss of family income owing to marriage is compensated by brides' family by paying a *bride price* that ranges around ₹ 12,000 to 15,000 in 2002. Many young boys remain unmarried owing to high *bride prices*. The status of women in *Barela* households is significantly higher than that of the non-tribal society. Women participate in economic activities equally as men do. Married females generally accompany their husbands if the entire family or a few members have to migrate seasonally for their livelihood.

Despite a relatively higher status of women, there appear to be powerful processes of socio-cultural norming within the society with the sanctioning of rule breakers ensuring conformity. Sanctioning was noted in the form of the exclusion of unmarried, of women without children, of widows and the disabled from social functions, and the use of domestic violence as a mechanism of control. The treatment meted out to unmarried, childless women, who fail to maintain the expected submissive and acquiescent behaviour, harassments, taunts and house being regularly pelted with stones and liquor bottles are not uncommon. There is evidence of strongly patriarchal gender relations where the space for women's jurisdiction and control was severely circumscribed. Women had no power in farm-management decisions – what crops to grow where; planting; weeding and harvesting times, were not permitted to sell agricultural output, and were not even in control of household decision-making down to the level of choosing what meals to cook. This is in the context of patrilocal youth marriages, where marrying at 15 is the norm and marrying younger not unusual. Young brides are expected to take on a disproportionate share of productive and reproductive tasks in her husband or parents-in-law's house. Wives are commonly 'disciplined' through repeated and sometimes severe beatings delivered by her husband if she is regarded as not working hard enough or not completing tasks in the required way. Young women look back on their pre-marriage adolescence as a period of plenty – they might occasionally be taken to the bazaar by their fathers and bought clothes and snacks – and leisure – they could sometimes refuse to work.

Livelihood Struggles

Around 1870 tribals were encouraged to stop shifting cultivation and settle down on forest land.[15] Most of land cultivated by *Barela*, even today, consists of a part of depleted forestland. Such encroached cultivation is essential to subsistence in land-starved economy. Encroachment though results in deforestation and soil erosion, it is the only way out when opportunities are none and resources are lacking. The necessity to encroach forestland need to be appreciated within the social frame that values agriculture and the autonomy it provides.

Agriculture is the main source of livelihood of the *Barela*. But agriculture is difficult in the hilly terrain for, cultivation is practised without terracing the slopes. As a result, only a small part of the available land that is relatively plain has capability of retaining moisture and exploiting its yield potential. Market oriented high yielding crops like cotton, soyabean and wheat are grown on these fertile plots. In rest of the slopes, that constitute bulk of the cropped area, traditional crops like maize, pulses, bajri, jowar and groundnut is grown. Agriculture is rainfed and energized wells serve less than 15 per cent of the cropped area during *rabi* for wheat. Since land productivity is poor and monsoon failures are frequent, livestock and migration constitute major coping mechanism. The ownership of livestock varies. Yardstick of wealth is the number of cattle, goats and hens that a family possesses. Goats are important assets that can be converted into liquid money during times of shocks. The forest by and large has depleted but wherever accessible is the source of fodder, fuel, fibre, fruit, house-building materials, medicines, etc.

Demographic pressures amongst the *Barela* have resulted in rapid fragmentation of agricultural land. The fragmentation of land has become a source of chronic poverty in the community. With poor resource base, seasonal migration provides much needed stability to the *Barela* households. There has been a long tradition of tribal migration in search of employment from the region. While market mechanisms have become more dominant, agricultural productivity depends on the availability of fertile land and use of seed-fertiliser technology on it. Fertile lands in the *Barela* villages are scanty. Thus, seasonal migration becomes necessary for monetary supplement to the limited production base. During scarcity years, even well off *Barelas* have to resort to migration. It is a necessity for about half of the households that have low access to land assets.

Contemporary Movements

Colonial marginalization of tribal interests in the *Nimar* valley has already been discussed in the preceding sections. After Independence, the ways of administrative set-up did not change, though the rational of development[16] did. Independent India inherited an economy pervasive of intense poverty. Agricultural production was stagnating and productivity was falling (Blyn, 1966). Industrial sector was small and its traditional manufacturing and trade was stunted. Moreover, the trade and infrastructure were designed to feed its colonial interests. Modern industry was discouraged and the regime flooded the Indian market with low cost industrial goods that further depressed indigenous industry. The capability of the industry to absorb the work force was marginal. Reduced death rates and increased pressure from growing population fragmented the land and landless class increased rapidly. The system of collecting agricultural tax reinforced these tendencies. Consequently, agriculture – the dominant sector of country – was characterized by a large labour-force tilling small and fragmented plots with seed varieties just capable to feed its growing population.

This scenario was responsible for a desire and hence choice of development strategy in India. Few pressing ideologies also influenced the choice. First, false optimism with respect to capabilities of agriculture originated due to good rainfall, and achievement of low targets fixed during 1951–56; Second, structural constraints of agriculture were wrongly identified as '*slack*' *between* average and higher levels of yields that some farmers have achieved (Government of India, 1959). It was wrongly presumed that the agricultural technology existed in the country and the '*slack*' was due to inadequacy of supplies and the manner of its usage; and lastly was the tendency to equate modernization with industrialization.

The debate over the development strategy after Independence was guided by these considerations. The prime need before the country was to 'accelerate the rate of material capital formation'. The limiting factor in this regard was low saving. It was argued that shortage of saving was mirrored in the inadequacy of production of capital goods. And, thus, came forward the theory behind Mahalanobis plan that considered source of growth was capital goods and the means of growth were allocation of resources for their acquisition. The more resources so allocated, the faster production capacity would grow (Mellor, 1967). The underlying assumption was that with a faster growth in production, benefits would trickle down to the masses and thereby ensuring distributive justice. But the growth remained too little to trickle down.

The situation further deteriorated with respect to distributive justice when second generation problems of new agricultural technology started emerging in mid-1970s. The new agricultural strategy created islands of prosperity amidst mass of poverty. Inequality across group of people and across locations got intensified. Tribals, marginal farmers and landless labourers were losers and so were the areas that remained outside the purview of new agricultural technology. The lopsided investment in Research and Development between irrigated and dry farming technology affected the tribal adversely who depended on dry farming. This capital-intensive approach resulted in inequality and concentration on the one hand and insensitivity and violent social disruption on the other. Alienation, deprivation and inequality, it can be argued, are inherent in the strategy of Indian development.

This pattern of development has fundamentally altered three crucial bases of production: water, land and forest.[17] Moreover, the tendency of the government to consolidate its power over resources is also shown in its support for large irrigation projects. These interventions have further affected tribal interests adversely. The critical relationship between the tribal, environment and development led to ideologically driven struggles that brought together concerns for conserving nature with issue of justice. The tribals of Madhya Pradesh, including *Nimar,* has a history of revolts (Dubey, 1998). In contemporary Madhya Pradesh, despite numerous interventions by the state, movements against state policy have been quite successful. Small informal loans supplied by *bania* during scarcity or input credit on failed crops with vivaciously high interest rates end up in *Barela* becoming a debtor and losing his land. The immigrant *Patidars* are settled on the fertile alluvial lands in the Narmada plains whereas hilly unfertile drylands are left to the *Barela*. The rapidly increasing *Barela* population moved into the forests that, since Independence, have come to be fully under state control. Tribals who cleared forest areas for cultivation now face charges of encroachment.[18] Control over forest is a major contention that has brought into play civil society institutions like the *Adivasi Mukti Sangathan* (AMS). On the other hand, displacement due to large dams in the region has rationalized the presence of the movements like *Narmada Bachao Andolan* (NBA), an NGO that has provided alternatives in existing development paradigm.

Development, environment and governance have been contested in these struggles in tribal South-Western Madhya Pradesh. These concepts have different meanings for the *Barela* and the state. This mismatch in the definition is contested by everyday practices; violent sometimes but in more sublime way bring out the contradictions of state actions relating to access to natural resources. State as the authority of development, rationalizes its action through projects of national interest and through interventions that rest on out-dated mode of land acquisition, makes the tribals powerless. The struggles against state are placed within the discourse of ecology and development as the case is with *Narmada Bachao Andolan* or are located against state's force and repression as in the case of *Adivasi Mukti Sangthan.* These struggles are able to mobilize *Bhil, Barela and Bhilala,* and have gained support from a number of institutions outside the region (Baviskar, 2001). The success of these initiatives is mixed in weakening of the state repression and development initiative.

The *Adivasi Mukti Sangathan* attributes tribal oppression to their powerlessness before state and market. Corrupt revenue officials, brutal policemen and foresters, poor education facilities and failing health services make up a system that marginalizes tribals. In the last three years, the political activities of AMS have brought it into direct confrontation with these power elite. The AMS has successfully compelled the government to retrieve tribal lands and other property that had been taken over by moneylenders. The campaigns of the AMS forced the government to suspend several corrupt revenue officers, policemen and forest officers.

To counter the AMS, the non-tribal deputy chief minister of Madhya Pradesh, late Subhash Yadav, organized the *Adivasi Samaj Sudhar Shanti Sena* (ASSSS) in 1997. Commercialization of country liquor replacing home made *Moudee*[19] has assumed notoriety in the *Nimar* tribal belt. The anti-liquor campaign of AMS had resulted in the closure of legal and illegal liquor vends in around 250 villages with considerable losses to both vendors and their protectors. One such 'injured party' was b*hanjgadia patel*, the hereditary Adivasi headman, of Kabri village and the block Congress committee president. The AMS took the battle to b*hanjgadia*'s own door when its members in Kabri declared that no liquor would be sold in the village during *Indal*, the most important Adivasi festival. The campaign turned violent and had to face state repression. The incident was reported in media as rivalry between two tribal groups. Unlike *Narmada Bachao Andolan*, the *Adivasi Mukti Sangathan* is declared by the state an armed struggle that is trying to misguide tribals (Baviskar, 2001).

The campaign of the Narmada Bachao Andolan started with Sardar Sarovar Project in Gujarat[20] in late 1980s and took a decisive form in Madhya Pradesh with the construction of 400 MW hydroelectric plant at Maheshwar. This project would submerge 61 villages, about 5000 hectare of rich agricultural land in *Nimar* plains that would adversely affect livelihood of 2500 submerging households. The NBA started mobilizing project affected persons (PAPs) in the submerging villages for futility of this unsustainable pattern of development that results environmental destruction as well as serious relocation and rehabilitation (R&R) problems from mid-1990s. The successful campaign around these issues forced the Madhya Pradesh government to review the project and suspend the work on the project in early 1998. The success of NBA campaign had three major factors. First, the Maheshwar campaign was an extension of a larger process against the state's unsustainable approach of development that brought together national and international NGOs, environmentalist and the PAPs. Second, it brought in forefront the issue of involuntary displacement, outdated mode of land acquisition, and human rights violation of the PAPs. Lastly, throughout the campaign was projected as non-violent struggle of tribals against environmental distraction.

The differences in these two struggles are acute. While Narmada Bachao Andolan campaign was instrumental in making the state realize its mistakes, the *Adivasi Mukti Sangathan* turned out as a violent campaign between fighting groups of tribals to gain supremacy over each other. Despite these differences, the effect of the two campaigns within the tribal community of *Nimar* has been binding. These campaigns did create social capital in the form of closer ties between the communities, despite serious economic differences. When it comes to non-tribal intervention in their affairs, no outsider would be able to create space, no matter how harmless it could be to their land and livelihood, if there is even an iota of misgiving. Notwithstanding the changes around them, this suspicion is neither unjustified nor detrimental to tribal livelihood.

Continuity and Change

After Independence, three important processes have brought considerable change in constitutive ideas and behavioural expectations of Barela .

Development interventions of state, political decentralization and seasonal migration have influenced the Barela social and economic outlook. In order to appreciate the struggles between continuity and change, each of these processes have to be located within the cultural construct that *Barela* employ to interpret them. Development for *Barela* brings images of large projects, displacement and associated hardship.[21] Otherwise, large sections of the Nimar tribals have missed the fruits of post-Independence development interventions, which have been poor both in terms of coverage and quality. But except for elementary education and Public Distribution System, other amenities like access to electricity, all weather roads, health services, drinking water and sanitation, irrigation, agricultural extension, rural co-operatives, etc. are poor. In fact, their remoteness to administration and civil society institution is overriding enough to allow these facilities to reach the area. What has, however, reached them is the fear of displacement due to development projects with administrative insensitivity that accompany them. Presence of administration – in the form of police, forest and revenue officials – is synonymous to corruption, repression and exploitation.[22] The experiences of development in *Barela* consciousness imprint mistrust towards non-tribals, caution and apathy towards state interventions and loss of land and natural resources.

The change in the form of technologically driven agriculture, though restricted to a small subset of area, is not entirely an outcome of state intervention either. It happened because of seasonal migration. Seasonal migration for *Barela* is not coping with scarcity alone[23] it is experiencing development that has by-passed them.[24] What a migrating *Barela* learns during his stay as a labourer either on irrigated farms of *Nimar* plains or on the farms of irrigated HB cotton growers of Khandesh or on the fields of irrigated paddy and sugarcane growers in south Gujarat is a main source of agriculture technology transfer. How to energize the well and distribute water; how to grow irrigated fertiliser-responsive cotton, soyabean and wheat; utilization of post-harvest technology of these market-oriented crops etc. is learnt during seasonal migration. No matter how much the *Adivasi Mukti Andolan* discredits it, this process of production of knowledge is creating space for non-tribal institutions that is inducing conversion of subsistence way of agriculture to a market driven agriculture.[25] The process is, however, internalized without any state support. In irrigated areas, the *bania* is providing agricultural credit without any security. The *Barela* are also able to repay the loans promptly at least during good agricultural years. But in the process, *Barela* have started attaching a high degree of dependence on non-tribal institution they loathed the most, the *market*. This is an ideological contradiction that is the handiwork of modernity. This emerging consciousness towards technological change – infuse with conditions of larger tracks of poor quality of land – produced ethos in which *bania* finds that land as a source of exploitation is not as remunerative for their money-lending business as it used to be during pre-Independence years.

The third important process that is imprinting the *Barela* consciousness is the process of decentralized governance. The logic of decentralized governance is to bring decision-making nearer to the masses. In last eight years of its working in the region, decentralization has brought considerable transformation. Traditional leadership and its social dominance has given a way to elected leaderships; many of roles that *patel* used to play have become redundant when identity of *Patel* is subsumed into *Sarpanch*. But when patels are unable to establish themselves as elected leaders, especially in a multi-village panchayats, decentralization has become a ground where traditional ideology would like to re-establish itself. This has resulted in divide and fractions in village polity. Social interests that used to be supreme are giving way to economic interests. Generation divide has sharpened with older people being sceptical to all economic changes, whereas the younger generation is receptive and adaptive to interventions and economic changes. Both sides with their experiences – marginalization and exploitation versus modernity and economic affluence – have stood to their ideological stand. But the divide is apparent.[26] Both the agents, the *Patel* with his social clout as well as the elected representative with his political clout and reach-up to high echelons of administration, are playing their respective roles. Changes are accepted slowly in *Barela* society with caution.

Images of modernity and changes are mirrored simultaneously with traditionality and *status quo*. The process is a continuum of mistrust and trust at one level but at another, it only reflects diversity and stratification in an apparently homogenous society.

Notes

I am grateful to B.R. Purohit, Amita Shah and Kate Bird for their comments on an earlier draft of the paper. However, all the errors remain mine. D.C. Sah is Professor Emeritus, MPISSR, Ujjain.

1. Sahu (1998) reports that 7 out of 46 tribes of Madhya Pradesh have status of primitive tribes. Gautam and Sisodia (2001) have argued that tribals in Madhya Pradesh are located in following zones: Eastern Zone comprises the districts of Surguja, Shahdol, Raigarh, Bilaspur and Sidhi; in the hills of Surguja, we come across the *Pahari Korwas*, who are recognized as the most backward of the primitive tribes of the state; in the Central Zone are the districts of Mandla, Betul, Chhindwara, Seoni and Balaghat wherein *Gond, Korku, Kol* and *Baiga* are the principal tribes; Southern Zone comprises Bastar district and parts of Raipur, Durg and Rajnandgaon fall

under this Zone. *Maria, Muria, Sawara, Halba* and *Bhatra* are the tribal groups of this area; South-Western Zone comprises Jhabua, Dhar, Khargone, Barwani, Ratlam and Khandwa districts wherein the *Bhils, Bhilalas, Patalias* and *Barelas* are the principal tribal communities; in North-Western Zone, there are *Saharia* tribal communities that inhabit districts of Shivpuri, Morena and Guna.

2. *Sanskritization* mirrors the social mobility in the form of entering into caste fold, acceptance of religious faith, and gradual movement to Hinduism without losing the tribal identity (Sarkar, 1986). In mixed caste villages where *Barela* are in majority, social groups like *Bhangi, Balai* and *Chamar* – all Scheduled Castes – are placed by the *Barela* in a lower social order.
3. *Bhilala* and *Barela* would not accept cooked food from *Bhil* but *Bhil* would accept these from the former.
4. Badwani, along with adjoining Khargoan and Khandwa districts, formed the part of 362 km long and 64 km wide valley with fertile soils in its plains. *Patidar* from Gujarat have settled in the *Nimar* plains a century back. This influx of *Patidar* displaced *Bhil, Bhilala* and *Barela* tribals from the plains to unfertile hills.
5. Shrivastav (1970) argues that the *Sisodias*, rulers of Badwani, trace their origins to Bappa Rawal, the founder of Mewar dynasty. One of his descendants established himself at the Avasgarh (Badwani) about twelfth or fourteenth century.
6. The first *Maratha* intrusion in the region was in late 1699. By 1755, the whole region, including parts of *Nimar,* came under their control. The turbulent *Bhil* were subdued with drastic measures. The rebels were brought to Khargoan and ordered to behave. Those who complied were presented with collars of honour and those who did not were beheaded (Shrivastav, 1970).
7. Rajput rulers of Badwani were treated with honour by *Mughals* and were given their original powers. These rulers in early eighteenth century, however, assisted *Maratha* invasion in the Malwa. British took over the state briefly from 1861 to 1873. From 1894 till 1910, the state was administered directly under the British Political Agent. During the First World War, the then Prince of the Badwani state, Ranjit Singh, served the forward line of France. In recognition, he was granted powers to rule again. In 1921 again, the prince received, with hereditary perpetuity, some more criminal powers. After his death, his minor son, Devi Singh was invested with administrative powers. Till Independence, the *Sisodias* ruled the state. In 1948, the state was merged in India. For details, see Shrivastav (1970).
8. The interest rate charged by the *bania* in the region is as high as 50 per cent for four months. A shock in the form of death of bread earner, prolonged illness or failed crop result in the tribal debtor losing his assets; land, silver and animals. The riches and affluence of trading *bania* community in towns of *Pati, Sendhwa* and trading centres like *Chacania, Dhanora*, etc. can be traced to exploitation of tribal by them.

9. In contemporary *Nimar* hills, a large part of cultivation is on encroached forestland. *Barela* villagers do not want to talk about when they settled on these upper hill lands. It is, however, recalled that the most recent tribal influx in the hills has been in last 75 to 100 years. A significant proportion of the resettled households have acquired land rights by 1970s. But about 10 per cent of encroaches are still fighting for their rights. Vast tracks of the *Nimar* hills are still uninhabited. Population pressures may encourage tribals to settle on these tracks for survival, fuelling a new confrontation with state.
10. *Adivasi Mukti Sangathan* activist Madhuri identifies the cash crops grown for the market in these hilly regions as one of the critical reasons of tribal indebtedness. The seeds for these crops are sold at an exuberant price. A crop failure brings a shock that puts the *Barela* in debt for at least three-four years if he has some fertile land. In case the farmer has poor quality land, asset depletion is a certainty. The situation may not have been significantly different a century back.
11. It has been argued that Quit India Movement left the tribal of the *Nimar* region rather untouched. The urban areas, nevertheless, had significant Congress following and political awakening (Shrivastav, 1970). The term 'Dacoit' had been an ominous connotation that British often used for the Freedom Fighter of 1850s in *Nimar* Hills (Dubey, 1998).
12. *Sulia Gotra* of Barela tribe is claiming themselves as Solanki by suffixing Singh to their names in the Pati hilly tracks. This is a sign of social mobility and *sanskritization*.
13. The training of a child starts from age five onwards. The first education to boys is to take cattle for grazing, by nine the boys are ready to be introduced to agriculture. By 14, boys can cultivate traditionally grown crops. Generally, girls between five and seven years have burden of caring for their younger sibling and gathering fuel-wood. Girls between nine and 13 years are generally engaged in fetching water, collecting fuel, helping their younger sibling. From 14 onwards, girls take up all the household chores including cooking.
14. Marriage could take place by selecting one of the following processes: In-service: Where the groom starts living in the bride's family when he cannot pay bride price; Exchange: Wherein the brother and sister of the family are married to the sister and brother of the other family; Settled: Marriage fixed by parents; *Bagodia*: Unmarried young couples chose their partners in a festival; Rajibhaji Abduction: Many a times bride is abducted by groom's family and marriage is solemnized after paying a price to bride's family known as '*Jagda*'.
15. The British made shifting cultivation illegal, reserved the forests and established sources of revenue there (Morse and Berger, 1992).
16. The economic critique of colonial past legitimized the option to govern the new nation-state; in order to legitimize their political authority, the Congress assumed the role of central allocator with an aim to remove inequality by a

process that resulted in rapid economic growth. The process required efforts and sacrifice by citizens. The *Dalits*, the small and marginal farmers, the landless labourers and the tribals were the groups that made the sacrifices.

17. This is how Madhavi, the *Adivasi Mukti Sangathan* activist, rationalizes the tribal movement against state repression.
18. The scale of the problem is reflected in the fact that in the *Nimar* hills many villages are identified as forest villages, i.e. lying outside the revenue system. In Pati taluka of Badwani district out of 106 villages, 46 are identified as forest villages. Rights of tribals in the forest villages are highly restricted by Forest department.
19. Commercialization of liquor is a recent phenomenon. As forests have dwindled and opportunity cost of fuel-wood increased many folds, *Moudee* – the homemade brew made out of *Mouda* (Bassia Longifolia L) flowers – making has become a costly affair. Consequently, purchase of country liquor has replaced Moudee brewing. *Bania* has also started liquor supply. A section of tribal population, about 5 to 7 per cent, is alcoholic. Country liquor is cheap but it is a cause of indebtedness for these households.
20. Sardar Sarovar Project, a large irrigation project costing the state ₹ 80,000 million in 1986–87 prices, is one of 30 major, 135 medium and 3000 minor dams planned on Narmada river. These projects will displace a large number of families from Madhya Pradesh. Resettlement and rehabilitation of state of the project affected persons has been casual, to put it mildly (Sah, 1997 and 2002).
21. The Indian experience with R&R of large project affected PAPs lacks completeness and had been apathetic to local needs and resources. The R&R policy is forced and its implementation creates visible and invisible raptures in the social fabric in the short run and impoverishment in the long run (see Sah, 1999).
22. Revenue officials are remembered for their extortion in land sales which cost the seller about ₹ 4,000 per acre or for land transfer to a son could be registered only after a bribe of ₹ 2,000 per entry. The police have duel images. First as an institution of settling disputes in such a way that each affected party has to bribe in order to resolve the dispute in its favour. Its second image is of a state apparatus that is used in intimidating involuntary relocation of PAPs. The forest officials connote a bureaucratic set-up that has denied *Barelas* access to natural resources. But if one can bribe them, limited access may be granted.
23. Rehabilitation of involuntary migration begins with shifting of PAPs and ends with reconstructing their broken socio-economic fabric in new environment. It is a prolonged and complex socio-economic and political process (see Sah, 1997).
24. In drought prone areas, migration also works as asset formation device. Successive droughts render agriculture as unsustainable livelihood option

and forces even large farmers to join the queue for doles. The marginal farmers and landless labourers accumulate assets due to their access to labouring options owing to migration.

25. This may also break the distrust syndrome with respect to non-tribals as noted above.
26. *Nimar* tribal belt is an economically divided lot. For example, in Pospur village in Pati taluka of Badwani district a group of young farmers is ready to take risk and associate themselves with schemes like *group financing* and *self-help group* activities. But the older generation wants no outsider especially state intervention on schemes like *social forestry* and *soil and water conservation* activities on common property land that further constrains their already constrained access to natural resources.

References

Bailey, F.G. (1960), *Tribe, Caste and Nation*, London: Oxford University Press.

Baviskar, A. (1995), *In the Belly of the River: Tribal Conflicts Over Development in the Narmada Valley*, Delhi: Oxford University Press.

——(2001), *Written on the Body, Written on the Land: Violence and Environmental Struggles in Central India*, Berkeley: Institute of International Studies, University of California Press.

Beteille, Andre (1998), 'The Idea of Indigenous People', *Current Anthropology*, Vol. 19, No. 2. pp. 187–191.

Blyn, G. (1966), *Agricultural Trends in India, 1891–1947: Output, Availability and Productivity*, Philadelphia: University of Pennsylvania Press.

Dubey, K.C. (1998), 'Tribal Uprising and Social Movements in Madhya Pradesh', in K.S. Singh (ed.), *Antiquity to Modernity in Tribal India, Volume 4: Tribal Movements in India*, New Delhi: Inter-India Publications.

Fernandes, W. (1999), 'Displacement of Tribals', in G. Pfeffer and D.K. Behera (eds), *Contemporary Society, Volume 2: Development Issues, Transition and Change*, New Delhi: Concept Publishing Company, pp. 78–91.

Gautam, R.S. and Y.S. Sisodia (2001), *Welfare Programmes and Tribal Development in Villages of Madhya Pradesh* (Mimeo), Ujjain: Madhya Pradesh Institute of Social Science Research.

Government of India (1959), *Report of India's Food Crisis and Steps to Meet it*, New Delhi: Ministry of Food and Agriculture.

Gupta, P.K. (1984), *Tribal Development in Madhya Pradesh*, New Delhi: Inter-India Publications.

Mellor, J.W. (1967), *The New Economics of Growth: A Strategy for India and the Developing Word*, Ithaca: Cornell University Press.

Morse, Bradford and Thomas Berger (1992), *Sardar Sarovar: The Report of the Independent Review*, Ottawa: Resource Futures International.

Raizada, A. (1984), *Tribal Development in Madhya Pradesh*, New Delhi: D.K. Publications.

Roy Burman, B.K. (1966), 'Questions Relating to Inclusion in and Exclusion from the List of Scheduled Tribes', *Journal of Indian Anthropological Society*, Vol. 1, No. 1.

Sah, D.C. (1997), 'Second Generation Problems of Involuntary Migration: Evidences from Sardar Sarovar Project', *Indian Journal of Agricultural Economics*, Vol. 52, No. 4, pp. 707–727.

——(2002), 'Crop Commercialisation and Migration', in G. Shah and D.C. Sah (eds), *Land Reforms in India, Volume 8: Performance and Challenges in Gujarat and Maharashtra*, New Delhi: Sage Publications.

Sahu, C. (1998), 'Madhya Pradesh', in C. Sahu (ed.), *Primitive Tribes of India*, New Delhi: Sarup & Sons.

Sarkar, J. (1986), *Social Inability in Tribal Madhya Pradesh*, New Delhi: D.K. Publications.

Shrivastav, P.N. (1970), *West Nimar: Madhya Pradesh District Gazetteers*, Bhopal: District Gazetteers Department.

Sinha, S.C. (1962), 'State Formation and Rajput Myths in Tribal Central India', *Man in India*, Vol. 42, No. 2.

Thakur, D. and D.N. Thakur (1996), 'Tribal in Central India', in D. Thakur and D.N. Thakur (eds), *Tribal Life in India*, Vol. 1, New Delhi: Deep and Deep Publications, pp. 99–121.

5

An Analysis of Tribal Movements in Contemporary Odisha

S.N. TRIPATHY

Tribal Resistance Movement was an integral part of freedom movement of Odisha against the British imperialism. In this historic struggle, the heroic roles played by some distinguished tribal leaders were Laxman Naik of Koraput, Ratan Naik of Keonjhar, Dora Bisoyee and Chakra Bisoyee of Ghumsur and Veer Surendra Sai of Sambalpur. Indeed, nothing could be more inspiring and edifying than saga of heroic struggle and sacrifice of galaxy of tribal personalities mentioned above (Panigrahi, 2011).

The *Khonds* of Ghumsur protested the British, as the latter interfered to stop the heinous practices by the formers. The British could not dare to enter into the remote hilly areas of the *Khonds*, because the latter launched guerilla warfare. The Khond chief Dora Bisoyee was the main target of the English soldiers (Report of J.A.R. Sterension, 1835). The British announced handsome reward to arrest the Chief. The Khonds killed a group of British troops, as the former were troubled by the latter. Chakra Bisoyee, another indomitable tribal leader of Ghumsur, dared to fight against the British troops. Although the British offered to pardon him, if he would surrender but there was no positive response (Padhy, 2001). The British could not capture Chakra, as he escaped from one place to another such as Angul to Ghumsur, then Sonpur, Kandhmal, Ganjam and Parlakhemundi. There exists a long and illustrious list of tribal resistance movement that took place in different parts of Odisha. But nothing could be more inspiring and edifying than the saga of heroic struggle and sacrifice of one single tribal leader of Koraput whose feats and exploits till today are without a parallel. This great tribal leader is no other than Laxman Naik of Koraput (Panigrahi, 2007). Having belonged to a *Bhuyan* tribe, Laxman Naik the illustrious tribal leader was born on 22 November 1899 in Tentuligumma of Malkangiri. He fought single-handed vehemently against the oppressive foreign rulers with consummate skill and rare passion of a fighter. He was the very fountain of grit, courage, and strength to countless followers and co–workers and shone by rare brilliance. He sacrificed all worldly comforts and did not bow before the pressure of the British imperialism. This tribal hero was not well educated, yet fully aware about the national movement. He was crying for the freedom of this country. He became more active when Gandhi's message reached Koraput. He became an active member of the Congress in enrolling as four '*anna*' or '*charanna*' member of the Indian National Congress. He played a crucial role in popularizing the Congress programme in Koraput. The people of Koraput and its surrounding areas, like Malkanagiri, Tentulipada, accepted him as the real hero and sacrificed themselves for the cause of national freedom. He promoted Khadi and made people aware of the Congress plan of action and took the charge of president of the Congress Primary Committee at Mathili in Koraput in 1942. He managed to mobilize the tribal people for various development works like constructing roads, building bridges and establishing schools. He asked the villagers not to pay the taxes to the British Government. During the Quit India Movement 1942, Laxman Naik was nominated to represent Mathili. He also offered individual *Satyagraha* with other seven friends in 1941 in Mathili Police Station area and used non-violence as a main weapon against colonial power. The tribal people called him 'Gandhi of Malkanagiri' (Devi, 1972). The Bonda tribes of this region were violent and belligerent and seized Mathili Police Station under the leadership of Laxman Naik. The angry demonstrators voiced patriotic slogans and as retaliation measure, the police lathi-charged the innocent tribal people of this area. Since Laxman Nayak was their leader, he was falsely implicated in a murder case of a forest guard and as a result, along with his sons and Congress workers, was sent to Koraput Jail. His trial was taken by the Additional Sessions Judge of Koraput session court and he was sentenced to death under Section 302 of IPC Later, he was sent to Berhampur Jail for execution. At the break of dawn on 29 March 1943, by 5.30 a.m. Laxman Naik gallantly marched towards the gallows (Ali, 1988). In this way, this great tribal leader resisted against the British imperialism and sacrificed his life.

Birsa Munda and His Movement

The British colonial system strengthened the transformation of the tribal agrarian system into feudal state. As the tribes with their primitive technology could not generate a surplus, non-tribal peasantry were invited by the chiefs in Chhotanagpur to settle on and cultivate the land. This led to the alienation of the lands held by the tribes. The new class of Thikadars (Contractors) was of a more rapacious kind and anxious to make most of their possessions. In 1856, the number of the Jagirdars stood at about 600, and they held from a portion of village to 150 villages. By 1874, the influence of the old Munda or Oraon chiefs had been almost completely effaced by that of the farmers, introduced by the superior landlord. In some villages the aborigines had absolutely lost their proprietary rights, and had been reduced to the position of farm labourers.

Birsa Munda, a dedicated tribal leader, a great freedom fighter along with the Munda reacted vehemently against the twin challenges of agrarian breakdown and culture change, through a series of revolts and uprisings. The movement sought to affirm rights of the Mundas as the real proprietors of the soil, and the expulsion of middlemen and the British. Birsa was treacherously caught on 3 February 1900 and died in mysterious conditions on 9 June 1900 in Ranchi Jail. Though Birsa Munda lived for a very short span of 25 years, he awakened the mind-set of the tribes and mobilized them in a small town of Chhotanagpur and was a terror for the British rulers.

Nature and Consequences of Early Tribal Movements

It is apparent from the aforesaid analysis that the history of Odisha has recorded scores of instances of such unequal battles, which became inevitable when imperialist forces came out with their mad craze for acquiring other's territories through the use of brute force, destroying the sovereignty and freedom of the free people and bringing in the process a holocaust to the lives of innumerable men, women and children. It is a battle between the evil designs of expansionism and the powerful instinct of self-presentation (Gomango, 1999).

It is immaterial as to what were the compulsions or motivations behind this resistance movement; it is immaterial if the tribal revolutionaries had no formal education and training in staging armed rebellions and had no common leadership to guide and encourage them to action. The unmistakable fact remains that they could no longer meekly submit to the intervention of the foreign rulers in their habitat, age old customs, rituals and cultural moors. Some of the tribal uprisings were directed against the mal-administration of the numerous feudal chiefs, the so-called *rajas*, *maharajas* who held ownership of large estates and lived on a policy of extortion and oppression. They acted as the representatives of the imperial power and all their action and conduct were directed at cementing the foundations of the foreign rule.

It is also evident from the above analysis that tribal communities have had an extensive history of struggle against the British during the colonial period. In the annals of Hunter in the annals of rural Bengal wrote of the Santhal rebellions; 'what we (British army) fought was not a war. So long their (Santals') drum went beating; they went on fighting to the last man.'About 20,000 Santals died and Hunter concludes, 'There was not a single sepoy (soldier) in the British army who did not feel ashamed.' The war of the Kondhs against British domination has also been extensively documented by the British administrators. The British sought to put an end to the rituals of human sacrifice of the Kondhs. Felix Padel (1995) aptly mentioned that the British, in fact, exaggerated the ritual and its violence in order to put gloss on their efforts to suppress this almost indomitable tribal community. Needless to mention, the British did not just sacrifice Kondh lives, they massacred them in thousands. Beginning at the middle of the nineteenth century, which also corresponded with the end of the stage of direct plunder, the British policy in India significantly became one of supports for landlords through whom the officialdom of empire sought to protect their dominations. Every now and then there was a deviation from this policy to accommodate the pressure generated by an unequal agrarian society which under the impact of the market, produced peasant movements, ... over the century, the peasants' ability to resist the landlord control of rent and produced increased and the structure of landlordism stood considerably weakened by the end of the British rule (Speech presented by Majid Siddiqi, JNU, 23 May 1997).

There are some important aspects of the tribal resistance movement which deserve mention. One is that the tribes have their own social, cultural and religious identity, their own taboos, make beliefs and peculiar compulsion of lifestyle and therefore, any attempt of the administration of an alien rule to make an inroad into the tribal society by way of reformatory and correctional changes, however laudable, is bound to be resisted by the tribes with all their individual and collective might (Pande, 1989b).

The second aspect of the resistance movement could be attributed to immigration of a chain of resourceful peasants, money-lenders, and scribes from the coastal plains to the tribal hinterland and the process of forced assimilation of the tribes with the economic policies pursued by the immigrants such as improvement of land, introduction of improved agricultural practices in places of the primitive agricultural system pursued by tribes. Alienation of land ownership of tribal *ryots* and eviction of tribal tenants was the direct and inevitable outcome of this process of invasion of crafty and unscrupulous traders and moneylenders and prosperous peasants from the plains into tribal areas and forced induction of the tribes into their ways.

The most dominant characteristic of the tribal resistance movement was that it was fundamentally an uprising against the foreign rulers and in that sense could be constructed to be the precursor of the national liberation movement which took a distinct shape and gathered momentum under the inspiring leadership of Mahatma Gandhi nearly one century later. The new policy introduced brought a radical change in the concept of land ownership. Tradition had conferred ownership or title to land on the basis of membership of a clan or tribe. The new policy put an end to this; it also put an end to attempts at land-grabbing by the leaders of a clan or tribe by force (Bhuyan, 2003).

Prima facie fair and equitable, this policy caused the replacement of the clan leader by new elite as an intermediary between the tribesmen and the alien government; it destroyed the traditional balance between the tribes and non-tribes. It also destroyed the traditional tribal economy and shattered the bonds which knit the different segments of a tribal society together. Such an unfortunate situation could have been avoided, had the foreign rulers pursued an enlightened and equitable land reforms policy which would have assured land to the tiller and protected his proprietary rights while discouraging rack renting and absentee landlordism. Instead, the land revenue policy of the British Government based on frequent settlement and revision of rent provided an impetus to the process of tribal land alienation, pauperization of the tribal peasantry and resultant unrest and violence in the tribal society.

If alienation of tribal lands in favour of non-tribal immigrants constituted an important factor of tribal unrest and uprising in the early part of the nineteenth century, it is no less today. It has no doubt enacted laudable legislative enactments like the Tribal Land Alienation Regulation of 1956 to arrest the process of grabbing of land of tribes by non-tribes but the process is going on unabated and often unnoticed. The crafty and resourceful members of the non-tribal community are responsible for such land-grabbing.

Land alienation coupled with denial of a fair and equitable return on the products of their hard labour have been responsible for misery and privation of members of the scheduled tribe community on an increasing scale. These injustices or deprivations could possibly have been compounded if industrialization of tribal areas on a scale or manner commensurate with their needs and conducive to their interests could have taken place by paying them just and fair compensation for acquisition of their land and by providing employment to them and their family members in the industrial establishments. Unfortunately, the reverse has happened leading to the total detriment of social and economic interests of tribes. This can be illustrated with a few examples. An area is given for prospecting and mining lease and the tribal loses his surface rights on the land he was used hitherto to cultivate for his own biological survival. His habitat is destroyed and he is pushed to the background to work under the mining contractor, under conditions subhuman living/bondage (Pande, 1989a). These contractors take over the tribal property, outrage the modesty of tribal women and devastate the very foundation of a quiet and placid tribal existence. These above acts force peace-loving tribes of Odisha to raise the banner of revolt in order to assert their rights for a better and fairer deal in the hands of development agencies.

Tribal Movements in Contemporary Odisha

For the last few decades and more particularly since 1990s, the issue of human rights – violation of rights to life and livelihood of tribal peoples – is a central concern. Therefore, the discourse on tribal movements and issues of tribal livelihood revolved around securing their well-defined rights on land and forest resources. This paper attempts to critically review major tribal policies and programmes of the state of Odisha. It tries to assess the impact of and changing perspectives regarding development programmes that affect the livelihood resources of the tribal people. The paper also tries to review various methods of articulation of collective concerns of tribal people with regard to the promotion and protection of their natural resources based livelihood.

The experience in Odisha shows that tribal peoples' protest movements, however well organized, have to take cognizance of the powerful interests of economic elite and industrial capital – both domestic and foreign – that wield considerable political power. Protest movements by the tribal people of Odisha in different pockets have attracted the attention of policy makers, bureaucrats, academia and activists across the world. These movements have contributed to strengthening the sporadic articulations by tribal people to organized protests and have led to the recognition that there is need to review the approaches and strategies of development interventions of the state as well as streamline the development programmes.

Since last more than two centuries, tribal communities, like many other non-tribal peasants and forest dwellers, have been witnessing the collapse of their multiple relationships with the land, the forest and water resources among themselves. The basis of their cultural ethos, their systems of meaning have faced the collective onslaught of outsider exploiters, and of foreign models of economic betterment which have been conceived without their participation and being implemented without their approval. The traditional territories of the tribal people have been subjected to incursions. Their lands are taken away in the name of national interest and economic development of the country. But in return, the tribes receive landlessness, impoverishment and long term degradation of the environment on which they totally depend.

Laws like Land Acquisition Act and the Indian Forest Act, etc. legitimize the continuing decline in access and control over forest resources that are considered as the basis of their subsistence economy. As a result of which, the tribes have continually fought for their rights and against their natural, social, economic and cultural resources being appropriated increasingly by outsiders and the State. Combined with the search for political autonomy, these agitations and fights assumed rebellious and militant forms in various regions, particularly in the North-East.

Demands range from creation of separate states, as in the case of Jharkhand and Bodoland to outright separation such as in Nagaland and Mizoram. Even since the pre-Independence era a series of tribal movements were witnessed. For instance, the Santal rebellion, the revolt by Birsa Bhagwan, the Praja Mandal Movement, the Tana Bhagat Movement, the Naxalbari Movement, the Jharkhand Movement etc. are all attempts by the tribal people to shake off the yoke of exploitation. The Khanwar tribes of Madhya Pradesh protested in 1957 against revenue collection and called upon the people to defy forest laws which violated their customary rights. Their slogan, 'Jungle Zamin Azad Hai', (forest and land are free gifts of nature) succinctly expressed the opposition to external control and commercial use. Naxalite movement, one of the outcomes of these type of exploitation, is the manifestation of the growing unrest among the tribal belts and activities of left wing extremists in the tribal belts of India.

For instance, the tribes, mainly peasants who were fraudulently deprived of their lands and means of livelihood along with their erosion of resources by the intrigues of the landlords started with greater ferocity the Naxalite movement in Andhra Pradesh. It soon spread like a wild fire to Telangana and Rayalseema districts. The movement got an impetus when Kondapalli Seetharammiah (KS) formed the Peoples War Group (PWG) on 22 April 1980. The group made rapid progress in a short time encashing on people's anger and resentment and spread its wings beyond Andhra to Odisha, Madhya Pradesh, Maharashtra, and Karnataka. In recent times, the organization has its deep-rooted presence in Bihar, West Bengal, Haryana, Delhi and Kerala. The tribes in many parts of the country fighting their battles relentlessly to protect their right to life, but the state has no hesitation in using coercive forces against the tribes who are struggling for establishing their rights. In the absence of state support and on the contrary; practically repressive measures being adopted by the state machinery to snatch away their traditional rights and life support system the tribes have no way out but to support the extremists and consequently they are unwillingly caught in the holocaust of a crossfire.

Understanding the Tribal Issues

Out of the total population, 8.2 per cent of the population in India constitutes the tribes. The states of Madhya Pradesh, Chhattisgarh, Maharashtra, Odisha, Jharkhand and Gujarat have more than half of the total tribal population of our country. The Scheduled Tribe population represents one of the most economically impoverished and marginalized groups in India.

Notwithstanding the fact that the Constitution of India prohibits discrimination on grounds of religion, race, caste, sex or place of birth (Article, 15) and it provides the right to equality (Article, 14), to freedom of religion (Articles, 25–28) and to culture and education (Articles, 29–30); the tribes in India, the oppression and appropriation of the tribal people by the economically and politically more powerful groups continued unabated.

At the root of the problem is the marginalization of tribes and their access failure to natural resources, especially land, forest and water. Low productivity, dispersed habitation, shifting cultivation, weak cooperative and marketing infrastructure, continued tribal land alienation leading to their dispossession and exploitation, physical complications etc. are some of the manifest features which characterize the tribal areas. The symbiotic relationship between the forests and the local dwellers was not recognized and the forest became property of the state. The tribes who have a lifelong relationship with the forests –which are their very homes, their religion and their culture – were conspicuous by its absence in the new frame. It is because of this basic lack of understanding, that there is a state of confrontation and regime of destruction in almost all tribal concentrated regions of India, which in the final analysis means great injustice to the tribal people. In recent decades, the perception of forestry has transformed because of the problem of deforestation, loss of bio-diversity, non-conservation of resources, non-protection of forest and lack of 'sustainable development'. Deforestation, exploitation and recurring droughts and other natural calamities drive the tribes into relentless grip of disease, suffering and starvation. About the decision which ends up destroying their land, livelihood and survival, leading to perpetual misery, the tribes are never consulted. These are voiceless people and unfortunately nowhere on the political agenda appear the restoration of their traditional rights to harvest and sell non-timber forest produce at fair and remunerative prices.

The Plight of the Displaced Tribes

Historically speaking, the inevitable sequel of all projects was displacement and displacement has been a saga of marginalization. But considering the escalating needs of the people, it is not possible to abandon all projects. As such, what is imperative is to conceive the possible implications of displacement while examining the social, economic and environmental aspects of the project as well as its viability. Of course, the cost-benefit analysis of the projects are usually undertaken before enforcement of a project, but the credibility of methods adopted, the procedures followed with regard to the evaluation of socio-economic costs involved in the projects, are subject to re-assessment. Even in most of the cases, a thorough scrutiny of costs in terms of loss of bio-diversity or ecological damages is never examined nor also the clearance from the department of environment and forests are adhered to.

The process of industrialization in India since the advent of twentieth century, the Tata Iron and Steel Company, Jamshedpur (Bihar), The Bokaro Steel Plant (Bihar), The Rourkella Steel Plant (Odisha), have detrimental impact on the tribes resulting in alienation of land, displacement and deprivation of this poverty-stricken community. Though the development activities in Odisha surged as early as 1950s, there were about 8,117 displaced families from 1446 villages because of development projects during the period 1950 to 1993. The UNDP estimates that till date more than one lakh people in Odisha have been displaced while 20 lakhs have been affected by development projects. Industrial projects like Rourkella Steel Plant (RSP), The Hindustan Aeronautics (HAL) and National Aluminum Company (NALCO) have displaced people, mainly the tribes (Fernandes, 1994; Tripathy, 2003).

In the tribal tracks of Andhra Pradesh, the Polavaram project threatens to displace more than 1.75 lakh people, mostly the Adivasis and will submerge 300 villages. The Adivasis in their present habitat, i.e. the schedule areas, enjoy a unique set of constitutional rights and privileges, which would no longer be available after they are uprooted. This project has been designed to impound water from Godavari and, apart from irrigating the coastal districts; it would also divert a portion of the stored water to the Krishna.

Sometimes, the marginalized are completely disenfranchised and disempowered to respond and only deal with challenges by coming up with what can be termed as coping mechanisms. In Madhya Pradesh, a survey conducted in Barwani district in 1998 found that 30 per cent of families rendered landless due to displacement migrated to Malwa, Gujarat, and Maharashtra. A second survey exhibited that the percentage of migrating families had increased to 46 in 2006. Similarly, impoverished tribes from Jhabua district in Nimad migrate to Godhra in Gujarat to work in quartz factories, but within 8 to 10 months of working in these factories, they contract 'silicosis', a deadly disease caused by inhalation of crystalline silica. As per one study carried out in just 20 villages in three blocks of Jhabua district, 128 persons have died and 277 persons are suffering from the disease. With respect to the Indore SEZ, youth from displaced tribal households have started to go to factories for daily wage labour, working under exploitative conditions of hard physical labour (Mehta and Tiwari, 2007): When it comes to the National Rural Employment Guarantee Scheme (NREGS), case studies show that neither the 100-day work promise, nor the promise of a wage of ₹ 60 per person for 7 hours labour is met. Often, three members of families work for 11 hours, to only get paid a sum of ₹ 60 in total. Often, employment is provided for 15 to 20 days and not for 100 days as promised (Mehta and Tiwari, 2007: 43–44). Further it has been pointed out that the homogeneous image of the tribes resulted in a planning process where their variability was neglected. Since tribal development ignored tribal worldview, non-tribal institutions, technology and skills were forced on them (Sah et al., 2008: 35).

The affected tribes have been deprived of modern fruits of development such as tap water, education, road, electricity, convenient medical facilities, etc. The majority of the project affected families (PAFs) were involved in rain-fed agricultural activities for their own sustenance. There is partial employment in forestry sector. Since the area is hilly with difficult terrain, they are wholly dependent on vagaries of monsoon and normally only a single crop is raised by them. Out of the PAFs of Madhya Pradesh who have re-settled in Gujarat, more than 70 per cent are tribal families. Majority of the total tribal PAFs are stated to have already been re-settled in Gujarat after having exercised their option. It is the contention of the State of Gujarat that the tribes in large number have responded positively to the re-settlement package offered by that state.

The Land Acquisition Act-1894 has the provision that the government is not bound to provide a displaced person anything but cash compensation if the concerned person can show the evidence of his land title, unfortunately, the tribes could not produce the same and as a result of which, they are usually deprived of the compensation. The elite have, therefore, through such pseudo developmental activities impoverished the earth of its natural resources. The earth's impoverishment has meant that communities who depend upon the natural base for sustenance have been deprived of their resources. This alienation cannot be described in terms of loss of material livelihood only; it is most profoundly the loss of culture autonomy, knowledge and power (Baviskar, 1995).

For the government and its agents of development, cash compensation seems to be the only panacea for the problems induced by displacement and the only policy for rehabilitation, whereas, in practice it is the most inadequate means for rehabilitation. No procedure and principles are laid down to estimate the costs, showing the arbitrariness of compensation. Apart from loss of land, the villager suffers loss from common property resources, forest produce, village grazing land, community centre, social security, and so on. The problem is more acute with the artisans, some of them may own land, but their major income is from their profession within the known community. There seems no provision with regard to their rehabilitation. Besides, the landless and the tribes are probably the worst sufferers.

The situation of the tribal people is all the more thorny, since the compensation is paid on the basis of land owned, the tribes who have no inclination to own land but use it as a common property fail to claim compensation on the basis of the lost common land. It's hard to believe that how land, natural resources, means of livelihood, social and cultural loss resulting from displacement can be quantified and compensated in monetary terms? And the non-quantifiable nature of numerous human and ecological costs is not even acknowledged? The government acknowledges the problem that, in tribal areas, where the displaced persons are given only cash compensation, the tendencies to spend the compensation amount by buying consumer goods and becoming destitute are common.

However, the voices of the displaced are no longer extraordinary. Echoed in virtually every displacement situations be it Tehri, Narmada, Singrauli or Keol Karo, only to name a few, they reveal what it means to be a 'displaced lot': loss of livelihood and traditional lands; demolition of homes; loss of social networks; severance from an eco-system that sustained them earlier and, above all, a feeling of powerlessness and insecurity for the future.

Displacement is a multidimensional phenomenon not confined to physical relocation; it reduces the 'quality of life' of the communities into sub human conditions. Displacement deprives of the vital sustenance of the tribal people who are dependent on the land, forests, common property resources (CPR), for their livelihood and finally their long term sustainability is also endangered. The detrimental effects of displacement are:

1. the alienation of the individual and community legal and customary rights and dislocation of the social and economic organization, and
2. the politics of legal and policy instruments that sanctions such disenfranchisement.

Cernea's impoverishment risk and reconstruction model proposes that 'the onset of impoverishment can be represented through a model of eight interlinked potential risks intrinsic to displacement.' These are: (i) Landlessness, (ii) Joblessness, (iii) Homelessness, (iv) Marginalization, (v) Food Insecurity, (vi) Increased Morbidity and Mortality, (vii) Loss of Access to Common Property, (viii) Social Disintegration, (ix) Loss of Access to Community, (x) Violation of Human Rights (Cernea, 1988).

Forcible Eviction of Project Affected Communities in Niyamgiri Hills (Kalahandi) and Resistance of Tribes in Odisha

Since a decade, the thickly forested and riverine region of Lanjigarh in Kalahandi (Odisha) is under severe pressure from mining development for bauxite deposits and alumina processing, by the British Vedanta Group, in collaboration with State of Odisha, Orissa Mining Corporation and also the Ministry of Environment and Forests. The proposed mining will severely degrade the Niyamgiri hills ecosystem which is a rich wildlife habitat and an important and recognized elephant corridor, endanger the Dongaria Kondh's self-sufficient forest-based livelihoods, and lead to the extinction of their culture over a period of time. More than 7 sq km of the sacred undisturbed forest land on top of the mountain that has been protected for ages by the Dongaria Kondh as sacred to their deity, Niyam Raja, and essential for the region's fertility; will be stripped off its vegetation, soil and rendered into a vast barren exposed land. Mining will build roads through the Dongaria's territories, opening the area to outsiders, a trend that is already threatening the rich biodiversity of the hills. The forested slopes of the Niyamgiri hills and the many streams that flow through them provide the means of living for Dongaria Kondh and Kutia Kondh, Scheduled Tribes that are notified by the government as 'Primitive Tribal Groups' and, thus, eligible for special protection. In addition, the Dongaria Kondh, whose total population is 7952 according to the 2001 census, are regarded as an endangered tribe. Schedule V of the Indian Constitution which enjoins the government to respect and uphold the land rights of Scheduled Tribes applies to the entire Niyamgiri hills region.

Since the Kutia and Dongaria Kondh are heavily dependent on forest produce for their livelihood, this forest cover loss will cause a significant decline in their economic well-being. It must be noted that the Vedanta proposal assumes that no displacement will be caused by the mining project whereas practically there is overwhelming evidence that mining will not only result in widespread resource displacement but may well permanently undermine the survival of the Dongaria Kondh.

When the Odisha Government says that the Vedanta Aluminium project would benefit the tribes, the tribal communities are against the development as planned by the government and are opposing the project. But, overlooking the grievances placed by the tribal people and neglecting their demands, the Government of Odisha rather uses its force to suppress the tribal opposition and make the project move ahead. At times, state police behaves like corporate goons and humiliate the tribals.

The Supreme Court of India imposed conditions on Vedanta Aluminium project to make a comprehensive plan for rehabilitation and all-round development of project affected tribal families before their displacement, which are to be monitored by the Government of Odisha.

The Forest Right Act (FRA) – whose rules were notified in January 2008 – did not see much progress till 2010. It was around this time that the MoEF refused forest clearance for Vedanta's phase II. In February 2010, stepping up their resistance to the controversial project, hundreds of Dongria Kondhs trekked to the abode of their presiding deity Niyam Raja on the Niyam Dongar (hill slopes) and designated it as inviolate. They carried out religious rituals and then put up a totem pole in the area. Since then, over a two-year period, the district government has tried to hasten the process and finalize individual claims under the FRA. Till the FRA came into force, millions of India's traditional forest dwellers were in the same spot that they have been since colonial times: bereft of any rights on the forest land that they have lived off for generations. This is the situation that the FRA attempts to change. For one, it allows claims to individual family titles of land occupied or cultivated forestlands that are considered 'encroachments'. For another, the law allows access to, as well as the use and selling of, forest produce that has been traditionally collected. This includes particular leaves that are used as leaf-plates, palm-tree juices, medicinal plants, and fruits. The forest rights law also gives a community – usually one village unit – the right to manage and protect forests it has customarily managed, even though these are government property.

The alumina refinery, capable of producing one million tonnes of alumina from bauxite per annum, has been operating since 2009 from the foothills of Niyamgiri. From 2007, Vedanta has been seeking clearance for a sixfold expansion of its refinery and 660 hectares of bauxite mining land over and above the existing 720 hectares granted in Phase I. This too has run into legal controversy, as it was granted clearance based on false information provided by Vedanta, namely that the land it wanted does not contain any forestland.

Niyamgiri Mountains of Lanjigarh area (Kalahandi district, Odisha state of India) is 4248 ft high. It is the source of 32 rivulets contributing to Vansadhara and Nagavali River flowing through Kalahandi and Rayagada. It contains elephant, sambhars, leopards, tigers, barking deers, various species of birds and other endangered species of wildlife in 672.018 hectares forest land. More than 75 per cent of the hill is covered by thick forests with an average density of 0.6. It has more than 300 species of plants, trees, etc. including about 50 species of medicinal plants (Wildlife Institute of India Report, 2006–2007). Six of the species are listed in the Red Data Book. These forests are yet to be surveyed properly for their floral and faunal wealth. This is because the bauxite is oolitic and pisolitic with high level of porosity resulting in high water retention capacity. It occurs beneath the laterite-capped plateaus and is characterized by the existence of a plateau supported by relatively impervious laterite layer with poor water retention capacity. Equally alarming are the observations on how the project affected communities were forcibly evicted and 'rehabilitated':

The tribal people have been displaced from their houses through physical eviction by the district administration. Many were beaten up by the employees of M/s Vedanta. The National R&R policy requires that land for land should be given after due process of consultation, particularly in the case of the tribals. Contrary to the above, cash compensation was offered to them which was not acceptable to many. The tribal people living on the plant site are mainly Kondhs who are illiterate and depend completely on their agricultural lands and forest for their subsistence. They have deep spiritual and cultural attachment to their ancestral lands and settlements. The displacement was opposed vehemently by them despite being offered large cash compensation by M/s Vedanta. In the face of resistance, the District Collector and the company officials collaborated to coerce and threaten them. An atmosphere of fear was created through the hired goons, the police and the administration. Many of the tribals were badly beaten up by the police and the goons. After being forcibly removed they were kept under watch and ward by the armed guards of M/s Vedanta and no outsider was allowed to meet them. They were effectively being kept as prisoners; the rehabilitation package for the displaced persons given by the user agency is not in the interest of sustainable livelihood of the local communities as no land has been given for grazing purposes, raising agricultural crops and carrying out other income generating activities, etc. The location of the rehabilitation colony has been decided totally ignoring the interest of the conservation of forests.

It has been observed that with the latest unanimous rejection from the gram sabhas of the tribes who resisted allowing the Niyamgiri for mining, Vedanta has signed agreements with the Governments of Chhattisgarh and Gujarat for ore to keep the Lanjigarh refinery – which had been closed for months before reopening two months ago – running. While both Kutia and Dongaria Kondh communities will be adversely affected by mining in the area, the likely negative impacts on the Dongaria Kondh are a particular cause of concern. The Niyamgiri hills are the sole and unique habitat of this tiny community. Any major disruption of their relationship with their environment is not only a serious violation of their rights under the Indian Constitution and forest laws, but also a grievous threat to their cultural integrity and their ability to survive as a distinct social group. Mining will destroy Dongaria Kondh livelihoods and culture.

The alumina plant and the mining project linked with it will have serious adverse effect on the flora and fauna due to mining, overburden dumping, construction of proposed road through the dense forests, liquid and gaseous effluents emissions, bright illumination, blasting with explosives, drilling and resultant vibration and dust, operation of heavy loading and unloading equipment, pollution, etc.

Thus, it is unanimously agreed that mining will severely degrade the Niyamgiri hills ecosystem which is a rich wildlife habitat and an important and recognized elephant corridor, endanger the Dongaria Kondh's self-sufficient forest-based livelihoods, and lead to the extinction of their culture over a period of time.

In the light of the above discussion, we can enumerate the multitude of factors which have contributed to the tribal unrest. Among them the important causes are enumerated as follows:

1. The prominence of tribal peoples' concerns stems from the realization that they have not benefitted from development projects, while the mainstream societies have prospered at their expense, pushing them deeper into the poverty trap. The forests of India are home to

significant numbers of forest-dependent people, mainly tribes whose socio-economic living conditions have not altered even after six decades of Independence. The traditional rights of local communities provide for subsistence and non-timber values that are usually unrecognized by the state-owned and controlled forest management agencies. In its mid-term appraisal of the Ninth Five Year Plan, documented that forests provided sustenance – non-timber forest produce (NTFP), small timber, fuel wood and fodder to 100 million forest dwellers out of which more than 60 millions are tribes. Ironically, the legislations pertaining to wildlife conservation and the establishment of national parks and wildlife sanctuaries deny them access and residence rights.

2. Most of the changes in the economic condition and lifestyle of tribal people have been caused by contacts with materially more advanced and politically more powerful populations. The improvement of communications, particularly the construction of motorable roads, as well as the intensified intervention of government agencies in more and more aspects of citizens' activities, have combined to undermine the independence of tribal societies. The degree of interaction with non-tribes varies according to both topographical and economic factors. Small groups in out-of-the-way places are less likely to be affected by contact with outsiders than settled communities close to a commercial highway or in the midst of agriculturally rich country. Where there are a few resources to attract settlers or traders, primitive tribes may be left in peace even though access to their habitat is not difficult, while in other areas the prospect of growing lucrative cash crops rapidly leads to fierce competition between the local tribesmen and rapacious immigrants.

3. Beyond the question of straight economic harm done to what is an economy under stress, two further effects of the failure of planned development projects are to be considered. Change in social relations is largely initiated by changes in economic environment. The end product is due to 'the interplay of many factors.' The economic change that has occurred is not a relative change in the environment but rather is an enlarging of economic networks with the outside world and the development of interdependence – a radical and absolute change in the economic environment, not a relative one; in fact, a change-over from isolation to interdependence. Over the decades, injustice of all types has individually and collectively frustrated tribal masses. Hence, in reaction to these undercurrents there is a crowd of social movements in the tribal area. Specifically, most of these movements are against the exploitation of natural resources, land encroachment, establishment of mega-development

projects and atrocities on tribes by different interest groups including the state, and so on. Their customary rights and privileges were denied. Thus, the tribes found them totally alienated from the administrative machinery and newly set up self-governing institutions and were denied opportunities of gainful economic activities. They suffered not only from poverty but also from a deep sense of insecurity. The tribes have been in the grip of insecurities and injustices through decades of neglect by the local administration.

4. It is reported that in many cases if voice of protest is raised by tribes and their supporters, instead of having respectful dialogue with them, attempts are being made to suppress these movements ruthlessly. And such ruthless incidences contribute to these movements. The net result of this process is perpetuation of rural unrest and violence. Some of these movements are highly local and some are working at the macro level. Some are exclusively headed and run by tribes and some are run by non-tribes. There are several social movements jointly organized by local tribes and the non-local non-tribes. While some of these movements are highly organized, systematic and structured but some are highly temporal, unstructured and emotion-ridden. Some have historical roots and some are recent in terms of its origin. Some of these movements are independent and autonomous and some have linkages with other social movements working in other parts of the country.
5. Dube (1998) argues that any 'development strategy that skirts around poverty, speaks of social justice in low whisper and underplays an endogenous creativity cannot be sustained … . The worst sufferers in the process will be the tribes, whose problems need sensitive handling. For them we need economically effective and culturally sensitive plans of participatory development. It would be suicidal to ride roughshod over tribal interests and ways of life in the name of national development. There has been a great overlap between our tribal areas and areas of abundant forest resources, and minerals. The last few years have seen several struggles by tribes and other local communities against mining which threatens their ecosystems and livelihoods.

Concluding Remarks and Policy Implications

In the light of this background, there is rationale on the part of the state to rethink and re-look the root of the problem. The state must take into note that it has been entrusted with the responsibility of protecting them, who can sustain on the good will and support of the state. A dialogue needs to be initiated with them for discharging, even though symbolic, the obligation as a part of the system and also in relation to the constitutional responsibility there is no other alternative but to get directly linked with their struggle (Sharma, 1990).

A perusal of the aforesaid analysis boils down to the fact that notwithstanding constitutional provisions and legislative measures to protect the interests of the tribes, particularly, in the article 164, 244, 244(A), 278, 330, 332, 334, 335, 338, 342 and 5th and 6th schedules of the Constitution aiming at development and protection of interest of tribes, the powerful exogenous forces of moneylenders, contractors, officials having their link with political personnel and police could exert dominant control and gratify the selfish greed of exploiting tribes. The poverty stricken, illiterate, innocent, simple tribes fail to withstand the countervailing exogenous forces and becoming prey to all types of exploitations. Despite the vast expansion of the formal credit system in India, the dependence of the rural poor on moneylenders continues in some areas especially for meeting emergent credit requirements. Such dependencies is pronounced in the case of marginal farmers, landless labourers, petty traders and rural artisans belonging to the socially and economically backward classes and the tribal population particularly in the resource-poor areas (Tripathy, 2007).

It has been observed that non-recognition of tribes over resources and restrictions on their use, alienation of tribes from the means of production, denial of due entitlement of labour, distressed payment of wages, and misappropriation of funds, have kept the tribes in the web of misery and starvation. In tribal dominated states in India, the life support system of the local tribes has been snatched away by non-tribes and state institutions, through the imposition of restrictions on the use of forests. As a result, tribal movement originated in fierce struggle of their rights (Tripathy, 2000).

The benefits of development has not percolated to the local tribal people, rather adversely affected their lifestyle, leading to the violation of human rights, miserable living standard of tribes, has restricted the community rights over natural resources, and their own forest resources, and finally, culminated to identity crisis of the tribes.

Secondly, the deregulation and privatization of mining and mineral sector is leading to the corporate sector, both Indian and foreign, entering this area which is mainly in the tribal regions. Already in Odisha, Jharkhand and Chattisgarh, the setting up of new projects to mine bauxite and other minerals has led to tribal people losing their lands. Their protests are met with brutal police repression. The trend of displacing the Adivasi people for industrial projects is getting heightened.

The State and the bureaucracy is not willing to adhere to the Samata judgement of the Supreme Court which has declared that in the scheduled areas (under 5th schedule), private industries or industrial enterprises cannot be set up without the consent of the tribes and such projects must be undertaken through the consent of tribal people.

As has been told earlier, one of the major problems for the tribal people is the exploitation by money lenders. Once they get into the bondage of usury they are reduced to the plight of serfs. This bondage is the most degrading aspect of tribal life. Hence, adequate credit must to be provided to tribes through cooperatives and bank loans so that the scourge of usury can be contained. Further, the minor forest produce which provide livelihood for the tribal people must be available for the tribes and they must own it. Cooperatives for marketing such produce have to be run by the government in cooperation with the tribes. Steps must be taken to protect the indigenous tribal knowledge of plants and their uses.

Strict enforcement of constitutional safeguards for the Scheduled Tribes must be carried out by taking over surplus lands above ceiling and distributing them to landless tribes along with other landless families, providing irrigation facilities in remote tribal areas, people's participation in forests through community management, etc. will go a long way in mitigating the miserable conditions of the tribes. Forest produce should be accessible to forest dwellers and neighbourhood tribal communities, ensuring provision of drinking water in remote hamlets must be a priority for ending hardships of tribal women. The state should ensure livelihood to the tribes when tribes are displaced from the original habitat.

A functional grass-roots democracy and people's participation in decision-making that benefits and harmonizes all interests, is probably the best possible way to complete the projects on time and keep the costs from escalating and minimizing the miseries of the affected. Development which cannot provide the basic necessities of life should be shunned and attempts be made for an alternate mode of development which should aim at providing roads in villages instead of flyovers in cities, schools in all places instead of five star hotels.

Protagonists of development should understand that it is not possible for the multinational companies to ameliorate the plight of the starving millions in the country. For greater equity in development, we need to forge a development strategy that takes into account the immense social, ecological diversity benefitting the tribes who are in the grip of unemployment accompanied by acute distress and poverty.

The Panchayat Extension to Scheduled Areas (PESA) Act 1996 has made it mandatory for the states having scheduled areas to make specific provisions for providing wide range of powers to the tribes for their development. The Act recognizes traditional customary rights over local natural resources. It accepts the validity of customary law, social and religious practices of community resources. Under PESA, the protective aspects have aimed at the preservation of their unique cultural traits, their rights on land and forests and safeguarding against inhuman exploitation. It empowered villages to protect community resources, control social sector functionaries, own minor forest produce, manage water bodies, give recommendations for mining leases, be consulted for land acquisition, identify beneficiaries for poverty alleviation and other government programmes and have a decisive say in all development projects in the villages. It empowered villages to protect community resources, control social sector functionaries, own minor forest produce, manage water bodies, give recommendations for mining leases, be consulted for land acquisition, identify beneficiaries for poverty alleviation and other government programmes and have a decisive say in all development projects in the villages.

Section 4 (M) of PESA authorizes the gram sabha to act in all areas where the tribals face threat to their survival and welfare because of their continued exploitation. The PESA creates legal space for direct community action, and therefore, PESA directly confers ownership to the gram sabha on Minor Forest Produce (MFP) which has been a support for their survival. But it has been observed that this right has been neglected or violated rather than adhered to. The commercial value of MFP has been appreciated resulting in the nationalization of MFP and, thereby, optimizing the state's revenue.

Thus, despite PESA, as well as several other protective legislations in the tribal regions of our country, there has been extensive violation of fundamental rights and human rights of the tribal people. The second hindrance lies in the inability of the poor peasants to make their voice heard in the face of elite domination of the traditional power structures.

The ingrained problem of elite domination can hardly be resolved, unless the poor tribes themselves can exercise enough bargaining power and be organized so that their collective voice can be audible to the irrigation executives and bureaucrats. It is lamentable fact that the purpose of the PESA Act has not been completely understood either by the political leaders or by the bureaucracy. People at large are also not aware of the provisions of PESA Act except in those areas where the NGOs are seriously working with the people.

The Act clearly prohibits the state to make any law, which would not be in consonance with the customary law, social and religious practices and traditional management practices of community resources. It has clear provisions that the gram sabha or the Panchayats at the appropriate level shall be consulted before making the acquisition of land in the schedule areas for development projects. Such consultation and consent of the gram sabha is mandatory on the part of the government much before the settlement and rehabilitation of persons affected by such projects in the schedule areas. Thus, PESA aims at ensuring significant protection against any arbitrary, discriminatory, and motivated action of the state relating to land acquisition and resettlement and rehabilitation (R and R) in tribal regions. It has been revealed that the local administration in league with the company officials was indulging in deliberate falsehood. In the consultation of gram sabha the method adopted is dubious as the consent was obtained through coercion and brutal force (Das, 2005).

The area affected by extremist movement is the region of Central India with concentration of tribal population, hilly topography and undulating terrain. The area has much less density of population than the plains. The failure to provide infrastructure and services as per national norms is one of the many discriminatory manifestations of governance here. These disparities result in non-available/poorly provided services. The removal of these disparities should be among the top priorities to convince people living in these areas that they are equal citizens and that they matter in national life.

1. There is no denying that what goes in the name of 'naxalism' is to a large extent a product of collective failure to assure to different segments of society their basic entitlements under the Constitution and other protective legislation. Therefore, what is required is to identify specifically the processes and causes contributing to continued tensions and alienation in areas of unrest and discontent, such as widespread displacement, forest issues, insecure tenancies and other forms of exploitation like usury, land alienation and imperfect market conditions and suggest specific steps to reduce the tensions and causes of discontent.
2. There is need to identify causes for persistent and abysmally low social and human development indicators and suggest steps for bringing these on par with the rest of the country in a time bound manner.
3. There is need to examine and suggest an appropriate strategy for ensuring peace and life with dignity and for resolution of conflicts in areas of chronic unrest. Also there is need to take measures to upgrade the levels of governance and strengthen public service delivery in these areas, through suitable administrative and institutional reform and mechanisms for prompt redressal of grievances.
4. There is need to suggest measures for ensuring time bound achievement of livelihood security, health and nutrition security, food security etc. and also suggest changes in Central and State Legislations impeding the achievement of these objectives. This is due to fact that so long as the tribes and all other sections don't feel stakeholders in the development of the country, naxalism will continue uncontrolled.

In view of their abject poverty and century old tradition of depending on forests and, moreover, due to lack of alternative viable option for livelihoods, the indigenous tribal people have to retain their traditional right over forest resources. The tribes as forest dwellers conceived themselves as the trustees of forest resources, preserving the forest for the benefit of future generations. Nobody can disown the role of tribal women in the preservation of bio-diversities in the tribal areas. Based on their traditional knowledge of protecting and conserving forests for generations, tribes adhere to sustainability principle by the economic and rational use of the minor forest produces.

Land, water, forests, environment, husbandry, etc, are in many ways common to all the states in the region and in meeting the challenges arising from them a collective approach in terms of thinking, research, policy formation and planning at the scientific and technological levels will prove immensely useful.

Moreover, any use of force in the name of law and order against the people, who are fighting for establishing their right to life, who are struggling against the paradigm of development which is not only iniquitous, but is contravention of the law of the land, is against the spirit of our Constitution as well as against human rights.

Taking into consideration the prevailing state of tribal affairs, unfortunately India seemed to have not done well in respect of building up an inclusive society as far as our tribal population is concerned. The important reason being the sheer number of tribal groups, i.e. approximately 635 tribal groups and subgroups including 73 primitive tribes, consisting of about 8.2 per cent of India's population and their spread in different areas of the country.

The absence of mainstreaming of their skills in arts and crafts as a source of income in our tribal development strategy further adds woes as they are then constrained to leave their homes for far flung urban areas in search of livelihood. Over the decades, it is seen that increasing levels of out-migration amongst tribes for want of employment opportunities is acquiring ever high proportion in keeping with the rise in their population. This out-migration for daily wages in the fields like construction and labour work, hotel industry, house maids or small business is not only responsible for their poor and inhuman standard of living as they earn less even after working for longer hours, since they fall into the trap of exploitation in terms of bonded, forced labour and human trafficking, etc. involving the tribal women. It is no strange that these areas are witnessing increased number of Left wing militancy, widely known as Maoism. These incidents point not only to their lack of empowerment in the present sense but also calls for reorienting the development strategy for the tribal upliftment, which will at least ensure them a decent standard of living and full enjoyment of rights.

References

Ali, S.M. (1988), 'Biplabi Saheed Laxman Naik' (in Oriya), *Souvenir*, Bhubaneswar, December. Quoted in N.P. Panigrahi, 'Tribal Resistance movement in Orissa', *Orissa Review*, Government of Orissa, August, 2011, pp. 52–57.

Baviskar, Amita, (1995), *In the Belly of the River*, New Delhi: Oxford University Press, p. 36.

Bhuyan, S.K. (2003), *Tribal Economy and New Projects*, Calcutta: Center for Studies in Social Science Research, p. 93.

Cernea, Michael M. (1988), 'Involuntary Resettlement in Development Projects: Policy Guidelines in World Bank Financed Projects', World Bank Technical Paper No. 80, World Bank, Washington, D.C.

Das, Vidya (2005), *PESA: A Reality, National Consultation on PESA Act*, Rayagada: Agragamee.

Devi, B. (1972), 'Se – EK – Sphulinga' (in Oriya), Cuttack, p. 164.

Dube, K.C. (1998), 'Tribal Uprising and Social Movements in Madhya Pradesh', in K.S. Singh (ed.), *Antiquity to Modernity in Tribal India, Volume 4: Tribal Movements in India*, New Delhi: Inter-India Publications.

Fernandes, W. (1994), *Development Induced Displacement in Tribal Areas of Eastern India* (Mimeo), New Delhi: Indian Social Institute.

General Report of J.A.R. Sterension to the Board of Revenue (1835).

Gomango, K. (1999), *Life Style of Tribals and Social Habits*, Bhubaneswar, p. 103, quoted by Dr N.P. Panigrahi, 'Tribal Resistance Movement in Orissa: Some Reflections', *Orissa Review*, August 2011.

Government of India (2004), *Report of the Expert Group on Prevention of Alienation of Tribal Land and its Restoration*, New Delhi: Ministry of Rural Development.

——(2008), *Development Challenges in Extremists Affected Areas (Report of an expert group to Planning Commission)*, New Delhi: Planning Commission.

Mehta, J. and V. Tiwari (2007), *Agriculture Policy of Madhya Pradesh: An Analysis*, Pune: National Centre for Advocacy Studies (NCAS).

Padel, Felix (1995), *The Sacrifice of Human Being: British Rule and the Kondhs of Orissa*, Delhi: Oxford University Press.

Padhi, Sakti and Nilakantha Panigrahi (2011), 'Tribal Movements and Livelihoods: Recent Developments in Orissa', CPRC-IIPA Working Paper No. 51, New Delhi: Chronic Poverty Research Centre, Indian Institute of Public Administration.

Padhy, S.C. (2001), 'Tribal Resistance to Imperialism', *Freedom Movement Prelude to Sequel*, Bhubaneswar, quoted by Dr N.P. Panigrahi, 'Tribal Resistance Movement in Orissa: Some Reflections', *Orissa Review*, August 2011, p. 33.

Pande, B.N. (1989a), 'Contours of Present Tribal Society', quoted by Dr N.P. Panigrahi, 'Tribal Resistance Movement in Orissa: Some Reflections', *Orissa Review*, August 2011.

——(1989b), 'Genesis of Tribal Resistance Movement in Orissa', *On Development and National Integration*, Bhubaneswar, p. 48, quoted by Dr N.P. Panigrahi, 'Laxman Naik: The Leader of the Leaders', *Orissa Review*, August 2006.

Panigrahi, N.P. (2007), 'Tribal Leader Laxman Naik of Koraput and His Uprising', *The Quarterly Journal of the Mythic Society*, Vol. XCVIII, No. 1, January–March, p. 84.

——(2011), 'Tribal Resistance Movement in Orissa: Some Reflections', *Orissa Review*, August.

Sah, D.C., Ashish Bhatt and Tapas K. Dalapati (2008), *Chronic Poverty in Remote Rural Areas: Evidence from Central Tribal Belt of India* (Mimeo), Ujjain: Madhya Pradesh Institute of Social Science Research and New Delhi: Planning Commission, Government of India.

Sharma, B.D. (1990), *Report of the Commissioner for Scheduled Castes and Scheduled Tribes*, Twenty Ninth Report, 1987–89, New Delhi: Government of India.

Tripathy, S.N. (2000), *Glimpses on Tribal Development*, New Delhi: Discovery Publishing House.

——(2003), 'Problems of Displacement and Development', in S.N. Tripathy (ed.), *Economic Development and Problem of Displacement*, New Delhi: Anmol Publishing.

——(2007), *Tribal Development: Issues and Policy Options*, New Delhi: Anmol Publishing.

Wildlife Institute of India Report, commissioned by the MoEF (2006–07), *Studies on Impact of Proposed Lanjigarh Bauxite Mining on Biodiversity Including Wildlife and its Habitat*.

6

Contradiction between Natural Resources and Development

A Key Issue for Contemporary Unrest in Tribal Areas of Madhya Pradesh

Y.G. JOSHI

The interlinking of the resource rich but economically poor areas with the economically prosperous urban areas under the globalized market economy has now initiated a process by which the resources and cheap labour is being drained out from these poor area towards already prosperous areas. At the global level, due to the technological advancement and networking, the natural resources of the poor countries are being drawn into prosperous countries for profit maximization, while the desired reverse flow of capital to the source area is relatively week. At the national level this process of internal colonialism is enriching the already rich areas at the cost of marginalized natural resource rich 5th schedule tribal areas. In a sense, the resource-rich 5th schedule areas have not been able to link themselves to the mainstream economy to take a real advantage of their natural resources, but on the contrary, they are being pushed to disadvantaged position due to this linkage. Therefore, the natural resources for them do not mean the same, as perceived by the people of the developed parts of the country.

Viewed in the context of contemporary tribal unrest resulting into various tribal movements occurring in different tribal areas of India, including the parts of Madhya Pradesh, one of the key issues is the draining off of resources from these areas on the one hand, and the resultant fall out of the negative impact of the development process in terms of environmental degradation, impoverishment and displacement, on the other.

The tribal dominated region of Vidhyachal, Satpura, Mahadev and Maikal of Madhya Pradesh also presents a scenario of a similar equation between resources and development, which is quite different than perceived in the developed parts. The objective of the present paper is to present this dimension of the inverse relationship of resources and development which is in the root of the discontent of the local population. For an ease of presentation the content of the paper has been divided into the following three parts:

1. Theoretical context of the relationship between resources and development.
2. The tribal belt of Madhya Pradesh and its resource base.
3. The scenario of socio-economic development of the area, under the emerging globalized market economy.

Theoretical Context of the Relationship between Resources and Development Resource

Resources are the aspects of bio-physical environment and are that portion of total stock that could be used under specified technical, economic and social conditions (Haggett, 1975). These substances existed in the environment since geological times but they could function as resources, only when man perceived their utility and developed technologies for their exploitation. Natural resources existing in some areas are only passive elements of production. Factors of other group are the attributes of man and society. These factors not only determine the availability and exploitability of natural resources but also their distribution and utilization. When viewed with reference to the tribal areas, the primary natural resources are – forest, land, water and minerals. Out of these, water, forests and minerals are such resources which are transferable, that is, they may be siphoned out in the name of national development or utilization in other demand areas. Viewed in the local perspective, it is always possible that the local population may not derive any benefit out of these resources, but on the contrary, may be adversely affected by the environmental fall out and the problem of displacement. Out of these natural resources, land is the only resource which could not be transferred out, however, viewed in the perspective of social development and justice, it will have to be seen who controls the better quality of land in the area and from the environmental point of view it has also to be analysed how far the quality of land resource is being adversely affected by land degradation caused due to the exploitation of resources and industrialization.

Development

We all know that the word 'development' has a much wider coverage, as compared to economic growth', which merely means increasing capacity of the economy to satisfy the wants of its members and may be measured in terms of GDP or GNP. Conceptually, the term development has undergone a number of changed interpretations, including, economic development, social development, sustainable development, human centred and inclusive development. In the concept of sustainable development, which is largely based on the concern for environment and future generation, sociologists have added the concept of 'socio-cultural sustainability' based on the principals of human dignity, equality and social justice (Gangarade, 1998) that includes the elements like improving social quality of life, elevation of moral fabric and invoking wider participation (Sharma, 1998).

However, while all the above perceived models of social development, environmental sensibility, inclusive growth, and people's participation may look impressive and desirable, in actual practice it is the economic model, based on infusion of capital, infrastructure and integration with market forces and urban demand, that dominates the scene, and the aspired social agenda is pushed in the background.

The Equation of Resources and Development

Economic development is a complex phenomenon that depends on a myriad of spatial and non spatial factors; natural resources being one of them. Merely existence of a natural resource cannot induce development. It depends on various human elements, ranging from individual participation, attitude and wants to various attributes of culture, such as, technological innovations, legal, political, financial, institutional and bureaucratic set-up. Resource availability is exploited through techno-feasibility and socio-political accessibility and, therefore, its relationship with development is a complex process that should not be analysed with a world view, but with reference to specific area and people in question. With reference to the development scenario of underdeveloped areas and under privileged people, their situation of underdevelopment should not be viewed to be due to lack of natural resource, or simply neglect, but to have been actively produced by exploitative processes (Frank, 1967). It has also been argued that in the present politico-economic structure, those people who are conscious of their rights and those areas which are dominated by such people get the benefits of developmental efforts, irrespective of existence or non-existence of natural resources (Sundaram, 1983).

Natural resources and development do not mean the same for all, hence should be viewed differently with reference to different areas and different people. Natural resource rich areas do not mean developed areas. The proponents of 'dependency theory' argue that resources flow from the 'periphery' of poor and underdeveloped states and regions to the 'core' of wealthy states and regions and, thus, poor regions and states are impoverished and the rich ones are enriched by the way poor areas are linked to the markets of the developed countries or developed urban areas (Munck and O' Hearn, 1999). This paradox of the inverse relationship of natural resources with development, termed as 'poverty in plenty' or 'rich lands and poor people' is clearly discernable in the Indian context. If the areas of forests, mineral wealth, watersheds and tribal habitations in India are mapped together, they will overlay one another on almost the same area, and surprisingly, these are also the homes of India's poorest population. This paradox of poverty and poor economic growth in areas of abundant natural resources has been dealt with in detail by the proponents of the 'resource curse thesis' (Auty, 1993). This situation can more or less be perceived throughout the Central tribal belt of India, especially in the mineral rich belt. The exploitation of forests and minerals of these areas are not benefitting the local population, but on the contrary, they are being adversely affected by environmental degradation and displacement. Therefore, these local aggrieved groups of people have been referred to as 'victims of development' or 'refugees of development' (Fernandis, 1993).

Tribal Belt of Madhya Pradesh and Its Resource Base

Madhya Pradesh is the home of the largest tribal concentration in the country. It has a concentration of 14.5 per cent of India's tribal population, which is 20.3 per cent of the total population of the state. If all the tribal subgroups are included, their number in the state is 46. Six are the principal tribal groups which are respectively, Bhil, Gond, Kol, Korku, Saharia and Baiga who together constitute 92.2 per cent of the total tribal population. Baiga, Saharia and Bharia of the state have been included in the list of primitive tribal groups by the government of India; now named as 'particularly vulnerable tribal groups' (PVTG).

It has been stated that most of the tribal groups of Madhya Pradesh have in-migrated from outside and initially these occupied the plane areas. Till the twelfth century, when the Rajput kings established their control on Madhya Bharat, tribals controlled this region. Even up to sixteenth century, the territory of Gond kingdom existed in the Mahakoshal region. Later on, the Mughals established their control on this area. In this process of conflicts, the tribals shifted to interior forested areas, for safety.

From the regional point of view, the existing tribal belt of Madhya Pradesh extends in the Vidhyachal, Satpura, Mahadev and Maikal region. Table 1 and 2 lists out the 19 districts and 136 Blocks that have been designated as tribal districts and Blocks by the State administration.

Table 1

Tribal Districts of Madhya Pradesh

S.N.	*District*	*S.N.*	*District*	*S.N.*	*District*
1	Sheopur	8	Burahanpur	15	Dindori
2	Ratlam	9	Hoshangabad	16	Anuppur
3	Jhabua	10	Betul	17	Shahdol
4	Dhar	11	Chhindwara	18	Sidhi
5	Barwani	12	Seoni	19	Umaria
6	Khargone	13	Balaghat		
7	Khandwa	14	Mandla		

Source: Department of Scheduled Tribes Development, Bhopal

Table 2

Tribal Blocks of Madhya Pradesh

S.N.	*Tribal Zone*	*District Name*	*Total Blocks*	*T.D. Block*	*S.N.*	*Block Name*	*Block Code*
1.	Saharia Zone	Sheopur	13	1	1.	Karahal	01
2.	Western Region	Ratlam	6	2	1.	Sailana	02
					2.	Bajna	03
3.	Western Region	Dhar	13	12	1.	Dhar	04
					2.	Nalchha	05
					3.	Tirla	06
					4.	Sardarpur	07
					5.	Manawar	08
					6.	Dharampuri	09
					7.	Gandhwani	10
					8.	Bakaner (Umarban)	11
					9.	Kukshi	12
					10.	Nisarpur	13
					11.	Bagh	14
					12.	Dahi	15
4.	Western Region	Jhabua	6	6	1.	Jhabua	16
					2.	Rama	17
					3.	Ranapur	18
					4.	Petlawad	19
					5.	Thandla	20
					6.	Meghanagar	21
5.	Western Region	Alirajpur	6	6	1.	Alirajpur	22
					2.	Sondawa	23

Cont'd...

... Cont'd

				3. Katthiwada	24
				4. Jobat	25
				5. Udaigarh	26
				6. Bhavra	27
6. Western Region	Khargone	9	7	1. Khargone	28
				2. Gogaon	29
				3. Bhagwanpura	30
				4. Segaon	31
				5. Bhikangaon	32
				6. Jhiranya	33
				7. Maheshwar	34
7. Western Region	Badwani	7	7	1. Badwani	35
				2. Pati	36
				3. Thikri	37
				4. Rajpur	38
				5. Pansemal	39
				6. Sendhawa	40
				7. Niwali	41
8. Western Region	Khandwa	7	1	1. Khalwa	42
9. Western Region	Burhanpur		1	1. Khaknar	43
10. Central Region	Betul		7	1. Betul	44
				2. Chicholi	45
				3. Ghoradongari	46
				4. Shahpur	47
				5. Bhainsdehi	48
				6. Aathner	49
				7. Bhimpur	50
11. Central Region	Hoshanga bad	7	1	1. Keshla	51
12. Central Region	Chhindwa ra	11	4	1. Tamia	52
				2. Jamai	53
				3. Bichhua	54
				4. Harrai	55
13. Central Region	Seoni	8	5	1. Kurai	56
				2. Lakhnadon	57
				3. Chhapara	58
				4. Kahanapas (Ghansaur)	59
				5. Dhanaura	60
14. Eastern Region	Mandla	9	9	1. Mandla	61

Cont'd...

... Cont'd

				2. Mohgaon	62
				3. Ghughri	63
				4. Nainpur	64
				5. Bichhiya	65
				6. Mawai	66
				7. Niwas	67
				8. Narayan Ganj	68
				9. Bijadandi	69
15. Eastern Region	Dindori	7	7	1. Dindori	70
				2. Amarpur	71
				3. Karanjiya	72
				4. Samnapur	73
				5. Bajag	74
				6. Mehadwani	75
				7. Shahpura	76
16. Eastern Region	Balaghat	10	3	1. Baihar	77
				2. Paraswada	78
				3. Birsa	79
17. Eastern Region	Shahdol	5	4	1. Sohagpur	80
				2. Gohparu	81
				3. Burhar	82
				4. Jaisinghnagar	83
18. Eastern Region	Anuppur	4	4	1. Anuppur	84
				2. Pushprajgarh	85
				3. Kotma	86
				4. Jaithari	87
19. Eastern Region	Umaria	3	1	1. Pali	88
20 Eastern Region	Sidhi	5	1	1. Kusmi	89
	Total	136	89		

Out of the above 19 districts, Jhabua, Barwani, Dhar, Mandla and Dindori are the districts whose more than 50 per cent of population is tribal; in Jhabua the per cent tribal population is 86.8. There are 89 development blocks in the state which are designated as tribal blocks (Map 1), besides, there are 26 MADA pockets and 30 clusters which are included in the tribal sub plan area.

Based on the resource base, the tribal areas of Madhya Pradesh may be divided into following two regions:

1. *Saharia and western tribal region* – Low rainfall, deficient in natural resources of forest and minerals, excessive population pressure as compared to available resources, and resultant large scale seasonal migration.

Map 1

Madhya Pradesh: Tribal Development Blocks

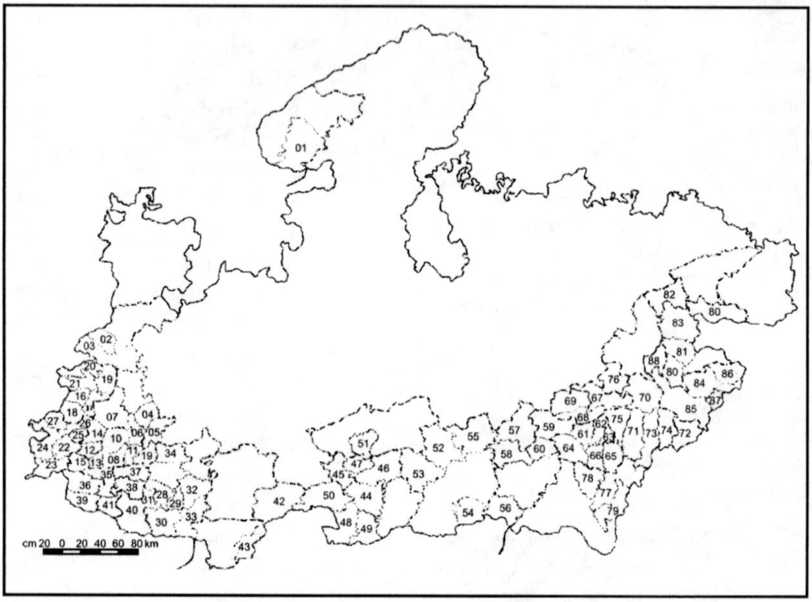

Source: M.P. Scheduled Tribes Development Department, Bhopal

2. *Satpura, Mahadev and Maikal region* – Medium to heavy rainfall, rich in forest and mineral resources but less accessible and relatively economically backward area.

Viewed with reference to land resource, the entire tribal belt is the rugged hilly region of Vidhyachal, Satpura, Mahadev and Maikal, where soils are stony, less deep and due to sloppy terrain, are subject to rapid erosion. In Jhabua there is a vast stretch of rugged terrain, known as, '*Raath land*'. In Balaghat, Mandla, Umaria and Sheopur, cultivable land is less than 30 per cent and the fields are fragmented. Besides, in the entire tribal belt, a large chunk of good quality of agricultural land is under the control of non-tribal farmers. That is why, in spite of the fact that landlessness among the tribal farmers is relatively less, due to low agricultural productivity and increasing pressure of population on agriculture, sustaining the family on agriculture alone has not been possible in a majority of cases. Frequent losses due to monsoon failures make the agricultural resource increasingly risky, resulting in the condition of 'chronic poverty'. In a comprehensive study conducted in the interior locations of South-Western Madhya Pradesh, about two-third of the tribal families were found to be under the grip of chronic poverty (Sah and Shah, 2003).

The source of all the major rivers, like, Narmada, Tapti, Son, Ken, Wainganga, and Chambal lie in the tribal areas. As such, any environmental degradation occurring in these source areas, will hit the entire catchment region. With respect to water resources, the Saharia and Bhil dominated entire tribal region is a low rainfall tract, where rainfall is less than 100 cm. With low rainfall, its variability is also high. Due to sloppy terrain, low retention, and percolation, the runoff rate is higher. This results into drying off of available water resource and resultant water scarcity condition, even with minor shortage of rainfall. A majority of the tribal development blocks of the Sheopur, Jhabua, Dhar, Barwani, Khargone and Burahanpur are covered under the Drought Prone Area Programme (DPAP) of the Government of India. The underground water level in this area has also gone very deep, and during summer a majority of wells and tubewells go dry, resulting in a scarcity of even drinking water. In Jhabua and Nimar belt, during drought years, cases of widespread looting and illegal felling of trees are often reported (Joshi, 2008).

The average rainfall of Betul-Chhindwara is 100 to 120 cm, which increases to 160 to 180 cm in Balaghat-Mandla; the highest rainfall of above 200 cm is recorded around Panchmarhi. In the central and eastern part of the tribal belt, despite higher rainfall, due to higher runoff on the sloppy surface, the availability of water for rabi season is limited.

Wells, tubewells and tanks are the principal source of irrigation in the area. Excepting the Narmada and Wainganga basins, in the rest of tribal region, the irrigation is on a limited scale and, therefore, the area is largely single cropped. In the Mandla-Dindori tract, the area irrigated is even less than 10 per cent.

Excepting the deforested central and northern tracts of Jhabua, the entire tribal belt of Madhya Pradesh is rich with respect to forest resources. Noticeable within this is the forest belt extending from Alirajpur-Barwani to Satpura, Mahadev and Maikal ranges. In the districts of Barwani, Burahanpur, Balaghat, Mandla and Umaria the area under forests is more than 50 per cent of the total geographical area, against the state average of 30.7 per cent. According to the forest department of Madhya Pradesh, out of the total forest area 19.4 per cent are teak forests, 4.2 per cent are Sal. 0.5 per cent is bamboo and 22.8 per cent are mixed forests. Besides timber, fuel wood and bamboo, forests are the source of tendu leaves and a variety of minor forest produce, like harra, gum, sal seed, etc. According to the annual report 2009 of the Forest Department, the revenue from the forest was ₹ 6890 million. As far as the benefits derived by the forest dwellers from the forests is concerned, they derive some income from fuel wood, collection of tendu leaf and minor forest produce, and wages. However, various micro level field studies conducted in different parts of tribal belt clearly indicate that today the contribution of forests in the household income is meagre, and it is decreasing every year (Joshi, 2004; Rai, 2009; Sen, 1999; Mahor, 2005). The figures available in the government reports also clearly indicate that the forest dwellers get only a negligible share of the total revenue earned by the state. The report of the Indian Forest Institute, 2009 brings out that during 2003–04, the earning of the state from the sale of timber, bamboo and khair was ₹ 5100 million, against which the total help rendered as *Nistar facility* to the forest dwellers was just ₹ 67 million, that is, merely 1.3 per cent (Verma and Kumar, 2009).

A majority of the mineral producing areas of the state lie in the tribal region. Coal, manganese, bauxite, copper and dolomite are the principal minerals mined in the state, which generated revenue of ₹ 6400 million as per the report of 2006–07. Out of this, the revenue from coal alone was 95 per cent. The Sohagpur-Singrauli-Umaria-Korar coal belt lies in the eastern tribal districts of Shahdol, Sidhi and Umaria, while the Satpura coal fields of Kanahn, Pench and Tawa valleys and of Patharkheda lie in Betul and Chhindwara districts. Maikal plateau of Mandla, Dindori and Shahdol districts produce best grade bauxite, while the Malanjkhand mine of Balaghat is one of the richest copper mines of the country. The important manganese rich belt lies in Balaghat and Chhindwara districts, while the mines of dolomite are situated in Mandla, Balaghat, Sioni, Chhindwara and Jhabua.

No doubt these minerals play an important role in the development of the state and the country, however, how much of these benefits goes to the local tribal population is a debatable issue. The ground reality is that the problems of environmental degradation, pollution, erosion of economic base and displacement are more or less common in all the mining areas.

Present Scenario of Socio-economic Development and Problems

The inverse relationship of natural resources and development is clearly discernable in the tribal belt of Madhya Pradesh, that is, despite being rich in mineral, water and forest resources, the tribals of these areas are most backward with regards to socio-economic development. With an increased pace of development and linkage with market economy, the pressure on natural resources of these areas is ever increasing, resulting in adverse environmental fallout, erosion of traditional economic base and displacement on the one hand, and increasing regional disparity, on the other. A study of natural resources and development conducted in this area, points out that the utilization of the natural resources has not been made for the development of these areas but their wealth has been drained out for increasing the wealth of the prosperous and urban areas of the State (Sharma, 2008). The World Bank Report has reported this situation as 'mirage of mining and growth' and holds that, as far as the mining areas of Central India are concerned, the mining dependence is associated with retarded economic performance, higher levels of poverty, lower growth rate, higher levels of mortality, malnutrition, and morbidity in the source areas (Shrivastava, 2006). Extreme poverty in some cases has compelled the tribals to permanently leave their home land in search of work. In one study it has been reported, that only in Delhi, more than 60,000 tribal girls from Jharkhand and adjoining Jaspurnagar of Madhya Pradesh, are working as domestic servants (Gupta, 2007).

Land acquisition, displacement and the related discontent and violence is the contemporary serious problem in the tribal areas. The economic reforms have triggered 8–9 per cent rate of an expected growth which demands exploitation of the country's mineral and head water resources; the largest part of which lies in the 5th schedule areas. Every new industrial, mining, power, dam, rail-road or port project or related township that intrudes into these areas and call for land acquisition, create great controversy, tension, opposition, and violence. During last 15–20 years, the private real estate players related with eco tourism, resorts and amusement parks are also making deep inroads in the tribal dominated tracts. Even the eco-parks and the wildlife protection area programmes which do not directly displace people, restrict their entry and, thus, reduce their access to forest produce. This results into impoverishment of the forest dwellers (Geisler, 2003). Thousands of people have been displaced due to the construction of dams on the Narmada and its tributaries, and a majority of these are tribals. According to one report, up to the year 2010, nearly 100 thousand of the displaced were still waiting for rehabilitation (Sharma, 2010). In between hundreds of adverse reports brought out by the activists and the clarifications and denials published by the government agencies, one thing is quite clear, that whatever has been done in the name of rehabilitation, has been too less and too delayed.

Hundreds of micro-level studies have been conducted and a number of Ph.D dissertations have been written to evaluate the affectivity of different government programmes in different parts of the tribal areas of Madhya Pradesh. Though, due to different ecological and socioeconomic conditions, their results may vary, however, it has clearly been observed that, at the ground level, even after more than six decades of Independence, we have failed to fulfil our constitutional commitment towards the tribals and meet their aspirations. The exploitation in different forms still exists, the pace of economic development is slow, and the gap between them and other communities is ever widening. Though it cannot be said that there has been no positive change in the human development parameters of these area, however, one thing is certain that the overall situation is still far from being satisfactory.

Some of the common indicators derived from secondary data and a number of micro-level studies that depict an overall sorry state of affairs in the tribal areas of the state, may be listed out as follows:

- The economy of the tribals in many parts is still based on survival compulsions. The ratio of families living below poverty line is very high and a significant area is in the grip of chronic poverty.
- At one place when the resource base is ever declining, the population growth in these tribal areas has been very fast. The growth of population in Jhabua district had been second highest after Indore, which is a highly urbanized district. In the absence of a desired rise of employment in the tertiary sector, the rapid growth of population is putting extra pressure on the decreasing land resources.
- Though there has been an improvement in the economy of the tribals, the gap between them and the other sections of the society, and even within their different groups, has widened.
- In spite of the fact that three-fourth of their work force is engaged in agriculture, the agricultural produce is not sufficient to give them round the year sustenance. Food security is still a serious concern for at least three to four months.
- The contribution of the forests in their household economy has drastically reduced.
- There has been an apparent downward occupational mobility. The one time self-sufficient household economy now largely depends on wage paid employment. Many of the onetime cultivators are now part time ones, and a major share of their income is derived from wages earned as unskilled labourers, both from nearby and distantly located places.
- Despite rise in literacy, there has not been perceptible rise in the skill component. The contribution of the service and self-employment sector is negligible, even much lower than that of the Scheduled Castes.
- In spite of various legislations, large scale alienation of land is still taking place, resulting in displacement.
- Seasonal migration to urban areas, mines, brick kilns, industries or rich agricultural areas has now been an established coping strategy to mitigate the deficit or to fight the adversities.
- Together with lower efficacy, the government expenditure on various programmes, targeted at improving the economic condition of the people, largely failed to induce a self generating multiplier impact. In many places the condition of dependency syndrome is observable.
- Barring certain exceptions, the PDS system which is basic to their survival, is not delivering desired results.
- High child mortality, more deaths during pregnancy and delivery, high mortality due to preventable diseases, like, malaria, jaundice and diarrhoea are some of the indicators which depict the poor reach and ill accessibility of basic health facilities.

In the last, it may be concluded that the equation between natural resources and the aspired level of development is negative and unfavourable as far as the tribal areas of Madhya Pradesh are concerned. This situation is in the root of discontent that triggers conflicts and movements against various large scale industrial, mining and infrastructural projects. In the contemporary globalized market economy where the resource-rich tribal areas are under a constant threat of resource depletion, land acquisitions and displacement, their concerns should not be underestimated, ignored, or perceived with an overall consideration. No sustainable development of the state or the nation is possible, unless the concerns of the local population are seriously attended to.

References

Auty, R.M. (1993), *Sustainable Development in Mineral Economics: The Resource Curse Thesis*, London: Routledge.

Fernandis, W. (1993), 'Indian Tribals and Search for an Indigenous Identity', *Social Change*, Vol. 23, Nos. 2–3, pp. 33–42.

Frank, A. (1967), *Capitalism and Underdevelopment in Latin America*, New York: Monthly Review Press.

Gangarade, K.D. (1998), 'Environmental Crisis: A Challenge to Modern Civilization for Secularization of Environmental Stewardship', in Y.G. Joshi and D.K. Verma (eds), *Social Environment for Sustainable Development*, Jaipur: Rawat Publications, pp. 51–85.

Geisler, C. (2003), 'A New Kind of Trouble: Evictions in Eden', *International Social Science Journal*, Vol. 55, No. 1, p. 175.

Gupta, R. (2007), *Tribal Contemporary Issues: Appraisal and Intervention*, New Delhi: Concept Publishing Company.

Haggett, P. (1975), *Geography: A Modern Synthesis*, New York: Harper and Row.

Joshi, Y.G. (2003), *Food Security Measures to Check Felling of Trees in Tribal Areas of M.P.*, Unpublished Report, Mhow: Dr B.R. Ambedkar National Institute of Social Science Research.

——(2004), 'Economic Development of Primitive Tribal Groups: A Study of Baigas of M.P. and Chhattisgarh', in D.C. Sah and Y.S. Sisodia (eds), *Tribal Issues in India*, Jaipur: Rawat Publications, pp. 195–229.

——(2008), 'Perceptions and Management of Droughts by the Tribals and its Planning Implications', in S.N. Chaudhary (ed.), *Tribes and Their Indigenous Knowledge: Implications for Development*, Bhopal: Indira Gandhi Rashtrya Sangrahalaya and Delhi: Pratibha Prakashan, pp. 63–96.

——(2010), 'Indebtedness and Land Alienation among Tribals of Madhya Pradesh', in S.N. Chaudhary (ed.), *Tribal Economy on the Cross Road*, Jaipur: Rawat Publications, pp. 119–65.

Kumar, Pramila and S.K. Sharma (2010), *Madhya Pradesh: Ek Bhougolic Adhyayan*, Bhopal: Madhya Pradesh Hindi Granth Academy.

Mahor, Rajesh (2005), *The Development Process of the Saharia Tribes with Reference to Changing Livelihood Base* (in Hindi), Unpublished PhD Dissertation, Indore: Devi Ahilya Vishwavidyalaya.

Munck, R. and Danis O' Hearn (eds) (1999), *Critical Development Theory: Contributions to a New Paradigm*, New York: Zed Book Ltd.

Rai, Ajay (2009), *Evaluation of Changing Relation of Tribals with Forests with Special Reference to Betul-Chhindawara Plateau* (in Hindi), Unpublished PhD Dissertation, Indore: Devi Ahilya Vishwavidyalaya.

Sah, D.C. and Amita Shah (2003), *Chronic Poverty in Remote Rural Areas of South-Western Madhya Pradesh* (Mimeo), Ujjain: MPISSR and Ahemedabad: GIDR.

Sen, H.B. (1999), *Socio-economic Change and its Future Trends with Reference to Development Programmes: A Study of Bharia Tribes of Patalkot* (in Hindi), Unpublished PhD Dissertation, Indore: Devi Ahilya Vishwavidyalaya.

Sharma, S.K. (2005), 'Man, Environment, Resource and Development: A Search for Interrelationship in Madhya Pradesh', *Indian Cartographer*, Vol. 25, pp. 23–31.

Sharma, S.L. (1998), 'Sustainable Development: Socio-cultural Imperatives', in Y.G. Joshi and D.K. Verma (eds), *Social Environment for Sustainable Development*, Jaipur: Rawat Publications, pp. 35–51.

Shrivastava, S. (2006), *Economic and Social Challenges of Mineral Based Growth in Orissa*, New Delhi: World Bank.

Sundaram, K.V. (1983), *Geography of Underdevelopment*, New Delhi: Concept Publishing Company.

Verma, Madhu and Vijay Kumar (2009), *Natural Resource Accounting of Land and Forestry Sector for M.P.*, Bhopal: Indian Institute of Forest Management, p. 132.

7

Contemporary Social Movements in Tribal Regions of Central India

S.N. CHAUDHARY

About 80 per cent tribes of the country live in states of Central India like Jharkhand, Odisha, Chhattisgarh, Madhya Pradesh and Rajasthan. These tribes are from different linguistic, racial, economic and social categories. Some are numerically inferior but others are numerically superior. Some are highly vulnerable but some are relatively in a better position. Inspite of these variations on certain issues they are similar in different ways. Most of them live in villages. They depend on primary sources for livelihood. The rate and magnitude of backwardness is very high among them and most of them are historically found in the natural resource-rich areas. Most of them have enjoyed symbiotic relations with nature and today all of them are experiencing negative consequences of the break-down of symbiotic relations with nature. Further, whether these tribes are the original inhabitants of the places where they are settled today or they are the in-migrant population it may be controversial but it is beyond doubt that during last several centuries gradually intensity of their interaction with non-tribal cultures and traditions have significantly increased. There are certain gains of this process. There is an emergence of tribal elites. There is direct impact on mortality rate. There is improvement in enrollment and literacy rate. There is class formation among them, although the process is slow in comparison to the scheduled castes. The number of tribal representatives in formal political institutions have increased. The number of tribal welfare and development projects and schemes have also increased. But the intensity of pain and miseries is more widespread. There is massive degeneration of their identity. The support base, both material and non-material, has experienced serious degeneration. Coping mechanism of different types have largely failed to arrest the degeneration process. Even the constitutional provisions and state initiatives are not able to arrest the ongoing pauperization in a successful manner. Civil society initiatives, including social and environmental movements, have also badly failed to arrest pauperization.

However, there are a section of scholars (Atal, 2012: 6) who are of the view that such criticism gives the impression that development has done nothing positive and, in the fact, development efforts have further worsened the life of tribals. Implicit in it seems to be the plea that the process needs to be halted almost instantly. Such a position makes an interesting copy for a political statement, but also misguides the common man. But the highest number of illiterates, mal-naurisheds, poor, their massive dependence on primary sources of livelihood, day by day diminishing status of their sources of livelihood etc; support the counter argument.

The paper is an attempt to underline history of dispossession, emergence of protest movements and institutional mechanisms to question the degeneration as well as to repair the fractured state of affair with reference to tribal masses of Central India. The paper is divided into four parts. Opening part describes richness of tribal culture and their cordial relationship with local ecology and environment. It also covers environmental degradation and their gradual move towards insecurity and deprivation zone. Part second examines process and consequences of the establishment of mega-development projects on tribal economy, livelihood and their culture. The third part briefly examines some of the social and ecological movements going on in tribal regions which have emerged to address plights and miseries of tribes and regions resided by tribes. Towards the end, some of the institutional steps taken during the era of globalization, particularly for the restoration of human rights and dignity of tribes, have been examined.

I

It is very difficult to locate zero point in the history of social change and social transformation because the process of continuity and change in society and its different elements and traits is an ongoing phenomenon. But for logistic purpose a benchmark in history needs to be identified to regulate academic discourse in a proper perspective so that a comprehensive understanding of social change is made possible and some reliable conclusions may be drawn for further investigation. Therefore, when we use the word 'contemporary' in the tribal context, inorder to analyse social movements, we are primarily concerned with those social movements which have obviously occurred since Independence. Therefore, in principle, scope of the paper is primarily not to discuss social movements which have taken place during the British or pre-British days. This does not mean underestimation of historical conditions and circumstances which may be held responsible for the origin and perpetuation of movements either as a necessary or sufficient condition during the post-Independence period. Of course, ongoing social movements (including unrest) needs to be understood in relation to the past but it is not essential that every present movement may have its roots in the past. Hence, to devote more on nature and dynamics of contemporary movements only passing references of movements before Independence have been made and more focus is on movements which have taken place after Independence.

If we restrict to the cases of social movements in the tribal areas, it seems that its history is very old. It goes back to the pre-British days. For example, the rise of the Marathas from the mid-seventeenth century onwards for the first time led to serious inroads into the Bhil homelands. In order to develop trade and settled agriculture so as to boost their revenue, they carried out sustained campaigns against the Bhils[1] who refused to agree to this incursion into their lifestyle. Peasants and traders from Gujarat and Maharashtra were encouraged to settle in the Bhil regions and forests were cleared to bring land under the plough. Thousands of Bhils were massacred when they rose in revolt against this policy (Manohar, 2001). Kol revolt (1832–33), Bhumij revolt (1832), Santal revolt (1855), Birsa Munda Movement (1895–1900), Tana Bhagat Movement (1915), Jharkhand Movement (1950) in present Jharkhand state, Juang Movement (1837–1856) and Kaujhar Movement (1891–93) in Odisha state, Naga revolt in 1940s and Gond revolt against British Raj (1911) and Movement for Separate Gond State (1940) in Madhya Pradesh may be taken as few examples (Chaudhary, 2013: 21). Many more examples of similar movements from different tribal belts of Central India may be quoted. Most of these social movements were against high handedness of the local and non-local administration and vested interests.

During the British period, these social movements largely aimed at social reform, eradication of different evil practices which were perceived as dysfunctional by local level tribal and non-tribal social reformers. These movements were also against exploitation of different types by the British Raj and local level non-tribals, who were subsequently termed as Diku (enemy) in certain pockets of the country in the nineteenth century. Actually Kol revolt and Birsa Munda movement, mentioned above, were against the imposition of the concept of private property in land in the present Jhakhand state. These movements led to introduction of Chhotanagpur Tenancy Act-1908, Wilkinson Rule of 1833 in Kolhan Area and the recognition of Manjhi system of the Santhals in the Santhal

Pargana Settlement (Amendment) Regulations of 1908. These legislations not only provided legitimacy to the tribal land tenure system but also recognized the communal land ownership system like Mundari Khuntkhatti Dari system (Areeparampil, 2002: 39). This does not mean that movements directed to ecological and environmental issues were completely absent from the scene during the British period (Chaudhary, 2013: 21).

But after Independence there is a trend of departure from the earlier genesis of social movements. During post-Independence period because of number of external forces, the amount of acculturation between tribal society and non-tribal society have massively increased and it is further increasing. Tribal areas have been perceived as a heaven of natural resources by the industrial houses, nation-state and other investors. This thinking with having its roots in the past, have gradually become dominant in the development discourse today. As a result, hundreds and thousands of development projects have been either established in tribal areas itself or even if they are established outside the tribal area, for raw material these projects are directly or indirectly dependent on tribal locations. Ever increasing number of industries and projects in tribal areas from 1950s onwards have already led to massive exploitation of natural resources even without critical examination of its cultural, economic and environmental consequences on the society in general and locals in particular. In the ongoing model of development, which is capitalistic in nature, with having strong faith in the top-down approach of development with its roots in the British period, there is no scope and space for cultural, social, ethical, environmental and botanical issues. Nadkarni (1987) rightly said that economic planning in India has paid little attention to the ecological constraints to economic expansion or to the impact of environmental degradation on livelihood and work. Only economic issues are provided the front seat in the development debate and decision. The idea of either 'industrialize or perish' given by Visvesvaraya[2] (1920) became the buzzword in the development discourse since the beginning of the Second Five Year Plan for which underdevelopment was essentially perceived as a consequence of insufficient technological progress (GOI, 1956: 6).

This model of development was followed by the Government of India for modernization and development in different sectors. It was also followed in the field of science and technology. Industrial policy was formulated keeping this objective into consideration. These steps subsequently increased number of industries of various types in the country in general and in the tribal areas in particular. Thousands of jobs were created in these industries. Skilled personnels from across the country joined these industries. Most of them were non-tribals. The door of employment for tribals is virtually closed for want of required skills and qualification. Besides easy availability of raw materials, there are other factors which have historically enabled industrial houses to establish their projects in tribal areas. Because of mining and industries, thousands of tribes have lost their land. It was said that they have lost land in favour of 'national development'. According to Barik (2013: 85) 'a little more than five lakh cases of tribal land alienation were registered, covering an area of 9.02 lakh acres in 12 states. And of this 2.25 lakh cases went in favour of tribals where 5 lakh acres of land was involved. Also, 2 lakh cases covering 4.18 lakh acres of land area were restored to the tribal petitioners. Tribals had to go to the court of law for restoring their land'.

The concept of national development was defined primarily in economic term. Per capita income, GDP, GNP, percentage of industrialization and urbanization, etc. were perceived as indices of development. No emphasis was given on the issues of equity and justice, ecological stability and environmental sustainability. As a result, traditional sources of livelihood of tribals such as water, forest and land (*Jal, Jungle* and *Zamin*) their culture, tradition or what may be called 'Identity' etc; were forced to reach to the critical stage. Needless to mention that tribal identity was formed in the light of their natural surroundings and if condition of natural resources decreases identity is also like to disintegrate. Tribals at large are the involuntary victims of degeneration.

Indigenous knowledge practiced by tribals since long in their day-to-day activities are either about to die or loose its utility (Chaudhary, 2008). Even if it is found, it is massively misappropriated by the vested interests without any benefit to the locals who have retained and preserved these knowledge since long.

Revisiting identity with the help of modern education, cultural organizations and vote bank politics is not at all mass based and, therefore, largely ineffective. It appears that tribals have become an outsider, unwanted or uncalled for in their own homeland. Increasing number of non-tribals in tribal dominated areas, where development projects have been established, and near exclusion of tribals from the new opportunity of livelihood created by these initiatives is an example of tribal exclusion and marginalization in their own homeland. It also appears that gradually tribals have lost their access to and century old natural and autonomous control over land and water based natural resources. Because of poor bargaining power of tribal masses, poor bargaining power of tribal representatives or tribal elites and apathy on the part of state and its functionaries working at the grass-roots level, tribals at large have been forced to reach to the stage of insecurity, deprivation, marginalization and dependence in different walks of life during last decades inspite of the presence of number of constitutional provisions, tribal development projects, presence of NGOs in tribal areas, seasonal out-migration by tribal themselves as a coping mechanism, rehabilitation policies of the government, promises made by investors through attractive phrase like 'corporate social responsibilities' and expansion of market forces, etc. in major parts of the tribal world. Only small number of tribals have been able to reap benefits of development promised under different schemes. Only few tribals, particularly those who are educated, depend on salary and live in urban areas with having some amount of modern network, have been benefitted. But more than 90 per cent tribals live in villages with having poor safety net and bargaining power. They are at the bottom of the development process. Those few who have been benefitted by the development process have been made dependent prone. In the absence of most of the Human Development Indices (HDI) tribals at large have been further forced to become like a marginal man (Desai et al., 2010). Their socio-economic condition is inferior in comparison to scheduled castes (Chaudhary, 2010). Their human rights are violated every now and then primarily by the state and the industrial houses (Dungdung, 2013). They have become what Cernea (1988) called the victim of landlessness, joblessness, homelessness, marginalization, food insecurity, increased morbidity and mortality, loss of access to common property, social disintegration, loss of access to community resources and violation of human rights. In short, only few of them have been able to improve their quality of life by availing fruits of development in a tenable manner but majority of them are failed to avail benefits mainly due to problems at the delivery level and a section of them have been pushed to the insecurity zone.

II

Instead of needful correction in the ongoing development projects keeping in view of the tribal interest, the entire tribal locations were opened for investors and industrial houses during globalization period. Globalization was formally introduced in India in the middle of July 1991. Both in principle and in practice, it has further added fuel to the fire to the ongoing development or what Padel (2013) called 'investment induced displacement', degeneration and marginalization of tribes by increasing the number of various types of industries and development projects in tribal areas. States who are rich from natural resources point of view have fearlessly signed countless number of MOUs with investors and industrial houses. According to Dungdung (2013) in Odisha state alone, for example, more than 90 memorandum of understanding (MOUs) has been signed with corporate houses. These initiatives are likely to industrialize and strengthen the state but, on the other hand, locals are also likely to suffer and become deprived. The chairperson of National Human Rights Commission, K.G. Balakrishnan, apprehended, 'As Odisha is emerging as an industrialized state, we apprehend more cases of human rights violation' (as quoted by Dungdung, op. cit., p. 162).

According to Iyer (2013), in a span of less than a decade, the Government of Jharkhand for example, has signed well over 100 MoUs. Notable among these are Arcellor-Mittal, Jindal, Essar, Tata Hindalco, Abhijit group and so on. According to a human rights report published by Jharkhand Human Rights Movement (JHRM), the state government of Jharkhand has so far signed 102 MoUs that go against the 5th schedule of the Constitution that guarantee to tribals their right over the land they live in. The Jharkhand Industrial Policy-2001 and the Jharkhand Vision Document-2010 strongly wish to exploit its natural resources by making it investor-friendly by providing various concessions and government help to industrial houses by acquiring land for private industrial estates and making it available at acquisition cost.

The same process of industrialization and signing of MoUs with investors and subsequently displacement is going on in the neighbouring states of Chhattisgarh[3], Odisha, Madhya Pradesh, Andhra Pradesh and Maharashtra. According to the Annual Report 2007–08 of the Ministry of Rural Development, a total of 105,491 cases alleging alienation of 1,04,742 acres of land have been filed in the court in Odisha. An estimated 104,644 cases were disposed of by the court. Out of these, 61,431 cases were disposed of in favour of tribals and 56,854 acres of land was restored to tribals. What will happen to the human rights of the locals, mostly tribals, in these states? Who will ensure the future of forests, water, land, climate, biodiversity and so on which are immediately and directly responsible for the survival of tribal masses? How to insure survival of tribal masses, their culture and tradition and their geographical space under the given economic and political scenario? Padhi and Panigrahi (2011: 16) documented consequences of deforestation and displacement in Odisha. More or less similar is the situation in other parts of Central India. They said, 'The impact of massive deforestation has been observed in the life-way processes of tribal people and can be categorized as environmental effects, social effects and economic effects. The social effects of deforestation restrict tribal people's access to the forest and affect their religious activities, life-cycle rituals, customs, practices and habits. Similarly, the economic effects of deforestation have drastically influenced the traditional livelihood resource of tribal people, which were providing them with food and economic security'. These are some of the critical issues which needs to be examined and resolved in the interest of tribals in particular and country in general.

Of course there are some areas where the amount of forests as well as NTFPs are found in plenty but poor tribals are today far away from these resources. It seems that during globalization period maximum parts of these resources are grabbed by the agents and representatives of market forces. Tribals have now no access to these resources. It is claimed that rehabilitation policy was adopted for the welfare of the displaced. But it appears that functioning of rehabilitation measures is not upto the mark (Chaudhary et al., 2013). There is wide gap between what is promised and what is performed. It appears that the implementing agencies are not serious on these issues. But the theoretical question is, even if implemented honestly, can any scheme rehabilitate, social, psychological and cultural displacement? In many cases tribals are either forced to displace themselves or they are terrorized to out-migrate so that land encroachment drive is not opposed strongly (Dungdung, 2013).

It seems that injustice of all types generated by globalization and related forces and schemes have individually and collectively frustrated tribal masses. Institutional initiatives taken during last decades are by and large failed to arrest the amount of frustration of tribes particularly tribal youths. There is no ray of hope from any corner to restore their environment and human rights. Sometimes it appears that either tribals or their non-tribal advocates fight a lost battle. The amount of frustration is high in those areas where so-called alternatives of traditional livelihood are totally missing and coping mechanism to adjust with the adverse situation is either ineffective or beyond the reach of tribal masses.

III

Hence, in reaction to these frustration and anxieties there is a crowd of social movements[4] in the tribal areas today. These social movements are basically collective response to injustice, both historical and contemporary, committed on tribes and their socio-environmental heritage and life supporting resources by external forces. And over the time, number of these external forces and atrocities committed by them on tribes have increased many fold. Tribal social movements are today broadly of two types viz., secessionist movements and reformist movement. The former is not found in Central India. There is no movement in favour of separate state in tribal belt. But there are movements against the functioning of the state and corporate houses working in tribal areas.

Some of these social movements are highly local and some are working at the macro level. Some are exclusively headed and run by tribals and some are run by non-tribals. There are several social movements jointly organized by local tribals and the non-local and non-tribals. While some of these movements are highly organized, systematic and structured, others are highly temporal, local and focused. Some movements are highly emotion-ridden. Some have historical roots and some are recent interms of its origin. Some of these movements are independent and autonomous and some have linkages with other social movements working in other parts of the country. Hence, in spite of some structural and compositional differences, these movements are socio-economic, political and civilizational. Case studies of some clearly reveals that these movements are correctional in nature. They do not put question mark on the existence of the state rather they do not agree with the functioning of the state. They perceive functioning of the state in favour of alien interest i.e. in the interest of the market forces or DIKUS of different varieties. Hence, they are in favour of change in the system and not change of the system. These movements may also be perceived as advocates of human rights and dignity of tribal masses. On the basis of objectives, these protest movements are also of different types. And, whether it is primarily addressed to social and economic exploitation or ecological and environmental degradation, development, displacement, rehabilitation and deforestation, these movements have become very popular these days. These movements have now drawn some attention of both print and electronic media. However, there is a serious criticism that the modern media is pro-elite and it is not sensitive to the concerns of tribal areas and tribal masses (Dungdung, 2013)[5].

Precisely, most of these local level social movements are against the exploitation of natural resources, land encroachment, establishment of mega development projects and atrocities on tribals by different interest groups, including the state and implementation of the so-called rehabilitation policy in dishonest manner and so on. It is reported that in many cases if voice of protest is raised by tribals and their supporters, instead of having respectful dialogue with them, attempts are being made to suppress these voices ruthlessly. Many times participants and sympathizers of these movements are termed as extremists. Many among them are made victims of state violence. Many of them are put behind the bar for indefinite period. And such incidences contributes to prolonged protest movement by tribals and others in the tribal world. The net result of this process is further perpetuation of rural unrest and violence. For instance, from 2001 to 2012 total 4759 naxal incidents took place in the state of Jharkhand alone in which 424 policemen, 602 citizens and 1019 naxals (total 2055 people) were killed (JHRR, 2007: 12). More or less similar is the situation in Chhatisgarh state. Large number of innocent tribals, police personnels, para-military force personnels, so-called naxalites and their supporters and others have been killed in Chhattisgarh during last two decades. It raises some ethical questions that instead of engaging in the meaningful dialogue in a peaceful manner both the state and the extremist groups are constantly engaged in violence, how they may be termed as legitimate and pro-people?

The naxalite movement most often follow undemocratic means to establish their hegemony. If they kill innocent tribals it cannot be justified in a legitimate manner. There is a point of view that even poor policemen, poor tribal informers and those locals who do not submit before them are perceived as agents of the state. Since they are perceived negatively therefore, no matter if they are rich or poor, tribal or non-tribal and local and outsider, they become victims of naxalite violence. More or less similar is the situation with the state. Even if dialogue is initiated by the state they seldom obey the agreement.

There is a preconceived notion among change agents, particularly the state that tribal society is relatively static, their needs and demands are limited, the local resources are capable enough to meet their limited needs. Their ecological and environmental base is still sound and, therefore, movement launched by them in favour of their human rights are not seriously taken. Their voice is grossly unheard.

But the pertinent question is that through violent means are both the state and extremists successful in storing/restoring human rights of tribal masses? There are views, observations and descriptions available to show their failure in restoring dignified life of tribals. Rather there are number of studies and narratives to prove that both of them have miserably failed on this front, many areas in the states of Central India are declared as disturbed areas. State is almost invisible in these areas. However, it claims that welfare measures are not effectively functioning in these areas due to disturbance created by naxalites. To what extent this claim is valid and acceptable? To search answer of this question one can go to the history of the movement. History reveals that after its birth in 1967 in the West Bengal, the movement did not directly reach to the tribal belts of Central India. For couple of decades it was confined to the non-tribal areas and in the due course of time due to push and pull factors it moved to the areas which are tribal, forest and mountain dominated. One of the pull factors available in the tribal areas since the British days was ever decreasing quality of life of tribal masses. Pauparization increased over the time as the process of acculturation with non-tribal traditions increased. It encouraged naxalites to enter and expand their support base in tribal areas. According to the report *Tribal: Victims of Development Projects*, 'The naxal violence in the tribal areas of the country is not because they invited or harbored the naxal groups. It flourished mainly because the political class and the administrations left them utterly neglected. The armed naxals occupied the vacuum and started ruling through terror and extortion of money from everyone who had something to offer them. Hence, they became rulers of the areas where police or government officials did not dare to go' (p. 19).

Naxalites also made promises to enhance tribals' quality of life which enabled them to trust each other. Already several years have gone but to what extent have these promises been translated into action? What benefits tribals at large have received from naxalite movement? Studies on this issue provide a rather negative picture. Most of the studies conclude that instead of improvement there is constant decay in the quality of life of tribal masses. In most of the cases, the movement has contributed to violence at the local level. Normal life of tribals are badly affected. In the areas where naxalites dominates innocent villagers are perceived as sympathizers and supporters of these movements. As a result, in many cases they become the victim of police atrocities. Actually tribes are forced to remain confined on a thin line between the Maoists and the state administration. They are exploited by both of them. Many tribals have been killed by naxalites for not obeying their order. Any meeting, called by naxalites is an unsaid compulsion for villagers. They have no option but to attend the meeting. And if they attend the meeting state administration brand them as naxalites or their supporters and the security forces go after them. For instance, in an anti-naxal operations in Saranda forest of Jharkhand state, which is inhabited by tribes, the deployed central and state forces devastated several homes, killed innocent people and did not even spare food that was in possession of tribals. They arrested 33 villagers but the police failed to provide any evidence against them. Every now and then search operation is conducted by the police. Edible and non-edible items are destroyed. Tribals are beaten, abused and in several cases their women are humiliated. In certain cases tribals are forced to out-migrate permanently in order to reduce amount of resistance created by them at the time of displacement and land acquisition drive launched by the state and corporate houses.[6] Because of fear psychosis created due to insecurity, tribals are pushed to move and remain in the insecurity zone from social, psychological and economic point of view.

Naxalite movement is not the only movement which is going on in tribal areas. There are host of environmental movements. Some are against land encroachment, the others are for respectful rehabilitation package, some are for dignity and respect, the others are against mega-development projects. This is clear from brief case studies of following movements:

Narmada Bachao Andolan (Save Narmada Agitation)

This movement was started in 1970s in favour of human rights of common people including tribals in the affected areas of Madhya Pradesh and Gujarat. The movement was not only against the increase in the height of the Bandh on the Narmada river which will displace thousands of villagers but it was also in favour of proper rehabilitation of beneficiaries. The movement received support from well known environmentalists of the country as well as abroad. In fact the main reason behind the World Bank's withdrawal of funding to the project was due to international pressure. The Japanese environmentalists convinced their government to discontinue the release of grant to the project. In America also environmental groups suggested the government to discontinue the grant. Similar voice of protest came from other countries of the world. As a result, World Bank discontinued its further aid to Sardar Sarovar. The entire Narmada Valley Project is dislinked from World Bank. Hence, this movement may be perceived as a success story which was created because of pressure from different corners on the donor agencies.

Kalinganagar Movement (Odisha)

Kalinganagar is a small town in Jajpur district of Odisha. The area has been declared as Industrial Development Corporation of Odisha. It acquired land from public for setting of steel plants. Needless to mention that minerals like iron-ore and chromite are located closer to this area. Tata signed MoU to set up a six MMTPA steel plant in this town with an investment of approximately ₹ 1,54,000 million. There are number of other industries located in and around this small town. In two Blocks of the district namely Sukinda and Danagadi there are significant number of tribal population. Huge amount of land have been acquired by the government both from villagers and different government departments. Locals do not like the factory because of number of cultural, environmental and economic reasons. They apprehend that the company will disown the promises which they will make for rehabilitation. About thousands of people have agitated on different occasions against this project. The conflict between locals and TATA along with police is going on. Police is strictly following the dictation of higher authorities which are in favour of TATA and against the legitimate interest of locals. In between, the government of Odisha is trying its best to earn crores of rupees out of this deal. Villagers also apprehend that those tribals and others who are cultivating the land but who do not have *patta* cannot get any rehabilitation package and therefore they are agitating and the movement is going on.

Lanjigarh, Niamgiri Movement Against Vedanta Alluminia Ltd

Vedanta is an England based investment company. It is working in different sectors in certain parts of India. It has planned to establish a refinery plant in Lanjigarh, Odisha. The area is inhabited by number of tribes like Dongaria, Kondh, Kutia Kondh and Desia Kondh. These tribals are since long dependent on forest and ecology of Niamgiri hill for their cultural and economic requirements. Except for the forest and forest produce, they do not have other sources of livelihood. Once the hill is permitted for digging, the tribals have to move from this place and in this way they have to die. Hence, they are strongly opposing their displacement. The area is under 5th schedule and the government is playing all politics to organize meeting of gram sabha and take their permission to allot the hill to the concerned company. The area is also dominated by maoists and they are supporting tribals in their class war. The company is promising a number of packages to the people. Number of committees constituted to look into the matter have also rejected the idea to allot the hill and forest to the Vedanta. And the conflict is going on between tribals, their supporters, free thinkers and maoists on the one side and the Vedanta and the state on the other side. In the mean time, the Supreme Court of India has strongly directed the state government to produce complete facts before the gram sabha and it has said that the final decision will be taken by concerned gram sabha only and the battle is going on.

Movement Against GMR Energies

Power producer GMR Energies plans to build a 1200 MW Thermal Power Project in Raipur district of Chhattisgarh. They have decided to invest about ₹ 5,500 crores in this project. For this purpose the power company needs more than 1100 acres of land but this effort is strongly opposed by farmers on health ground. For this purpose, a public hearing meeting was organized on 15 January 2009 but it was strongly opposed by locals. Villagers said that they are already facing serious health problem due to pollution caused by industrial units in the neighbouring Siltara Industrial area but government officials and GMR Energy officials are trying to convince people in favour of the project. They are quoting the features of Chhattisgarh industrial policy which says that those who will give land for industries will be given job and attractive compensation. But villagers do not trust them and tug of war is going on between them since 2009.

There are number of consequences of these movements. These consequences are both functional and dysfunctional as well as intended and unintended from environment, culture and human rights perspective. Sometimes mega-development projects are either delayed or withdrawn due to protest as it has happened in the case of Sardar Sarovar Project or, the catchment area of the movement becomes conflict prone or number of welfare schemes are introduced by the state. Sometimes welfare schemes are halted. For instance, Narmada Bachao Andolan (Save Narmada Agitation) was for complete stopping of the dam, resettlement and rehabilitation benefits to the oustrees and so on (Wood, 1993). These demands were supported by many environmentalists and reputed social workers. It was because of international pressure created particularly by environmentalists of Japan and USA that the World Bank was forced to withdraw its financial aid to the Sardar Sarovar Project on Narmada river. In the year 2000 the Andhra Pradesh Government passed a G.O (No. 112) to transfer forest lands to industries like Reliance and ITC Bhadrachalam through the village institutions of Van Sanrakshana Samitis. Strong protests from NGOs and opposition parties who highlighted the government's back door approaches to privatization of forest resources led to hasty withdrawal of the proposals. Similarly in Jharkhand, Arcelor-Mittal had to face challenge pased by tribals against their effort to acquire about 11,000 acres of land, of which 8,800 acres is required to set up a 12 million-tonne steel plant and 2,400 acres for establishing a township. The tribals claimed that the land identified by Arcelor-Mittal for the steel project is agricultural land and tribal lands are not transferable to non-tribals. A tug of war is going on between these two stake holders and the project has been halted.

But in spite of sustained protest by tribals against displacement and mega development projects, it appears that the movement is forced to largely remain ineffective. It happens that in several cases the so-called development process is halted or delayed but in exceptional cases such projects are withdrawn. According to Annual Report (2007–08) of Ministry of Rural Development, GoI, more than 5 lakh cases of tribal land alienation were registered, covering an area of 9.02 lakh acres in 12 states. And of this, 2.25 lakh cases went in favour of tribals where 5 lakh acres of land was involved. Also 2 lakh cases covering 4.18 lakh acres of land area were restored to the tribal petitioners. Tribals had to go to the court of law for restoration of their land. As a result, the establishment cost of these ongoing projects substantially increases which encourages change agents to compromise on the rehabilitation package. And in such cases also ultimately it is the locals who are made victims of the development process. Further, if we look into the history of mega-development projects in tribal locations, it appears that from 1991 onwards, there is massive increase in its number. This clearly shows that in spite of continuous protest, there is an increase in the number of development projects in tribal areas and in most of the cases because of logistic reasons the doors of these projects are virtually closed for local tribals who are poor and in most of the cases illiterate. Even if educated they lack technical skill and, therefore, the openings into these industries and mines, etc. are practically closed for them. Also, as stated earlier, these development projects have massively eroded local ecological and environmental bases which have forced local tribals to become alien and marginalized in their own homeland.

In response to social and ecological movements in tribal areas and increasing cases of violence by naxalites, in order to provide safe passage to the investors and in order to correct historical injustices to the tribes popular steps have been taken by the state during globalization period. Important among these are (1) Panchayat (Extension to Scheduled Areas) Act (PESA), (2) Scheduled Tribes and other Traditional Forest Dwellers (Recognition of Forest Rights) Act-2006. Theoretically, these two initiatives are pro-tribal and pro-tribal areas but the grass-roots experience is not praise-worthy. Rather the picture is alarming. This is evident from the following observation:

Panchayat (Extension to Scheduled Area) Act-1996

This is popularly known as PESA. This Act came into force on 24 December 1996. It empowers gram sabha in the designated areas to safeguard and preserve the traditions and customs of the people, their cultural identity, community resources and the customery mode of dispute management. Features of this Act are:

1. The village councils *(panchayats)* and *gram sabhas* have ownership of the minor forest produce.
2. *Gram sabhas* approve beneficiaries under poverty alleviation programmes.
3. Before any land is acquired for development purposes, it is mandatory to have consultation with the *gram sabhas* and *panchayats.*
4. Recommendation of the *gram sabha* or the *panchayat* at the appropriate level is mandatory for granting any prospective licence or minig lease for minor minerals.
5. Requirement that the state governments change their existing laws wherever these are inconsistent with the central legislation.

This Act is applicable in the districts and Development Blocks declared as Schedule V area in the states of Andhra Pradesh, Gujarat, Himachal Pradesh, Madhya Pradesh, Chhattisgarh, Maharashtra, Odisha and Rajasthan. With some modification it is also working in Jharkhand State.

But to what extent the Act fulfilled the purposes for which it was enacted? There are number of studies. However, in most of these studies it has been underlined that it was a near failure intervention. The Act could not become 'mainstream' policy (Sinha, 2011), some states had misinterpreted the concept of Gram Sabha and equated it with the meeting of the Gram Panchayat (*The Telegraph*, Guwahati edition, 9 April 2012). In the case of Pachwara coal mines project of Jharkhand State at no point of time, starting with the survey and the recent exercise of acquisition, any consultation in any form with the affected Santal and Paharia households, the villagers and the gram sabha was made (Iyer, 2013), the purpose of PESA has not been understood either by the politicians or by the bureaucracy. People at large are also not aware of the provisions of PESA except in those areas where the NGOs are seriously working (Tripathy, 2013). PESA is supposed to protect against any arbitrary, discriminatory and motivated action of the state relating to land acquisition, resettlement and rehabilitation in tribal region but it has been observed that the local administration in league with the company officials was indulged in deliberate falsehood. In consultation of gram sabha, the method adopted is dubious as the consent was obtained through coercion and brutal force (Das, 2005). According to Sisodia (2009), at the grass-roots level the situation is not as per the assumed goal of this endeavour. The level of participation of people has been very low, meetings of gram sabha is rarely held and even if held it was merely a formality without fulfilling the quorum. The grass-roots experience suggest that majority of the panchayat representatives and villagers are not aware of the quorum required for gram sabha meetings. The reasons behind the low attendance of people are engagements of the people in agriculture and labour, migration, groupism, scattered habitation etc. Gram sabha has been empowered to safeguard and preserve the traditions and customs of the people, cultural identity and customary mode of dispute resolution. But it is not done. Also, in the name of traditions and customs, social evils like use of liquor and dowry are getting place in society.

The Scheduled Tribes and Other Traditional Forest Dwellers (Recognition of Forest Rights) Act-2006

This Act was passed on 18 December 2006 and notified on 31 December 2007. Some of the specific features of the Act are as under:

1. Right to hold and live in the forest land under the individual or common occupation for habitation or for self-cultivation for livelihood by a member or members of a forest dwelling Scheduled Tribe or other traditional forest dwellers.
2. Community rights such as nistar, by whatever name called, including those used in erstwhile Princely states, Zamindari or such intermediary regimes.
3. Right of ownership, access to collect, use, and dispose of minor forest produce (includes all non-timber forest produce of plant origin) which has been traditionally collected within or outside village boundaries.
4. Other community rights of uses or entitlements such as fish and other products of water bodies, grazing (both settled or transhumant) and traditional seasonal resource access of nomadic or pastoralist communities.
5. Rights including community tenures of habitat and habitation for primitive tribal groups and pre-agriculture communities.
6. Rights in or over disputed lands under any nomenclature in any state where claims are disputed.
7. Rights for conversion of *pattas* or leases or grants issued by any local council or any state government on forest lands to titles.
8. Rights of settlement and conversion of all forest villages, old habitation, unsurveyed villages and other villages in forest, whether recorded, notified or not into revenue villages.
9. Right to protect, regenerate or conserve or manage any community forest resource which they have been traditionally protecting and conserving for sustainable use.
10. Rights which are recognized under any state law or laws of any Autonomous District Council or Autonomous Regional Council or which are accepted as rights of tribals under any traditional or customary law of the concerned tribes of any state.
11. Right of access to biodiversity and community right to intellectual property and traditional knowledge related to biodiversity and cultural diversity.
12. Any other traditional right customarily enjoyed by the forest dwelling Scheduled Tribes or other traditional forest dwellers.
    12.1 *Title rights* – i.e. ownership – to land that is being framed by tribals or forest dwellers as on 13 December 2005, subject to a

maximum of 4 hectares; ownership is only for land that is actually being cultivated by the concerned family as on that date, meaning that no new lands are granted.

12.2 *Use rights* – to minor forest produce (also including ownership), to grazing areas, to pastoralist routes, etc.

12.3 *Relief and development rights* – to rehabilitation in case of illegal eviction or forced displacement; and to basic amenities, subject to restrictions for forest protection.

12.4 *Forest management rights* – to protect forests and wildlife.

Number of studies are now available to show impact of this Act on distribution of lands to tribals and other forest dwellers. According to Chaudhary (2014) in Madhya Pradesh, for example, till March 2010, altogether 4,04,591 claims were received from both individuals and community, but only 1,09,000 (about 25%) claims were cleared. Altogether 3,59,502.09 acres of land were allotted under 89,035 titles. It is also claimed that the *pattas* distributed are not accepted as negotiable instruments for receiving subsidies or accessing bank loans.

Hence, it can be said that in spite of continuous social movements of different types in tribal regions of Central India, in favour of human rights of tribes and protection of ecology and environment the outcome is not praiseworthy. Institutional initiatives have also failed to restore human rights and dignity of tribes. It seems that social movements of all types, environmental degradation, pauperization of tribal masses as well as establishment of mega development projects, all these, which are antagonistically related to each other is going on side by side and the state which is theoretically democratic and welfarestic, is either silent or it is with the industrial houses, growth process and so on. It has either joined hands with the corporate houses or it has decided to be indifferent. Hence, under the given socio-political regime they along with their ecological base have to move towards insecurity and deprivation.

Notes

1. According to Padel (1998), the Bhils, Hos and Konds were forced to submit to British rule in the early nineteenth century in similar wars of conquest or 'pacification'. The Munda (Kol) uprising of 1831–32 and the santhal *bul* (rebellion) in the 1850s point to the great increase in exploitation that took place after British rule was imposed in tribal areas: *diku* ('foreigner', non-tribal) landlords, merchants and moneylenders had established a hold over Mundas and Santhals that made them work the land that had been theirs virtually as serfs, to create a profit and to pay the revenue demanded by the East India Company. This was the period when the Company, in the

face of much opposition, forced farmers in the Gangetic Plain to grow opium for the lucrative trade with China.

2. Visvesvaraya (1920) said: 'Indians will have to choose whether they will be educated or ignorant whether they will come into closer contact with the outer world and become responsive to its influences; whether they will be organized or disunited, bold or timid, enterprising or passive, an industrial or an agricultural nation; rich or poor; strong and respected or weak and dominated by forward nations.'
3. In Chhattisgarh, since the beginning of globalization, 121 MoUs have been signed. The total proposed budget of all these MoUs was ₹ 1,92,126 crore. About half of them have already started functioning. In Madhya Pradesh, 324 MoUs were signed of which 12 MoUs have been implemented and 18 are in process. The areas where MoUs have been signed are agriculture and food processing, forest and herbal industries, infrastructure, minerals, power, textiles and tourism. In Odisha, 235 MoUs were signed during the above period. These were in the following sectors: Air products (04), Alumina and Aluminium (12), Aviation (01), Cement (26), Ferro products, (09), Food processing (08), Mining (03), others (13), Paper (05), Pelletisation (14), Petroleum (05), Power (63) and Steel (72) (Source: Different website sources of the concerned state governments dated 24 June 2014).
4. Many Indian scholars have conceptualized and classified social movement. Important among them are Ghanshyam Shah (2004), P.N. Mukherji, (1977), T.K. Oommen (2010) and so on. All these scholars perceived the movement as a non-institutional collective response in favour of the collective cause in violent or non-violent manner. These movements are apolitical.
5. Dungdung (2013) observed that because of five reasons media of Jharkhand, for example, is not faithful either to the tribals or to the interest of the state. These reasons are: (a) the builders and developers, who are mainly engaged in the real state business in the state, also run TV news channels. They are strongly opposed to Chhotanagpur Tenancy Act (CTA) 1908, Santal Pargana Tenancy Act 1949 and PESA Act 1996 which prohibit land transfer to them, hence they criticize these Acts, (b) media has a clear corporate business interest in the name of development of Jharkhand, (c) nearly 90 per cent journalists in the state are outsiders and from upper castes. They have mutual adjustment with builders and industrialists who are non-tribals and also from outside the state, (d) media still treat Jharkhand as a part of Bihar, hence, in most of the TV channels and newspapers of Jharkhand more time and space is provided to Bihar related issues in comparison to Jharkhand issues, and (e) most of the consumers of Jharkhand media are originally outsiders and therefore, their concerns are more important for the media in comparison to the concerns of the state and its original population, particularly tribals.
6. Iyer (2013: 60) rightly said: 'The spread of militant left radicalism in the central Indian states of Jharkhand, Odisha and Chhattisgarh is not a sudden

eruption. It is also not primarily a law and order problem. It is a political movement which needs to be contextualized in the objective overall current situation of the people involved, which creates conditions for its emergence.'

References

Atal, Yogesh (2012), 'Tribal Unrest, State Policies and Empowerment in Contemporary India', keynote address (unpublished) in a National Seminar during 21–22 March, IGRMS, Bhopal.

Areeparampil, M.S.J. (2002), *Struggle for Swaraj*, Chaibasa, Jharkhand: Tribal Research and Training Centre (TRTC).

Barik, B.C. (2013), 'Globalization, National Development and Tribal Identity', in S.N. Chaudhary (ed.), *Globalisation, National Development and Tribal Identity*, Jaipur: Rawat Publications.

Cernea, M.M. (ed.) (1988), *Putting People First: Sociological Variables in Rural Development*, London: Oxford University Press.

Chaudhary, S.N. (2008), *Tribes and Their Indigenous Knowledge: Implications for Development*, Bhopal: Indira Gandhi Rashtriya Manav Sangrahalaya and New Delhi: Prathiba Prakashan.

——(2010), *Tribal Economy at Crossroads*, Jaipur: Rawat Publications.

——(2012), *In Search of Sustainable Development: Scenario in a Tribal Village of Madhya Pradesh*, New Delhi: Serials Publications.

——(2014), 'In Between Deprivation and Dependent Economic Development: The Case of Tribal Women of Madhya Pradesh', in S.N. Chaudhary (ed.), *Tribal Women: Yesterday, Today and Tomorrow*, Jaipur: Rawat Publications, pp. 206–224.

Chaudhary, S.N. (ed.) (2013), *Globalisation, National Development and Tribal Identity*, Jaipur: Rawat Publications.

Chaudhary, S.N., M. Mishra and M. Sharma (2013), *Adivasi Gramo Me Tikau Vikas Ka Yathartha*, New Delhi: Concept.

Desai, S.B., A. Dubey, B.L. Joshi, M. Sen, S. Shariff and R. Vanneman (2010), *Human Development in India: Challenges for a Society in Transition*, New Delhi: Oxford University Press.

Dungdung, G. (2013), *Whose Country is it Anyway?: Untold Stories of the Indigenous Peoples of India*, Kolkata: Adivaani.

Das, Vidya (2005), *PESA: A Reality, National Consultation on PESA Act*, Kashipur, Rayagada, Orissa: Agragamee.

Government of India (1956), *The Second Five Year Plan*, New Delhi: Planning Commission.

Guha, R. (2011), 'Apni Tradesio Se Azadi Ke Intezar Mey Adivasi', *Dainik Bhaskar*, Daily Newspaper, Bhopal, August 15.

Iyer, K.G. (2013), 'Globalisation, Jharkhandi Identity and Rural Transformation', in S.N. Chaudhary (ed.), *Globalisation, National Development and Tribal Identity*, Jaipur: Rawat Publications, pp. 57–81.

Jharkhand Human Rights Report (2001–2011), Ranchi.

Manohar, D. (2001), *Bagh Ke Bacche Hai Ham (We are the Children of the Tiger)*, Hosangabad: Disha Samvad.

Mukherjee, P.N. (1977), 'Social Movement and Social Change: Towards a Conceptual Clarification and Theoretical Framework', *Sociological Bulletin*, Vol. 26, No.1, pp. 39–59.

Nadkarni, M.V. (1987), 'Agricultural Development and Ecology: An Economist's View', *Indian Journal of Agricultural Economics*, Vol. 42, No. 3, pp. 359–75.

Oommen, T.K. (2010), 'Social Movements I: Issues of Identity and Social Movements II: Concerns of Equality and Security', in T.K. Oommen (ed.), *Readings in Sociology and Social Anthropology*, New Delhi: Oxford University Press, pp. 39–40.

Padel, F. (1998), 'Forest Knowledge, Tribal People, Their Environment and the Structure of Power', in R.H. Groove, V. Damodaran and S. Sangwan (eds), *Nature and the Orient*, New Delhi: Oxford University Press, pp. 891–917.

——(2013), 'Tribal Identity and Real Development in a Rapidly Globalising World', in S.N. Chaudhary (ed.), *Globalisation, National Development and Tribal Identity*, Jaipur: Rawat Publications, pp. 23–36.

Padhi, S. and Nilkantha Panigrahi (2011), 'Tribal Movements and Livelihoods: Recent Developments in Orissa', CPRC-IIPA Working Paper No. 51, New Delhi.

Shah, G. (2004), *Social Movements in India: A Review of Literature*, New Delhi: Sage Publications.

Sinha, Ratnawali (2011), 'Governance in the Scheduled Areas: Expectations and Realities', *Man in India*, Vol. 91, Nos. 3–4, pp. 429–40.

Sisodia, Y.S. (2009), 'Panchayat Raj in Scheduled Areas After Implementation of PESA: Evidences from Western Tribal Belt of Madhya Pradesh', in S.N. Chaudhary (ed.), *Tribal Development Since Independence*, New Delhi: Concept.

Tribal: Victims of Development Projects – India's Forced Displacement Policy and Practice; obtained from website https: //socialissuesindia.wordpress.com

Tripathi, S.N. (2013), 'Paradox of Development and the Plight of Tribes in India', in S.N. Chaudhary (ed.), *Globalisation, National Development and Tribal Identity*, Jaipur: Rawat Publications, pp. 95–113.

Visvesvaraya, M. (1920), *Reconstructing India*, London: P.S. King & Son Ltd.

Wood, J.R. (1993), 'India's Narmada River Dams: Sardar Sarovar Siege', *Asian Survey*, Vol. XXXIII, No. 10, October, pp. 968–984.

8

Sustaining the Environment

The Adivasi Way

RAVI P. BHATIA

Two issues have come to centre stage in today's discourse on the issue of the developmental paradigm in India – (1) the effect on the environment and the ecology and (2) the impact on the tribal populations living in remote areas of certain parts of India. In order to uplift the large parts of our population from penury, deprivation and backwardness, massive developmental activities are going on in the country. These include starting welfare schemes like schools, hospitals, etc. and construction of dams, setting up of industries, building roads and other infrastructural projects. These projects entail acquiring villages, farmlands, forest lands and water bodies for construction of dams, setting up of industries and mining activities etc. which lead to deforestation and displacement of people especially the tribal populations of the country. Environmental damage is another inevitable consequence.

Degradation and damage to the environment have acquired urgency in view of the familiar problems of pollution of the air, the soil and water all over the country. In addition, global warming, climate change, rising sea levels, unpredictable weather conditions are also a cause of concern. This is directly due to not only the massive developmental activities that are taking place for boosting the Indian economy and pushing economic growth but also our tendency of over exploiting the resources of the earth and the careless attitude that we have acquired in disposing of industrial and domestic waste.

The adverse impact of these activities on the tribal population of the country is all too obvious and tragic. Millions of people living in the regions where development projects are continuing, especially in the remote regions populated by Adivasis, are adversely affected. Water bodies like ponds, lakes and rivers and pasture lands have become polluted; trees are axed and forests become out of bonds for these people. According to the Forest Act, all forests are now the property of the state and any person entering these forests without permission is treated as a criminal. Forests provide Adivasis sustenance in the form of minor forest produce for survival and livelihood – timber, bark, fruits, etc. Thus, the forest laws have deprived these Adivasis from entering and using any minor produce that forests provide.

These tribal people are displaced from their traditional habitats that they have been living in for centuries without adequate compensation or rehabilitation. Although large sections of these people are peaceful and silently accept the hardships imposed on them, a certain section has become politicized and occasionally resorts to violence.

As indicated above, degradation of the environment is due to several factors but not least due to the present means of economic development that leads to consumerism, to over exploitation of resources and wanton damage to our ecosystem.

The demands for a better life and amenities like electricity, roads, clean water, nutritious food, etc. of large number of peoples from many developing countries are genuine and urgent. All this calls for development to rid these people from backwardness, deprivation and poverty. The dilemma being faced by India and other developing countries is stark and at the bottom of environmental debate and controversy. Should large parts of the country develop and if so how? If the answer is yes, how should a country develop without the cost it has to pay in terms of deforestation, depletion of natural resources and pollution of air, water and soil? How should construction of dams, roads, railway lines and building of other infrastructure take place while taking care of the environment? How should mining activities proceed, again, without harming the environment and keeping the interests of the tribal people who inhabit these forests in mind?

It is often argued by some well-known economists trained in the western concepts of development that there is no alternative but to construct huge projects like big dams, industries and mines for poverty alleviation and job creation for the poor of India. This has definitely improved the conditions of certain sections of the poor in India as shown by Jagdish Bhagwati and Arvind Panagariya (2013). They demonstrate how growth was the strategy successfully deployed to reduce poverty in India.

A contrasting view is made by another distinguished economist Prabhat Patnaik. According to him (2013), despite significant growth in GDP in the last few decades, its benefits have not reached the poorest sections and 'absolute poverty has increased during the economic boom in the first decade of this century'. This growth based developmental process has problems – the adverse impact on the eco systems of our country and the increase of disparities between the affluent and the poor.

It is obvious that we need to follow an environmental friendly development model so that we may improve the conditions of large numbers of people and yet protect and preserve the environment. How this degradation could be reduced and prevented is briefly discussed in this essay. We need to learn from the tribal populations of our country how they have been living in their natural habitats without damaging the environment.

Damaging our Environment

The Adivasis believe that the environment is a living entity that needs care and sustenance and so they use minimal resources that are available in or near their villages – the forests, lakes, pasture lands etc. In fact they do not consider themselves and their animals distinct from the environment; they are as much part of it as the trees lakes, ponds, hills are. Thus the protection of the environment is as natural as the protection of their families and animals.

The environment being a living body implies that the earth does not consist of just rocks, hills or sand or things inert, but is alive – water flows, breeze blows, glaciers melt and form again, even mountains rise although very slowly; earthquakes and volcanoes are active and there is movement, growth and decay – aspects that resemble living entities. Flowers bloom, plants and trees grow, fruit and food is produced, and seeds are again used in a fresh cycle of production of the vegetable and fruit kingdoms. Trees not only give us flowers and fruit for humans and birds; they also provide the oxygen that sustains, along with water and sunlight, all life on earth.

Before discussing how to learn from the tribal populations their lifestyles for survival, let us briefly list various aspects of environmental pollution and degradation of air, soil, water, rivers that have all become degraded to various degrees.

Industrialization, vehicular emissions, burning of coal for production of electric power, burning of garbage in incinerators all result in polluting the air. Large scale cutting of trees as developmental activities that takes place also leads to worsening the quality of air. In fact, two years ago a survey carried out by an international agency to measure the air quality found that among the 7o countries where the survey was carried out, the air quality of India was the worst.

Rivers, lakes, and other water bodies are also becoming polluted due to untreated industrial discharge into these water bodies. The situation has been aggravated by the indiscriminate dumping of domestic garbage into our rivers and lakes. Most of our major and minor rivers are polluted due to these factors. Use of chemical fertilizers and pesticides in agriculture are not only damaging the soil but also adding to water pollution.

As a result of environmental pollution climate change is also taking place with disastrous consequences like erratic weather conditions, frequent occurrences of landslides and cyclones, etc. According to a report of the UN body IPCC published in the *Indian Express* of 1 April 2014, climate change is resulting in severe damage in every continent and our oceans. The report warns that unless greenhouse emissions are brought under control, serious danger to human beings and our ecosystem will take place in the next two or three decades. Already environmental degradation is contributing to adverse impact on all forms of life. Several species of plants and birds are endangered and some have already becoming extinct.

Mining projects for coal, iron ore, bauxite and other minerals are also being vigorously promoted by the central government for boosting economic growth and employment without taking into consideration the impact on the environment and as a consequence on the livelihoods of local populations. According to Dutta (2014: 14), the decision to allow expansion of coal mines without environmental clearances and public hearing, the Ministry of Environment and Forest's role as a facilitator for the mining industry rather than as a custodian of natural resources and livelihood and health of local people. Since most of these projects are located in tribal areas, its adverse impact on them is becoming very severe. Not only is their health and livelihood affected, they are also forced to leave these areas without proper rehabilitation.

As a result of various infrastructural and developmental projects continuing in the country especially in ecological sensitive areas there have been conflicts over:

1. forests and hills
2. rivers and dams
3. tribal areas
4. mining operations

Forests and Hills

Gadgil and Guha (2007) have described at great length how with the establishment in 1864 of the Indian Forest Department the control and management of the forests were taken over from the community's hands to the colonial government. This led to serious social, economic dislocation of the tribals and villagers living in these areas. These people who had access to forests for centuries for their livelihood and survival were suddenly deprived of timber, firewood, fodder, and minor forest produce such as fruits and leaves. They further said, 'Throughout the colonial period popular resistance to state forestry was widespread and sustained … . In 1913 a government committee in the Madras Presidency (South India) was struck by the hostility towards the Forest Department. A British official wrote that 'forest administration consists for the most part in a running fight with the villagers'. Protests, some sporadic and some organized, occurred regularly against the denial of access to forest and its produce which the villagers considered were their customary rights.

The resentment and protests have increased since 1947 when the country became free from the British colonial rule. The advent of technology and organized exploitation of forest lands has made the conflict between customary requirements and commercial interests sharper. As a result, the social and economic conditions of the tribal populations and local villagers have become worse. They are deprived and helpless and feel their sense of peace, welfare and dignity is being constantly violated with this state intervention of 'their' forest homelands.

Rivers and Dams

Conflicts over the building of dams over rivers have been a recurrent theme in several parts of India over the last more than four decades. Small and large dams have already been constructed or being expanded over several Indian rivers – *Ganga* (Ganges), Narmada, Alaknanda, Bhagirathi and others. Proponents of dam construction, including some industrial houses, claim that besides providing water to arid regions, production of electric power that is vital in today's situation will also take place.

Vociferous opposition to dam construction is being constantly voiced and demonstrations and protests are a regular feature of the injustice felt by the poor people by this construction. It is pointed out that tens of thousands of people especially the tribal populations are being displaced from their traditional homes to areas that are unproductive and unfamiliar. Even this often does not happen as alternate lands, that are promised when land is acquired, are not provided. The compensation given for acquiring land is low and often delayed for years on end. This causes the displaced persons and their families resentment, distress and unhappiness resulting in a feeling of being cheated by powers over whom they have no control. In addition to displacement, submergence of these areas destroys or damages the ecosystem and endangers pant and wildlife when dams are constructed. Several species of flora and fauna have already become extinct.

Conflicts in Tribal Areas

As indicated earlier many forests and remote regions especially in tribal areas have been taken over or encroached for building roads, railway lines, construction of dams or for mining and other similar activities. An article by the undersigned (Bhatia, 2010: 363–378) (5) underlines the close relationship of the tribal population with the neighbouring hills and forests. When their lands are taken over, the people feel deprived, resentful and helpless and sometimes indulge in violence. The situation as far as the tribal population is concerned is particularly alarming since they are heavily dependent on the neighbouring forests, hills, lands and water bodies for their survival. This has been poignantly summed up by Felix Padel and Samarendra Das (2010) in the following words:

Out of earth we are made and to earth we shall return. But how well do we know our earth? How well do we understand how it feeds us? Or what are we doing to it through mining? Our modern lifestyle depends on extracting and processing huge quantities of minerals and oil. But what is the real cost we are making our earth pay?

Adivasis are India's indigenous or tribal people. They developed a lifestyle and social structure close to the earth many centuries ago. Most still live by cultivating the soil and gathering food from the forest. They experience the costs of mining most acutely, and understand its consequences better than most … . It is relevant to repeat the evocative description of this relationship by the well known writer and activist Arundhati Roy in the Forward of this book (Padel and Das, 2010).

> The low flat-topped mountains of Odisha contain some of the largest deposits of the best quality bauxite in the world … . But these bauxite mountains have been home to the Dongria Kond tribe long before there was a country called India or a state called Orissa. The hills watched over the Kond. The Kond watched over the hills and worshipped them as living deities. Now these hills have been sold for the bauxite they contain. For the Kond it's as though God has been sold … .

Imagine the conditions of these thousands of people who will lose everything that they cherish in life. This book also describes how the mining for the metal aluminum has inexorably destroyed the lands and the hills in the Indian state of Odisha. More or less similar observation was made by Xaxa (2008):

> The harmony between natural and social worlds that the tribes had maintained for centuries was ruptured first during the colonial period and then in the post-colonial Forest Policy of 1952. Tribes were deprived of their traditional livelihood, culture and rituals without their consent.

This type of development obviously results in perpetuating social inequities and degradation of the environment. In the words of two environmentalists J. Bandyopadhyay and Vandana Shiva (2012: 237), 'The ecology movements make visible the externalities of development based on a particular ideology and reveal the inherent injustice and non sustainability …' They add: 'the imperatives arising from the right to survival create another direction for development that ensures justice and sustainability, equity with ecological stability'.

This deprivation, destitution and despair is leading to conflict and sporadic violence in the tribal belt of Odisha, Jharkhand, Chhattisgarh and parts of Bihar and Madhya Pradesh as detailed by Ravi P. Bhatia (2012: 9).

It is also leading to violence by some elements of tribals loosely called Maoists. In the last week of May 2013 as well as recently in March 2014 in Bastar region of Chhattisgarh, Maoists cadres have resorted to violence killing CRPF jawans and others whom they feel are betraying the tribal cause. One of their grouse is that while forest dwellers are denied their traditional right to collect minor forest produce, large tracts of forest lands have been handed over to corporate houses.

Conflicts over Mining Operations

Mining projects for exploitation of coal, iron ore, bauxite and other minerals have sprung up in many parts of the country especially remote areas like Odisha, Chhattisgarh, etc. inhabited by tribal populations. Some of these are owned by the government some by private corporations and some are illegal. There is also a demand for expansion of capacity of some mines which the government is allowing without adequate consideration of their adverse impact on the environment as well as on the local populations. As an example clearance recently given to Jindal Steel and Power Ltd. in Chhattisgarh is posing serious environmental and health hazard. Explosives used for blasting are causing serious health problems for the local populations forcing them to move out of these areas. In addition, when the mining operations start, vast number of trucks that will be used to ferry the coal from these mines will result in severe vehicular emissions and add to the health hazards. Similarly, the Mahan coal block in MP that was given clearance in September 2013 is resulting in severe health concerns due to the large quantities of fly ash emitting from the mines and flowing into the local *Garha* stream. Tribal communities have organized a massive rally against the mining operations without success. The government according to some activists is adopting dilatory tactics by going to court and asking for time to review these issues. Dutta (2014: 14) has reported that '176 mines in Odisha alone are located in dense forest areas. The MoEF (Ministry of Environment and Forests) had not given permission for diversion of forest areas in the case of 98 mining leases ...' This is a sad example of the mining operations and their adverse impact on the environment and local populations.

Features of Adivasi Lives

As we all know, a large number of tribal populations continue to live in relatively remote, inaccessible regions of Chhattisgarh, Jharkhand, Odisha, Madhya Pradesh, Andhra Pradesh, Maharashtra, etc. Some of the Adivasis have benefitted from the constitutional and legal provisions provided for their welfare and advancement in the Constitution of India. But a large proportion of these continue to live in these remote villages and forest lands in isolation and relative penury. Since they lived in isolation from the larger Indian society, they enjoyed autonomy of governance over the territory they inhabited. They also lived as a community – all the regions including the forest areas they inhabited were community property that they could not sell or dispose of.

As Xaxa (2014) writes 'they held control over the land, forest and other resources and governed themselves in terms of their own laws, traditions and customs ...' The colonial laws that were framed by the British and the uniform civil criminal laws introduced by the Indian Government after Independence were alien to tribal traditions and ethos and led to large scale encroachment of tribal regions resulting in displacement and alienation of lands from tribes to non-tribal peoples.

The tribal peoples were earlier able to use the forest produce such as timber, bark of trees leaves, fruits etc, for cooking, building their hutments and for other daily needs. Their survival and livelihood depended on these community resources. They were able to fish in local ponds and lakes,, they could hunt in the forest areas, they could also practice *jhoom* (shifting) cultivation in nearby areas that allowed lands to replenish themselves over time. There was a close-knit relationship of Adivasis with nearby forest lands and villages. The relationship was mutually beneficial. While the forest lands provided tribal people with sustenance and livelihood, the forests were protected by them from degradation and pollution. The question of over exploitation of natural resources did not arise since the Adivasis lived simple and frugal lives and did not indulge in wastage.

Their simple lifestyles, their close-knit relationship with the local environment – forests, soil, air and water bodies, all have led to the concept of sustainable development of the Adivasis. They were able to keep the rivers and water bodies clean for domestic, agricultural and for fishing purposes. Some trees were cut for domestic use and for occasional decorative and cultural purposes, but large scale deforestation was unheard of. The air quality was good since there was no industrial and non-biodegradable garbage that could pollute the air or water.

The concept of sustainable development was first formally introduced by the Brundtland Commission on environment and development in 1987 as a means of linking socio-economic and ecological considerations in a cohesive policy relevant structure. According to this framework, sustainable development is 'development that meets the needs of the present without compromising the ability of future generations to meet their own needs'. This concept was endorsed at the UN General Assembly in 1987. The concept was expanded in 1992 by the UN conference on Environment and Development UNCED, to include achievement of sustainable livelihood as a broad goal for poverty eradication.

Adivasis did not have access to modern technology such as electricity, railways, household gadgets etc. and so from our point of view they led what is generally called primitive lives. However, this primitive lifestyle allowed them to lead culturally enriching lives. They were adept in local knowledge systems such as having familiarity with certain herbs and plants for medicinal purposes, preservation of food, building of local temples elaborately carved with local figurines, construction of toys, decoration pieces, musical instruments and the like. They possessed a rich repertoire of traditional music and dance forms. I recently got an opportunity to see the Tribal Museum in Bhopal. It was constructed only about two years ago and was inaugurated in 2012 although some sections of the museum are still being added to it. Seeing its various sections one cannot help but admire the varied artifacts on display that have aesthetic and colorful beauty and resonance.

In an article published on 5 April 2014, *The Hindu* newspaper talks about a retired teacher of *Kunker* district of Chhattisgarh, Shiv Singh Anchla, who has donated 5 acres of his land to fellow *Gond* tribals. This has been done to 'nurture rare herbs, plants and trees on this land which otherwise are likely to become extinct, with few even recognizing the loss … . Tribal communities share a unique relationship with their natural as well as cultural heritage which unfortunately is dying a slow death.' The report adds that Anchla alerts the tribal communities to the looming threat and shares ideas to ensure that the next generation inherits the wealth they inherited from their forefathers …'. Adivasis knew how to keep their homes clean, their farms and water bodies unpolluted and how to retain a healthy relationship with their local environments. These are aspects that we need to learn from them and to emulate in contemporary situations.

Adivasis are increasingly becoming aware of the importance of education and simple technology. In some areas *anganbadi kendras*, primary and middle level schools for tribal children are being established. In Delhi, in a locality called Dwarka, there is a tribal hostel for Chhattisgarh youth for training and orienting these young persons to appear in different competitive examinations like the IAS, etc. The hostel is supported by the Chhattisgarh Government.

Gandhian Approach to Protection of the Environment

Apart from his contributions in diverse fields of politics, religious amity and basic education, Gandhi was also an environmentalist of his times – a person who wished to sustain and protect the environment. He led a simple and frugal life, did not waste anything and minimized his wants. Some of his sayings towards this objective are well known. He often said:

- Nature produces enough for peoples' needs but not for their greed.
- Characteristic aspect of modern civilization is an indefinite multiplicity of wants.
- The earth, the air, the land and the water are not an inheritance from our forefathers but on loan from our children. So we have to handover to them at least as it was handed over to us.

Gandhi was critical of modern civilization that leads to degradation of the environment. He wrote (*Young India*, 2.6.72): 'The distinguishing characteristic of modern civilization is an indefinite multiplicity of wants whereas earlier civilizations were forced to have an 'imperative restriction upon and a strict regulation of these wants ...'

Interestingly, a similar idea was expressed by an American *Chief Seathl* of the state of Washington in a communication to President Pearce of USA in 1855. He wrote 'We do not inherit the earth from our ancestors; we borrow it from our children'.

Gandhi also maintained his surroundings clean – whether at home or in the ashrams that he built and where he met many of his followers. He himself used to clean his own room and toilet and encouraged others to follow his example. According to Gadgil and Guha (2007: 113) 'The *Chipko* and the Narmada *andolans* (agitations) are outstanding examples of the living heritage of Gandhi in the contemporary environmental movement.'

Conclusions

We can say that the degradation of the environment is a cause of serious concern for all forms of life. We need to understand this clearly and help to reverse the economic paradigm that is being followed where we unconsciously consume more than what is needed. This should be understood clearly and this trend reversed.

The Adivasis have since pre historic times been living in harmony and in a close relationship with nature. For them the environment was a living entity that provided them with sustenance and livelihood and in turn that needed to be protected from pollution and degradation.

While developmental activities are needed to remove large sections of our populations from poverty and deprivation, the developmental paradigm has to be tailored such that it does not result in large scale destruction of the environment and dislocation of millions of Adivasis from their natural habitats. The Adivasis have been leading dignified lives based on their own laws and traditions. Their lifestyles were not primitive but were culturally rooted in their own knowledge systems and customs. We need to learn from their simple but enriching life styles. The Gandhian concept of simple living and avoiding waste and over exploitation of the natural resources are also aimed at the broad objectives of sustainability and equity and justice for the marginalized sections of our population including the Adivasis.

References

Bandyopadhyay, J. and Vandana Shiva (2012), 'Political Economy of Ecology Movements', in Rohan D'Souza (ed.), *Environment Technology and Development*, New Delhi: Orient Blakswan Pvt. Ltd., p. 327.

Bhagwati, Jagdish and Arvind Panagariya (2013), *Why Growth Matters? How Economic Growth in India Reduced Poverty and the Lessons for Other Developing Countries*, Columbia: Public Affairs Books.

Bhatia, Ravi P. (2010), 'Human Rights, Development of Maoist Affected Regions and Peace', *Gandhi Marg*, Vol. 32, October–December, pp. 363–78.

——(2012), 'Violence and Non-violence Today: How Gandhian Principles can Help in Reducing Violence', *Gandhi Marg*, Vol. 33, January–March, pp. 441–463.

Dutta, Sagnik (2014), 'The decision to allow the expansion of coal mines without environmental clearances and a public hearing illustrates the MoEF's role as a facilitator for the mining industry rather than as a custodian of a valuable natural resource', *Frontline*, February 21, p. 14.

Gadgil, M. and R.C. Guha (2007), 'Ecological Conflicts and the Environmental Movement in India', in Mahesh Rangarajan (ed.), *Environmental Issues in India*, New Delhi: The Darling Kindersley (India) Pvt. Ltd., pp. 385–428.

Padel, Felix and Samarenda Das (2010), *Out of This Earth*, New Delhi: Orient Blackswan Pvt. Ltd.

Patnaik, Prabhat (2013), 'Poverty has increased during period of economic growth, says economist', *The Hindu*, Newspaper, 20 May.

Xaxa, Virginius (2014), 'Constitutional Provisions, Laws and Tribes', *Yojana*, January, pp. 4–7.

——(2008), *State, Society and Tribes: Issues in Post Colonial India*, New Delhi: Pearson Longmans Publishers.

9

Sources of Deprivation and Styles of Mobilization

Contextualizing the Issues of Dispossessed Tribals in Contemporary Odisha

R.K. MOHANTY

The Problem

There is no dearth of literature on tribes in India or social movement as such. Roggeband and Klandermans have claimed that sociology has been the 'home front of social movement studies', the theoretical place where concepts imported from other disciplines have been re-elaborated and systematically integrated into formal models (2007: 6). But the concept of social movement has never remained a harmless one. To construct a typology of so variegated social movement is a formidable task. To quote Mukherjee (2013: 2) 'the South Asian experience in general, and the Indian, in particular, provide extraordinary rich experience of numerous varieties of social mobilizations over time'. There are various dimensions, several levels, overlapping bases and even paradoxical purposes. In most cases, one cannot insist on clear cut exclusive types but there is a need to take them as momentous through changing and shifting crystallizations in a continuum of socio-cultural contexts and processes. Several terms like collective mobilization, ethnic struggle, revolution, resistance, dissent, protest, uprising and rebellion cross and inter cross with the concept of social movement against which extreme cautions have been sounded by *gurus* on social movement like T.K. Oommen (2001), P.N. Mukherjee

(1977; 2013) and D.N. Dhanagare (2013; 2014). Their advice has been that there should be no confusion over the use of terms provided the meaning and context are clear.

Several theories/approaches/perspectives have come up on social movements over and above the classical Marxian conflict model such as ethnographic approach (Dhanagare, 2013: 178–79; Touraine, 1981: 139–49), resource mobilization (McCarthy and Zald, 1977; Jenkins, 1985; Gamson, 1975; Giugni, 2004; McAdam, 1996: 27), the political opportunities approach (Meyer, 2004; Tarrow, 2011), subaltern theory (Guha, 1982; Amin, 1982; Chatterjee, 2012) populist approach (Taggart, 2002), assemblage theory (De Landa, 2006; Srnicek, 2007; Anderson and McFarlane, 2011; Kumar, 2013) and new movement approach with their comments and counter comments. Dhanagare (2013), Kumar (2013) and Travaglino (2014) provide an updated critical assessment of the available theories to the best aid of researchers in the field. Oommen (1984: 48) persuasively argues that an adequate framework for the understanding of protests in a society should take into account its historicity, the elements of its current social structure and the goals the society pursues.

Coming to the tribal movements, there is little consensus over the nature and type of movements by and for tribes in India. The recent leanings are towards the new social movement approach (Frank and Fuentes, 1987; D'monte, 1989; Omvet, 1993; Oommen, 2001; Pattnaik, 2011; 2013). T.K. Oommen (2001: 2–3) has characterized a new social movement as non party, political grass-roots level popular initiatives that are single issue based and anti-systemic if not anti-state, collective actions that tend to evolve due to multiple perceptions of modernity as well as meaningful articulations of identities. There are multiple actors as well in new social movements with intellectuals, activists, students including the tribes themselves (Pattnaik, 2013: 54) who meaningfully collaborate to articulate movements' ideology in course of time. Dhanagare sums up the works of Habermas (1987) and Cohen (1985) saying that 'for both of them contemporary social movements have to be understood as channels of outlet for development of new values and identities and for projecting new development alternatives to the hegemonic linear model of development driven by modern technology' (2013: 187–88).

Several enabling provisions in the form of protective discrimination under the Constitution of India, legal frameworks for their implementation, a lot many strategic public policy initiatives are taken by the government both at center and states, but the tribes in Odisha continue to struggle for survival, justice, identity and dignity. The ground reality remains disturbing. The process of deprivation at the ground level really centre around certain core problems they continue to suffer such as poverty, unemployment, crony capitalism and repression, land issues, political nexus and forest department fury, illiteracy and lack of awareness of law and erosion of cultural and religious identity which have been arguably worst encashed by the Maoists to their best advantage in the name of fight against injustice. Accordingly the natural resource rich regions inhabited by tribes have become the hub of mobilizations and movements particularly in the context of various exploitative development projects like dams, irrigations, mining, power plants, railways and industries, most specifically since the early 90's. Local communities and their support base are convinced that they can no longer remain silent about this extractive development.

Against this backdrop is built the problematic for analyzing the contemporary tribal movements as the benign outcome of the history of discrimination (D1), deprivation (D2), dispossession (D3) and of late development induced displacement (D4). This paper looks at the ground level four Ds suffered by the tribals due to the historic conditions of core problems faced by them which have manifested in some form of response (style of mobilization) articulated by themselves and for them in due course. Deprivation (D1) is the result of a tribal community's historic placement in the society involving the realization of unjust socio-economic status gap between them and others regarding enjoyment of rights and privileges. Discrimination (D2) is the prejudicial treatment of restricting members of one group from opportunities or privileges that are available to another group, leading to the exclusion of the individual or entities based on logical or irrational decision making. Deprivation and discrimination are deeply historical and acutely perennial in case of the tribes in Odisha, nay the country. As for example, the concept of 'denotified tribes' (DNTs), was discriminatory which included the tribes that were originally listed as being inherently 'criminal' under the Criminal Tribes Act of 1871 of British-India. This act was subsequently repealed under a new Act called Habitual Offenders Acts of 1958 and mere change of nomenclature did not put discrimination to an end. Dispossession (D3) relates to the action by government, corporate and/or their agents to take out the tribal's land, home, hearth, forest and resources thereon which give meaning to their life and living. Displacement (D4) understood as the so-called cost of development, refers to the forced movement of tribal people from their locality or environment and occupational activities leading to loss of livelihood and consequent impoverishment.

Our four Ds are made analytically and logically separate though in some context somewhere there might be empirical overlaps. D1 and D2 are very historic in nature and, on the other hand, D3 and D4 have their reference to the project affected people (PAP) and those who suffered due to non-industrial forced land grabbing. The concern here is to understand and explain the nature and dynamics of contemporary tribal resistance movement in Odisha and as such it is not the intention to enter into development discourse in general or tribal development in particular. The conceptual overlaps, exclusives and the variations in the life cycle of such emerging collective actions are context specific and must not be construed as a problem in the analysis.

Accordingly the paper, after delineating the problematic, presents itself in five parts. The first part gives a broad overview of the tribal scenario in some of the major tribal districts of the state. The next part briefs four major mining and industrial projects and one land alienation issue in Odisha which have severely threatened their community, life and living. The third contextual part models out the sources of deprivation and the styles of mobilization providing necessary explanatory there to. The penultimate section attempts to locate the perspective. The final part of the paper looks back and winds up with summing up of the new social movement perspective for approaching and appreciating the tribal movement in Odisha. To that end, reliance is placed primarily on available books, papers published in journals, documents, research reports publications of various organizations, paper clippings, search engines, blogs and validation through discussion with experts in the field.

I

Tribal Scenario in the State of Odisha

For the purpose of this paper, tribe refers to the endogenous primordial solidarities living in close proximity to forest territories united by ties of descent from a common ancestor, community of customs and traditions, adherence to the same culture and language distinctly their own (see Xaxa, 1999a: 3589–96; 2011: 1–17). Indigenous peoples are defined partly by descent, partly by the particular features that indicate their distinctiveness from those who arrived later, such as their language and ways of life, and partly by their own view of themselves. It means the same as originally 'native' as against those who claim native.

Odisha has the third largest concentration of tribal population comprising 9.66 per cent of the total tribal population of our country. As per 2011 Census, the Scheduled Tribe (ST) population of the state of Odisha constitutes 22.8 per cent of the total population of the state and 9.7 per cent of the total tribal population of the country. Out of 62 STs, Khond is the most populous tribe with a population of 1,395,643 constituting 17.1 per cent of the total ST population. Gond is the second largest tribe, having a number of 782,104 (having 9.6 per cent share in the total ST population.) Six other tribes namely, Santal, Kolha, Munda, Saora, Shabar and Bhottada along with Khond and Gond constitute 64.2 per cent of the total ST population of the state. Bhumij, Bhuiya, Oraon, Paroja and Kisan having a population ranging from 248,144 to 321,592.

Together, they form 18.1 per cent. Five STs, namely, Bhumia, Binjhal, Koya, etc. having population in the range of 103,537 to 196,846 constitute 9 per cent of total ST population. Remaining 44 tribes alongwith the generic tribes constitute the residual 8.8 per cent of total ST population of the state. Five tribes, namely Chenchu, Mankidi, Desua Bhumij, Ghara, Tharua, are very small groups having negligible less than 500 population (Census of India, 2010: 207).

Odisha houses 13 Primitive Tribal Groups but only eight Scheduled Tribes are declared as Primitive Tribal Groups by the Government of India. Those tribes are Juang, Bondo Poraja, Lodha, Didayi, Mankidia, Birhor, Kharia and Soura. The Registrar General and Census Commissioner of India are not publishing the figures and data (Nayak, 2010: 203) of remaining five tribal ethnic groups, namely Kutia Khond, Dongria Khond, Lanjia Saura, Chuktia and Paudi Bhuyan. So far as development is concerned, these tribal groups are as marginalized as other eight and continue to be techno-economically backward, therefore, their demographic information deserve inclusion as primitive tribes.

For the purpose of analysis it has been decided to include 10 tribal districts namely Mayurbhanja, Keonjhar, Sundargarh, Kandhamal, Kalahandi, Koraput, Malkanagiri, Nawarangpur and Rayagada. The rationale behind choice of these districts is the following: (1) These are the districts where tribes are worst deprived; (2) The tribals of Odisha mostly inhabit the hilly regions of these disricts, mainly in close proximity to forests comprising near more than 45 per cent of population in these district and 60 per cent of the tribal population of the state; (3) these are the districts in which almost all of the Primitive Tribal Groups (PTGs) live for centuries, being far away from the mainstream in their relatively isolated, inaccessible, less fertile and less agriculturally productive regions of forests, hills and mountains; and (4) These districts have lowest female literacy, greater gender disparity and dismal retention with high drop out rate.

Several macro indicators of tribal development relating to education, health, employment, income and work participation points towards an adverse status of scheduled tribes vis-à-vis the general population (Table 1). The Scheduled Tribes comprise a decisive segment of the poverty struck population in the State of Odisha. Development of Scheduled Tribes has been given priority in successive Five Year Plans and of late, huge public expenditure programmes have been directed to achieve the objectives of tribal development in Odisha. However, the outcome of the administrative intent and legislative programme are not properly realised. The status of any social group is determined by economy – poverty, health-nutrition and literacy-education. The persistence problems of tribals in Odisha can be seen from the following HDI Report.

Table 1

Indicators of Human Development Index in Selected Districts of Odisha

District	*% ST to Total Population*	*Literacy Rate*	*Health Index*	*Income Index*	*Literacy Index*	*Edn. Index*	*HDI Value*	*HDI Rank*	*GDI Rank*
Malkanagiri*	57.43%	30.53	0.122	0.497	0.313	0.491	0.370	30	30
Mayurbhanj*	56.60%	51.91	0.782	0.489	0.524	0.647	0.639	09	06
Nawarangpur*	55.03%	33.93	0.340	0.453	0.343	0.516	0.571	26	25
Kandhamal**	51.96%	52.68	0.006	0.516	0.530	0.645	0.389	29	29
Rayagada*	55.76%	36.15	0.250	0.547	0.356	0.531	0.443	25	24
Sundargarh*	50.19%	64.86	0.692	0.618	0.652	0.740	0.683	04	02
Koraput*	49.62%	35.72	0.218	0.539	0.362	0.535	0.431	27	26
Keonjhar**	44.50%	59.64	0.340	0.547	0.598	0.704	0.530	24	20
Kalahandi**	28.65%	45.94	0.763	0.471	0.462	0.585	0.606	11	08
Bolangir	20.63	54.93	0.468	0.504	0.549	0.666	0.546	21	16

Source: Odisha Human Development Report, 2004 (compiled).

* Districts in whole are under Schedule V in Odisha

** Few Blocks/Tehsils under Schedule V in Odisha (Keonjhar, Telkoi, Champua, Barbil tahasils of Keonjhar district; Khondamal, Balliguda and G. Udayagiri tahasil of Khondamal district, R. Udaygiri tahasil, Gumma and Rayagada block of Rayagada district, Thuamul Rampur and Lanjigarh blocks of Kalahandi district). The total area of the Scheduled Areas of the state contains almost 70 per cent of Odisha's forest areas, even though they form only 44 per cent of the state area.

The eight districts of KBK region, comprising the district of Kalahandi, Nuapada, Bolangir, Sonepur, Koraput, Malkanagiri, Nawarangpur and Rayagada are considered as one of the poorest regions not only in the State but also in the Country with about 71.40 per cent of families living below poverty line. As estimated in Odisha Human Development Report 2004, the omen with any anemia is 74.7 per cent among tribal women, which is significantly higher than that for general population (54.4%) and Scheduled Tribes (66.3%). There are overwhelming literates among the tribes. Recognizing the Census 2001, the overall literacy rate of tribals is 37.37 per cent. This is significantly lower than that of the general population (63.08%) and is even lower than the literacy rate of 55.53 per cent among the Scheduled Castes. The literacy rate of tribal male is 1.48 per cent; which is much lower than the state average of 75.35 per cent. The female literacy rate of 23.37 per cent is also the lowest of all social groups in terms of literacy. When education is considered to be the heart of all development, it is evident that education scenario among scheduled tribes is in a very bad shape.

II

The Roots of Resistance and Mobilization: Five Case Narratives

The situation in Odisha is gradually worsening in every area where people have put up brave resistances against forcible land acquisition and mindless mining and notorious industrialization at the cost of life and livelihoods of millions of people. Alienation of tribal land in favour of non-tribals and outsiders, loss of control and access to livelihood support systems vital to existence, marginalizing and destituting tribal communities are the additional factors contributing to their resentment. A series of factors have created an atmosphere of helplessness and hopelessness in the state among the marginalized sections.

This section of the paper presents five case narratives relating to the roots of resistance and mobilization by and for the tribals in Odisha. The movements are ill-famous as Kashipur Movement in Rayagada District (Schedule V Area), Niyamgiri Movement in Kalahandi District (Schedule V Area), Anti-POSCO Movement in Jagatsinghpur District (Non-Schedule V Area), Kalinganagar Movement in Jajpur District (Non-Schedule V Area) and Narayanpatna Movement in Koraput District (Schedule V Area). These are five cases taken in order to analyse the typicality of the contemporary tribal movement in Odisha since 1990s.

Schedule V of the Indian Constitution which enjoins the government to respect and uphold the land rights of Scheduled Tribes applies to the entire Rayagada, Kalahandi and Koraput Districts, the three southern districts of Odisha. Special Assistance is also provided under centrally sponsored KBK Plans of Government of India and Biju KBK of the State Government in Odisha. Anti-POSCO Movement in Jagatsinghpur and Jajpur are two coastal districts not covered under Schedule V Area plans. Kalinganagar area Jajpur District has substantive number of tribal population and Anti-POSCO Movement affected only twenty two tribal household of the area. Kashipur Movement in Rayagada District and Niyamgiri Movement in Kalahandi District were fought over bauxite mining and refinery and related issues. Anti-POSCO Movement in Jagatsinghpur District and Kalinganagar Movement in Jajpur District were fought over establishment of Steel Industry related issues. Narayanpatna Movement in Koraput district is fought for against the land dispute, which remained unsettled for generations together. The uniqueness of this movement is that the leadership is from within the tribe themselves without the same being provided by middleclass-high(er) caste outsiders. Under the Chasi Mulia Adivasi Sangha (CMAS), they have categorically claimed that the land belonged to the indigenous people who have inhabited this land and forests since centuries, and mostly outsiders, with the help of police, bureaucracy and politicians have captured their land. CMAS is led and controlled by tribals and has a support base running into thousands, sometimes external support from Maoists. The tribals here have forcibly 'recovered' thousands of hectares of agricultural land from the landlords and redistributed them among the tribal community. Poverty, unemployment, illiteracy, land deprivation and exploitation of tribals were the common triggers threading all the above cited movements into one. Let us through some light on each of them.

Kashipur Resistance Against Alcan-Hindalco

The tribal and Dalit people in the area began their resistance in 1993 when they came to know that Utkal Alumina India ltd (UAIL) is being established in mineral rich Kashipur and adjoining areas of Rayagada District (undivided Koraput) for the purpose of bauxite mining in the Baphlimali hills and setting up of a factory for processing the same in a big refinery at a Kondh village named Ramibeda for producing alumina. The UAIL was a consortium consisting of two large Indian companies and one MNC viz Tata, Indal and Norway's NORSK Hydro. In the wake of persistent resistance against the UAIL between 1998 and 2000, Tata quit the venture. Then ALCAN (Canada) brought up a major share in its subsidiary INDAL and sold it to HINDALCO. Later, Norsk Hydro also withdrew from the project due to heavy pressure from Norwegian human rights activists and abundant public opinion in favour of popular mobilization. Norsk Hydro is the third biggest aluminium corporation in the world after Alcoa and ALCAN. They could not start with the construction of the factory for processing bauxite nor could they start the bauxite mining. Since then, it became a joint venture of the mining giants HINDALCO (of Aditya Birla group) (55%) and ALCAN of Canada (45%) and hence the nomenclature ALCAN-HINDALCO. Apart from UAIL, large corporate houses with interests in bauxite mining like LandT and RSB Metaltech started showing interests in Kashipur and Lanjigarh area to produce alumina.

The total cost of the project is estimated at ₹ 4,500 crores. Bauxite would be sourced through open cast mining from Baphlimali of Maikanch Panchayat, with an estimated 200 million tonnes reserve, and will be transported to the plant site 25 kms away at Doraguda in Kucheipadar Panchayat via a conveyor belt. The capacity of the plant would be 2.5 million tonnes per annum. The minor irrigation dam at Baghrijhola village would meet the water requirement. When this dam was constructed in 1984, people were told that it was for the development of the irrigation infrastructure in the region. The alumina generated at this refinery, proposed to be sold at US$ 85 a tonne, is estimated to be the cheapest globally. In the 22–23 years, before the alumina reserves get exhausted, the joint venture would reap a profit of at least ₹ 2,88,000 crores. The government will get royalties of ₹ 1,300–1,400 crores during that period.

The UAIL project acquired 2,865 acres of land of Kashipur block in 1995. This includes 1,000 hectares of land presently under cultivation, besides forests and the dangars, which are also used for farming. UAIL claims that the project will displace only 147 families from three villages of Domkarel, Ramibeda and Kendukhunti. The Norsk Hydro's estimate puts the number of Project Affected Persons (PAPs) at 750 families, and the Norwegian Agency for Development's estimate puts it at 60,000 persons. The Doraguda plant alone will directly affect 2,500 persons. Open cast mining in Baphlimali would adversely affect another 2,500 families in 24 villages in Chandragiri, Maikanch and Kodipari Panchayats.

All these developments added to peoples' fear of loss of land, livelihood and culture terminating in violent resistance. The Kashipur Block of Rayagada district is the land of primitive tribal communities like Kondh, Paraja, Penga and Jhodia. They realized that this bauxite mining project will poison and pollute the waters, destroy the hills and nature completely and uproot them and destroy the tribal way of life. In addition to this, rampant corruption in the district administration of Rayagada and failure of Odisha Tribal Development Programme (OTDP) and other poverty alleviation programmes such as Food For Work (FFW), Jawahar Gram Samridhi Yojna (JGSY), Employment Assurance Scheme (EAS), Pani Panchayat, etc. (Das, 2003: 81–84) makes Kashipur amenable to a mobilization for resistance (Pattnaik, 2013: 56).

On 15 December 2000 at the behest of UAIL with support from local administration, elites and outsiders tried to forcibly organize a meeting in support of the bauxite mining at village Maikanch. The people in Maikanch protested vigorously against this,saying that such meetings cannot be held in their villages against their wishes by outsiders under the banner of Prakrut Sampad Suraksha Parishad (PSSP) (meaning Natural Resources Protection Organisation). The people drove these outsiders out of there. Next day, on 16 December three tribal men were shot dead and dozens of people suffered bullet injuries in police firing. Women and children who remained behind the protesters and tried to stop the violent police but were not spared as per reports in press.

The protest in the Kashipur Block started against UAIL as the chief target, and was later carried further against other bauxite mining projects of BALCO, LandT and Sterlite Industries India Ltd (SIIL) in the same area which affected the life and living of more than 5,000 families in nearly 100 villages (Pattnaik, 2013: 57). Further, rampant corruption in the district administration of Rayagada and failure of Odisha Tribal Development Programme (OTDP) and other poverty alleviation programmes such as Food For Work (FFW), Jawahar Gram Samridhi Yojna (JGSY), Employment Assurance Scheme (EAS), Pani Panchayat, among others have driven the mobilization for resistance in the area. Massive deployment of para-military forces in December 2004 by the state machinery to suppress opposition and Maoist linkage led to further violent resistance. Kashipur Solidarity, a forum for the local people have detailed out the genesis and the implications of Kashipur Movement under the title 'Why Kashipur Burns'?

Extraction of alumina is banned in the developed countries because of the pollution that it causes. Open cast mining has always been severely criticized on environmental grounds. The people in the area through media projection and civil society campaign have come to realize the destructive ecological impact of bauxite mining and processing (Srikant, 2009). The mined bauxite ore needs to be converted into alumina first and this requires a large amount of water and energy and then they release everyday thousands of tonnes of red mud into the rivers poisoning and polluting them. On the other hand, after a few years of bauxite mining, hills and forests are destroyed forever through the opencast mining, blasting the hills completely; they would not exist anymore and with it vanish the ecosystem having perennial water streams as well. The project would cause the drying up of perennial natural springs, desertification of the area, landslides, flash floods, and loss of the natural habitat of the local fauna and flora that sustain the diverse indigenous communities in the region. All industrial mining are very destructive to ecology, to the tribal people but the production of aluminium leaves an even larger trail of destruction and despoliation than some other metals.

Lanjigarh Niyamgiri Movement Against Vedanta Alumina Limited (VAL)

Vedanta Aluminium Ltd is an associate company of the London Stock Exchange. The company's original name was Sterlite Industries (India) Ltd (SIIL). In December 2003, it was launched in the London Stock Exchange a subsidiary of Vedanta Resources plc (VRP) in order to build Lanjigarh refinery in Kalahandi district. Now it is working under the banner of Vedanta Alumina Limited (VAL), based in Mumbai. VAL is a leading producer of metallurgical grade alumina and other aluminium products, which cater to a wide spectrum of industries. VAL operates a greenfield 1.0 mtpa alumina refinery plant and an associated 75 MW captive power plant at Lanjigarh, Odisha. Both SIIL and the VAL are headed by a non resident Indian, Anil Agarwal. Tribal people like the Dongaria Kondh, and Kutia Kondh and Desia Kondh have lived in the Niyamgiri mountain range of Lanjigarh area from time immemorial. While the Kutia Kondh inhabit in the foothills, the Dongaria Kondh live in the upper reaches of the Niyamgiri hills. The Dongria Kondh call themselves Jharnia meaning those who live by the Jharana (streams) confined to Niyamgiri hill tracts covering the blocks of Kalyansighpur, Bissamcuttack and Muniguda in

Rayagada district. The immediate two neighbours of Dongaria Kondh are Kutia and Desia Kondhs. Desia Kondhs are plain dwellers. The debilitating levels of poverty here seem to have nurtured radical Left currents in the region heavily influenced by Maoists. In the backdrop of high impoverishment among the affected people, their loss of shelter, land and livelihood pushes many of them for migration or to starvation deaths.

VAL started mining bauxite from the Niyamgiri hills jointly with OMC as per the lease agreement signed between VAL and OMC in October 2004. The major share holders in VAL are Barclays, Deutsche Bank and ABN Amro. The aggregate investment of the project was approximately 10,000 crores. For this purpose, 723.43 hectares of land was required by the VAL. Out of which 232.75 hectares was private and most of this land belonged to the Kondhs. Most of the land is categorized as forest. According to the office of the Collector, Kalahandi, 12 villages of the Gram Panchayat Lanjigarh and Batelima will be affected by the proposed alumina refinery at Lanjigarh. From these villages, 60 families were to be displaced and 302 families will be affected as their land will be acquired for the project. But in reality, the plant displaced 102 families from their homes. Another 1,220 'project affected' families lost either all, or parts, of their farmland. So far, the project displaced two villages partially and two completely and the list will add on. Out of the 64 displaced households in Jaganathpur village, most of them are Kondhs who had been cultivating there for generations. On 23 January 2004, four tribal villages, Borobhota, Kinari, Kothduar, Sindhabahali and their agricultural fields, in south east Kalahandi district, were razed by VAL, and the villagers were forcibly evicted. Apart from large scale displacement of tribal people, Lanjigarh Movement countered the violation of environmental laws/forest conservation laws including Panchayats Extension to Scheduled Areas (PESA) Act of 1996 as its extensive mining in the Niyamgiri mountains threatened an entire ecosystem, implying even drying up of rivers flowing from the mountains.

The 8,000-strong Dongaria tribe residing in the foothills of the Niyamgiri hill in Kalahandi district have been carrying out a resistance movement against the mining of bauxite from the hill top on the ground that their tribal diety Niyamraja resides there and any mining activities would destroy their God and ecology and deprive them of the their main source of livelihood. Resistance movements in Lanjigarh also inspired tribal representatives of Karlapat region whose mountains are now being targeted by the mining companies. Vedanta is also facing stiff resistance from the villagers to their proposed 'world-class' university on the Konarka-Puri coast on a massive 6,000 acres of land allotted to the company by the state government allegedly from out of the land owned by the Jagannath Temple Trust, Puri. The protesting villagers have not allowed Vedanta to take possession of the land.

People across the globe have registered their protests against Vedanta. On 11 January 2013, parallel demonstrations took place in Odisha, London and New York where activists in hundreds raised slogans and upheld placards to denounce the corporate annexations of indigenous peoples' lands. Various grass-roots groups, including Phulbari Solidarity Group, Japan Against Nuclear, Tamil Solidarity and London Mining Network, along with Foil Vedanta gathered at Vedanta's London headquarters to add their voice to recent pressure for Vedanta to be de-listed from the London Stock Exchange for its poor corporate governance, illegal operations and major human rights violations. They shouted 'Vedanta out of London' and blew horns and whistles. Several parliamentarians and the former CBI Director Richard Lambert London have highlighted how Vedanta's listing is used for legal immunity to hide their corporate crimes. Likewise, in New York City, protesters gathered outside the United Nations headquarters to highlight the company's human rights crimes, displaying placards that read: 'Our Mountain! Our Rights! Vedanta: Give Up!'

The project has provoked a serious political conflict between the political parties like the ruling BJD claiming development and the opposition Congress opposing displacement. Amidst opposition and based on the Forest Advisory Committee report headed by N.C. Saxena the Ministry of Environment and Forest (MOEF) withdrew the environmental clearance for VAL on 24 August 2010. Following this, on 17 September 2010 the National Environment Appellate Authority (NEAA) also suspended the environmental clearance to VAL that was granted in 2009. Government of Odisha through OMC moved to the Supreme Court on April 2011 against MOEF's withdrawal of environmental clearance to VAL at Lanjigarh for its bauxite mining at Niyamgiri hills.

The Supreme Court of India while adjudicating a case on mining in Niyamgiri hills of Odisha, appreciated the Dongaria Kandhas for the first time appearing in the court as parties and directed the Odisha state government on 18 April 2013 to place issues concerning individual, community, cultural and religious claims of STs and TFDs before the gram sabha which would take decision on the project. A bench headed by Justice Aftab Alam observed 'STs (Scheduled Tribes) and other TFDs (Traditional Forest Dweller) residing in the Scheduled Areas have a right to maintain their distinctive spiritual relationship with their traditionally owned or otherwise occupied and used lands. Agriculture is the only source of livelihood for them apart from collection and sale of minor forest produce to supplement their income … . The law intends to protect custom, usage, forms, practices and ceremonies which are appropriate to the traditional practices of forest dwellers … forests have the best chance to survive if communities participate in their conservation and regeneration measures' (Writ Petition-Civil No. 180 of 2011).

The seventh gram sabha held on 29 July 2013 at Phuldumer village in Trilochanpur Panchyat under Lanjigarh Block passed a resolution rejecting the proposed bauxite mining in Niyamgiri hills as happened in six gram sabhas held earlier. All the 49 voters of the villages, including 32 women, out of the total 65 members spoke against the proposed bauxite mining in Niyamgiri. Want of bauxite from alternative sources and rejection by gram sabha has brought VAL to a standstill now.

Kalinganagar Movement Against Tata Steel Ltd

Kalinganagar is a geographical unit consisting of a compact landmass of Danagadi and Sukinda Blocks of Jajpur district of Odisha. Kalinganagar is neither a village nor a town. This is a name given to a geographical area by Industrial Development Corporation of Odisha (IDCO) where the Government of Odisha developed a steel-producers-hub. IDCO acquired the land from public, developed infrastructure for giving it to various industries for setting up Steel Plants. The process has started from the early 1990s and the ex-CM, late Biju Patanaik, took the lead role in promoting the steel-hub. He had invited first, Swaraj Paul, an NRI British industrialist to set up a steel plant which did not materialize though. Later, the industrial activity grew when his son Naveen Patnaik became the CM of Odisha. Minerals like iron ore and chromite are located closer to this area. The river Brahmani flows nearby giving water opportunity.

Tatas are one of the investors who had signed the MoU in 2004 to set up a 6 MMTPA steel plant in Kalinganagar, in two phases, with an investment of ₹ 1,54,000 million. As per the latest report, there are 12 industries at different stages of construction/operation in Kalinganagar which include public sector plant like Nilachal Ispat Nigam Ltd, private sector plant like Zindal Steel Ltd, MESCO etc. Tata Steel is setting up its steel plant here which would become operational by 2014 end as per the recent press release of the company.

The two Blocks – Sukinda and Danagadi – under which the area falls has a Scheduled Tribe population of 36.06 per cent and 28.19 per cent and Scheduled Caste population of 11.89 per cent and 22.31 per cent, respectively. The Scheduled Tribe population in the acquired area is much higher than the Block average. Of the tribes, people belonging to Ho community constitute nearly 80 per cent and rest of them belong to Munda and Santal communities. These communities are said to have come from Mayurbhanj, Keonjher, Ranchi and Singhbhum districts in different phases in late decades of nineteenth century and early decades of twentieth century and have settled here at the invitation of the then Sukinda King. A total of 3000 acres of land has been acquired by IDCO, of which 6900 acres are private land and the remaining area is said to be 'government land'. The Estate of Sukinda King was vested with the government which the tribals were cultivating.

Locals in Kalinganagar did not want to make way for the new factories. They believed that the government was not offering them enough compensation, and that guarantees of jobs and resettlement could not be trusted. Three giant plants were already up and running, their chimneys, gas flares and trucks throwing smoke and dust up into the air. In 2004 an organization to protect the interest of the people affected by the industrial complex was formed; it called itself *Sukinda Upatyaka Adivasi-Harijan Ekata O Surakshya Parishad,* which was later renamed, and remains such till date, as *Visthapan Birodhi Jan Mancha*, Sukinda. In October 2004, they expressed their concern and grievances about the hardships faced by them due to the emerging complex, and spelt out several demands; five demands meant for the people to be displaced, and six demands concerning the people already displaced. The salient features of the demands included (i) stop further construction in agricultural land; (ii) giving *patta* to the people settled before 1980 (iii) land acquired, but unused, be returned to the original owners; (iv) stop deliberate targeting of tribal/dalit villages for land acquisition; (v) the homestead land to be raised to one acre per displaced family; (vi) the parishad to have a say in rehabilitation matters; (vii) one job per displaced family. During 2005, the Visthapan Virodhi Jana Mancha (VVJM) resisted all kinds of activities – like land-survey, bhumipuja, leveling, boundary wall construction etc, relating to setting up of industries in the Kalinganagar Complex. Notice was served to the people for Public Hearing on Tata Steel plant to be held at Jajpur Road on 27 July 2005. On the other hand, on 23 July 2005, Tatas came to perform their bhoomipooja in the presence of District Collector and the SP. About 3000 people protested and held demonstrations at the site. The administration responded by lodging cases against some people and their leaders. Again on 7 October 2005, Tatas came, accompanied by police and district administration, for *bhoomipooja* and people protested. A constable was reportedly beaten up by the protestors and, according to the police, people snatched away his gun. On 25 October, Shri Rabindra Jarika, one of the leaders of the Jana Mancha, was arrested by the Jajpur police from Bhubaneswar. On 27 October people gheraoed the Kalinganagar police station protesting against the arrest of Rabindra Jarika. After this incident police have been trying to arrest the other leaders of the Visthapan Virodhi Jan Manch. When in first week of January 2006, Tata Steel started work on clearing land it had acquired, angry villagers armed with bows, arrows and axes, tried to block it. The state government tried to force people off land for a Tata Steel Ltd project. In a resulting battle which led to police firing on 2 January 2006, a policeman was hacked to death and 12 villagers were killed.

Village leader Chakradhar Haibru protested and complained that the government made a huge profit on the land by selling the site to Tata Steel in 2004–05 for a much higher one than the amount given to locals during

1992–94. The government allotted 1,960 acres to Tata Steel, reportedly at nearly 10 times the rate at which the landowners were originally compensated. There were serious grievances: extremely inadequate compensation for the land acquired, gross failures in resettlement and rehabilitation, and major shortcomings in the provision of jobs (Pandey, 2008: 614). Many of them, though in possession of land, have no *patta* (Record of Rights) and as such did not receive any money since their traditional rights to the land were not recognized as the last land survey and settlement in the area was done only in 1928. The movement is still on.

Anti-POSCO India Private Limited Movement in Jagatsinghpur

Pohang Iron and Steel Company (POSCO) project in Odisha is the largest foreign investment project ever in India. Commonly known as POSCO India, it is an Indian subsidiary of Korean conglomerate. POSCO signed a memorandum of understanding in June 2005 with the state government of Odisha to construct a mega integrated steel plant and modernization of Odisha's iron ore mines. According to the MoU, POSCO would invest ₹ 52,813 crore to build a 12-mtpa capacity steelworks and develop mines and linked infrastructure over three phases from 2007 to 2016 on the sea coast of Jagatsinghpur district of Odisha. During the first phase (2007– 2010), it would produce 4-mtpa and expand the final production volume to National Steel Policy (2005) and POSCO Steel Proposal 12-mtpa by 2016. Namboodiri (2012) has prepared a project report on social cost benefit analysis of the POSCO steel project in Odisha. In the MoU, the Government of Odisha has promised to provide adequate land, water, power, attached minor port, iron ore mines, SEZ recommendation, issue various clearances and facilitate assistance, and, generally, promise continuous and committed support to POSCO's venture in Odisha. The villagers of Dhinkia started blockade of the village to prevent government or POSCO officials from entering the village. Children became the first line of defense in the event of a police raid. As of June 2012, controversies and regulatory delays have prevented Posco India's Odisha project to proceed beyond the concept. POSCO India has no mining or manufacturing operations in Odisha.

This is an area of betel farming done on mostly forest land belonging to the state. Of the 1,620 hectares needed for the project, 90 per cent, or 1,440 hectares, is this contested forest land. When the project site was selected, the government did not consider that it would have to pay compensation for this land – it was encroached upon by the people and the government would simply take it back for the steel giant. But it was forest land and the people who lived there had cultivated on it for as long as they could remember. This then raised the tricky matter of the conditions under the Forest Rights Act that require people to give their consent to the project.

On 23 March 2008, the gram (palli) sabha of Dhinkia village (the statutory authority to initiate the process of recognition of rights under section 6(1) of the Forest Rights Act) passed resolutions initiating the process of claims for rights, and further demarcating the boundaries of the village's 'community forest resource' and declaring its intention to protect it, including it's resolve to deny consent to any diversion of this land. This forest land cannot now be disturbed without violating section 5 of the Act. West Bengal based web portal *Sanhati-Fighting Neo-liberalism* in its report dated 25 February 2010 says, 'Today US holders of POSCO stock greatly outnumber the South Korean shareholders. By far the largest block of shares in POSCO is the depositary receipts of Bank of New York Mellon, of which the largest holder is CITIGROUP. POSCO shares acquired for US$10 in 1998 sell for US$110 today. It is important for anti-POSCO activists to be aware that when they confront the various South Korean executives, or Odisha State politicians, or Chidambaram's paramilitary police, that behind them are their masters at CITICORP and the US Treasury'. If this is believed then the movement against the POSCO project is the frontline of the most critical global struggle of our time; to preserve an environment in which the next generations can thrive and against the primary enemy of humanity, imperialist capitalism.

The Union Ministry of Environment and Forests overruled its own dissenting committee to say it would have to trust the state government's version that all procedures were followed in determining that people in these villages were not entitled to this right to decide because they were not a traditional forest-dwelling community. With this sorted, the environmental and forest clearance was granted. Land acquisition for the project could proceed. But people who were not asked still said no. Local people are not 'employable' in such modern state-of-the-art plant which needs only a limited number of people in its operations. Not one time compensation but sustainable livelihood was demanded. This project affected a total of 22 tribal families, though large number of them was forest dwellers. The case of POSCO has been included in the list of narratives here to analyse the greater issue of development induced displacement and marginalization of forest dwellers rather than a case of tribal movement.

Narayanpatna Movement against Land Deprivation

Narayanpatna block is a hilly tract of land on the Odisha-Andhra Pradesh border. Almost 90 per cent of the 45,000 people who live in the block are tribes. For several years, according to the police, the block has witnessed violent attacks by Maoists – informers and contractors have been declared anti-people agents of the state and murdered with impunity and even police stations have been blown up. The November 20 firing took place in an extremely troubled land.

For more than 15 years, the CMAS has been working in Koraput district on two linked issues: the illegal and fraudulent grabbing of Adivasi land and alcohol addiction. With Adivasis' rights over ancestral land and the prohibition of transfer of land to non-Scheduled Tribes recognized by the Odisha Scheduled Area Transfer of Immovable Property Act and the Odisha Land Regulations Act, the CMAS mobilized Adivasis to take back land that they claim has been unfairly appropriated by nontribals.

The undivided Koraput district in western Odisha has acquired notoriety because of the Maoists literally taking over the dense hilly and forest areas, inhabited by tribal communities, still trapped in the vicious trap of infinite poverty, injustice and underdevelopment. The Maoists' presence stretch across the landscape and beyond to Ganjam, Malkangiri, Rayagada, and across the tense border zones of Jharkhand, Odisha and Andhra Pradesh.

Prafulla Samantra of Lok Shakti Abhiyan in a press release said 'non-tribals despite being only about eight per cent of the total population of about 38,000 in Narayanpatna block had been enjoying 85 per cent of the total land … . Many tribals including Nachika Linga's own family had to work as bonded labourers … . Tribals in the region over the years have lost their lands to several mega projects like Dandakaranya, Nalco, HAL, Indravati. And poverty persists.'

The community of 'sundhis' (the middle caste traders from outside) in the arrack business and contractors were trapping tribals in a debt trap, mortgaging their land and thereafter grabbing it. Tribals were often being used as virtual slaves and bonded labour in their own usurped land. Local officials, the tehsil office and police were in collusion with the land-grabbers. The tribals were treated with utter disdain. In 1994, tribal agitations reportedly started in Bandhugaon in the region for the first time over a land dispute. A tribal's land was grabbed to start an 'arrack business'. Six years later, upper caste landlords grabbed the land of three tribals after giving them petty amounts as loans. The tribals protested. They used every form of democratic means. They submitted a memorandum to the tehsildar, the District Magistrate and the Superintendent of Police of Koraput. They demanded that the 'arrack trade' and land-grabbing should be stopped.

The tribals here have forcibly 'recovered' thousands of hectares of agricultural land from the landlords and redistributed them among the tribal community. They have categorically claimed that this indigenous land belonged to the indigenous people who have inhabited this primordial land and forests since centuries, and mostly outsiders, with the help of police, bureaucracy and politicians, have captured their land. Under the Chasi Mulia Adivasi Sangha (CMAS), under the leadership of Nachika Linga with support from veteran CPI-ML leader Ganantha Patra. It is led and controlled by tribals and has a support base running into thousands, sometimes external support from Maoists.

No wonder the police could not move even as thousands blocked their way with bows, arrows and sickles, albeit peacefully, even while others actually started tilling the 'recovered' land. The movement has spread and acquired huge support base in the Koraput region, where scattered tribal communities share a strong chord of unity and angst with the tribals of Narayanpatna. The tribals, after years of condemnation, have refused to accept the logic of injustice anymore.

Indeed, thousands of cases are pending in different courts relating to tribal land encroachment in Odisha. Like in most tribal areas across the nation, revenue records or documents are not available – basically because tribals have been indigenous inhabitants of this land which belongs to them historically, and their land has been usurped by diabolical subterfuge using their poverty and illiteracy. More than 45,000 forest cases are pending against these poor tribals. How can the tribals fight the entrenched state machinery and this vicious nexus of the landlords, officials and police?

Table 2 presents a summary picture of the very nature of the five types of movements narrated in this section of the paper. Before going to details of the analysis on sources of deprivation and styles of mobilization, a schematic stock taking of the core issues of these movements, support networks and the continuity of the movement is considered worthwhile as done in the table.

Table 2

Support Base and the Continuity of Movements from 1990 Onwards in Odisha

S.N.	*Name of the Movement*	*Core Issues*	*Endogenous and Exogenous Support*	*Continuity*
1	Kashipur Movement Rayagada District (Schedule V Area)	Displacement due to bauxite mining and refinery; loss of land, livelihood and culture; environmental degradation	Activist networks in Odisha and in Delhi; CARE International, Local NGO; International support groups in Norway and Canada, Germany	(1994–2008)
2	Niyamgiri Movement Kalahandi District (Schedule V Area)	Displacement; loss of livelihood; environmental pollution; mining and crushing of sacred Niyamgiri; Damaging impact on Vamshadhara	CPI-ML (New Democracy), Samajwadi Jan Parishad, Green Kalahandi, Odisha and Delhi based activist networks, conservationist networks, lawyers in Supreme Court, international organizations (Survival International, UK, Action Aid) and networks, international celebrities, UK based activists	(2003–ongoing)

Cont'd...

...Cont'd

3	Kalinganagar Movement Jajpur District (Non-Schedule V Area)	Against TATA's Kalinganagar Steel Plant, displacement due to industries; protect land and livelihood; justice for the killing of 13 tribals in police firing	Activist groups in Odisha and outside; CPI-ML (New Democracy)	(2005–ongoing)
4	Anti-POSCO Movement Jagatsinghpur District (Non-Schedule V Area)	Displacement; loss of way of life and livelihoods; destruction of betelvine and fishery based economy	CPI, Activist networks in Odisha and elsewhere, Delhi based activist lawyers, activist groups in Bangalore, S. Korea and in US	(2006–ongoing)
5	Narayanpatna Movement Koraput District (Schedule V Area)	Alienation of land by non-tribal landlords; exploitation of tribals; against mining by companies	CPI-ML (Nachika Linga), activist groups in Odisha and outside	(2006–ongoing)

III

Contextualizing Sources of Deprivation and Styles of Mobilization

Traditionally, tribal communities have undergone drastic changes due to large scale migration, encroachment by outsiders and increasing vulnerability of the resources on which they have traditionally depended. Though many measures like scheduling of tribal areas, creasing land transfer and recognition of the rights over resources is encouraged by the Government of India. Yet, tribals are facing problems of land alienation, displacement, indebtedness and bonded labour. Many of the problems are rooted from their increasing attachment with dominant culture and lack of basic competence in education. The tribes in India suffered from the worst deprivation and exploitation and sought different solutions to their problems as per evidence in history.

The primary reason for their current uprising and collective action was for the loss of land while more so their culture and solidarity were threatened. There are few important aspects of the tribal resistance movement which deserve mention. One is that the tribals have their own social, cultural and religious identity, their own taboos, beliefs and peculiar compulsion of lifestyle and, therefore, any attempt of the administration/or an alien rule to make an inroad into the tribal society by way of reformatory and correctional changes, however laudable, is bound to be resisted by the tribals with all their individual and collective might. As said in the beginning, the mobilization of tribes is the collective reaction or the response to address and redress their deprivations which tend to emanate from certain core problems faced by the tribes in Odisha. With 'Human Development' being the focus on the radar of the world development community, there is a greater emphasis on the performance and progress of the social sector, the scope of which has expanded far beyond education and health in Odisha. There are bunch of socio-economic problems i.e poverty, unemployment, land dispute, displacement, distress migration, improper communication, food insecurity, corporate led repression, political nexus and forest department fury, which have come into notice in the areas affected by Left Wing Extremism (LWE). Explanation is important in this sensitive field of study and there is a lot to be learned, for there is a lot at stake. The explanatory is modelled around the following table for systematic appreciation of styles of mobilization in contemporary tribal Odisha. Before modelling out the dynamics, it is important to operationalize the nature of protests and the style of mobilizations that have tended to grow out of these deprivations. These are ameliorative, protective, protest and, resistance, transformative and alternative movements, found in varied contexts.

Ameliorative and protective styles are struggle for improvement of conditions over historic injustices. The protesters demand grant of special privileges made under the Constitution of India for the downtrodden and the underprivileged sections of society (in this context Scheduled Tribes). These are basically for abolition of discrimination, demanding governance to balance between weak and strong, to eradicate exclusion, hence called protective and positive discriminations.

Resistance and protest are certainly very different things. The goal of both is to somehow get rid of or prevent some sort of policy or law or action, or to speak out against a certain view or opinion. Protest is an expression or declaration of objection, disapproval, or dissent, often in opposition to something a person is powerless to prevent or avoid: a protest against increased taxation. Resistance is the act or power of resisting, opposing, or withstanding. Protest is different from resistance because to me, when I think of protesting I think of people getting together to avoid something they don't want to happen and using signs and shouting things. We've read things with many signs of protest and resistance from colonial times. Resistance is an action when a group of people are on an offensive side. Protesting is when a group of people are trying to stop something from being enforced, but protesters are on a defensive side. Protest tends to be more passive and resistance is more aggressive. A protest could be some sort of a rally, people with picket signs, or even the writing of a newspaper article. A resistance would tend to be something more like a riot, or the refusal to abide by a law. The difference between the two mainly stems from the idea that a protest is generally going to focus more on spreading a message, or simply making it clear that there is dissatisfaction with the subject matter, while a resistance actually does something to show this dissatisfaction. Resisting a law would be acting the opposite way the law is forcing you to, while protesting against the law would be doing something that proves your opposition, such as boycotting goods, or holding signs outside of a place accused of doing something that went against what you thought was right.

Transformative styles are oriented towards breaking the silence over historic injustices by building an inclusive movement where adversaries become allies in order to safeguard the common interest and mitigate common challenges. Successful transformative justice movements draw on strategic contributions by a diversity of people. Transformative mobilization seeks safety and accountability without relying on alienation, punishment, or state or systemic violence, including incarceration and policing. Alternative styles signal the politicization of movements that have been struggling for the rights of poor and marginalized sections of tribal and rural society. It protests against the 'false' globalization in which the rich and powerful are benefitting at the expense of the poor and marginalized. Ameliorative and protective movements have a longer history but the dynamics of transformative, alternative styles, protests and resistances tend to give newer dimensions to the styles of such collective mobilization in the context of tribes in Odisha since early 1990s onwards.

Table 3

Sources of Deprivation and Styles of Mobilization in Contemporary Tribal Odisha

Core Problems	*Ground Level Deprivations*	*Styles of Mobilization*
Poverty	Bondage, indebtedness, malnutrition, lack of health care, inadequate living standard (such as inadequate drinking water, fuel, toilets, electricity, housing, and equipment)	Ameliorative and protective
Unemployment	Compulsive migration, low wage, exploitation, commodification of labour	Ameliorative and protective
Crony capitalism and repression	Co-ordination of capitalists with global extractive capital leading to depletion of tribal resources, neo-patrimonial tendencies, elite advantage at the cost of tribals and their environment, facing false cases, being dissuaded by false promises of development	Protest and resistance

Cont'd...

...Cont'd

Land issues	Violation of tribal right in the name of public Interest, Eviction and Displacement, No or Inadequate Compensation, Land Mortgaging and Sale, Encroachment by outsiders, Loss of patta through Land Acquisition, Loss of land through survey and settlements, Uncertainty over unsurveyed areas, Non-Distribution of wasteland, Loss of rights on forest land and forest products, Ban on shifting cultivation, Lack of regularization of eligible encroachments	Protest and Resistance
Political nexus and Forest Department fury	Apathy and Party Interest of politicians, Bribery and Scam, Poor Implementation of Forest Laws, Ineffective forest officials, Controlling Gram Sabhas	Protest and Resistance
Illiteracy and lack of awareness of law	Inadequate Resources, Schools without teachers, Poor retention and drop outs, Leasing out teaching, Linguistic barrier	Protective and Transformative
Erosion of cultural and religious identity	Loss of indigenous Identity, Influx of Outsiders, Cultural Submergence, Loss of Home, hearth and place of worship, Top-Down development without considering the requirements of locals	Protest, Resistance and Transformative
Maoist advantage	Fear of Police and Maoists, Mobilization Networks, Allurements, Involuntary recruitment in Maoist groups	Alternative and Transformative

Poverty

Odisha suffers the ignominy of having the highest poverty rate among Scheduled Tribes (STs) in India, with nearly three-fourths of its tribal population below the official poverty line in 2004–05. With Scheduled Tribes in the state falling behind other groups on practically every development parameter, there is an increasing recognition in policy circles to focus on their development. The spatial and social concentration of poverty among the tribals and Dalits living in interior districts of Odisha is the outcome of the historical processes of exclusion and discrimination that have been among the pronounced features of the social economy of the region (Mehta, 2010). Poverty is spatially and socially concentrated in Odisha and as such the incidence of poverty in the north and south Odisha continue to remain high compared to coastal districts (De Haan and Dubey, 2005; Mishra, 2009; Panda, 2008). As such Kalahandi, Balangir and Koraput (KBK) are more or less recognized as synonymous with mass poverty, starvation and hunger deaths (Currie, 2000; Lokadrusti, 1993). But the exclusion from and unequal access to state-initiated anti-poverty measures also has significant bearing on such outcomes. Human Development indicators in the conext of tribal districts in Odisha given in the first section of this paper vouchsafe this. Poor tribals are at the high risk of vulnerabilities like bondage, indebtedness, malnutrition, lack of health care, inadequate living standard (such as inadequate drinking water, fuel, toilets, electricity, housing, and equipments).

The state needed a development model that could create jobs and alleviate poverty of every segment of society. Unfortunately, the model chosen was heavy industry, high investment and sophisticated technology based, requiring extensive exploitation of the natural and mineral resources (Ray and Katzenstein, 2005). This resulted in a damage of the livelihood of the communities that had sustained them for generations on the common property resources (CPRs). To consider displacement as the inevitable but unfortunate outcome of an otherwise benevolent development process is to deemphasize the structural and historical connections between dispossession and 'development' of a certain kind. It is important to recognize that many of those who have been displaced in Odisha, and also elsewhere, have been dislocated not because of a mega-event like the construction of a dam or an industry, but because of a rather gradual but systematic undermining of the basis of their livelihoods. It is important and imperative to understand both these aspects together to understand the protests by poor people in their proper perspective.

It needs to be understood that hunger and extreme poverty do not persist because of the states' failure to recognize them as real issues, rather, it stems from neglect and insensitivity toward the victims in the process of policy implementation. The collaboration with private partners, exportation of forest and timber products, and undertaking of 'development projects' often caters to such influential minorities at the expense of local populations. In the process, tribal poor have gone poorer with livelihhod at stake. This is none the less evidenced in all the five case narratives given in the Table 3. People who are indisputably poor are left out of the BPL list, PDS do not reach in the name of area being inaccessible, eating inedible forest food, health care is beyond their reach against which people express dissatisfaction and seek amelioration. Civil society and media campaign mobilize people demanding protective discrimination. The basic objective of all these arrangements is to bring tribal people out of poverty and to free them from exploitation by non-tribals. Development districts are home of hunger. Developing an alternate path, however, needs a paradigm shift, both in thinking and in implementation. It needs different stakeholders to come together, beyond their ideologies, to work in a cohesive manner with a long-term vision and most critically with community participation.

Dongaria Kondh in the Niyamgiri area face acute shortage of food in the post-sowing monsoon period (July–September) and again around March when the *kharif* harvest has been exhausted. In such situations, consumption of mango kernels is the usual practice to compensate the staple food shortage. It is being used after a series of cleaning procedures to get rid of toxicity, which is added to the *mandia* preparation in place of rice. They were also taking local alternative non-food varieties like wild tubers, leaves, mushrooms, tamarind seed powder that contribute as rainy foods since generations as coping measures of food insecurity. Moreover, the powder from the pith of sago palm is being used commonly. In the past, they were able to cover most of the shortfall with foods gathered from the forests. Due to depletion of forest resources and aggressive mining activities, the livelihood base is shrinking and compels them to depend upon purchased foods to meet the food deficit. Many households have become caught in a debt trap because of the precariousness of food security. The government schemes such as the targeted PDS, special schemes under food safety net and rural development schemes like SGRY, MGNREGS, and OTELP, etc. have limited impact on poverty and food security in this region.

They adopted traditional shifting cultivation (*Podu or Jhoom*), since they are poor and illiterate and away from winds of modern agricultural technology and economy. The agriculture or podu cultivation provides food security only for 150 days in a year; for another 157 days people are dependent upon forest resources (Kumar and Kerr, 2012; 2013). They collect the non-timber forest produce such as *jhudang, kandul, kating, alsi*, mustard, etc. Public works like construction of road, watershed works, etc. provides wage employment for 25 days in a year. To meet food requirements, during the agricultural lean period, villagers take loan from the local money lenders. Rate of interest is decided on the basis of the urgency of the need which may cross over monthly 10 per cent interest. For 70 days in a year, villagers are dependent upon loan to purchase foodgrains. Villagers take loan during agricultural lean period from the money lender and return it during the harvesting period i.e. in November to December (Mohapatra, 2012: 55).

In the absence of the medical health care system, the tribal villagers employ traditional knowledge of the causes-cure of ailment, and consult their Disari, the medicine man, at times of need. Tribal villagers from Rengapalli and Bandhuguda village adjoining to the red mud pond of Vedanta plant, facing many health hazards since 2003–2004 soon after the mining activities started in this region. Villagers from these two villages reported that about 16 people have died of TB and many of them are suffering from TB, skin disease and dust infection. There are two large red mud ponds that contain caustic water that comes out in the process of refining bauxite from the VAL plant. This hard smell affects the adjoining villages and causes many health problems (Mohapatra, 2012: 54).

With the increase in the level of poverty, the level of debt increases. The burden of debt passes on from generation to generation. While borrowing money, the borrower does not pay attention to his repaying capacity and for him even a little debt becomes a trap out of which he cannot come out. Tribals borrow money to satisfy their food needs during off season. They tend to take loan for food, family and festival expenditure such as marriage, birth, death, ceremonies, rituals, worship and treatment of diseases. A large number of tribals are highly addicted to wine for which they tend to borrow money from the *sahukars* (lender). Even they mortgage their agricultural land to meet the expenditure of the wine. At last, they fail to repay the loan amount and surrender before the *sahukar* as a *goti*. He has to work for *sahukar*'s family without any financial benefit. When the poor tribals fail to repay the loan amount, the whole family from generation to generation works under the money lender known as *goti (*bonded/free labour*)*. Again the master possesses the land of the tribal borrower and employ him as a *goti* who works in that agricultural land as well as in master's home. Indebtedness has caused excessive migration of tribals to other districts and states. Indebtedness has generated psychological frustration among the tribals and encouraged them to turn violent and join extremist outfit.

The leader of *Chasi Mulia Adivasi Sangha*, Nachika Linga was also working as a *goti* under *sahukar* known as Kantha Parida in Koraput. With the passage of time he was very much displeased with the nature of work and the ill bondage system. So he decided to quit from the house of his master and vowed to fight against the *goti* cult. Then he also decided to release his brother from this *goti* system. So he moved from hill to hill and collected tamarind in huge amount and sold it in the market which offered him good cash to release his brother from *goti*. Nachika mobilized people to renounce *goti* and to work in their agricultural land. As said already in this paper, *Chasi Mulia Adivasi Sangha* (CMAS) became the frontal organization which strongly fought against the landlords, money lenders and *daru mafias* (wine peddlers) with the basic objective of returning the land to the tiller. Therefore, this movement is popular as 'land to tiller movement' under the banner of *Chasi Mulia Adivasi Sangha* at Narayanpatna and Bandhugaon block in Koraput district. Unfortunately, the tribals are facing oppression and repression in the course of struggle for their rights. The tribals were inhumanly exploited in the hand of greedy landlords who deceive them by snatching their age-old property. On one side, the state officials and on the other side the *shahukars*, contractors and *sundhis* together are building a 'counter movement' in a most heinous manner by forming so called peace committees to suppress the *Adivasi* Movement.

Unemployment

Due to the growth of population of tribal and other forest dwellers, there is scarcity of agricultural land for shifting cultivation and settled cultivation. Again due to restriction of forest land, large number of people failed to continue their shifting cultivation for which they tend to remain unemployed. Further in tribal areas, land is very limited in comparison to the population, the rate of job expansion could never have been as high as population growth would have required, thus creating the unemployment situation for a large number of persons who depend on agriculture in rural areas. Again in backward districts particularly tribal districts most of the people are engaged directly or indirectly in agricultural operation.

The seasonal nature of employment provides employment facilities to the tribal people. During the sowing and harvesting period, they are fully employed and for the period between the post harvest and before the next sowing they remain unemployed. In southern districts of Odisha, the fragmentation of land has created a great obstacle in agricultural operation. As land is fragmented and agricultural work is being hindered, the people who depend on agriculture remain without work. This has an adverse effect on the employment situation and the poverty of villagers.

It needs to be noted that while the price for the acquired land, provision of homestead land and assistance for housing building has been fixed by the government, the provision of jobs to the displaced families is not made obligatory for the companies, in the guidelines. But, people have been promised of it by the government/politicians at different times before displacement. Unfortunately, not more than 10 per cent local people are being employed in these units. At no stage, the government has considered, 'land for land' as a rehabilitation measure for the affected families.

The Central Government's flagship rural employment scheme under the Mahatma Gandhi National Rural Employment Guarantee Act (MGNREGA) has major flaws on the ground as indicated by widespread evidence in the area. Either the NREGA work is stopped abruptly by the authorities or the workers are not paid the due amount for their labour or workers do not get an unemployment allowance which is stipulated under the Act. Hardly any progress has been made on the proposed NREGA work so far. Generally, there is very little awareness among Dalits and Adivasis about the rules that govern the Act. Many villagers have not received the job card yet, and most of the job card-holders do not have any work at all. Due to lack of closer monitoring and better auditing of the scheme fudging of records and corruption has become the norm in the daily life. Villagers are exploited by contractors and junior engineers. The new proposal of the Rural Development Department to set up an ombudsman to oversee NREGA complaints is appreciable in this connection (Mohapatra, 2012: 54). Although the rules stipulate that the BPL survey has to be conducted every five years, the 2007 survey has not been carried out so far. Another setback to the poverty amelioration programme in the region has been the erroneous identification of the poor, with corruption playing a big role in the faulty distribution of BPL cards.

Unemployment is one of the major problems in the affected areas because teen age youths are inclined towards ideology of LWE (Left Wing Extremism) whenever they fail to earn at least for their day-to-day maintenance (Pradhan, 2012: 99). Later on this leads to several problems like high frustration on government mechanism, strengthen emotional attachment with extremely poor valunerable groups and so on. The large investments in corporate sector industrialization in Odisha seem to have made little difference in employment of project affected people. These industries are increasingly capital intensive and generate little new employment. The mining sector has shown a drop in employment, even though production has increased manifold (Kumar, 2014: 66). Similarly, new industrial projects for refining minerals require much less manpower. Moreover the local populace do not possess the skill or edication to fit into the job requirement of these multinational companies. Thus, the promise of employment did not benefit the local people and instead outstripped by livelihoods lost through state-facilitated displacement and environmental disruption. Given the low employment needs of these industries, lost livelihoods are not compensated for by employment in the projects. The compensation received in cash and kind soon runs out, and many of the displaced are left destitution and hunger (Mohanty, 2011: 67–73). Landless labourers and those not having titles over land have been the worst victims of such involuntary displacement. A majority of them have joined the urban informal sector as casual labourers. Thus, irrespective of their stated objectives, most of these 'development projects' have created a class of dispossessed people without any livelihoods security.

Crony Capitalism

After the economic reforms of 1991 in which India took the path of rapid and indiscriminate industrialization, Odisha turned into a sort of 'laboratory' for the neo-liberal agenda, putting huge pressure on the state's forests, water sources, and energy supply (Sahu, 2010a). Rules for investments, capital ownership, expatriation of profits and leasing polices for minerals were relaxed, opening the doors for large scale crony capitalism. Kundan Kumar who has researched and published extensively on the extractive sector in Odisha writes, 'The political ruling class and the state apparatus have smoothly merged into a coalition with global exploitative capital. The outcome is a crass crony capitalism (the state-corporate nexus) and capture of the state apparatus by the extractive sector. The local administration and police often act as executive arms of companies' (Kumar, 2014: 70). Kohli characterizes states like Odisha as being dominated by neo-patrimonial tendencies wherein the political elites use the state's authority and resources primarily for personal gain or to benefit a narrow political interest, rather than for the greater interest of the tribals (2012: 150–55). Metal factories, power plants, dams and mining units sprouted like mushrooms all across the state, especially in forest areas. Communities everywhere are resisting being sacrificed at the altar of development. In many cases, people have been able to halt the progress of industry, putting the brakes on the disruption of their lives and livelihoods: Kalinganagar, Kashipur, Jagatsingpur, Niyamgiri are just the recent names. Nearly 50,000 forest-dependent people were forcibly evicted from their homes in the 1980s and 1990s to make way for the multi-purpose Upper Indravati Hydroelectric Project in Nawarangpur district that submerged 11,000 hectares of prime forest, one of the most diverse wildlife habitats in Asia. The displaced forest communities had no option but to retreat to the banks of the reservoir. The road that came with the project, tearing into the heartland, ensured that the remaining forest around the reservoir was wiped out by the timber mafia, in connivance with forest officials, in less than a decade. It has gone to the pages of history that the 50,000 displaced forest-dwellers lost whatever livelihood base they were left with. In Odisha, the extent of forest area diverted for non-forestry use since the 1940s would be close on 200,000 hectares; most of them inhabited for generations by forest-dependent tribal populations. Between 1980 and 2007 alone, according to government records, the area of forests diverted for non-forest activity was close on 35,000 hectares, and this does not include vast tracts of forest promised in MoUs but not yet transferred by the state to industry. After witnessing the devastation at Lanjigarh, the Dongrias are now putting up a strong resistance; deferring Vedanta's 'mining happiness' to the ambitious past.

Armed with a liberalized mining policy, the Government of Odisha has been zealously inviting investors compromising the interest of the state and its people (Kumar, 2014). During the last decade, the state of Odisha has signed 43 MoUs. Notable among them are international and Indian corporate heavy weights, namely POSCO (Korea), Vedant Aluminium (UK), Rio Tinto (UK), BHP Billition (UK-Australia), Alcan (Canada), Hindalco, Jindal, Tata and Sterlite. Further, the state government went on working overtime to appease the investors such as managing permission for companies from the central government at Delhi and simplification of lease procedure for quick processing which led to public unrest and mobilizations. The large-scale development projects and policy of denial of access to forest resources were interventions of greater magnitude and scale than reservation and other affirmative action programmes developed for the welfare of the tribal people. Such intervention offset all that was desired to be achieved by affirmative action programme. Rather, affirmative action has been pushed through alongside the processes that further deteriorated their existing social base and further exposing their vulnerability and deprivations (Xaxa, 2011: 13; 1999b: 1519–24). Protection and mitigation of the adverse impacts of development were not enough for indigenous people who did not opt for such projects in the first place. Fallout of these negative impacts, over the years, has forced them to build up their own distinct movement in order to survive.

Displacement forced these tribals to move out of their habitat, whether it is individually and formally owned, or a traditional, customarily, and collectively owned area. Resistance began when the people were involuntarily displaced in backward tribal districts of Odisha without proper rehabilitation package. Forced displacement has aggrieved the mass for collective resentments against the administration because they lose their land and livelihood sources. Cernea explained 'Forced displacement is a painful social pathology regardless of whether it is caused by justified development programmes or by atrocious conflicts such as internal civil wars, inter-state wars and violent ethnic persecution. Development induced forced displacements and war-conflict caused forced displacements emerge from different causes, but share profound similarities in their effects, not only differences' (2009: 49–76).

The process of alienating the forest dwellers from their sustenance began in the colonial age and continued after Independence (Fernandes, 2004a). Underdeveloped by the colonialist to turn it into a supplier of capital and raw material for the Industrial Revolution in Britain and a captive market for its finished products, after Independence national development became India's major task. Planned development launched in 1951 concentrated on the building of an industrial base without questioning the colonial pattern of development. Vidya Das (2003: 81–84) analyses politics of development in Kashipur context. When India needed a development model that could create jobs and alleviate poverty of every segment of society, the model chosen was heavy industry, high investment and sophisticated technology based, requiring extensive exploitation of the natural and mineral resources. It, thus, became an attack on the livelihood of the communities that had sustained themselves till then on the common property resources (CPRs). Their alienation from the CPRs that the colonial forest and land laws had started got intensified in the name of planned development with no alternative provided to them. Thus, far from solving the problems of poverty and unemployment, it increased inequalities and caused environmental degradation (Das, 2003: 81–84). Indications are that liberalization intensifies these processes and will cause greater poverty and destroy more natural resources (Kurien, 1996: 36–38).

Whenever there is resistance, the government comes down on its own citizens with a heavy hand. Greater the resistance, greater tended to be the repression of the government. The police firing at Maikanch that led to the loss of three tribal lives in December 2000 is still fresh in the public memory. Earlier in 1997, there was a police firing at Sindhigaon, Gopalpur where people protested against the proposed steel plant by the Tatas. There are a series of ongoing conflict between the two sides: between the one favouring 'industrialization', led by the government, and those opposed to it. These movements reinforced people's belief in community strength, women's abilities, and environmental consciousness. Villagers were able to protect their indigenous productive forces. Their agitations have proved that a people's movement against globalizing forces can make a meaningful path to preserving indigenous sources of livelihood.

The district administration along with the company authorities launched an intensive public disinformation campaign to expose the resistance as misguided and manipulated the public opinion in favour of the projects through media. For example, in village Kendukhunti in Kashipur block, people were told by the surveyors that the survey was being carried out for the children's education project. For a long time, the tribal people were kept in darkness and being supplied with vague answers by the surveyors (Patnaik, 2013: 78). Further, to counter the environmentalists' allegations the UAIL claims to have conducted several technical studies, like, (Environmental Impact Study) EIA and environmental management plans by the Engineers India, SEIA study by NIRD Hyderabad, Mixing Depth Studies by the Department of Oceanography and Meteorology of Andhra University, impacts of discharges of treated effluents by the Industrial Toxicology Research Centre, Lucknow, etc. But none of these reports are made public. Padel and Das (2010: 594) term it as 'manufacturing of consent'.

It is ironical that the poorest tribal people suffer the worst poverty amidst plenty of natural resources. The tribal communities are forced to bear the massive burden of development. The material and cultural resources, institutional access and dense networks and connections across locations and scales that elites can otherwise draw on to obtain favourable policies and changes are not typically available to the deprived, discriminated, dispossessed and the displaced, particularly the tribals in our country. The high modernist developmental state with its tendency for top-down reconstruction of societies through the instrumentality of the bureaucracy, though democratic and welfarist sees poor people as passive subjects of development instead of active citizens participating in governance.

Land Issues

The process of land alienation has gained momentum over the years through different patterns and sources. The informal society of tribals is perennially in conflict with the legal, administrative and economic structures of formal system based on the written word and individual ownership (*patta*) to which they have been pushed into. Violation of tribal right in the name of public interest, eviction and displacement, no or inadequate compensation, land mortgaging and sale, encroachment by outsiders, loss of *patta* through land acquisition, loss of land through survey and settlements, uncertainty over unsurveyed areas, non-distribution of wasteland, loss of rights on forest land

and forest products, ban on shifting cultivation, lack of regularization of eligible encroachments. To quote Xaxa, 'The right to property of one has been the right to dispossession of property by another. The paradox is that dispossession has invariably been of tribes' (2011: 5). Tribals and Dalits have been exploited in backward districts of Odisha due the following reasons: (1) poor governance; (2) weak redressal mechanism; (3) indifference from administrators and bureaucracy in dealing with tribal grievances; (4) harsh and unfriendly forest laws and regulations; (5) lack of legislation to prevent the passing of tribal land into the hands of non-tribals; (6) lack of credit facilities; (7) ineffective government measures to rehabilitate tribal population; (8) delay in implementation of recommendations of different committee; and (9) discrimination in implementation of reform measures.

The principle of land reforms was guided by the value of social justice which sought to ensure equitable/minimum entitlement to land and prevent concentration of landownership. In addition, it was also treated as part of uplifting large number of backward communities from oppression and dispossession, as land was central to the issues of social relations, social interactions and determination of categories at the grass-roots level (Ambagudia, 2010: 60).

The commitments/promises made by successive governments at different times on land reforms, promising land to the landless, have never been implemented in the area (Das, 2006). The Land Acquisition Act of 1894 (Amendment, 1984) does not give the owner of land (seller) the right to say 'no' as the land is acquired for 'public interest'. The owner can only contest about the price fixed by the buyer (the government) and take the matter to the court of law and has to accept whatever the court of law (again, the same government) decides about the price of land. Whereas, when dealing with a private buyer one has the option to negotiate the price and say 'no' if the price doesn't suit him/her. The irony is the land acquired by the government, under the LA Act, for 'public purpose' is actually meant for private companies. On one hand, industrialiszation is projected as the panacea to widespread poverty, unemployment and underdevelopment of the state. On the other, people, particularly the socially and economically underdeveloped ones, feel the threat of displacement and loss of a secured livelihood (whatever little they have) due to this industrialization. And this constrains them to oppose it.

For listing of name in the list for compensation, the local *Amin* (land surveyor) demands bribe which people could not afford. Even people who had received compensation money for their land couldn't buy land as land price suddenly increased many times in the surrounding area, due to the prospects of industrialization.

Senapati (2013) found out that the land allotted by Steel and Mines Department before signing the MoU with 49 industries in the state was highly irregular. Similarly, Pandita (2011) observed that land allotted to

Vedanta Company for establishing its university was curiously interesting. CAG Report (2013: 15–47) clearly identified the following problems in the land policy of the state government.

1. The state government has not made attempts to assess availability of natural resources prior to allowing industrial projects.
2. No policy or guidelines for assessing the need as well as other inputs like land, water and minerals, attracting entrepreneurs to the state through open competitive bidding, signing of MoUs with promoter companies for setting up industries in the state was formulated.
3. The Department of Steel and Mines has signed MoUs with promoter of industries and made commitments without assessing the actual availability of land, water and minerals. There was no exercise to scrutinize the land category (whether agriculture, irrigated or double cropped) and no consultations were held with other departments like Revenue and Disaster Management, Water Resource, Agriculture department and district collectors before signing the MoUs.
4. Checks of MoUs and concerned files revealed that promoters themselves have selected the sites and applied for acquisition subject to their suitability. No exercise was conducted by the government to ascertain the availability of government land to ensure barest minimum acquisition of agriculture land. Sites for setting up of industries were identified by promoter companies and got regularized by applying through IPICOL and IDCO.
5. The promoters concerned have mortgaged the allotted land in different banks to avail loans though no such commitment was made in MoUs. The Revenue Department has not even authorized IDCO to give such permission for creation of mortgage by the promoters.
6. No record could be provided to audit by IPICOL and IDCO and Steel and Mines Department to show that due diligence has been exercised to examine the proposal of promoters and benefits that would accrue to the state and that would be extended to the particular project proponent before signing of MoU.

The linkages between catastrophic land grabbing and the classic processes of land alienation explain staggering deprivations suffered by especially the tribals of the state. Land grabbing in Odisha has ensued through varied roots, such as land acquisition for mining, industrial, military and infrastructural projects, including SEZs; conversion of forest lands to agro-industrial plantations; state-initiated enclosures for conservation projects as well as illegal enclosures by non-native outsiders. Interestingly, another way by which non-tribals are acquiring tribal land is by marrying tribal women (Xaxa, 2004: 362). In view of the fact that there is a restriction on the alienation of land from tribes to non-tribes, such methods have become fairly pronounced. The irony of the fact is that often after such transactions, non-tribal men have deserted simple tribal women (Behura and Mohanti, 2009). This in itself came to be an emotive issue among tribes in view of the long struggle that they have waged against the alienation of tribal land (Xaxa, 2004: 362).

Further, the systematic undermining of livelihoods resources (such as forests, grazing field, water bodies); reorganization of property rights over resources (such as forest, agricultural land, village commons, tanks, ponds, lakes and rivers) and exclusion of a section of the population; endemic non-responses by the state to natural calamities (such as recurring droughts, famine) also create vulnerabilities among the resource dependent population. The consequent 'voluntary' land transfers that are found in the backdrop of such livelihoods crises are essentially part of a process of dispossession-in-slow-motion (Mishra, 2011). In the more recent period, diversion of water from agricultural to industrial use, declining agricultural productivity as a result of industrial pollution and the over-all impacts of neo-liberal reforms have further reduced the bargaining power of the small and marginal farmers. The response of the tribals took various forms, from gradual submission to rebellion.

Political Nexus and Forest Department Fury

The laws aimed at protecting indigenous peoples have, however, numerous shortcomings and their implementation is far from satisfactory. The policies and schemes implemented by successive governments at the Centre and the state have further worsened the situation. The challenges to their civil, political, social, economic and cultural rights have been critical today, insofar as they perpetuate extreme form of deprivation in many ways.

Forest is the principal source of livelihood of the tribals and they collect their food, fodder, fruits, medicines, shelter, rituals, recreations and cultural activities all come from the forests. 'Minor forest produce' includes all non-timber forest produce of plant origin including bamboo, brush wood, stumps, cane, tassar, cocoons, honey, wax, *lac*, *tendu* or *kendu* leaves, medicinal plants and herbs, roots and tubers. These products are very valuable for the market. Unfortunately, due to lack of proper market facility, the tribals sell those valuable products to the middlemen in cheap rate and the middlemen sell it in higher price. This way the tribals are exploited and do not get the real price of their product.

When the FD provides legal backing to JFM committees dominated by local elites, politically weak local forest users are often excluded from forest access and use (Behera and Engel, 2006). Elite dominance and resource capture have been reported in almost all studies of JFM and negative impacts on the poor have been widely documented (Kumar, 2002; Kumar and Kerr, 2013).

Table 4

Recognition of Forest Rights Act-2006 in Odisha till 31.01.2014*

Nature of FRA implementation	*Status till 31.01.2014*
(1) No. of claims filed at Gram Sabha level	5,45,279 (5,34,275 individual and 11,004 community)
(2) No. of claims recommended by Gram Sabha to SDLC	4,51,516 (4,46,195 individual and 5,321 community)
(3) No. of claims recommended by SDLC to DLC	3,55,351 (3,50,238 individual and 5,113 community)
(4) No. of claims approved by DLC for title	3,48,990 (3,44,017 individual and 4,973 community)
(5) Number of titles distributed	3,28,580 (3,25,449 individual and 3,131 community)
(6) Extent of forest land for which title deeds issued (in acres)	6,66,050.11 (5,14,886.02 individual and 1,51,164.09 community)
(7) No. of claims rejected	1,39,519 (1,38,905 individual and 614 community)
(8) % of titles distributed over number of claims received	60.25%

* Certain forest land in the State is unsurveyed and detailed maps/records are not available

Source: Government of Odisha, SC and ST Welfare Dept (Compiled)

The Panchayat (Extension to the Scheduled Areas) Act-1996 (or simply the PESA Act-1996) made it mandatory for the Fifth Schedule areas to make legislative provisions in order to give wide-ranging powers to the tribals on matters relating to decision-making and development of their communities. Politically, it gives radical governance power to the tribal communities and recognizes their traditional community rights over local natural resources. It not only accepts the validity of 'customary law, social and religious practices, and traditional management practices of community resources', but also directs the state governments not to make any law which interfere with these. Accepting a clear-cut role for the community, it gives wide-ranging powers to gram sabhas. *The spirit of PESA is to strengthen the role of the tribal community by empowering gram sabhas so that the tribal community land is not taken away without the informed consent of the community.*

As per PESA, the gram sabha will be involved in approval of development plans and programmes, all decisions related to land acquisition as well as rehabilitation of affected persons, and in management of the minor forest produce. Implementation of the law has been severely hampered by the reluctance of most state governments to make laws and rules that conform to the spirit of the PESA Act. Weak political will has allowed the bureaucrats to continue to work as usual and PESA provisions have remained appealing on paper only. Padel and Das (2010) document the extensive collusion, between politicians/bureaucrats and the private companies, which has displaced scores of tribals from their land they inhabited for ages. The most glaring act of bureaucratic subversion is about the concept of ownership of minor forest produce (MFP).

Forest officials argue that the power of gram sabhas can extend only to the forest located within the revenue boundaries of a village. The ground reality is that a reserved forest is generally not located within the revenue boundary of a village. The spirit of the law is clearly to provide the usual access to MFP from forests located in vicinity of the village.

Another argument against giving ownership of MFPs to gram sabhas is that it would lead to destruction of forests. Therefore, the ownership of MFP should mean the right to net revenues from MFP, after retaining administrative expenses of the Forest Department. This is also contrary to a whole body of empirical evidence of JFM and community control of forests. While the forest dwellers are the most suited people to entrust the well-being of the forests along with all their biodiversity, such fanciful interpretations have almost killed the concept of ownership and control of local resources by the gram sabha giving rise to resistances, mobilization and protests. There is yet another widespread tendency to see land and natural resources separately mooted largely by transnational corporations. Unguarded gram sabhas are controlled by the Forest Department (FD) officials. Complains are also received that though Scheduled Caste and Scheduled Tribe Welfare Department is the nodal agency, the decisions and actions are carried on by FD without the knowledge of and consultation with the nodal department.

When the 5th schedule provisions offer protection to tribal culture and their traditional way of living, which is reaffirmed by various others laws including the PESA and Forest Rights Act, the idea is to allow them freedom to manage their socio-cultural affairs on their own. Since their lifestyle is intrinsically centered on land and surrounding natural resources, vital for their survival, it is clearly implied that they should be in the position to assert control on land, forests, and natural resources. Ground reality, however, is strikingly different. It is a fact that the average size of the land holding by the tribals has been shrinking due to the State led acquisitions and the ill-designs of powerful non-tribal land mafia despite the fact that the sale of tribal lands to the non-tribals in the Scheduled areas is prohibited. During post liberalization-cum-privatization, alienation of tribal land has become more perceptible and attack of natural resources of their regions has become rapacious.

The Forest Department, by contrast, comes down with bestial fury against the tribal organizations. In Rayagada, a women's group formed a society of 50–60 tribal women to make brooms and sell them for a better price through this society. The Odisha Forest Department, saying that the society was not licenced, promptly confiscated their brooms and prosecuted the women (Dandekar and Choudhury, 2010; Rosencranz and Lélé, 2008). Various paper industries have been engaged, under the guise of 'labour contractors', for working bamboo areas. The forest produce is being leased out to the industry. These attempts to rob the tribals of their resources are criminal, especially when it occurs in places like Kalahandi and Koraput districts where starvation deaths among tribals are legendary. Police stations not hospitals are constructed in the area as the company wants police stations, which can protect their interest not the tribals during the protest against land acquisition. Roads are made for police and company vehicles to move not for buses to ply, people claim (*The Hindu,* 2010).

Joint Forest Management (JFM) relates to a partnerships in forest management involving both a village committee known as the Forest Protection Committee (FPC) and the Forest Department who enter into a JFM agreement. The policies and objectives of Joint Forest Management are detailed in the Indian comprehensive National Forest Policy of 1988 and the Joint Forest Management Guidelines of 1990 of the Government of India. Villagers agree to assist in the safeguarding of forest resources through protection from fire, grazing, and illegal harvesting in exchange for which they receive non-timber forest products and a share of the revenue from the sale of timber products.

The majority of actors in the anti-tribal forest laws movement strongly believe that rights must be recognized and the insecurity, distress and disaffection in their homelands in the absence of legal recognition of their rights, which grows day by day must end (Prabhu, 2005).

The Scheduled Tribes and Other Traditional Forest Dwellers (Recognition of Forest Rights) Act-2006,was notified into force on 31 December 2007. On 1 January 2008, this was followed by the notification of the Rules framed by the Ministry of Tribal Affairs to supplement the procedural aspects of the Act. The law concerns the rights of forest-dwelling communities to land and other resources, denied to them over decades as a result of the continuance of colonial forest laws in India. India's forests were governed by two main laws, the Indian Forest Act-1927 and the Wildlife (Protection) Act-1972. The former empowers the government to declare any area to be a reserved forest, protected forest or village forest the latter allows any area to be constituted as a 'protected area', namely a national park, wildlife sanctuary, tiger reserve or community conservation area.

Under these laws, the rights of people living in or depending on the area to be declared as a forest or protected area are to be 'settled' by a 'forest settlement officer.' This basically requires that officer to enquire into the claims of people to land, minor forest produce, etc. and, in the case of claims found to be valid, to allow them to continue or to extinguish them by paying compensation.

Studies have shown that in many areas this process either did not take place at all or took place in a highly faulty manner (Prabhu, 2005). All the hilly tracts of Odisha were declared government forests without any survey (Kumar, 2014), ignoring forested landscapes; histories of injustices and appropriations often aggravates conflicts and marginalization of forest dwellers (Kumar and Kerr, 2013). In Odisha, around 40 per cent of the government forests are 'deemed reserved forests' which have not been surveyed (Kumar and Kerr, 2013). The Campaign for Survival and Dignity described the final form of the law as 'both a victory and a betrayal' in their official statement on the occasion. There have been numerous complaints regarding the manner in which the Act has been implemented after its notification. For instance, in September 2010, the Council for Social Development, a New Delhi based think tank, released a 'Summary Report on Implementation of the Forest Rights Act' which stated that:

'All of the key features of this legislation have been undermined by a combination of apathy and sabotage during the process of implementation. In the current situation the rights of the majority of tribals and other traditional forest dwellers are being denied and the purpose of the legislation is being defeated. Unless immediate remedial measures are taken, instead of undoing the historical injustice to tribal and other traditional forest dwellers, the Act will have the opposite outcome of making them even more vulnerable to eviction and denial of their customary access to forests ... both the Central and the State governments have actively pursued policies that are in direct violation of the spirit and letter of the Act' (Sethi and Mukul, 2008).

Those whose rights are not recorded during the settlement process are susceptible to eviction at any time. This 'legal twilight zone' leads to harassment, evictions, extortion of money and sexual molestation of forest dwellers by forest officials, who wield absolute authority over forest dwellers' livelihoods and daily lives (Gopalkrishnan, 2005). Almost 46 per cent of the land in scheduled areas has been categorized as forests without proper survey and settlements, and thousands of square kilometres of shifting cultivation areas as well as permanent cultivation areas have been included as under forest category (Kumar and Choudhury, 2005). The Forest Department has taken up an incredible 52,800 hectares of plantations in the undivided Koraput district only. Much of this plantation is taken up on land already being cultivated or under shifting cultivation by tribals. The lack of legal title of tribals on most of the land cultivated by them aggravates this situation (Kumar and Choudhury, 2005).

The mainstream opposition political parties like Congress and Bharatiya Janata Party including radical communist groups (particularly CPI-ML New Democracy, CPI-ML Red Flag and CPI-ML Liberation) are very active in all the resistance movements in Odisha. On the one hand, mainstream opposition political parties are opposing the industry and mining projects and, on the other hand, are competing with each other and the ruling Biju Janta Dal for securing contracts for their respective supporters (Pattnaik, 2013: 61). The local tribal people are allegedly threatened (Sarangi, 2002: 3241) by these parties acting as the company's agents engaging themselves as private army, to leave their land for the industry so as to facilitate their grabing the contracts for construction. Some form of mud throwing and counter blaming also goes on. Similarly, while the ruling party wanted to carry the Niyamgiri Movement to New Delhi for a sit down protest in front of the Supreme Court for a verdict in favour of the company led by local MLA, subsequently the local MP from the Congress party (ruling at the centre) mobilized the central government and its machinery against Vedanta Alumina (Pattnaik, 2013: 61). Even Committee reports are believed to have been influenced by the Congress leader. Allegations of political nexus are abundant in literature. Powerful companies pushing extractive projects are able to call on high offices such those of the prime minister, finance minister, chief minister, and top bureaucrats for intervention. Pandita (2011) alleges that Vedanta is alleged to be one of the major contributors to the ruling Biju Janata Dal (BJD) the ruling party in the state. Many of the company and mining concerns are owned by politician members of Indian parliament. Relatives of politicians and bureaucrats responsible for decisions and regulation are alleged to have been provided jobs by companies (Kumar, 2014: 70). Similarly it is reported that the use of criminals and goons, often linked to local political leaders and contractors, makes it difficult to pin blame on companies or the government. Companies liberally fund groups that can coerce resistance movements (Kumar, 2014: 70).

Supreme Court of India in its judgment on 18 April 2013 said the tribal's 'dependence on the forest being almost complete, the violation of the specific protections extended to their 'habitat and habitations' by the Forest Rights Act-2006 are simply unacceptable' (Writ Petition (Civil) No. 180 of 2011–Odisha Mining Corporation Ltd. vs Ministry of Environment and Forest).

Illiteracy

Education has always been a determinant of one's income and upward mobility. Quality of schooling and years of college education help raise productivity and entitle students to their jobs and earnings. Provision of education right from the primary stage assumes significance. This is where the deficit starts in the under-developed regions of the state. With a very poor infrastructure and absence of the requisite number of teachers, students in the backward districts/regions have frustrating experience in the schools. Most of the students, as they come from socio-economically disadvantaged communities like the Scheduled Castes and Scheduled

Tribes, are scared of the teachers (fear of corporal punishment) and do not find anything interesting to hold them onto the schools and gradually they start withdrawing from the schools and start looking for jobs in the job market which can offer them only low paid ordinary jobs. Curriculum dissemination do not fit local tribal language requirements. Teachers appointed in tribal scools lease out their teaching by paying cuts from their salary in connivance with school headmasters.

The tribals do not have any knowledge about the formal laws of the state. Due to lack of awareness campaign, they sometimes break the formal law like cutting the tree and collecting charcoal from the jungle for which they are punished. This creates discontent and frustration among the tribals and they provoke the action of the forest officials and they continued their organized resistance, protest groups, and social movements.

In places where tribes had still control over land, massive transfer of land took place from tribes to non-tribes through such measures as fraud, deceit, mortgage, etc. Since tribes had no practice of record keeping, as they did not have the knowledge of reading and writing, non-tribes took advantage of it forging evidence and documents in their favour. The local administration, which was manned by the non-tribes, worked hand in hand with their ethnic kinder men to ensure smooth transfer of land from tribes to non-tribes. The court language was alien to tribes and they had absolutely no idea of what was going in the court.

The tribals are illiterate and ignorant about their rights and privileges. Due to ignorance they have been the worst sufferers. The current state of movement is thus (1) to pressurize the government for a drastic amendment to the existing laws to fix the the loopholes, (2) to move the government for proper implementation of some well meaning laws like PESA Act 1996, FR Act 2006, (3) to pressurize the government for abolishing certain anti-tribal laws like Land Acquisition Act 1894, Mines and Mineral (Development and Regulation) Act 1954, Bihar and Odisha Excise Act 1915, (4) to pressurize the central and state government for proper implementation of fifth schedule to the constitution, (5) to push vigorous governance reforms so as to ensure proper and prompt delivery of benefits of various laws and schemes to the people, (6) sensitizing the MLAs and MPs belonging to various tribal communities on the anti-tribal nuances in various schemes, (7) to create a support base for the resistance movement in tribal areas against landowners, exploitative money lenders, nexus between vested interests and administration, liquor *mafias* and police atrocities and finally (8) to mobilize the government machinery for imparting training to the young educated tribals on the use of RTI Act for bringing in transparency and accountability in the system of governance.

The Supreme Court of India, in its judgment vide Writ Petition (Civil) No. 180 of 2011 on 18 April 2013, opined: 'Many of the STs and other TFDs are totally unaware of their rights. They also experience lot of difficulties in obtaining effective access to justice because of their distinct culture and limited contact with mainstream society. Many a times, they do not have the financial resources to engage in any legal actions against development projects undertaken in their abode or the forest in which they stay. They have a vital role to play in the environmental management and development because of their knowledge and traditional practices. State has got a duty to recognize and duly support their identity, culture and interest so that they can effectively participate in achieving sustainable development' (Para 39, Odisha Mining Corporation Ltd. vs Ministry of Environment and Forest).

Cultural Identity

The resistance movement by the tribal people raised a number of significant questions related to the issues of Rehabilitation and Resettlement (RandR), environmental degradation, ecological imbalance and the poor agricultural productivity of this drought-prone area (Fernandes, 2004b). In addition to violation of economic rights, a great deal of the moral content of such resistant in tribal Odisha is derived explicitly from cultural issues pertaining to their vanishing religio-cultural life, of identity, of spiritual links to land and environment and of loyalty to mythological as well as historical ancestors (Pattnaik, 2013: 62). The Supreme Court of India in its judgment on 18 April 2013 said, 'Religious freedom guaranteed to STs and the TFDs under Articles 25 and 26 of the Constitution is intended to be a guide to a community of life and social demands. The above mentioned Articles guarantee them the right to practice and propagate not only matters of faith or belief, but all those rituals and observations which are regarded as integral part of their religion. Their right to worship the deity Niyam-Raja has, therefore, to be protected and preserved' (Writ Petition (Civil) No. 180 of 2011).

Cultural factors behind resistances in tribal areas relate to: (a) attachment to the place and (b) cultural identity (Pattnaik, 2013: 62). Sentimental and emotional attachment to the place is associated with the local culturally significant term '*Bhita Maati*' meaning mother earth (see Patel et al., 1988). Leaving the land of forefathers is like leaving the mother deserted. Forefathers were the value-givers, norm-setters and institution-builders which subsequent generations are to follow completely and unquestionably. In the Saura tribe, for example, if a woman remains unmarried after attaining adulthood (if not proposed to by someone for marriage), she is forced to marry a plant, and her remarriage is performed like that of a widow (Pattnaik, 2003: 149–52). Attachment to a place virtually refers to a repository of embedded life experiences that are not separable from the feelings and sentiments associated with the place. When several betel vines of Nuagaon village under POSCO area were demolished in August 2010, *Bhita Maati Surakhya Janmanch* (BMSJ) vehemently protested. Similarly some of the Dongaria Kandhas visited New Delhi for the first time to appear before Supreme Court of India (Writ Petition (Civil) No. 180 of 2011) to demonstrate the value of their attachment to the place and for the protection of *Bhita Maati*. Similarly *Bhita Maati* is the only claim of *Chaasi Mulia Adivasi Sangha* led by tribal Nachika Linga who claims that tribal land is theirs and not that of outside grabbers. The process of getting attached to a place, thus, involves the behavioural, cognitive and emotional embeddedness of individuals in forging the link between their socio-cultural and physical environments (Pattnaik, 2013: 62). The beliefs, practices, sentiments, memories, ideas, values and meanings associated with everyday life in a particular setting come to constitute an important dimension of a groups' identity (Oliver-Smith, 2001: 61–69).

These tribes in the project areas or the areas grabbed by outsiders (Narayanpatna) are the natives of the forest and mountains. Their indigenous identity is associated with the community sentiments, forests, hills and mountains. The tribal identity is expressed through their distinct cultural forms and practices such as dress patterns, language, rituals, festivals, ornaments, tattoo songs/dances, *mahuli* (country liquor) and their spiritual life. Physical relocation of tribal population away from *Bhita Maati* is a complex sentimental issue signalling adverse implications for their identity, culture and customary livelihood. Burial ground and graveyard is held very sacred by them and they feel tortured if alienated from the place. Tribal culture, way of life, folklore, religious practices are inextricably linked with their relationship with nature, different from the mainstream society. Displacement often leads to a sudden onslaught of dominant values threatening the very basis of their cultural identity because culture, which is rooted in a particular place, cannot be easily 'reconstructed' in another place. Resettlement after displacement not only relocates groups/communities in space but also remakes them. Often the community is reconfigured in certain ways and the local culture is pressed for a change, as it gets linked to regional and national market systems. Visualization of this itself engenders resentment and subsequent collective resistance among the affected people (Pattnaik, 2013: 63). Digging mines is believed to be crushing the heart of the mother earth locally called in Lanjigarh as *Dharni Penu* (Earth Deity).

Supreme Court of India, in its judgment vide Writ Petition (Civil) No. 180 of 2011 on 18 April 2013, opined, 'Gram Sabha has a role to play in safeguarding the customary and religious rights of the STs and other TFDs under the Forest Rights Act. Section 6 of the Act confers powers on the gram sabha to determine the nature and extent of 'individual' or 'community rights'. In this connection, reference may also be made to Section 13 of the Act coupled with the provisions of PESA Act, which deal with the powers of gram sabha … . We are, therefore, of the view that the question whether STs and other TFDs, like Dongaria Kondh, Kutia

Kandha and others, have got any religious rights i.e. rights of worship over the Niyamgiri hills, known as Nimagiri, near Hundaljali, which is the hill top known as Niyam-Raja, have to be considered by the gram sabha. Gram sabha can also examine whether the proposed mining area Niyama Danger, 10 km away from the peak, would in any way affect the abode of Niyam-Raja. Needless to say, if the Bauxite Mining Project (BMP), in any way, affects their religious rights, especially their right to worship their deity, known as Niyam-Raja, in the hills top of the Niyamgiri range of hills, that right has to be preserved and protected. We find that this aspect of the matter has not been placed before the gram sabha for their active consideration, but only the individual claims and community claims received from Rayagada and Kalahandi Districts, most of which the gram sabha has dealt with and settled'(Para 56 and 58, Odisha Mining Corporation Ltd. vs Ministry of Environment and Forest). Now, gram sabha decided and as such VAL and mining operations have been stopped.

Maoist Advantage

It is our long neglect to develop the tribal areas which has created large pockets of alienation against the government and these pockets have become the spawning ground of Maoist terrorism. The governments concerned have to take note of the genuine grievances of the tribals and deal with them in a sympathetic manner. There has to be a system for a prompt enquiry into all allegations of excess and it is here that activists like me can contribute to reach the base realities and unveil the truth. Extremism cannot be effectively countered without modernizing and strengthening our rural policing and the rural presence of the intelligence agencies. Not only the affected areas but also the tribal areas and coastal belts, which have not yet been affected by the Maoist virus, have to be developed on a crash basis in order to prevent the spread of the virus to them. There has to be an equal focus on several entities like education, employment, immediate settlement of disputes, environment protection and even providing security to the deprived, discriminated and dispossessed.

The helplessness and naivety of tribal people, their socio-economic exclusion, and their exploitation and harassment by state bureaucracy provides an ideal ground for Naxals or Maoists or left-wing-extremists to propagate their ideology of anti state armed-struggle (Pradhan, 2012). The conditions of 4Ds discussed earlier provide ideal fertile ground for their activities to both sustain and flourish. The tribal community finds some sympathetic voices among the Maoists who have often taken up their issues against the powerful landlords or helped them take revenge by supporting them (Gupta, 2006). Thus, some tribals join their cadre to settle scores and others find the ideology attractive. Those who don't agree don't speak out for fear of the barbaric modes of Maoists punishments. Even women and girls join Cadre out of desperation. Some of them being abused in Maoist camps come on to surrender before the police. Their sufferings do not end, neither is full surrender package delivered nor are they safe on their appointment as home guards (Padhi and Pradhan, 2013). The increasing penetration of Maoist insurgency in Odisha has come as a boon to the state. It is also alleged that the government has used every opportunity to portray the resistance movements as being linked to the Maoists (Kumar, 2014: 71).

Padel and Das (2010) have shown how companies split tribal communities by bribes and coercion, such that a division emerges between 'accepters' and 'refusers' (Dandekar and Choudhury, 2010; *The Hindu,* 2010). The autonomous and non-violent resistance of tribals to destructive mining has often been misrepresented by the state, corporate interests, and even by the media at times to label it as a 'Maoist threat'. Then this label is used 'to crush all kinds of spontaneous opposition of tribals to be displaced' leaving them displaced and left to the mercy of fate. Nothing would deal a bigger blow to the Maoists than participative development by, for and of the tribal communities.

Locating the Perspective

The current discourse on tribal movements and tribal empowerment mainly revolves around securing well-defined rights to land and forests through participatory practices. The understanding of development is being questioned at the grass-roots level by various struggles from the standpoint of tradition and culture. At a more fundamental level, the question of abuse of tribal people's rights to land (vita maati), life and living, is of central concern. Tribals' and forest dependent communities' demands for greater access and rights to forest resources are often dressed up in discourses of democratic governance and claims to citizenship. Thus while asserting claims over natural resources through protests and resistance, they use the language of rights and entitlement rather than efficiency or equity. The affected/displaced people are still objecting to any form of displacement. They are promoting adoption of a land-for-land strategy, conferring absolute rights in the form of a share for tribal people in companies' profits. Decentralization and citizens' participation have emerged as core strategies to achieve sustainable and just natural resources governance. They tend to oppose any form of detribalization. However, it is important to recognize that, by the very nature of the issues involved, tribal people's protest movements, however well organized, have to contend with the powerful interests of a local economic elite and industrial capital – both domestic and foreign – who wield considerable political power. In this section, the paper looks back to question raised initially and tries to locate the explanatory or the perspective as to how these ground level deprivations manifest in different styles of grass-roots mobilizations. Before proceeding further a brief overview of the available theories needs to be brought in order.

An ethnographic approach (field view) emphasizes on meeting, interacting with activists participants and leasers of movements to have direct knowledge of their inter relationship and activities, whether it is an ongoing movement or it is the one that has been consigned to the history. The researchers probe the stages of developments of the movements, the ups and downs witnessed in the course of its mobilization, its methods of agitation, agenda of demand and targets, goals and objectives, movements leaders ideologies and the sources of inspiration of the participants (Boushel and Meuleman, 2013: 49–62; Dhanagare, 2013: 178–79; Touraine, 1981: 139–49). Canadian sociologist Dorothy E. Smith (2005) has used the method of institutional ethnography in order to analyse the current debate on social media activities in the context of political participation.

The resource mobilization approach examines movements as a part of organizational dynamics strategic problems of having to appeal diverse constituencies to demand resources and also control mass insurgents behaviour (Jenkins, 1983: 527–63). It looks at the importance of social movements' formal institutions/organizations, micro-structural processes, material resources and tactics as preconditions to the emergence and development of a movement (McCarthy and Zald, 1977). Resource mobilization scholars demonstrate that sponsorships and resources from established organizations were needed in order to overcome the free-rider problem and induce political participation (Jenkins, 1985). Those movements which were able to mobilize resources from external sources and offer incentives to their members were more likely to succeed (Gamson, 1975). They appear as a part of the political process.

Political opportunities approach to social movement indicates that if the existing socio-political system is vulnerable to a challenge, it creates an opportunity for the movement members to take up the challenge and try to use this opportunity to push through a social change. Meyer (2004) quoting Tarrow (1989) stresses that political opportunity is consistent, but not necessarily formal or permanent – dimensions of the political struggle that encourage people to engage in contentious politics. Protesters come to be characterized as rational actors, intent upon weighing costs and benefits of participation. At a more macro level, the political opportunities approach emphasized the role of the opportunities afforded by the political context on emergence and development of social movements and their outcomes (Giugni, 2004; Tilly, 1978). Although the notion of political opportunity has proved to be a challenge to define (Kriesi, 2004), there is a certain consensus that encompasses the relative openness of the political system, the formal and informal set of power relations among potential allies and the degree of state repression (McAdam, 1996: 27).

Subaltern theory looks at the elementary and substantive forms of mobilization in which the protest of the deprived and hitherto marginalized sections whether peasantry or the tribals that have a long history of subjugation and suppression (Guha, 1982; Amin, 1982). Subaltern scholars strive to pursue 'history told from below' and mobilize in order to be heard by means of their political actions, effected in protest against the discourse of mainstream development and, thereby, create their own, proper forms of modernization and development. Chatterjee (2012: 47) recognizes the limitations of subaltern theory and prefers populist approach to understand mass protests (Dhanagare, 2013: 186). Populism is marked by passionate appeals to 'the people' to build a unified coalition. These uprooted and atomised masses get attracted to direct mobilizing appeals by charismatic leaders. Referring to the writings by Taggart (2002), Taguieff (1993) and Canovan (1991), Dhanagare persuasively opines that the populist approach, if not a theory, is not in much use in Indian sociology of social movements (2013: 195). He further goes on to argue, 'In modern democratic societies, populism is best seen as an appeal to the people-'heteronomous or politically subordinate masses. The people are against the established structure of power and also against the dominant ideas and values of the society' (Canovan, 1991: 3). Therefore populist movements are of the people but not of the system (Dhanagare, 2013: 199). In view of dearth of research on populism and populist movements in India, while re-examining various theories on social movements in India, D.N. Dhanagare opens six sets of questions for posterity to examine and find answers in course of their research (2013: 218).

Assemblage theory contends that social movements are also assemblages that come together by the actions of diverse actors. Many of the important concepts in social movement theory, such as mobilizing structure, resource mobilization, repertoires of contention, and opportunity structures (Tarrow, 2011), can be explained in terms of assemblage theory (Srnicek, 2007). Existing interpersonal networks of individuals and groups are precursors to social mobilization, and constitute the substrate or mobilizing structure for movements (Srnicek, 2007). Social movements can be visualized as emergent "individuation" from existing networks of relationships as common grievances are articulated, shared, and become the basis of action. Articulation of shared grievances, claim-making, stories, narratives, written memoranda, etc. are the expressive elements that stabilize i.e. help in territorializing the assemblages and correspond to the scaffolding of collective mobilization in social movement mechanism.

Very recently the theory of assemblages (De Landa, 2006; Srnicek, 2007; Haynes, 2012; Anderson and McFarlane, 2011) have been systematically used (Kumar, 2013: 2) to analyse the Niyamgiri struggle, and to illustrate how additional avenues of inquiry and practice such as the interplay of scale, contingency, structure, and agency, are opened by considering social and material formations as assemblages. He argues that traditional social movement theories can be reworked through assemblage theory, while reducing conceptual confusions and allowing incorporation of powerful insights to examine social movements and contentious politics (Kumar, 2013: 9). The assemblage theory visualizes entities such as state or capital as dynamic assemblages of diverse, heterogeneous elements, individuated through historic processes. Assemblages of state and capital operate at multiple interlinked scales and locations, contain centralized hierarchies, and can draw upon power of various kinds, forming 'powerful assemblages' (Allen, 2011). The assemblage theory allows for the diversity and divergences within actors, focuses on identification of the actual relational mechanisms functioning at the micro-political scale, and explains the capacities of the social movement assemblage as emerging out of interactions between constituents. The key activists were critical to the maintenance of the assemblage for mediating in case of contradictions between the various constituents of the assemblage. The Niyamgiri struggle can be seen as an assemblage of heterogeneous constituents located in diverse places and scales that hold together without being an essential totality (Kumar, 2013: 8).

The 'new social movements' interpretations treat social movements as both symptoms of, and solutions to, the contradictions inherent in the modern super-bureaucratic society. Social movements articulate the tension between the expanding spheres of human autonomy and growing regulation inherent in the logic of postindustrial development. This contradiction is reflected in new conflicts which, according to Habermas, 'no longer arise in the areas of material reproduction; they are no longer channeled through parties and organizations … . Rather, the new conflicts arise in areas of cultural reproduction, social integration and socialization' (Habermas 1987: 34).

D.N. Dhanagare and J. John (1988: 1089–92), while attempting a critique of 'nine thesis' of Frank and Fuentes (1987: 1503–10), sum up the features and the importance of new social movement theory. The new social movements are basically grass-roots level mobilizations which are apolitical. The implicit assumptions in a new social movement theory is that this movement doesn't necessarily attack the exploitative character of the existing power structure and class based power relations nor do they aim at altering the power relations whether within liberal democratic system of representative governance or in autocratic authoritarian regimes (Dhanagare, 2013: 189; for details of characterization of new social movement theory please see Tucker, 1991: 92–94; Omvedt, 1993: xv-xvii; Pattnaik, 2013: 53–78; Dhanagare, 2013:187–191). These movements took up the issues of livelihood, opportunities, dignity and development for and by landless, unorganized labour in rural and urban areas, Adivasis, Dalits, displaced people, peasants, urban poor, small entrepreneurs and unemployed youth.

In line with the briefs of seven theories sketched above, it can safely be said that social movement scholars have developed impressive theoretical and methodological artillery for facing the epistemic challenges related to the study of social movements. The succession of approaches in social movement studies has also bequeathed the field with a diverse range of nits and levels of analysis. Indeed, these different approaches are not necessarily incompatible and can be seen as highlighting different dimensions of social movements (Travaglino, 2014: 9). This variety is a testimony to the complexity inherent in the field of social movements. It is also a clear sign of the lively and healthy status of research on the theme. New approaches and themes continuously emerge, which enrich our understanding of social movements and stimulate theoretical and methodological debate (Travaglino, 2014: 14).

This paper presents the five cases of tribal resistances mobilizations and movements out of which four relate to the protests against forced industrialization and development (two are mining industry based such as Kasipur and Niyamgiri and two are against steel industry such as Kalinganagar and Jagatsinghpur and one relates to land grabbing of Narayanpatna). These are grass-roots mobilizations stemming out of the 4 Ds conceptualized as ground level deprivations pertaining to the core problems faced by the ever exploited marginalized trbals both in coastal as well as the tribal districts of Odisha. Taking the literature, theoretical and substantive accounts and the data presented, the viability of new social movement theory appears acceptable. A close look at the characteristics of assemblage theory reveals that it is closest to the theory of new social movement. The authors of assemblage theory also nowhere have named or contested the new social movement approaches. The other theories have more of critics and lack inclusivity so as to explain the trajectory of tribal movement or the styles of mobilization discussed in this paper. Space prevents to go into the details of criticisms (for detailed reading criticisms please see Tucker, 1991: 921–94; Oommen, 1984; Omvedt, 1993: xv–xvii; Pattnaik, 2013: 53–78; Dhanagare, 2013: 187–91; Travaglino, 2014: 9; Kumar, 2013: 3). Thus, the next attempt is to show as to how the trajectory of tribal movement or the styles of mobilization meet most of the theoretically identified features of new social movement approaches.

IV

New Social Movements: The Perspective

This study attempts to confirm the following features of new social movement.

1. The tribal movements analysed here are grass-roots movements. These types of collective mobilizations are basically well supported bottom-up movements against top-down industrialization based on crony capitalism and more so for scrapping the project, saving the environment, stopping displacement, returning land and forest rights to the natives and protecting the tribal cultural identity.
2. These types of collective mobilizations grew with the awe-inspiring actions of many diverse actors located in different places. Multiple actors like social activists, intellectuals, media persons, human rights groups, film makers, freelance writers, students and lawyers provide leadership roles with the support of local influentials. And those who direct these movements are mostly middle class intellectuals, professionals and activists, largely non-local and very few local tribal in leadership role. The grass-roots level participants are mobilized in large numbers and as such this is not only 'by' tribals but also 'for' them.
3. Success of these movements is realized through protracted leadership with mobilized networks of relationships as common grievances are articulated, shared, and become the basis of action. Apart from local protests, photographs and videos depicting the torture of innocent tribals reached long distances through internet and media publicity, generated ripples of effect and emotions and sympathy at far off places. Accordingly, this movement is attributed as translocal mobilization. The combination of many small victories builds the momentum for success.
4. Among the strategies adopted by the so-called new social movements, there is a strong reliance on digital technologies and new media. The role of social media in shaping the public perception and in generating mass political action is not only reflected in our study but also is now being increasingly debated (Boushel and Meuleman, 2013) in movement discourse. Needless to mention new social movement approach emerged differentiating itself from Marxian class based movements.
5. The actors, sympsthizers and participants of new social movement in our context do not represent a homogenous group as against homogenous tribal identity for which they fight. The ideologies, strategies and beliefs of many of these actors were divergent, and often disengaging. Ideological differences of various actors, individual and institutional, zoom out and skip over the irrelevant details through their involvement in the movement. Concerns for indigeneity, human

rights, conservation, and social justice crisscrossed with each other in varied contexts. Yet, these contingencies and mobilities occurred within stabilized landscapes, institutional arrangements, discourses and power relationships. Histories of discrimination (D1), deprivation (D2), dispossession (D3) and of late development induced displacement (D4) mattered, and 'intentional stance' of individuals and institutions became apparent.

6. The new social movements are also conceived as non-party political forums, based on grass-roots popular initiatives and single issue based anti-systemic if not anti-state movements. These are distinct and they operate almost wholly outside the traditional political party system.
7. The new social movement mobilizes and opposes the repressive measures of the government administration in the state of Odisha, and their connivance with corporatism or their mercenaries. Some of the members in the ruling party and the opposition members along with their agents play dubious role to satisfy their individual interests or hidden party agenda.
8. The go-between institutions such as civil society institutions like NGOs and other activist organizations) play a significant role in fomenting these movements and also bring these movements into fruition for attaining the specific objectives. The resources, energy and creativity of diverse actors helped building scaffolding of collective mobilization for getting their demands fulfilled. They organized blockade (*nakabandi*), sit-in demonstrations (*Dharanas*), protest public meetings (*Sadharan Sabha*) and protest marches and road shows (*padyatra*) street play (*nukkad natak*) that form part of the repertoires of contention of the emergent movement. Articulation of shared grievances, claim-making, stories, narratives, written memoranda, e-mails, on net photo transfer geared up the movement. Protracted mobilization triggers the transition from tribal silence and inaction to mass voice and action.
9. These are essentially anti-systemic against 4Ds and not anti-regime movements. The social movements emerging out of conflicts and renewed attention over sharing natural resources like land/forest, water etc. concerns for ecology/environment, human rights, cultural identity, (all five cases) given in this paper and land grabbing (land grabbing including Narayanpatna case). The formation of a collective identity was seen as essential to the assignation of common meanings to events.
10. They do aim at bringing about change in state apparatus and various social institutions towards attaining distributive justice in sharing economic resources and services (compensations and claim of rights of project affected people and the victims of land grabbing) and is being called micro-movements. The actors from the middle class try to bring about changes through different means such as writings,

mobilizing people in a methodical/strategic manner, using media in their favour and the like (e.g. extensive reporting and wide publicity in newspapers, magazines and journals).

11. These movements are apolitical and do not confirm any membership formalities of political parties. There is a spontaneous interest base mobilized on the basis of issues of morality, justice and equity. The importance of emotions and group-based emotional appraisal in motivating or inhibiting political mobilizations and actions (Jasper, 2007) in new social movements can not be overlooked. Likki (2013) shows that subjective concerns about material needs and identification with the social movements distinctly and independently predict two fundamental motivations to engage in collective actions in the indigenous movement, namely group-based emotions and beliefs about social problems. In fact, concerns about social problems and intensity of group-based emotions in our cases as well were more strongly related to the participation among individuals who expressed both high degree of indentification and high concern about material needs.
12. These movements have their own life and continuity is contingent upon the fulfillment of the specific objectives. One notable outcome of the Kashipur movement, i.e. formulation of the Comprehensive RandR Policy of the Government of Odisha dated 20 May 2006 as the Government of Odisha had no such policy prior to this. Niyamgiri area is now silent after rejection of the project by Gram Sabha. Movement on land issues, however, in all project areas are going on as it is.

Thus, the new social movement perspective for the purpose of this paper in the context of tribal Odisha means those characterized by grass roots, bottom-up, issue based, mass, micro, anti-systemic and apolitical movement with multiple actors, strategic network, strong reliance on digital technologies and new media, protracted mobilization and group based emotional appraisal against all forms of discrimination (D1), deprivation (D2), dispossession (D3) and development induced displacement (D4). At the end, the paper intends to conclude with a statement from Robert K Merton who said 'we may have many concepts but few confirmed theories; many points of view, but few theorems; many approaches, but few arrivals. Perhaps some further changes in emphasis would be all to the good' (Merton, 1981: 52).

* Acknowledgement: I sincerely thank Prof. D.N. Dhanagare for having given his approval on the initial scheme of the paper and time-to-time feedback during writing of the draft. Prof. Binay K Patnaik, Director ISEC, Bengaluru deserves special thanks for his support in this endeavor of mine. Thanks are in the same quantum due to Prof. S.N. Choudhury, Professor and Rajiv Chair, Barkatullah University, Bhopal for having initiated me to this theme of research.

References

Allen, J. (2011), 'Powerful Assemblages?', *Area*, Vol. 43, No. 2, pp. 154–57.

Ambagudia, Jagannath (2010), 'Tribal Rights, Dispossession and the State in Odisha', *Economic and Political Weekly*, Vol. XLV, No. 33, pp. 60–69.

Amin, Shahid (1982), 'Small Peasant Commodity Production and Rural Indebtedness: The Culture of Sugarcane in Eastern UP: 1880–1920', in R. Guha (ed.), *Subaltern Studies*, Vol. I, New York: Oxford, pp. 39–87.

Anderson, B. and C. McFarlane (2011), 'Assemblage and Geography', *Area*, Vol. 43, No. 2, pp. 124–27.

Arnold, David (1982), 'Rebellious Hillmen: The Gudem Rampa Rebellion 1839–1924', in R. Guha (ed.), *Subaltern Studies*, Vol. I, New York: Oxford, pp. 88–142.

Behera, B. and S. Engel (2006), 'Institutional Analysis of Evolution of Joint Forest Management in India: A New Institutional Economics Approach', *Forest Policy and Economics*, Vol. 8, No. 4, pp. 350–62.

Behura, N.K. and K.K. Mohanti (2009), 'Tribe Vis-à-Vis Land: Critical Appraisal of the Issue and Option in Odisha', in A.B. Ota (ed.), *Development Induced Displacement and the Tribes*, Odisha: SCSTRTI.

Boushel, C. and B. Meuleman (2013), 'Hash Tags, Ruling Relations and the Everyday: Institutional Ethnography Insights on Social Movements', *Contemporary Social Science*, Vol. 9, pp. 49–62.

Brass, Tom (1991), 'Moral Economists, Subalterns, New Social Movements, and the (Re-) Emergence of a (Post-) Modernized (Middle) Peasant', *The Journal of Peasant Studies*, Vol. 18, No. 2, pp. 173–205.

CAG Odisha (2013), Report on Commitment Made in MOUs for Setting Up of Industries in Odisha and Acquisition/Allotment of Land Thereof, as on March 2011, Chapter II, Comptroller and Auditor General of India (CAG).

Canovan, M. (1991), 'Trust the People: Populism and the Two Faces of Democracy', *Political Studies*, Vol. XLVII, No. 1, pp. 2–16.

Census of India (2011), Provisional Population Total, Directorate of Census Operations, Bhubaneswar, Odisha: Government of India.

Cernea, Michael M. (2009), 'Financing for Development: Benefit-Sharing Mechanisms in Population Resettlement', in Oliver-Smith Anthony (ed.), *Development and Dispossession: The Crisis of Forced Displacement and Resettlement*, Santa Fe: School for Advanced Research Press, pp. 49–76.

Chatterjee, Partha (2012), 'After Subaltern Studies', *Economic and Political Weekly*, Vol. XLVII, No. 35, pp. 44–49.

Cohen, J.L. (1985), 'Strategy or Identity: New Theoretical Paradigms and Contemporary Social Movements', *Social Research*, Vol. 52, No. 4, pp. 663–716.

Currie, Bob (2000), *The Politics of Hunger in India*, Chennai: Macmillan India.

D'Monte, D. (1989), 'Green at the Grassroots', *Seminar*, Vol. 355, March, pp. 16–20.

Dandekar, Ajay and C. Choudhury (2010), *PESA, Left Wing Extremism and Governance: Concerns and Challenges in India's Tribal Districts*, Anand, Gujarat: IRMA.

——(2013), *PESA, Left Wing Extremism and Governance: Concerns and Challenges in India's Tribal Districts*, New Delhi: Ministry of Panchayati Raj, Government of India.

Das, Prafulla (2006), 'Resistance and Tragedy', *Frontline*, January 10.

Das, Vidhya (2003), 'Kashipur: Politics of Underdevelopment', *Economic and Political Weekly*, Vol. 38, No. 1, pp. 81–84.

De Haan, Arjan and Amaresh Dubey (2005), 'Poverty, Disparities, or the Development of Underdevelopment in Odisha', *Economic and Political Weekly*, Vol. XL, Nos. 22–23, pp. 2321–29.

De Landa, M. (2006), *A New Philosophy of Society: Assemblage Theory and Social Complexity*, New York: Continuum.

Desai, S. et al. (2006), 'In the Margins: Social Inequalities in Children's Educational Outcomes in India', Paper presented at the Annual Meeting of the Population Association of America, Los Angeles.

Desor, S. (2013), *Citizens' Report on Community Forest Rights under Forest Rights Act*, by Kalpavriksh and Vasundhara (eds), in collaboration with Oxfam India, an output of Community Forest Rights Learning and Advocacy Process.

Dhanagare, D.N. (1994), 'The Class Character and Politics of the Farmers Movement in Maharashtra during the 1980s', *The Journal of Peasant Studies*, Vol. 21, Nos. 3–4, pp. 72–94.

——(2013), 'Understanding the New Farmers' Movement in Maharashtra: Towards an Analytical Framework', *The Eastern Anthropologist*, Vol. 66, Nos. 2–3, pp. 163–218.

——(2014), *The Writings of D.N. Dhanagare: The Missing Tradition: Debates and Discourses in Indian Sociology*, Hyderabad: Orient Blackswan Pvt. Ltd.

Dhanagare, D.N. and J. John (1988), 'Cyclical Movement Towards the Eternal: Nine Thesis on Social Movements', *Economic and Political Weekly*, Vol. XXIII, No. 21, 21 May, pp. 1089–92.

Fernandes, Walter (2004a), 'Forest Issues, Forest Dwellers and Emerging Situations', Paper presented at the National Seminar on Human Origins, Genome and People of India, New Delhi: Anthropological Survey of India, 22–24 March.

——(2004b), 'Rehabilitation Policy for the Displaced', *Economic and Political Weekly*, Vol. 39, No. 12, pp. 1191–93.

Frank, A.G. and M. Fuentes (1987), 'Nine Theses on Social Movements', *Economic and Political Weekly*, Vol. 22, No. 35, pp. 1503–10.

Gamson, W.A. (1975), *The Strategy of Social Protest*, Belmont, CA: Wadsworth.

Giugni, M. (2004), *Social Protest and Policy Change: Ecology, Antinuclear, and Peace Movements in Comparative Perspective*, Lanham, MD: Rowman and Little?eld Publishers.

Gopalakrishnan, Shankar (2005), 'Missing the Woods for the Trees', *Combat Law*, Vol. 4, No. 4, June–July, pp. 11–14.

Government of Odisha (2004), *Odisha Human Development Report*, Bhubaneswar: NCDS.

——(2012), *Economic Survey 2011–12*, Bhubaneswar: Department of Planning and Co-ordination.

Guha, Ranajit (1982), *Elementary Forms of Peasant Insurgency in Colonial India*, New Delhi: Oxford University Press.

Gupta, Tilak D. (2006), 'Maoism in India: Ideology, Programme and Armed Struggle', *Economic and Political Weekly*, Vol. XLI, No. 29, 22 July, pp. 3171–76.

Habermas, Jürgen (1987), *Theory of Communicative Action, Volume Two: Liveworld and System: A Critique of Functionalist Reason*, Translated by Thomas A. McCarthy, Boston, Mass.: Beacon Press.

Haynes, P. (2012), *Networks are Useful Description, Assemblages are Powerful Explanations*, Valencia: Spanish National Council of Scientific Research (CSIC) and the Polytechnic University of Valencia (UPV).

Hazra, A.K. (2002), 'History of Conflict Over Forests in India: A Market-based Resolution', Working Paper Series, New Delhi: Julian L. Simon Centre of Policy Research, Liberty Institute.

Jasper, J.M. (2007), 'Cultural Approaches in the Sociology of Social Movements', in B. Klandermans and C. Roggeband (eds), *Handbook of Social Movements Across Disciplines*, New York: Springer, pp. 59–109.

——(2011), 'Emotions and Social Movements: Twenty Years of Theory and Research', *Annual Review of Sociology*, Vol. 37, pp. 285–303.

Jenkins, J.C. (1983), 'Resource Mobilization Theory and the Study of Social Movements', *Annual Review of Sociology*, Vol. 9, pp. 527–63.

——(1985), *The Politics of Insurgency: The Farm Workers Movement in the 1960s*, New York: Columbia University Press.

Kriesi, H. (2004), 'Political Context and Opportunity', in D.A. Snow, S.A. Soule and H. Kriesi (eds), *The Blackwell Companion to Social Movements*, Malden: Blackwell, pp. 67–90.

Kumar, K. (2006), *Dispossessed and Displaced: A Brief Paper on Tribal Issues in Odisha*, Bhubaneswar: Vasundhara.

——(2013), 'The Sacred Mountain: Confronting Global Capital at Niyamgiri', *Geoforum*, http://dx.doi.org/10.1016/j.geoforum.2013.11.008

——(2014), 'Confronting Extractive Capital: Social and Environmental Movements in Odisha', *Economic and Political Weekly*, Vol. 49, No. 14, pp. 66–63.

Kumar, K. and J.M. Kerr (2012), 'Democratic Assertions: The Making of India's Recognition of Forest Rights Act', *Development and Change*, Vol. 43, No. 3, pp. 751–71.

——(2013), 'Territorialisation and Marginalization in the Forested Landscapes of Odisha, India', *Land Use Policy*, Vol. 30, pp. 885–94.

Kumar, K. and P.R. Choudhury (2005), *Socio-Economic and Legal Study of Scheduled Tribes Land in Odisha*, Bhubaneswar: Vasundhara (World Bank Sponsored).

Kumar, S. (2002), 'Does 'Participation' in Common Pool Resource Management Help the Poor? A Social Cost–Benefit Analysis of Joint Forest Management in Jharkhand, India', *World Development*, Vol. 30, No. 4, pp. 763–82.

Kurien, C.T. (1996), *Global Capitalism and the Indian Economy*, New Delhi: Orient Longman.

Likki, T. (2013), 'Unity within Diversity: A Social Psychological Analysis of the Internal Diversity of the Indignados Movement', *Contemporary Social Science*, Vol. 9, pp. 15–30.

Lokadrusti (1993), 'Boden: A Societal Appraisal (A Socio-Economic Study of Twenty Hamlets in Boden Block, Kalahandi District, Odisha)', Lokadrusti, Khariar.

McAdam, D. (1996), 'Conceptual Origins, Current Problems, Future Directions', in D. McAdam, J.D. McCarthy and M.N. Zald (eds), *Comparative Perspectives on Social Movements: Political Opportunities, Mobilizing Structures, and Cultural Framings*, Cambridge: Cambridge University Press, pp. 23–40.

McCarthy, M. and M.N. Zald (1977), 'Resource Mobilisation and Social Movements: A Partial Theory', *American Journal of Sociology*, Vol. 82, pp. 1212–41.

Mehta, S.K. (2010), 'Including Scheduled Tribes in Odisha's Development: Barriers and Opportunities', IHD-UNICEF Working Paper No. 9, New Delhi.

Merton, R.K. (1981), *Social Theory and Social Structure*, New York: The Free Press (Third Indian Edition).

Meyer, D.S. (2004), 'Protest and Political Opportunities', *Annual Review of Sociology*, Vol. 30, pp. 125–45.

Mishra, Deepak K. (2011), 'Behind Dispossession: State, Land Grabbing and Agrarian Change in Rural Odisha', Paper presented at the International Conference on Global Land Grabbing from 6–8 April at the Institute of Development Studies, University of Sussex.

Mishra, Srijit (2009), 'Poverty and Agrarian Distress in Odisha', Working Paper No. 6, Mumbai: IGIDR.

Mohanty, Bidyut (2008), 'Dimension of Issues in Education of Children at Elementary Level Due to Repeated Displacement: Case Study of a Village-Chikapar', Koraput, Odisha: Society for Promoting Rural Education and Development (SPREAD).

Mohanty, Biswajit (2005), 'Field View', *Seminar*, No. 552, August.

Mohanty, R. (2011), 'Impact of Development Project on the Displaced Tribals: A Case Study of a Development Project in Eastern India', *Orissa Review*, September–October, pp. 67–73.

Mohapatra, G. (2012), 'Hunger and Coping Strategies among Kondh Tribe in Kalahandi District, Odisha', *Transcience*, Vol. 3, No. 2, pp. 51–60.

Mohapatra, L.K. (2009), 'Displacement of Tribal People with Land Resources for Development Projects: Their Rights and Entitlements for Rehabilitation', in A.B. Ota (ed.), *Development Induced Displacement and the Tribes*, Odisha: SCSTRTI.

Mukherji, P.N. (1977), 'Social Movement and Social Change: Towards a Conceptual Clarification and Theoretical Framework', *Sociological Bulletin*, Vol. 26, No. 1, pp. 39–59.

——(2013), 'Social Movement, Conflict and Change: Towards a Theoretical Orientation', *ISA e-Symposium in Sociology*, pp. 1–14.

Namboodiri, Udayan (ed.) (2012), *Social Cost Benefit Analysis of the POSCO Steel Project in Orissa*, New Delhi: National Council of Applied Economic Research (NCAER).

Nayak, A.N. (2010), 'Primitive Tribal Groups of Odisha: An Evaluation of Census Data', *Odisha Review* (Census Special), Vol. LXVII, No. 5, pp. 202–05.

Oliver-Smith, Anthony (2001), *Displacement, Resistance and the Critique of Development: From the Grassroots to the Global*, Final Report prepared for ESCOR R7644 and Research Programme on Development Induced Displacement and Resettlement, Refugee Studies Centre, University of Oxford.

Omvedt, Gail (1993), *Reinventing Revolution: New Social Movements and the Socialist Tradition in India*, New York: M.E. Sharpe Inc.

Oommen, T.K. (1984), 'Sources of Deprivation and Styles of Protest', *Contributions to Indian Sociology*, Vol. 18, No. 1, pp. 45–61.

——(2001), 'Multiple Modernities and the Rise of New Social Movements: The Case of India', *Indian Social Science Review*, Vol. 3, No. 1, pp. 1–16.

Padel, Felix and S. Das (2010), *Out of This Earth: East India Adivasis and the Aluminium Cartel*, Hyderabad: Orient Blackswan.

Padhi, S. and N. Panigrahi (2011), 'Tribal Movements and Livelihoods Recent Development in Odisha', Working Paper No. 51, New Delhi: Indian Institute of Public Administration and Chronic Poverty Research Centre.

Padhi, Ranjana and P. Pradhan (2013), 'India: Women in Resistance Struggles in Odisha', *Mainstream Weekly*, 3 August, pp. 15–23.

Panda, M. (2004), 'Poverty in Odisha: A Disaggregated Analysis' (Draft), Mumbai: Indira Gandhi Institute of Development Research.

Panda, Manoj (2008), 'Economic Development in Odisha: Growth without Inclusion', Working Paper No. 25, Mumbai: IGIDR.

Pandey, Balaji (2008), 'The Kalinganagar Tragedy: Development Goal or Development Malaise', *Social Change*, Vol. 38, No. 4, pp. 209–16.

Pandey, Gyanendra (1983), 'Rallying around the Cow: Sectarian Strife in the Bhojpur Region: 1888–1917', in R. Guha (ed.), *Subaltern Studies*, Vol. II, Delhi: Oxford University Press, pp. 60–120.

Pandita, R. (2011), *The Curious Case of Vedanta University*, Delhi: Open Media Network Pvt. Ltd.

Patel, Sujata et al. (1988), *Bheeta Maati-Our Soil, Our Earth, Our Home: A Report on Missile Base and Struggle*, Delhi: PUDR, August, Record No. CL 010015.

Patnaik, A.K. (2003), 'Sabara Sampradayaravivaha Pratha', *Parab 2003*, Koraput: District Council of Culture, pp. 149–52.

Pattnaik, B.K. (2011), 'Collective Mobilization by the Development Induced Displaced: Studies in Contemporary Tribal Resistance Movements from Odisha', *Eastern Anthropologist*, Vol. 64, No. 4, pp. 333–70.

——(2013), 'Tribal Resistance Movements and the Politics of Development-Induced Displacement in Contemporary Odisha', *Social Change*, Vol. 43, No. 1, pp. 53–78.

Prabhu, Pradip (2005), 'The Right to Live with Dignity', *Seminar*, No. 552, August, pp. 14–19.

Pradhan, S.K. (2012), 'Unemployment Magnitude and Left Wing Extremism', *Odisha Review*, Vol. LXVIII, No. 9, pp. 98–101.

PUCL (2006), *Police Firing at Kalinganagar: A Report by People's Union for Civil Liberties*, Odisha: PUCL.

Radhakrishna, R. and S. Ray (2005), *Handbook of Poverty in India: Perspectives, Policies and Programmes*, New Delhi: Oxford University Press.

Ray, R. and M.F. Katzenstein (2005), *Social Movements in India: Poverty, Power and Politics* (Introduction), Oxford, UK: Rowman and Littlefield Publishers.

Roggeband, C. and B. Klandermans (2007), 'Introduction', in B. Klandermans and C. Roggeband (eds), *Handbook of Social Movements Across Disciplines*, New York: Springer, pp. 1–12.

Rosencranz, A. and S. Lélé (2008), 'Supreme Court and India's Forests', *Economic and Political Weekly*, Vol. 43, No. 5, pp. 11–14.

Sahu, S.K. (2010a), 'Destroyed by 'Development': Community Forests of Odisha', *Infochange News and Features*, Part IV, April, pp. 1–6.

——(2010b), 'The Taming of the Wilds', *Infochange News and Features*, Part III, March, pp. 1–7.

Sarangi, D. (2002), 'Surviving Against the Odds: Case of Kashipur', *Economic and Political Weekly*, Vol. 37, No. 31, pp. 3239–41.

Senapati, A. (2013), 'Will Fight POSCO till Last Breath', *Down To Earth*, CSE Web Net, 17 May.

Sethi, Nitin and A. Mukul (2008), 'Forest Act Notified, Tribals Unhappy', *Times of India*, January 2.

Shah, Amit (2010), 'Patterns of Poverty in Remote Rural Areas: A Case Study of a Forest-based Region in Southern Odisha in India', ODI Working Paper 325, Westminster Bridge Road, UK: Overseas Development Institute.

Smith, D.E. (2005), *Institutional Ethnography: A Sociology for People*, Oxford: AltaMira Press.

Srikant, P. (2009), 'Tribal Movement in Orissa: A Struggle Against Modernisation?', Working Paper No. 215, Bangalore: The Institute for Social and Economic Change.

Srnicek, N. (2007), 'Assemblage Theory, Complexity and Contentious Politics: The Political Ontology of Gilles Deleuze', Unpublished MA Thesis, University of Western Ontario.

Taggart, P. (2002), *Populism: Concepts in the Social Sciences Series*, New Delhi: Viva Books.

Taguieff, P. (1993), 'Political Science Confronts Populism', *Telos*, Special Issue, No. 103, pp. 9–42.

Taradutta, D. (2001), *Tribal Development in India (Odisha)*, New Delhi: Gyan Publishing House.

Tarrow, S. (1989), *Power in Movement*, New York: Cambridge University Press (Second Edition).

Tarrow, S.G. (2011), *Power in Movement: Social Movements and Contentious Politics*, Cambridge: Cambridge University Press.

The Hindu (2010), 'PESA Implementation Not up to the Mark', Bhubaneswar, 26 July.

Tilly, C. (1978), *From Mobilization to Revolution*, Boston, MA: Addison-Wesley.

Touraine, Alain (1981), *The Voice and the Eye: An Analysis of Social Movements*, New York: Cambridge University Press.

——(1985), 'An Introduction to the Study of Social Movements', *Social Research*, Vol. 52, No. 4, pp. 749–88.

Travaglino, Giovanni A. (2014), 'Social Sciences and Social Movements: The Theoretical Context', *Contemporary Social Science*, Vol. 9, No. 1, pp. 1–14.

Tucker, K.H. (1991), 'How New are New Social Movements', *Theory, Culture and Society*, Vol. 8, No. 2, pp. 75–98.

Vasundhara and Kalpavriksh (2012), *A National Report on Community Forest Rights under Forest Rights Act: Status and Issues*, Bhubaneswar: Vasundhara and Pune: Kalpavriksh.

Xaxa, V. (1999a), 'Tribes as Indigenous People', *Economic and Political Weekly*, Vol. 34, No. 51, pp. 3589–95.

——(1999b), 'Transformation of Tribes in India: Terms of Discourse', *Economic and Political Weekly*, Vol. 34, No. 24, pp. 1519–24.

——(2004), 'Women and Gender in the Study of Tribes in India', *Indian Journal of Gender Studies*, Vol. 11, No. 3, pp. 345–67.

——(2005), 'Politics of Language, Religion and Identity: Tribes in India', *Economic and Political Weekly*, Vol. 40, No. 13, pp. 1363–70.

——(2011), 'Tribes and Social Exclusion', Occasional Paper No. 2, Department of Sociology, Delhi School of Economics, Delhi University.

Zald, M.N. (1996), 'Culture, Ideology and Strategic Framing', in D. McAdam, J.D. McCarthy and M.N. Zald (eds), *Comparative Perspectives on Social Movements: Political Opportunities, Mobilizing Structures, and Cultural Framings*, Cambridge: Cambridge University Press, pp. 261–75.

Zimmerman, Kristen (2013), *Movement Pivots*, Oakland, CA: Movement Strategy Center.

10

Impacting Development Thought and Practice through Bhili Cultural Rejuvenation

RAHUL BANERJEE

A fairly well established fact today is that the institutions set up under the provisions of the Constitution of India for the protection of the Adivasis have not functioned properly and various laws and policies enacted from time to time for this purpose have not been implemented primarily due to the wrong development policies adopted by the state which have tended to strengthen rather than weaken the political and economic power of the non-Adivasis vis-à-vis the Adivasis (Sharma, 2001). The state has also failed to provide good and adequate education services which has resulted in the Adivasis remaining unequipped to negotiate the complexities of the modern centralized system of governance into which they have been forcefully integrated (Banerjee, 2003). The poverty induced by these wrong development policies has adversely affected the nutritional levels of the food intake of the Adivasis and, combined with the lack of good and cheap health services, has led to a decline in their general health (Rahul, 1997a). Moreover, an even greater lack of both education and health services for the women has meant that they have not been able to smash age old patriarchal structures and their consequent lack of reproductive rights has led to a population explosion putting further pressure on already scarce resources. All these factors have combined to produce a scenario wherein Adivasis are being continually exploited by the improper functioning of the modern market system which has increasingly penetrated into their subsistence lifestyles and being forced to live on the edge (Rahul, 1997b). The condition of the Bhil Adivasis of Western Madhya Pradesh provides ample evidence of this decay.

The Bhils have not only lost their natural resource bases but with the undermining of their subsistence agriculture based lifestyle that this has led to, they have lost confidence in their own indigenous culture too. Poverty has led to community links breaking down and there has been a continuous downgrading of their culture by non-Adivasi oppressors. Even their Gods are losing their shine as more and more Bhils have begun to worship Hindu or Christian gods and goddesses. The final blow has come in the form of dam building on the River Narmada which seeks to destroy completely not only the Bhils' habitat but also, by displacing them into areas populated largely by non-Adivasis, their unique culture.

The Bhil Adivasis have a rich oral folklore. There is the creation of myth centred on the river Narmada in some cases and in others on the goddesses and gods Velubai, Rani Kajal and Indiraja which is sung during the Diwasa festival allowing the Bhils to partake of the products of their lands during the *kharif* season. Then there is the myth of the goddess Kansari, who represents the staple cereal sorghum, which is sung at the time of the celebration of Indal which is a festival of thanksgiving to nature for having been bountiful with her harvests. Finally there is the myth of Kalorano, the god of rain which is sung to appease him when the rains play truant during the monsoon season. Apart from these major myths, there are a number of other stories. Their contents reflect the close empathic relations that the Bhils have traditionally had with their habitat given the fact that their very existence is directly dependent on the munificence of nature. This rich and valuable oral literary corpus has the potential for reviving not only the belief of the Bhils in themselves and, thus, motivating them to better participate as equal citizens in political and economic processes but is also capable of providing theoretical and practical clues towards the formulation of a more sustainable agriculture based developmental model than the one that is dominant today. However, this valuable heritage is in danger of being lost forever as the younger Bhils today have little regard for the traditional Bhil culture and its rich oral heritage given its inability at present to secure them a viable livelihood.

An Innovation that is Systems Changing

Historically, a major medium for the positing of a strong identity by any community has been its language. All literate cultures have thrived by developing a rich literature to strengthen their language. However, Adivasi cultures being non-literate have not been able to do this and so have fallen behind and face extinction. Today, the lack of entertaining written literature in the Bhili language has resulted in most literate Bhils switching over to Hindi instead. So transcribing the voluminous folklore of the Bhils and publishing it will provide the literate Bhils with enough reading materials of quality to entice them back to their mother tongue. New literature and the further development of the written Bhili language and a revival of their decaying culture will then follow as the night follows the day. The modern Indian languages have all developed in this way. Moreover, the experience of using the traditional myths and tunes in conveying modern developmental and cultural messages has shown that they are extremely effective for this purpose. This innovation is being done by various social and political developmental organizations in the Western Madhya Pradesh region which are all affiliated to the federation Adivasi Ekta Parishad (AEP) which is active in the four contiguous states of Rajasthan, Madhya Pradesh, Gujarat and Maharashtra. Transcription of the whole of the folklore will also allow a systematic study of it and, thus, offer many more opportunities for innovation. The folklore is amenable to creative interpretation and copious material in support of the theory and practice of alternative, decentralized and sustainable development can be culled from it.

There is, for example, the creation of myth sung in the villages near the Narmada which detail how God was suddenly beset with the idea to build the universe and he looked towards Relu Kabadi the woodsman to go into the jungle and fetch him wood. Thus, starts the whole story of how slowly all the animals and plants are created and finally the rivers Narmada and Tapti. These rivers finally meet up with the ocean Dudu Hamad in marriage and in the process of their journey all the various villages, hills and valleys are created. The whole song gives a sense of the vastness of nature and the strength of natural processes and inculcates a respect in the listener for these. This is in direct contrast to the hubris of modern man who has tried to subordinate nature to his own ends and given rise to the serious environmental problems that face him today. The Adivasis have been sufferers of this process. Thus, by popularizing their creation myth and emphasizing that their worldview is much more 'rational' in the present context of serious ecological degradation will go a long way towards increasing their self-esteem.

Similarly, there is another story in one of the epic songs about a woman who has to answer for having questioned the authority of her husband. She is brought before the Panchayat which is the traditional all male dispute resolution forum. There the panches decree that she be punished for her disobedience and order that her tongue be cut off and given to the husband to swallow. The tongue then gets stuck in the throat of the husband where it has remained ever since. This story has been picked up to depict the extent to which the Bhil society is patriarchally oppressive of women. At the same time, the fact that the tongue has got stuck in the husband's throat offers the chance to the woman to recover it and so establish her right to speak out for her needs. This is the motif that has been used to organize the Bhil women to fight against diverse patriarchies inside the home and outside. Literature, especially religious literature of an allegorical character, has tremendous power to motivate people to act to change their socio-economic condition. Unfortunately, for Adivasis in Central India in general and the Bhils in particular there has not been any significant effort till now to transcribe and use their rich oral literature.

Thus, what is being done here by the AEP and its affiliates is the systematic creation of a new written literature and performing arts of the Bhils not only for their value in themselves but more for their utility as a crucial developmental tool through the transcription of their rich oral folklore by their own organic intellectuals who have risen from the process of the struggle to improve their socio-economic condition. While in the case of other modern Indian languages such forums sprung up by themselves, in the case of Bhili, a special effort has to be made because it is not a written language and being the product of an indigenous culture which is under threat of extinction requires protective promotion.

The penetration of market oriented consumerist culture has led to the breaking down of traditional communitarian bonds not only in urban societies but also in remote agrarian societies like those of the Adivasis. Thus, the social system prevalent at present promotes cut throat competition among its members and hampers collective action. This in turn leads to violence and crime. This is extremely harmful for society as a whole. So it is of utmost importance that Adivasi societies which still retain communitarian social practices be encouraged to thrive and creatively build on these practices so that society as a whole can draw on this valuable resource to counter the threat of evolving into a consumerist mono-culture. For instance there is no sense of belonging in the cities these days leading to the problem of alienation. This is then sought to be corrected through identification with fundamentalist religious organizations which tend to divide society further into narrow communities. Thus, the present new intervention by conserving and positively developing one of the sources of rich communitarian culture, development and governance, that of the Bhils, will be a radically systems changing one in the long run.

The form of politics that has come to dominate the globe now is that of first past the post competitive centralized electoral liberal democracy. In this system, central governments of nation-states tend to over ride the lower level governments. The local government institutions at the small town and village level suffer most as their needs and aspirations are sacrificed for the development of mega cities and industrial centres. The net result is that there is tremendous destruction of the environment and the livelihood opportunities of the urban and rural poor. This kind of political system is also extremely divisive socially as it tends to pit communities and groups against each other in the fight to gain control of state power which is crucial to secure a good livelihood. Thus, it is imperative that a more decentralized and localized form of democratic politics be promoted which works through consensus rather than by competition. The present intervention will provide an impetus for the revival of the traditional village council led management of affairs which is central to the lives of the Bhil Adivasis and the eventual evolution of an alternative decentralized political system globally as an antidote to the ills of the present centralized one.

At the micro level of Western Madhya Pradesh this new intervention will over time contribute to the ongoing movement of the Bhils for attaining a strong self-identity based on a rich written literature that is capable of contending with the literature and culture of the non-Adivasis and, thus, give them social equality with their oppressors. This will in turn help them to negotiate the modern political and economic systems on equal terms with the non-Adivasis and thus gain a fair share of the developmental cake.

At the macro level this new literature being the product of an agricultural society will first of all provide intellectual and cultural support for the ongoing national and worldwide efforts for the revival of agriculture which is in crisis all over the world leading to serious problems of food and livelihood security. The modernization of agriculture based on artificial inputs has proved to be a failed enterprise and there is a growing trend towards the revival of sustainable organic agriculture. This is especially important for India which is primarily an agricultural country. The main agricultural areas in India have all come under the sway of modern agriculture and have lost the traditional seeds and processes and are suffering from severe erosion of soil quality and water sources.

The Bhils still retain traditional knowledge in this regard and a strengthening of their culture will lead to a strengthening of their agriculture too. At present, the worldwide movement for sustainable agriculture lacks a mass base and a supporting culture which will help it to thrive. Sustainable ariculturists are perceived as quixotic deviants rather than as proponents of a serious alternative system. The AEP has actively promoted a sustainable agriculture based socio-econono-political system as a comprehensive and viable alternative and the present intervention by strengthening its cultural dimensions will contribute positively to this movement. At a later point of time, an alternative agriculture based system of development that is less destructive of nature can develop from these preliminary efforts.

Finally agricultural societies are all highly religious given their dependence on nature and the need to placate forces which are beyond their control. This is why despite the Nehruvian project of building a secular society and the specific injunction that the state will not function in support of any religion, in practice the majority of Indian society having rural agricultural roots has remained deeply religious and all the mainstream parties, including the Communist Party of India in Bengal, have to a greater or lesser extent promoted Hinduism. However, of late this has become overly problematical due to the aggressive fundamentalism of the Sangh Parivar. The Hindu fundamentalist organizations have embarked on a proselytization campaign of the Adivasis in violation of their fundamental right to follow freely their own religion as guaranteed under Article 25 of the Constitution. The converted Adivasis do not get an equal status with the high caste Hindus but are inducted into Hindu society as menials who are even today treated as untouchables by the latter.

The reality of the power of religion in pre-modern agricultural societies has to be acknowledged and fundamentalism has to be countered through promotion of religious diversity. Religious diversity is as much a desired value as cultural diversity for the survival of the human race. The revival of their literature which is traditionally highly religious will automatically lead to a revival of the Bhili animist and nature friendly religion and provide them with an effective antidote to the proselytizing thrust of the fundamentalist Hindu organizations.

A New Developmental Intervention

The two broad prevalent modes of developmental intervention for the improvement of the socio-economic condition of the Adivasis in particular and the rural population in general among NGOs, social movements and the government are that of service delivery and political empowerment. The interventions in the cultural sphere mainly through the use of audio-visual media like street theatre for the purpose of information, education and communication (IEC) have not been independent developmental interventions but have subserved the above mentioned two modes and the lack of a written literature of the Adivasis has hampered these efforts. Thus, despite over two decades of developmental and empowerment interventions, the impact in terms of creating a self-confident Bhil population capable of pinpointing and solving their problems independently has been less than desirable.

The intervention of the AEP makes a quantum jump both horizontally and vertically from the current practice. Horizontally, it makes the original assertion that the creation of a new living literature of the Bhils from their traditional folklore is itself a new and major developmental intervention that can parallel the prevailing two modes in the case of Adivasi development because of their lack of a literate culture. Vertically this intervention will result in considerably improving the content and style of the IEC campaigns which are a necessary part of the prevailing two modes of intervention. Moreover, the experience of service delivery and political mass organization has shown that these processes rarely become self-supporting and have to be constantly reinforced with funding and professional assistance by outsiders. In this respect, the creation of a literature has historically been a self-sustaining process once the initial critical mass of writers and readers has been established either through voluntary efforts or by some organized action.

This brings us to the existing interventions in the field of culture. Anthropologists Amita Baviskar (Baviskar, 1995) and Engelbert Stiglmayer (Stiglmayer, 1970) have studied some Bhili myths from an academic anthropological perspective so as to better understand the social dynamics of the Bhils. Jyotindra Jain has also studied some of these myths to assess their aesthetic qualities and to determine their relationship with the mainstream Hindu culture (Jain, 1984). Christian missionaries too have transcribed some of the myths but not in any sustained manner and not with the objective of the creation of a new literature. Similarly, the government departments of tribal development too have from time to time attempted to publish reading material in Bhili dialects but these too have been haphazard and have necessarily lacked a mass character.

The decade of the 1990s has seen yet another academic project launched by Ganesh Devy for the study of the languages of the Adivasis of northern Maharashtra and Gujarat (Devy, 2003). In this externally funded venture a biannual journal is published by turns in four different Bhili dialects meaning that new written material is produced in a particular dialect only once in two years. Moreover, there is little attention being paid to the transcription of the folklore of the Adivasis. Thus, this effort has spread itself thin by dealing with too many languages and so the output in terms of new literature in any of these is quite minimal and lacks the necessary critical mass of writers and readers to pose a strong challenge the hegemony of Marathi and Gujarati as the dominant languages.

The AEP effort, therefore, builds on all these previous interventions while giving them a new and purposeful thrust of reviving Bhili culture with the intention of positing it as a vehicle of sustainable development. The intervention, thus, seeks to protect and build on the fundamental right to culture of the Bhils guaranteed in Article 29 of the Constitution of India. The Muslims and Sikhs have taken advantage of this provision but there has been no such specific cultural rights intervention among Adivasis in the central Indian region. Thus what is being implemented by the AEP is a best practice framework for Adivasi cultural renewal that can not only rejuvenate the living conditions of the Bhils but can be gainfully replicated for the development of other Adivasi cultures.

The Overarching Social Problem Being Addressed

This intervention addresses the serious problem that the culture of the Bhils is considered to be sub-human by the non-Adivasis of the region and even the modern Indian state seeks to destroy the culture of the Adivasis nationally by introducing a uniform modernizing sweep through its developmental and educational policies. The problem assumes a vicious circle as the Bhils internalize this devaluation and tend to reject their culture. Given that most Bhils are not able to imbibe the modern non-Adivasi culture in a successful manner, this further reduces their ability to fight effectively in the competitive political and economic systems that prevail at present and leaves them even more disrespectful of their own culture.

The extent of this dehumanization of the Bhils can be illustrated with an example. There was a great Bhil rebel named Tantia who fought the British and their subservient upper caste Hindu landlords valiantly in the latter half of the nineteenth century for over a decade and a half. He was a Robin Hood like character who used to distribute the loot from his raids on the British and the landlords among the poor Bhils. Thus, Bhil women used to consider him to be their brother and used to tell their children that Tantia 'mama' (maternal uncle) would bring gifts for them. He was finally apprehended by the British through treachery and hanged after a summary trial. Following the British, the non-Adivasis of the region regarded him not as a freedom fighter but as a dacoit. Later, the term 'mama' too lost its value and degenerated into a pejorative name for the Bhils. The Bhils who have lost independent livelihood opportunities over the last century and a half are today forced to migrate to nearby cities and rich agricultural areas for employment. Thus, the Vadodara–Kota passenger which runs on the main Mumbai–Delhi trunk rail route is most of the time filled with Bhils going up and down from their homes to their places of work and back and has come to be called the 'mama gari'.

When the process of forming a forum for the revival of Adivasi culture was begun, the major problem faced was the sense of shame that the educated Adivasis felt about speaking and writing in Bhili in public places. A pamphlet in Bhili was published to popularize the whole idea. Even senior literate Adivasis would go into peals of laughter on reading it. The process of reading the pamphlet itself proved to be laborious as there is no written literature in Bhili dialects. What more can be indicative of the extent of decay of a language than this reluctance of the literate Bhils to converse and write in it. Simultaneously, the illiterate Bhil masses are being wooed away by television and they do not spend as much time as they used to do to celebrate their own festivals. There is an increasing tendency to celebrate Hindu festivals such as Ganesh Puja and Durga Navaratri instead.

This lack of a positive self-image is a major obstacle in the search for a viable system of livelihood for the Bhils. Consequently, the core of the intervention draws from the glorious history of the European and modern Indian cultural renaissance movements and posits that the solution to this problem lies in the creation of a strong new literature using the rich classical resource of the Bhils' oral folklore as the cornerstone of the process of revival of a Bhili culture that can rival the dominant non-Adivasi culture in all respects and so provide the Bhils with an equal cultural footing in their struggle for emancipation. At a higher level, the successful implementation of this intervention will provide a replicable blueprint for the strengthening of non-literate Adivasi cultures nationally and worldwide and so maintain cultural diversity. Indeed the whole point of the present intervention is to chart out a map for the revival and promotion of Adivasi cultures in a sustainable way through mass participation.

As mentioned earlier the problem of the marginalization of Adivasi culture is closely linked to the proliferation of a consumerist monoculture worldwide which is proving to be dangerously harmful for future human development. Thus, by seeking to strengthen Adivasi cultures the present idea seeks to address this serious problem of loss of cultural diversity on a global scale as will be described in detail later.

The Main Systemic Problem Being Addressed

The most serious systemic problem that the developmental initiatives in the Western Madhya Pradesh region in particular and in Adivasi areas in general have been unable to resolve is that they have not been able to inspire the Adivasis to devise and then implement their own solutions to their problems of social, economic and cultural deprivation due to the culture of silence which stifles their articulation and innate genius giving rise to the problem of social devaluation described above. Invariably schemes and plans that have originated elsewhere have been dumped on the Adivasis with the result that not only has any sustainable process of development not evolved but that the Adivasis have continued to remain mute recipients of the crumbs thrown to them. This has meant that the age-old exploitative structures have continued to hold sway. In many cases new developmental initiatives have been sabotaged by the non-Adivasis who have been entrusted with their implementation.

For instance, watershed development schemes have not addressed the basic lack of land resources with the Adivasis in the region which has meant that even after successful completion of these schemes the Adivasis have not been able to augment their incomes to higher levels sufficient for sustainable living from these small holdings because the enhanced production is not sufficient for the purpose. The response of the government has been the introduction of jersey cow based milk production and vermiculture. These, however, have failed because there is insufficient wasteland available for fodder development enough to make these latter schemes successful. The net result is that the Adivasis who took government loans to start these projects are now in debt which they cannot possibly repay. This is, in fact, the situation with most subsidized poverty alleviation schemes of the government. The failure of the Integrated Rural Development Programme to bring about any widespread sustainable income generation due to this inability to take into account the views of the beneficiaries has been well documented.

Similarly political empowerment interventions have addressed agenda close to the heart of the activists without paying attention to the actual demands of those who are being organized leading to the eventual dissipation of these movements. A very good example of this is the Narmada Bachao Andolan. The movement initially started by addressing the genuine fear voiced by the Adivasi oustees of the Sardar Sarovar dam that they would be displaced from their lands without proper rehabilitation. Later, however, the movement was converted into a battle to stop the construction of the dam altogether mainly on the basis of the ideological predilections of the non-Adivasi activists who led the movement. The pressure of the movement forced the government to better the rehabilitation package on offer and the Adivasis plumped for this but the activists went on fighting for the no-dam option with lesser and lesser people. This lack of articulation of the Adivasis has meant that the two decades of work put in by various development and empowerment organizations has not been able to bring about self sufficiency in the Bhils.

This lack of articulation can be seen also in the lack of effective implementation of two very important statutes. The 5th schedule of the Constitution of India provides for special governance of the notified scheduled Adivasi areas in a state on the recommendations of the tribal advisory council comprised of Adivasi legislators. Similarly, the Panchayati Raj Extension to Scheduled Areas Act (PESA) provides for the Adivasi gram sabhas to be paramount in deciding on the use of the resources of the village and in resolving disputes. However, in reality these two powerful statutes are not being implemented in the way they should be because the Adivasis and their elected representatives are not able to press for this in any articulate manner (Banerjee, 2014).

The urgent need, therefore, is that the Adivasis be able to articulate their felt needs and act in an organized manner in accordance with their own genius so that they are fulfilled. The publication of literature in Bhili dialects addresses precisely this problem of lack of articulation among the Bhils. The Bhils are now writing about their problems and their culture and history in independent public fora that are funded by their own contributions and a tremendous process of increasing articulation has been set into motion. The confidence created by this intervention among a new class of Bhili intellectuals has also lead them to write in other languages in the mainstream media.

The present intervention is, thus, an initial step in the direction of building up the ability of effective articulation of Bhil Adivasis as a prelude to breaking the deafening culture of silence that muzzles them. The vast Bhil masses remain unheard because what they say does not carry enough cultural clout to make any impact.

There are many NGOs and people's organizations in Western Madhya Pradesh doing worthwhile work in the spheres of service delivery and political empowerment. There is a significant population associated with these organizations either directly as beneficiaries or participants or indirectly as well wishers and supporters. Workshops organized by these agencies and the AEP to critically analyse the results of the work done by them over the past decade and a half have clearly brought out the need for a concentrated intervention on the cultural front to give a wider base to their activities and also to counter the negative attitudes of the administration, the Hindu fundamentalist organizations and the non-Adivasi development workers and social activists. This is the basis of the present intervention in this direction, the most important being the researching of the history of famous Bhil martyrs like Khajya Naik, Motia Bhil, Tantia Bhil, Chitu Kirar and others. Sustained lobbying and mass celebrations of the martyrdom of these heroes has resulted in their being acknowledged as freedom fighters of repute and the recognition that the Bhils had played a major resistive role against the British. Similarly, Bhili songs and stories and modern versions of these have been recorded and published.

Positive Local Impact of the Intervention

A narrative will bring out the way in which people's lives can change from a cultural initiative. The Adivasis in Potla village in Dewas district were held in thrall by the only sahukar in the village who used to rule their lives in all respects. Some of them heard of the plans for holding the martyrdom celebrations of Tantia Bhil and came and told the rest of the villagers about it and distributed the pamphlets and booklets on Tantia's brave deeds to the educated Adivasi youth. The result was that the villagers decided to participate in the yatra to Tantia's Samadhi. For this they needed to hire a truck to carry their possessions and they contacted their *sahukar* who initially agreed to give them his truck on hire. But on the day of their setting out the *sahukar* declined to give them the truck and also threatened not to give them any loans for the forthcoming cropping season.

This incensed the villagers so much that they decided to socially boycott the *sahukar* and his family and made alternative arrangements to participate in the yatra. There was no need for activists to go and organize the people as it just took a few pamphlets and a general milieu of cultural revival to bring about the end to generations of servitude. The emancipatory power of literature and its capability to bring about a positive change in the life of the oppressed has been established time and again throughout history and the French Revolution is the well known example in this regard. The American freedom fighters were influenced by the writings of Thomas Paine to rebel against the British. The freedom fighters for India's Independence too were motivated by the publication of new and liberating literature. Indeed, the Dalits in this country have been far more enterprising in this regard as compared to the Adivasis of the central and western Indian regions.

The important thing is that this new literature must be published as part of a general milieu of emancipatory socio-economic change. The work of the various civil society organizations of the Bhils over the past two decades in general and the activities of the AEP in particular have created such a milieu of change and it only needs a systematic and well articulated ideology for its further expansion which the present intervention intends to provide by encouraging the people to hark back to their rich oral folklore and their nature friendly animist beliefs and practices.

Potential for Wider Application

All over the country and even worldwide Adivasi cultures are on the verge of extinction. This has something to do with the decline of indigenous agriculture on which these cultures were based and with the homogenizing culture of western consumerism which has been popularized through television soap operas, sports broadcasts and commercials. A global market is sought to be created for the products of the industrial West by washing away local cultural influences from the brains of people through this powerful cultural onslaught of western consumerism.

For instance the tremendous concentration of the audio-visual media on the Cricket World Cup in South Africa in 2003 seeped through to a remote Adivasi village in the region where an old woman who did not know anything about cricket still lamented the fact that India had lost the final. The irony is that nationalism is being promoted through an unproductive symbol such as cricket when such poor people as this Adivasi woman are on the edge of starvation because of a lack of viable livelihood opportunities just to sell various consumerist products of industry. A victory in the final would not in any way have improved the living conditions of poor people in this country but a major improvement in their condition brought about by the adoption of more appropriate development policies would automatically ensure that we win more accolades in the international arena in sports which are played by more countries of the world than cricket.

This erosion of cultural diversity has come to be recognized as a serious impediment to the future of the human race. Thus, my innovation by stressing that the Adivasi culture and the agricultural base from which it springs have the potential to offer an alternative to this destructive homogenization of culture and livelihoods has vast areas of application not only in the preservation of Adivasi cultures but also that of the culture of more so called advanced societies. The AEP innovation provides a best practice framework for carrying out such a revival and preservation of cultural and livelihood diversity.

The Larger Impact of this Innovation

It is difficult to state exactly how many people have already benefitted from the implementation of the innovation so far. The people who are consciously involved with the various organizations that are a part of this process number about one hundred thousand. However, many Adivasis who may not be openly supportive of these efforts due to various reasons secretly go along with the process and try to move it forward in many ways. Thus people even in remote areas have heard of the revival of the Tantia festival and have drawn heart from it without having participated in it. Many mainstream Adivasi political figures from all parties have asserted in public fora that the revivalist movement of the Bhils is a positive development and some have even participated in the programmes of the AEP. The pressure created by the AEP so far has forced the government to take note of rising level of awareness of the Adivasis and initiate beneficial development policies which have helped the whole of the Adivasi population of the four states of Western India which is close to 12 million.

Today, we have a globalized world with far flung nations and communities tied together by trade in commodities and services, cross border manufacturing, financial transfers and also a massive communications industry. Thus, it is relatively easy for the more well endowed societies to press their social, economic and political thought on those who are not so advantaged. This process is happening at all levels from the village to the global. We have a situation in which cultural production is taking place in the affluent west and being broadcast for consumption by the world at large. The western cultural icons and agencies dominate the powerful medium of television, the newer and equally powerful medium of the internet as well as the various printed media.

This cultural domination favours the economic interests of the various corporate behemoths that control the world economy. It is in the interests of these corporations that the cultural tastes of the population of the whole world are homogenized. This has created a critical situation for human survival with the loss of diversity in the biological, economic and social spheres in addition to the cultural sphere. As mentioned earlier the only way in which this dangerous cultural homogenization and erosion of diversity caused by thoughtless industrialism can be challenged is by rediscovering the virtues of traditional agriculture and the culture that it gave rise to. Today it is the indigenous people worldwide who still retain the skills and knowledge of traditional agriculture and the accompanying culture. Thus the work of the AEP by reviving and conserving the indigenous Bhil culture will challenge the dominant system of development and governance which is increasingly being adopted at all levels from the local to the global. Since centralization and homogenization invariably necessitates violence which is so evident in various forms today the AEP's stress on decentralization and difference presents a prospectus for peace and amity worldwide. This intervention, therefore, will impact development thought and practice and make it more amenable to the evolution of sustainable living and working patterns in the future at all levels from the local to the global.

References

Banerjee, R. (2003), 'Status of Informal Rural Financial Markets in Adivasi Dominated Regions of Western Madhya Pradesh', Working Paper No. 2, Department of Economic Analysis and Research, Mumbai: National Bank for Agriculture and Rural Development.

——(2014), 'Actualising Adivasi Self Rule: The Only Panacea', *Yojana*, Vol. 58, No. 1., January, pp. 22–25.

Baviskar, A. (1995), *In the Belly of the River: Tribal Conflicts Over Development in the Narmada Valley*, New Delhi: Oxford University Press.

Devy, G.N. (2003), *Painted Words: An Anthology of Tribal Literature*, New Delhi: Penguin.

Rahul (1997a), *Target Free but Not Oppression Free*, Indore: Free Press, 24 March.

——(1997b), 'Reasserting Ecological Ethics: Bhils' Struggles in Alirajpur', *Economic and Political Weekly*, Vol. 32, No. 3, pp. 87–91.

Sharma, B.D. (2001), *Tribal Affairs in India: The Crucial Transition*, New Delhi: Sahayog Pustak Kutir Trust.

11

Conservation Ethos and Consequent Environmental Movements and Biodiversity Governance in Tribal Areas of India

DEBASHIS DEBNATH

Social movements are non-institutional legal or illegal collective action, starting from protests, agitation, demonstration strikes, etc. leading to minimal organization to achieve some goals on principals. Social movements encompass social transformations or change with some political actions. Sociologists do not differ social movements from the political movements. The former talk about the autonomy and the latter's views are based on state of power. In India, social movements are categorized into peasants, tribals, Dalits, women, students, etc. on the basis of the organization, leadership and issues.

Tribals are ethnic groups having their own cultures – dialects, lifestyles, social structures, rituals, values – differing somewhat from those of the dominant non-tribal peasant social groups. At the same time, most of them are settled agriculturists and social differentiations have developed among them. Their agrarian problems were and are, to some extent, the same as those of other non-tribal peasants. Studies are now available to show how a section of tribes have, in course of time, become peasants (Upadhyaya, 1980; Shah, 1984; Pathy, 1984). After the invasion and intrusion into the lands of Indian sub-continent by the British Raj, tribal revolts broke out to challenge alien rule. In the early years of colonialization, no other community in India offered such heroic resistance to British rule or faced such tragic consequences as did the numerous Adivasis' Communities of now Jharkhand, Chhattisgarh, Odisha and Bengal. Tribal movements have been, by and large, associated with the tribes that are numerically large and relatively advanced. The relatively advanced tribes are associated with tribal groups that make their living from agriculture, especially settled agriculture. Hence, many scholars treat tribal movements as peasants' movements (Gough, 1974; Desai, 1979; Guha, 1983). Conversely it is held that small, isolated and primitive tribes have little potential for learning and sustaining a movement. At best they are expected to react to issue over land and forests on which they are greatly dependent for their livelihood (Singh, 1982). K.S. Singh joins issue with these scholars and political activists. He argues such an approach tends to gloss over the diversities of tribal social formations of which tribal movements are a part both leaving structurally related (1985: 119). Because of the concentration of the tribals in certain areas, their social and political organization and relative isolation from the main stream, their leadership pattern and modus operandi of political mobilization may differ from those of other peasants. K.S. Singh has edited two volumes on Tribal Movements in India (1982–83). He divides the movements into three phases. The first phase was between 1795 and 1860, and coincided with the rise, expansion and establishment of the British Empire. The second phase covers the period of colonialism, 'during which merchant capital penetrated into tribal economy affecting their relationship with the land and forest'. The third phase deals with the period from 1920 till the achievement of Independence in 1947. During this phase, the tribals not only began to launch the so-called separatist movement, but at the same time, participated in nationalist and agrarian movements. K.S. Singh classified the tribal movements into: (1) movements for political autonomy; (2) agrarian and forest-based movements; (3) sanskritization movement; and (4) cultural movements based on script and language.

Numerous uprisings of the tribals have taken place beginning with the one in Bihar in 1772 followed by many revolts in Andhra Pradesh, Andaman and Nicobar Islands, Arunchal Pradesh, Assam, Mizoram and Nagaland. The important tribes involved in revolt in the nineteenth century were Mizos (1810), Kols (1795 & 1831), Mundas (1889), Daflas (1875), Khasi and Garo (1829), Kacharis (1839), Santhals (1853), Muria Gonds (1886),Nagas (1844 & 1879) and Konds (1817).

Different scholars have evolved different typologies of tribal movements. Tribal movements have been classified on the basis of geography, chrolonology and objectives or issues. Hence, these are classified into: rebellion, revolts, insurrection or reforms. Mahapatra (1972) applies the typologies widely used for social movements to tribal movements: (1) reactionary; (2) conservative; (3) revisionary or revolutionary. The reactionary movement tries to launch a movement to bring back 'the good old days', whereas the conservative movement tries to maintain the status quo. The revisionary or revolutionary movements are those which are organized for improvement' or 'purification' of the cultural or social order by eliminating 'evil' or 'law' customs, beliefs or institutions, Surajit Sinha (1968) classifies the movements into (1) ethnic rebellion; (2) reform movements; (3) political autonomy movement within Indian union; (4) secessionist movement and (5) agrarian unrest. K.S. Singh (1983) makes more or less the same classification except that he uses the terms sanskritization instead of reform movement and cultural movement instead of ethnic movements. There is no substantial difference among the scholars who use different typologies. Mahapatra excludes political movements whereas others do not. These typologies do not include the recent movements around issues of forest rights and environment and displacement of the tribals due to development programmes of the state and market. By the turn of the twentieth century, K.S. Singh observes:

'In recent years, with the rise of the international movement of indigenous people in the past modernist phase' the focus has shifted to self determination or self management of the resources, identity and ethnicity. The environmental movement has focused on communities in situ, their relationship to require their rapport with nature, their worldview. Therefore, with the growing concern for environment, particularly biodiversity, pluralism, ethnicity and identity – all are now inter-related the tribal movements are assuming a new character. They are now becoming more and more identity-based movements with various issues concerning control over resources etc. being considered as ramification of this central issue (1998: 9–10).

After Independence, tribal movements may be classified into three groups (i) movement due to exploitation by outsiders. Most of the tribal movements were result of oppression and discrimination, neglect and backwardness and apathy of government towards tribal problems. (ii) movements due to economic deprivation (like those of Gonds in Madhya Pradesh and the Mahars in Andhra Pradesh, and (iii) movements due to separatist tendencies (like those of the Nagas and Mizos). The tribal movements may also be classified on the basis of their orientation into four types: (i) forest-based movements, (ii) socio-religious movements or social-culture movements (iii) movements seeking political autonomy and formations of states (Nagas, Mizos, Jharkhand), and (iv) agrarian movement, Naxalbari Movement-1967 and Brisadal Movement 1968–69. During the second half of the nineteenth century, the whole of

Chotanagpur underwent a tremendous change. The old Munda system of Khuntakatti tenure gave way to a new and alien system of exploitation by the landlords known as jagirdar and thikadar. In 1895, Birsa Munda of Chalkad started a movement. In him the Munda found the embodiment of their aspiration. He gave them leadership, a religion and a code of life. He held before them the prospect of Munda Raj in place of foreign rule. Reformative movement was found among the Mundas under powerful leadership of Dharli Aba, who preached Hindu ideals of ritual purity, asceticism and criticized the worship of priests.

In the Tana Bhagat Movement, an attempt was made to emulate the way of life of the Hindu higher castes. It emerged among the Oraon of Chotanagpur; Bihar. It tried to raise the status of its members in the eyes of the surrounding Hindu society and was characterized by a large scale incorporation of Hindu belief-practices into its ideology. Hence, this movement was in favour of sanskritization.

Environmental Movements

All the environmental aspects are more or less peripheral to the contemporary social movements in India. These ecological or environmental movements have widened their focus from basic survival needs to habitat conservation or management, and these are grouped under tribal or peasant movement in community conserved areas. Omvedt (1993) and Wrignaraja (1993) called them new social movements, as the ecological aspects are problems associated with peasants and tribals where survival is attached to the status of natural resources. Hence, the environmental movements, unlike the West, are meant for the survival of the poor. The environmental movements can be divided into two: (1) Macro – the main objective is to influence the policy, and (2) Micro – the movements aim at a result oriented sustainable development practices.

Macro-Level Environmental Movements

The macro level movements are addressed to the broader ecological dimensions of development. These movements took initiative for environmental protection. Some such popular movements are as follows:

The origin of modern environmentalism and environmental movements in India can be ascribed to Chipko Movement in central Himalayan region in the early 1970s. The roots of this movement are found in the early decades of twentieth century. The movement was launched from the protests for the benefits of the forests, especially the right to fodder should go to the local people (Bahuguna, 1990). However, the origin of Chipko (chipak jayenge – to hug) has taken place during the year 1973. The form of protest was instrumental in driving away the private company from felling the trees. With its success, the movement has spread to other neighbouring areas and then the movement is popularly known as Chipko Movement internationally only during 1970s. This movement started towards concentrating on ecological issues such as depletion of forest cover. Chipko Movement with its wide following and success, though modest in achieving some of its objectives, can be formed as a watershed in environmental movements in India. This in fact kindled the environmental aspects of development and gave rise to numerous conflicts and protests over natural resources and ecological issues. The basic attributes to three important aspects are:

1. The close links to the livelihoods of the local people especially women where contribution to household's subsistence and anti-alcohol campaign.
2. It has strictly adhered to the Gandhian tradition of non-violence.
3. Simplicity and sincerity of the leaders like Shri Sundarlal Bahuguna and their access to the national leaders like Smt Indira Gandhi.
   (i) The other popular environmental movements of importance in India are Tehri Dam, Silent Valley and Narmada Valley projects.
   The longest struggle among the anti-big dam protests was the opposition to Tehri Dam being constructed on the river Bhagirathi in the Garhwal region. Another one was one of the early successes of environmental movements, which is the Silent Valley hydroelectric project in Kerala. This movement was fought primarily on environmental grounds and mostly at the intellectual level organized by the Kerala Sahitya Parishad in collaboration with Wildlife Conservationists. The major concerns of this movement were the adverse environmental impact on Silent Valley, one of the last surviving natural tropical forests in India and protecting a rare breed of monkey, lion-tailed Macaque.
   The most popular movement in the environmental listing of India is the movement against the Narmada River Valley Project. The movement was initiated by the state human rights activists toward proper rehabilitation programmes for the dam displaced or oustees (mostly tribals) along with the damage in ecological resources. The movement, however, gained public interests after joining of eminent social workers. The Narmada Valley Movement also known as 'Narmada Bachao Andolan' started with addressing the problems of livelihoods of local people (tribals), traversed into human rights issues and focused on environmental concerns while suggesting an alternative development paradigm.

Micro-Level Environmental Movements

In this section two micro-level movements can be mentioned:

Self-Initiated Forest Protection

In the mean time, since 1960s, the tribal communities in tribal lands have taken their initiative to protect the forestlands, both Reserved Forest (RF) and Protected Forest (PF), for natural regeneration. Attempts are being made to protect about 40,000 hectares of forests of Odisha, Bihar (present day Jharkhand), Gujarat, Rajasthan, Karnataka, Madhya Pradesh (and also Chhatishgarh), and Andhra Pradesh (SPWD, 1993). These village groups (see Table 1) have started protecting forest patches adjoining their village in response to resource scarcity. In a personal communication to Mark Paffenberger, Madhu Sarin, a freelancer in Society for the Promotion of Wastelands Development (SPWD), commented that during that time indigenous people protected 6,00,000 hectares of forest land whereas the government became successful in planting trees in only 5,000 hectares of revenue land under social forestry project (Poffenberger, 1995).

Table 1

Reported self-initiatives committees in different parts in India

State	*Number of Village organiza-tions*	*Area protected (in Ha.)*	*Legal status of forest*
Himachal Pradesh	2,000	23,556	Panchayat, community
Odisha	5622	74,000	RF & Keshra
Karnataka	23	665	RF & PF
Jammu & Kashmir	101	5434	Demarcated Land
Tamil Nadu	100	5,550	RF & Revenue
Uttaranchal	4058	2,20,000	Panchayat
West Bengal	1684	2,00,000	RF & PF

Source: Ravindranath et al., 2000.

Pani-Panchayat (Water Council)

This is located in Maharashtra. It was initiated by the Ralegaon Sidhi experiment as an integrated movement of environment and development. Ralegaon Sidhi was commenced by Shri Anna Hazare, behind the success based on the philosophical path of Gandhi and Vivekananda, where he used religion and cultural factors to bring the desired change in a degenerated society. He started people-centric movement to achieve the goals of sustainable development by banning the forest sterilization, prohibition, ban on grazing and ban on tree felling. The approach of Pani Panchayat (Water Council) is somewhat different from that of Relegaon Sidhi. In the former, the importance was given to soil conservation and water harvesting mechanisms in drought prone region. The project demonstrated the impact of a watershed development in the drought prone regions through watershed management approach. However, the success of the above micro-level movements is also attributed to other factors like socio-economic homogeneity of the villages, particularly in the economic life.

Legacy of Tribal Movements and Tribal Land Alienation

Before advent of the British Raj, the forest was the common property resource. So these tribal groups utilized the forest products for their traditional livelihoods following some social norms, cultural practices and religious affiliation. The sacred groves, trees, and ponds reflect such pristine culture centred round the forest resources. Hence, the phase can be expressed by sustainable use with religious affiliation. This traditional indigenous forest management system was gradually shattered by the British Policy of 'Scientific Forestry' since 1855, which imposed the state management of forest under full control by an organized department. The silvicultural system was applied as tending operation for coup felling of valuable timbers. The first forest policy which came in 1894 made two major enunciation – first, the cultivation are stronger than the claims of forest preservation and second, the public (material) benefit through teak extraction for the industrial purposes such as ship building in Royal Navy and railway slippers laying and bridge constructions. In 1865 Forest Act, an attempt was made to regulate the collection and preservation of forest products in a desired direction by the British Administration which subsequently became anti-forest and anti-locals who were organically related to forest.

The commercial exploitation of forests was encouraged at the cost of forest dwellers in the name of national interests. The colonial government issued permits to professional contractors to harvest the timbers. The forest department was strengthened to regulate people's rights over forestland and produces with the enactment of Indian Forest Act 1927. That is still in practice. The consequences of various policy, laws or acts are the depletion of forest resource, shrinkage of forest areas, loss of bio-diversity and ecological imbalances. It caused various tribal revolts and enactment of criminal tribes' act.

The National Forest Policy in 1952 was just an extension of old policy followed during the colonial period. Rigid restrictions were also imposed on the forest dwellers and others to exploit the forest resources on which their cultural traditions and economy depend. The regulations were imposed on the ground with the assumptions that forest dwellers were solely responsible for the destruction of forest resources.

The Central Indian forests and its vicinity are inhabited by tribals. But in the last century and a half they have shared a common fate of dispossession and oppression. Long years of colonial and post-colonial subjugation have increased pauperization and oppression and alienation of these peoples. Over the last century, the Forest Department has used cheap and often forced labour of the tribes to convert rich mixed forests into pure teak forests, so that the commercial value of the forest increases. Legal and illegal felling of the trees by the forest department and the contractors has decimated the forests. More important, the traditional control of the tribal society over the use and maintenance of the forests has been dismantled; the tribal people's access to the forest resources has been severely restricted or altogether finished. Given the fact that in marginal lands access to forest resources is a major means of livelihood, establishment of the control of the government and its Forest Department over the forests constitutes a major blow to the tribal peoples. In the last 50 years over 90 lakh people have been displaced due to various projects in India and a huge majority of them belong to the tribal. The forest lands were out of reach for the government for years as they never even thought of venturing into those regions. Hence, there was no development in the region. Today, the tribal question has jolted the people who have conscience. It needs a thoughtful and sensible understanding as why there is unrest in the entire tribal belt of Central India. Let us first have a look at the government records.

According to Ministry of Rural Development, 3.75 lakh cases of tribal land alienation were registered covering 8.55 lakhs acres of land. Out of the above, 1.62 lakh cases (43.2%) were disposed of in favour of tribal covering a total of 4.47 (55. 28%) lakh hectares of land; 1.55 lakh cases covering an area of 3.63 lakh acres were rejected by the courts on various grounds; 57,521 cases involving 44 lakh acres of land are pending in various courts of the country (Report quoted in 'India and the Rights of Indigenous people published by ILO). There is huge mining in these regions. Forests are out of reach for tribals now. The areas where they developed their culture and nurtured India's huge forest are now under the government control. There was no attempt to bring them into national mainstream. Health, road network, schools, PDS, communications were out of bounds for them. For years, tribal suffered in the abject and shameless neglect by the Indian state and, hence, different forces entered there to 'liberate' them.

Community Mobilization Under Movements' Spirits

As discussed above, under micro-level environmental movements there is formation of self-initiated forest protection groups in various indigenous lands by the local tribal groups, which was later estimated to be over 58,000 odd village organization. A.K. Bannerjee, the then Divisional Forest Officer (Silviculturist) of East Midnapur Forest division, took initiative to develop village partnership with the Forest Department in the forest management, which had been the legacy of centralized, controlled, custodial timber-harvesting and revenue earning forestry state management to people-centred, people responsive, popular democratic Participatory Forestry. West Bengal Forest Department first declared the resolution of Forest Protection by the village people. Following this in 1990s, the

Government of India resolution under the heading 'Joint Forest Management' (JFM) was passed on 1 June 1990 by a circular No.6.21/89-FP from the Secretary, Ministry of Environment & Forest, providing guidelines for the 'involvement of village communities and voluntary agencies in the regeneration of degraded forests'. This is a paradigm shift from traditional forest management system to the community based participatory forest management system. The definition of forest management has been elaborated encompassing the totality of administrative, economic, legal, social, technical and scientific approach for the utility, conservation, and sustainability of forests.

In the Joint Forest Management Programme, a number of village institutions were formed to promote a partnership between the state and local communities to manage forests for the benefit of the people and state and to make livelihood strategies for the people to strengthen the economy of poor tribals. This people-centred forest management has developed a partnership business to change the existing forest conditions at the local level, pattern of forest to bolster collective action for bio-diversity conservation. According to some sources, so far it is seen that 64,000 forest protection committees are working in 28 states covering a forest area of over 14 million hectares.

In the JFM process, a number of social impacts and sustainable livelihoods approaches have taken place (Debnath and Das Gupta, 2003: 49):

- Local level village committees.
- Involvement of all sections in decision-making process.
- Participatory protection mechanism.
- Organizational development and institutional process.
- Conservation practices for bio-diversity.
- Preparation of micro-plans.
- Innovative approaches for socio-economic development.
- Promotion of indigenous knowledge and technology.
- Collective consciousness for sustainable use of natural resources.
- Affirmation of common property resources.
- Social equity and women empowerment.

Tribal Movements and Livelihoods

Since Independence, the Government of India provided the especial human rights values in the Constitution of India giving them special status for provision of privileges in the country's Constitution. In the identification of tribal identities, emphasis was laid on their culture and technology. It is well known that access to forest land and forest produce plays a critical role in the livelihood of the tribal people. However, instead of nurturing tribal livelihood, developmental interventions in India have mainly resulted in curtailment of tribal people's access to traditional sources of livelihood. The situation of tribal people in the state of Odisha is no different from those in other states of the country. Recently, the state has witnessed increasing tribal resistance and protests against state encroachment on their land rights.

Discussing the impact of state interventions on the livelihood of the tribal people, the authors note that because of faulty land-reforms in the post-Independence era, tribal people have lost significant amount of land over which they had customary usufructuary rights since time immemorial. Regarding land use and tenure systems, the authors argue that over the decades, because of denial of rights over shifting lands, restrictive forest policies, loss of land, etc. the practice of shifting cultivation – a major source of tribal people's livelihood – has declined.

Since the British Regime, even in the report of Dhebar and Shilo Ao's Commissions, the forest related policies of the government too had severely curtailed the tribal people's access to forest and forest produce. Instead of protecting the rights of the local people, declaration of several reserve and protected forests have been done without settlement of rights or providing adequate recognition of rights on land used for shifting cultivation. Further, deforestation associated with various development projects, such as mining, dams, etc. have adversely affected tribal people's livelihood resources – the mainstay of their food and economic security. In addition, unfair trade practices of traders, middlemen and forest contractors have resulted in tribal people not getting remunerative prices for sale of non-timber forest produce (NTFP).

Several forestry projects aided by International Donor agencies have been launched with the ostensible aim of restoring forests to degraded stretches and preserving bio-diversity with the cooperation of the tribal people. However, most of these projects have been severely criticized by several organizations. It seems that the projects in effect seek to increase the control of the Forest Department and further reduce the access of traditional forest users. It seeks to oust communities settled for generations in the midst of dense forests (which now are being designated as national parks and sanctuaries) on the plea that they are a threat to the effective conservation and preservation of the natural flora and fauna.

Forest Rights

Under the Scheduled Tribes and other Traditional Forest Dwellers (Recognition of Forest Rights) Act-2006, the Government of India recognizes and vests the forest rights and occupation in forests lands in forest dwelling Scheduled Tribes and other traditional forest dwellers who have been residing in such forests for generations but whose rights could not be recorded. It also recognizes the responsibilities of the Forest Dwelling Scheduled Tribes (FDST) and other traditional forest dwellers for sustainable use, conservation of biodiversity and maintenance of ecological balance and, thereby, strengthening the conservation regime of the forests while ensuring livelihood and food security to them. It reported that under the FRA, like all tribals who depend on forests for livelihood, the Baigas, too, are entitled to rights over forestland … . Even after the FRA was in place, the Forest Department took over the land of 41 Baiga families of Masna village. 'In August 2011, the Baigas presented their case before the gram sabha (village council) claiming forest rights. The village council approved their demand and forwarded it to the district administration for further action. But the administration refused to accept the Baigas' claims over the forestland, 'The government has taken over our land and enclosed it with barbed wire fencing,' says Bajrahin Bai, a villager. 'The officials say we are Naxalites and harass us in whatever way they can.' To oppose what they claim is a sustained assault on their rights to the forests where they have been living for generations, the Baigas from Masna have been waging a 'jungle satyagraha' movement since 9 August 2012.

Conclusion

Tribals of India are basically simple and peace loving people. Various studies on tribal movements highlight the militancy of Adivasis in various struggles during the pre- and post-Independence period. Tribal movements are heterogeneous and amorphous in nature, varying in character and orientation. This is because they have invariably tried to address a wide range of issues. They also point out that the line between the changing nature of issues that the tribals raised in the past and the present movement is thin and getting blurred as tribals become peasants. Few scholars believe that Adivasis, because of their locale and dependence on natural resources, are closer to nature. They respect nature. Hence, their struggles are considered as a part of environmental struggles. In the past, studies on tribal movements, particularly of the nineteenth century largely focused on their land and forest rights. However, during the last three decades, issues of identity and ethnicity are increasingly emphasized. Though the number of studies on tribal movements is large, only a few are intensive and well documented.

Since the last two decades, government efforts and intervention have been taken place for the participatory process in forest management and development in the tribal areas from the point view of livelihood securities and protection management by the local peoples. The political and legal implications have been observed in recognizing their rights on the forest lands as well as vest their interests in sustainable use and conservation practices. But the oppression and exploitation have been reduced to that extent as expected and the tribal movements have been suppressed to give them the real rights and the value of the conservation ethos and practices. The government intervention has been taken place to run the project bearing the high cost of the administration depriving these people who are the primary beneficiaries and key actors for the conservation of forest resources and the increase of the forest lands.

References

Bahuguna, Vimala (1990), 'The Chipko Movement', in Lina Sen (ed.), *A Space within Struggle: Women Participation in Peoples Movements*, New Delhi: Kali for Women.

Debnath, D. and S. Dasgupta (2003), *Social Impacts and Poverty Alleviation in Joint Forest Management Projects in Madhya Pradesh*, Proceedings of International Workshop on JFM form 19–20 June, Vigyan Bhavan, New Delhi.

——(2006), 'Livelihood Generation and Poverty Reduction Attempts in Joint Forest Management Activities in Madhya Pradesh', *International Forestry Review*, Vol. 8, No. 2, pp. 241–50.

Desai, A.R. (ed.) (1979), *Peasant Struggles in India*, Delhi: Oxford University Press.

Gough, Kathleen (1974), 'Indian Peasant Uprisings', *Economic and Political Weekly*, Vol. IX, Nos. 32–34, 10 August, pp. 1391–1412.

Guha, R. (1983), *Elementary Aspects of Peasant Insurgency in Colonial India*, New Delhi: Oxford University Press.

Mahapatra, L.K. (1972), 'Social Movements in India', in K.S. Singh (ed.), *Tribal Movements in India*, Vol. 2, New Delhi: Manohar Publications, pp. 399–409.

Omvedt, Gail (1993), *Reinventing a Revolution: New Social Movements and Socialist Tradition in India*, Armonk: M.E. Sharpe.

Pathy, J. (1984), *Tribal Peasantry: Dynamics of Development*, New Delhi: Inter-India Publications.

Poffenberger, M. (1995), 'India's Forest Keepers', *Wastelands News*, August–October, pp. 65–79.

Ravindranath, N.H., K.S. Murali and K.C. Malhotra (2000), *Joint Forest Management and Community Forestry in India*, New Delhi: Oxford and Calcutta: IBH Publishing Pvt. Ltd.

Shah, G. (1984), *Social Movements in India: A Review of Literature*, New Delhi: Sage Publications.

Singh, K.S. (1982), *Tribal Movements in India*, Vol. I, New Delhi: Manohar Publications.

——(1983), *Tribal Movements in India*, Vol. II, New Delhi: Manohar Publications.

——(1985), *Tribal Society in India: An Anthropo-historical Perspective*, Delhi: Manohar Publications.

Sinha, Surajit (1968), 'Tribal Solidarity and Messianic Movements: A Review Article', *Contributions to Indian Sociology*, Vol. II, New Series, pp. 112–118.

SPWD (1993), *Joint Forest Management: Concepts and Opportunities*, Proceedings of the National Workshop, New Delhi, August.

Upadhyaya, Ashok (1980), 'Class Struggle in Rural Maharashtra (India), Towards a New Perspective', *Journal of Peasant Studies*, Vol. 7, No. 2, January.

Wrignaraja, Ponna (1993), *New Social Movements in the South: Empowering the People*, Berkeley: University of California Press.

12

Left-Wing Extremism in PESA Area

Causes, Consequences and Addressing the Challenges

SWAPAN KUMAR KOLAY

Economic prosperity and well-being is only possible with sustained economic growth and distribution of fruits of growth among social groups and regions in a sustainable manner. The internal security theoretically provides these conditions happen true. Of the 106 Left-wing extremist (LWE) affected districts in the country today, 32 are PESA districts, according to official estimates. Drawing on a four decade old movement of militant left politics, the CPI (Maoist) was formed in September 2004, by merging the Communist Party of India (Marxist Leninist) and the Maoist Communist Centre. Its spread currently extends across significant parts of Bihar, Jharkhand, Odisha, Chhattisgarh and Andhra Pradesh, leading to the term, 'The Red Corridor'. This includes the epicentre of the banned party's base in the Dandakaranya region, a vast forested area on the borders of Andhra Pradesh, Chhattisgarh, Maharashtra and Odisha. While the senior leadership of the party is mostly drawn from non-tribal communities, much of the rank and file comes from local villages and has built on their grievances emanating from the non-implementation of PESA. The CPI (Maoist), which is the major Left-wing extremist organization, is responsible for most incidents of violence/killings in PESA locations. Almost all the conflicts underlying such violence are decades old, with strong local roots (Acharya, 2006: 320).

The LWE problem has roots running way back to the colonial period. They grabbed all natural resources from the people who are actual owners of those resources. The British rulers promoted different administration which was not acceptable to the local people.

The Zamindari system was adopted during the British Raj wherein a piece of land was given to a Zamindar and in return, he was required to pay a certain amount to the company or the state. The Zamindar did not cultivate the land himself; this had affected the poor tribal people who were directly embraced with the land. The deprived tribal people adopted different forms of agitation. Later, the Indian Government changed the governance strategy and helped the tribal toward empowerment, but the strategies bounced back due to systemic problems. Thus, the state government, the contractors, and street level bureaucracy fully exploited the tribals, bringing down their status to that of encroachers in the forests. The *jal* (water), *jungle* (forest) and *zamin* (Land) are the primary survival resources of the tribal; these resources are invariably exploited by the government and private players. The poor lack ownership of or access to assets such as land, water, forest, a dwelling unit, credit, literacy, longevity, voice and capital both physical and social (Mehta and Shah, 2001), may revolt against the state. The rehabilitation and payment of compensation for lands and assets acquired from the tribal for various purposes have been very poor. For certain tribal families, it has meant generations of resettlement without being given any compensation. This has led to deprivation and marginalization of the people. However, the industrialization was not the answer for the prey tribal. Moreover, 'In areas influenced by the Naxalite Movement the poor have started exercising their right to vote' (Bharti, 1990).

Even during post-Independence, the agrarian reforms did not reach the tribal areas. The solutions like *Bhoodan* and *Gramdan* were not effective for the empowerment of the tribal. Corruption, vote bank politics and atrocities against the Scheduled Castes and Tribes played havoc with the economic and social fabric of the society. The malfunctioning of government machinery in terms of inefficiency, corruption and exploitation was largely considered as the main factor behind the creation of a power vacuum as well as a space for LWE to take root in the country. Iyer (2009) looks at all terrorist incidents in the Indian subcontinent and infers that lagging regions are more prone to conflicts. Maoist insurgents engage in systematic attacks on development works in an effort to undermine the government's authority and perceived effectiveness. They have targeted school buildings, railways, roads, and power and telecom infrastructure (MHA, 2010: 17).

Many government programmes did not reach the tribal due to poor governance. However, the PESA was the answer to such problems, although it did not served expectedly. The LWE further argue that in the light of the state's insensitivity towards the problems of the weaker sections, only their party's ideology and methods can resolve the exploitation faced by the tribals. Government analyses the development deficit roots in the Left-wing extremism affected districts:

1. More than three-fourth of the people living in the PESA area have a low standard of living index.
2. Female literacy for most districts is below the national average.
3. Less than one-fourth of the population lives in pucca houses.
4. Less than one-third of the population have an electricity connection.

But while party proclamations and the evidence of poor development and governance support this hypothesis of economic liberalization fuelling socio-economic disparities, resulting in political extremism, it is necessary to note that the Maoist like all political outfits, seeks political power. One civil rights worker in the PESA area of Khammam, (Andhra Pradesh) reflected on this altering nature: 'When the LWEs first came here decades ago, their work was much needed, they agitated for better rates for *tendu* leaves sold by the Adivasis and for minimum wages. But today, the party has become corrupt, power hungry and intolerant of any difference.' Another advocate said, 'We also fight for the same issues as them, namely the dignity of the tribal, and the upholding of the Constitution by the powerful. But we adopt non-violent methods, and so we seem like a threat to the Maoists.'

However, the LWE today have a dual effect on the ground in PESA areas. By virtue of the gun they wield, they are able to evoke some fear in the administration at the village/block/district level. They, consequently, prevent the common villager's powerlessness over the neglect or violation of protective laws like PESA e.g. warning a *talathi*, who might be demanding bribes in return for fulfilling the duty mandated to him under the Forest Rights Act, a trader who might be paying an exploitative rate for forest produce or a contractor who is violating the minimum wage. It was found to be violating the Forest Rights Act (FRA), the Forest Conservation Act, the Environment Protection Act and the Panchayats (Extension to Scheduled Areas) Act, which applies to STs covered under the 5th schedule of the Constitution of India (Nai Azadi Udghosh, 2010).

On the other hand, the LWE ideology is brutal and cynical. It attacks perceived class opponents and even carries out political assassinations, e.g. panchayat members from rival political parties, who might have proximity to the administration and are seen as exploiters of the people or a political threat. Further, the party's violence is now resulting in an armed response from the state with the nebulous aim of ending LWE influence on the ground and extending the state's control villages in their control. As a result of this, there is increasingly no middle ground in PESA areas and communities here face violence and displacement.

The atrocities of LWE was not accepted by some areas in Chhattisgarh and similarly the extra-constitutional Salwa Judum's scorched earth policy have also induced displacement which current policies are not adequately responsive to. This effort made many LWEs workers to move to places like Khammam in Andhra Pradesh or Malkangiri in Odisha. These are also 5th schedule areas, these displaced communities are treated as non-citizens at the best, or Maoist supporters at the worst. What is the effect of all this on PESA's implementation? Such conditions of tumult have disrupted normal life, rendering PESA meaningless on the ground. While security personnel do not have a direct role in the implementation of PESA, the effect of the current militarization means they must concentrate power in their hands in order to win the armed conflict. PESA did not envisage this extreme scenario, and so its provisions are not geared to address such challenges. Therefore, it is necessary for policy makers to ask if and how the state's security aims can be reconciled on the ground with respect towards a law like PESA, which emphasizes devolution of power to tribal people.

The efforts of the central and state government in militarization of the PESA area has to be reviewed with the local people who are facing the direct problem. The irony is that the administration is blaming the LWE and the local people are blaming the administration for the poor implementation of the programmes and policies for the empowerment of the tribes. A comprehensive and holistic approach to the problem needs to address not only immediate dangers posed by armed men, but also infrastructure needs and economic development, provision of basic services, more effective democratic representation, and the quality of governance (Christensen and Lægreid, 2007).

The data accentuated that these districts (see Table 1) are badly affected by the LWE insurgence movement. The government interventions have not yielded results; however, the people are at the risk. These incidents are slowing down the development and empowerment process.

Table 1

Districts Affected by Left Wing Extremism

S. No.	*State*	*District*
1	Andhra Pradesh	Visakhapatnam
2	Bihar	Gaya
3	Bihar	Jamui
4	Chhattisgarh	Balrampur
5	Chhattisgarh	Bijapur
6	Chhattisgarh	Sukma
7	Chhattisgarh	Kanker
8	Chhattisgarh	Narayanpur
9	Jharkhand	Chatra
10	Jharkhand	Garhwa

Cont'd...

...Cont'd

11	Jharkhand	Gumla
12	Jharkhand	Latehar
13	Jharkhand	Palamau
14	Jharkhand	West Singhbhum
15	Madhya Pradesh	Balaghat
16	Maharashtra	Gadchiroli
17	Odisha	Gajapati
18	Odisha	Kandhamal
19	Odisha	Koraput
20	Odisha	Malkangiri
21	Odisha	Nuapada
22	Odisha	Rayagada
23	Uttar Pradesh	Sonebhadra
24	West Bengal	Midnapore West

Source: Minister for Rural Development, Government of India, New Delhi, 2013

From Table 2, it is evident that Chhattisgarh is the most troubled state, followed by Jharkhand, Odisha, West Bengal and Bihar, in that order, and have recorded the highest number of fatalities (see Table 3) in the past three years. Thus, these four states could be termed as the most affected states, where as Maharashtra and Andhra Pradesh have recorded considerable number of fatalities and could be ranked next in intensity. Thus, in all, the Maoist problem is spread across these seven states like Chhattisgarh, Jharkhand, Odisha, West Bengal, Bihar, Maharashtra and Andhra Pradesh, while in states such as Uttar Pradesh, Uttarakhand, Delhi, Haryana, Punjab, Rajasthan, Gujarat, Tamil Nadu, Karnataka and Kerala, the movement is in the organizational and therefore infancy phase. Available reports also indicate that some rudimentary Maoist activity has also been detected in Jammu and Kashmir and Assam, where the LWE were said to have investigated if the ground conditions are favourable to launch the movement there.

Table 2

State-wise Fatalities in Maoist Violence, 2008- 2010

State	*2008*				*2009*				*2010*			
	Incidents	*Civ*	*SF*	*LWE*	*Incidents*	*Civ*	*SF*	*LWE*	*Incidents*	*Civ*	*SF*	*LWE*
Andhra Pradesh	92	45	1	37	66	18	0	18	100	24	0	16
Bihar	164	52	21	15	232	47	25	16	307	72	25	20
Chhattisgarh	620	157	85	66	529	163	127	137	625	171	172	102
Jharkhand	484	169	38	50	752	140	68	76	501	132	25	49

Cont'd...

...Cont'd

Maharashtra	68	17	5	7	154	41	52	23	94	35	10	3
Madhya Pradesh	7	0	0	—	1	0	0	—	7	0	1	—
Odisha	103	28	73	32	266	36	31	13	218	62	17	25
Uttar Pradesh	4	0	0	2	8	2	0	2	6	1	0	—
West Bengal	35	19	7	1	255	144	14	9	350	221	35	61
Others	14	3	1	3	5	0	0	—	4	0	0	—
Total	1591	490	231	213	2268	591	317	294	2212	718	285	276

Source: Lok Sabha Secretariat, New Delhi

Table 3

State-wise Left Wing Extremist Violence from 2009 to 2012

State	*2009*		*2010*		*2011*		*2012*	
	Incidents	*Deaths*	*Incidents*	*Deaths*	*Incidents*	*Deaths*	*Incidents*	*Deaths*
Andhra Pradesh	66	18	100	24	54	9	67	13
Bihar	232	72	307	97	316	63	166	44
Chhattisgarh	529	290	625	343	465	204	370	109
Jharkhand	742	208	501	157	517	182	480	163
Madhya Pradesh	1	0	7	1	8	0	11	0
Maharashtra	154	93	94	45	109	54	134	41
Odisha	266	67	218	79	192	53	171	45
Uttar Pradesh	8	2	6	1	1	0	2	0
West Bengal	255	158	350	258	92	45	6	0
Others	5	0	5	0	6	1	8	0
Total	2258	908	2213	1005	1760	611	1415	415

Review and Monitoring Mechanism

The government has instituted a number of review and monitoring mechanisms for different aspects of LWE problem and the measures needed to deal with it. These include:

1. A Standing Committee of Chief Ministers of states concerned, under the chairmanship of the Union Home Minister, to work out a coordinated strategic policy and tactical measures to deal with the problem simultaneously on political, security and development fronts.
2. A Review Group (earlier called Task Force) under the Cabinet Secretary to review efforts across a range of development and security measures.
3. A Coordination Centre chaired by the Union Home Secretary to review and coordinate the efforts of the state governments, where the state governments are represented by the Chief Secretaries and the Director Generals of Police.

4. A Task Force under the Special Secretary (Internal Security), Ministry of Home Affairs, with senior officers from Intelligence Agencies, Central Armed Police Forces and State Police Forces, to monitor and coordinate counter-LWE efforts.
5. An Empowered Group of Officers under the Chairpersonship of Member-Secretary, Planning Commission has been set up by the government to over-ride or modify existing instructions on implementation of various development programmes and flagship schemes, having regard to the local needs and conditions in Left-wing extremist affected areas. The affected states have been asked to constitute an Empowered Group in the state also.

Specific Measures Taken by the Government of India (GoI)

Government of India (GoI) has taken concrete measures both security related and development related to counter the LWE. The GoI deployed forces under the green hunt in the tribal dominated and PESA area. The effort yielded results to reduce the LWE insurgence movement but hindering the development and empowerment process of the tribal communities.

Security Related Measures

1. Deployment of Central Armed Police Forces (CAPFs) Battalions of CAPFs are currently deployed for assisting the state police in the states of Andhra Pradesh, Bihar, Chhattisgarh, Jharkhand, Madhya Pradesh, Maharashtra, Odisha, Uttar Pradesh and West Bengal.
2. CoBRA Battalions: Battalions of Special Force trained and equipped for counter insurgency and jungle warfare operations, named as Commando Battalions for Resolute Action (CoBRA) have been raised as a part of the Central Reserve Police Force (CRPF). These Battalions have been deployed in the LWE affected States.
3. Security Related Expenditure (SRE) Scheme, under the Union Government, reimburses the expenditure relating to ex-gratia payment, training and operational needs of security forces, as also for assistance to Left-wing extremist cadres who surrender in accordance with the surrender and rehabilitation policy of the state government concerned, community policing, security related infrastructure for village defense committees and publicity material. An allocation of ₹ 207.54 crore has been made in BE 2012–13 under the Scheme, out of which 171.56 crore has been spent up to 28 February 2013.
4. Fortified Police Stations: The central government has been implementing a scheme to assist the state governments in construction/strengthening of 400 Fortified Police Stations at the rate of 2 crore each in Left-wing extremist affected districts on 80:20 basis. Under this Scheme, ₹ 220 crore was released to the states during

2010–11 and 2011–12. In the current year 2012–13 (Upto 28 February 2013) 136.50 crore has been released.

5. Scheme for Special Infrastructure: The Scheme for Special Infrastructure in Left-wing extremism affected states was approved in the 11th Five Year Plan, with an outlay of 500 crore, to cater to critical infrastructure gaps, which cannot be covered under the existing schemes. These relate to requirements of mobility for the police/security forces by upgrading existing roads/tracks in inaccessible areas, providing secure camping grounds and helipads at strategic locations in remote and interior areas, measures to enhance security in respect of police stations/outposts located in vulnerable areas, etc. So far, ₹ 445.82 crore has been released to the states under the Scheme (₹ 100 crore in 2008–09, ₹ 30 crore in 2009–10, ₹ 130 crore in 2010–11 and ₹ 185.82 crore in 2011–12).
6. India Reserve Battalions: The Left-wing extremism affected states have been sanctioned India Reserve (IR) battalions to strengthen the security apparatus of the state. 37 IR battalions were sanctioned to nine affected states, of which 33 have been raised. One IR Battalion each in Andhra Pradesh, Jharkhand and Maharashtra has been converted into Specialised India Reserve Battalions (SIRBs). Besides, nine new SIRBs have been sanctioned to the LWE affected states of Andhra Pradesh (1), Bihar (1), Chhattisgarh (2), Jharkhand (2), Odisha (2) and Maharashtra (1).
7. CIAT Schools: During the 11th Plan period, a scheme was approved to set up 20 Counter Insurgency and Anti Terrorist (CIAT) Schools, four Schools in Assam (see Table 4) and 16 in LWE affected states. The Ministry of Home Affairs is providing an amount of ₹ 1.5 crore to each school for development of infrastructure. The Ministry is also bearing recurring expenditure thereon and for equipment up-gradation. The land for these schools is provided by the state governments. They would also provide administrative support for running the Schools.

Table 4

Counter Insurgency and Anti Terrorist Schools sanctioned in LWE affected States

Name of the State	*Original Allocation*	*Revised Allocation*	*Functional*
Bihar	4	3	3
Chhattisgarh	4	4	4
Jharkhand	4	4	2
Odisha	4	3	2
West Bengal	0	1	1
Total	16	15	12

8. Recruitment in Central Armed Police Forces (CAPFs): In order to wean away the potential youth from the path of militancy or Left-wing extremism, recruitment guidelines have been revised to permit 40 per cent recruitment in CAPFs from the border areas and areas affected by militancy or Left Wing Extremism.

Development Related Measures

1. Monitoring of Implementation of Flagship Programmes: The Planning Commission has been monitoring the implementation of Flagship Programmes in 82 Integrated Action Plan (IAP) districts and also reviewing the progress of implementation through video conferencing of the following schemes:
   (i) Pradhan Mantri Gram Sadak Yojana (PMGSY); (b) National Rural Health Mission (NRHM); (c) Ashram Schools; (d) Mahatma Gandhi National Rural Employment Guarantee Act (MGNREGA); (e) Sarva Shiksha Abhiyan (SSA); (f) National Rural Drinking Water Programme (NRDWP); (g) Rajiv Gandhi Grameen Vidyutikaran Yojana (RGGVY); (h) Integrated Child Development Services (ICDS); (i) Indira Awaas Yojana (IAY); (j) Scheduled Tribes and Other Traditional Forest Dwellers (Recognition of Forest Rights) Act-2006.
2. The Planning Commission is implementing the Integrated Action Plan (IAP) for 82 selected tribal and backward districts for accelerated development. The aim of this initiative is to provide public infrastructure and services in these affected/contiguous districts. Originally, a sum of ₹ 25 crore and ₹ 30 crore was released to 60 districts during the financial years 2010–11 and 2011–12 respectively. This Scheme has now been extended to 22 more LWE affected districts, taking the total coverage to 82 districts. A total amount of ₹ 5,440 crore has been released to the districts concerned under the Scheme till 28 February 2013.
3. The Ministry of Road Transport & Highways is implementing the Road Requirement Plan-I (RRP-I) with an outlay of ₹ 7,300 crore for LWE affected areas to build road stretches of 5,477 km in 34 worst LWE affected districts. The stretches for Phase II of Road Requirement Plan have been finalized by the Ministry of Home Affairs in consultation with the Ministry of Road Transport & Highways based on the priority indicated by the State Governments. The Phase II of the proposed Road Requirement Plan involves a total of 5,624 km of road stretches along with bridges at an estimated cost of ₹ 9,400 crore.
4. Under the Prime Minister Gram Sadak Yojana (PMGSY), the norms for maximum length of bridges has been increased from 50 mts to 75

mts and the population norm of 500 for habitations coverage under PMGSY has been relaxed to 250 for LWE affected areas. Also, the minimum tender package amount under PMGSY has been reduced to 50 lakh.

5. Provision of funds on a 100 per cent grant basis (against a 50:50 ratio has been approved for LWE affected districts) for establishment of hostels for Scheduled Tribe girls and boys as well as Ashram Schools in Tribals sub-plan areas.
6. The Ministry of Environment and Forests has given general approval under section 2 of the Forest (Conservation) Act-1980 for diversion of forest land in LWE affected areas from 1.00 hectares to 5.00 hectares for activities like schools, dispensaries/hospitals, electrical and telecommunication lines, drinking water, water/rain water harvesting structures, minor irrigation canal, nonconventional sources of energy, skill up-gradation/vocational training center, power sub-stations, rural roads, communication posts; and police establishments like police stations/outposts/border outposts/watch towers in sensitive areas and laying of optical fiber cables, telephone lines and drinking water supply lines.
7. Under the Indira Awaas Yojana (IAY), the ceiling of per unit cost has been increased of IAY house from 45,000 to 48,500 for LWE affected districts.
8. Effective Implementation of the Provisions of the Panchayats Extension to the Scheduled Areas Act-1996 (PESA) and the Scheduled Tribes and Other Traditional Forest Dwellers (Recognition of Forest Rights) Act-2006 has been emphasized time and again with the state governments concerned. The Ministry of Tribal Affairs have issued comprehensive guidelines to State Governments/UT Administrations on 12 July 2012 for expeditious recognition of forest rights under the Forest Rights Act-2006 and have also amended the Scheduled Tribes and other Traditinal Forest Dwellers (Recognition of Forest Rights) Rules 2008 on 6 September 2012 to strengthen the same.
9. Civic Action Programme: Under this scheme financial grants are sanctioned to Central Armed Police Forces (CAPFs) to undertake Civic Action Programme in the LWE affected States. This is a successful scheme which aims to build bridges between the local population and security forces. During the financial year 2012–13, an amount of ₹ 20 crore has been provisioned for Civic Action Programme, out of which ₹ 13.27 crore has been released to CAPFs upto 28 February 2013.
10. Surrender and Rehabilitation Policy: At present the rehabilitation package, inter alia, includes a stipend of 2,000 for three years, vocational training, immediate grant of 1.5 lakh and incentives for surrender of

weapons. Revised guidelines offering better financial package for surrender-cum-rehabilitation of Left-wing extremists, inter alia, offering an immediate grant of ₹ 2.5 lakh for top LWE cadres and ₹ 1.5 lakh for hardcore LWE cadres including a monthly stipend of ₹ 4,000 each for a maximum period of 36 months is likely to be implemented soon.

11. Central Scheme for Assistance to Civilian Victims/Family of Victims of Terrorist/LWE/Communal violence: The broad aim of the Scheme is to assist families of victims of Terrorist, Communal and LWE violence. An amount of ₹ 3 lakh is given for each death or permanent incapacitation to the affected family under the scheme. The amount of ₹ 3 lakh would be put in a fixed deposit account in a nationalized bank for a minimum lock-in period of three years. The interest on the above sum would be credited directly by the bank to the beneficiary's saving account on a quarterly basis. At the end of the lock-in period, the principal amount of ₹ 3 lakh would be transferred directly to the saving account of the beneficiary. The financial assistance is released by the District Magistrate/Deputy Commissioner/Collector on behalf of the state government. This amount, is subsequently, reimbursed to the state government by the Ministry of Home Affairs. During the year 2012–13, an amount of ₹ 4.71 crore has been released by the Ministry of Home Affairs.

Policy Recommendations

- The corruption is one of the giant problems at the grass roots. The people are fully negative to the problem but not the government. The government needs to tackle corruption to sustain developmental activities for the empowerment of the people in unreached areas. And for this purpose, mass awareness programme should be launched at the village level under the leadership of local NGOs, colleges and schools.
- The government should implement the welfare activities simultaneously with counterinsurgency measures.
- The information dissemination regarding development and welfare of the people is more important than guerrilla warfare and curbing the Maoists.
- Besides the armed warfare activities, the government needs to negotiate with the LWE to emit the rebellion against the government.
- The government expenditure is mostly limited to the fortification of the police stations and procurement of arms and ammunition. The coordination among the forces on the ground is clearly missing and their mobility has been curtailed due to geographical constraints.
- The state must re-establish connectivity with local and tribal people as this can hit the LWE the most where it matters. The process of development must also have a human face to prevent tribal alienation.

- The security forces can only deal with the problem but not solve it. As far as the dialogue is concerned, a lot of negative connotation has been attached to the term 'dialogue'.
- It is a political war, wherein the current political system is being questioned by a group, which believes that another alternative system is good for society. It is important to convince the people and neutralize the belief that revolutionary politics is necessary and relevant.
- The government has failed to exploit the media to expose the true brutality of the LWEs. The LWE has exploited the media much better than we have. If someone produces a video called blazing fields, it goes all over the world. Perhaps, the government should start its own Indian Media blitzkrieg or the media could take some proactive actions towards this.
- We have to have different strategies for differently affected areas. Since they are targeting democracy, we should use democracy to target them.
- A political issue like the LWE conflict with socio-economic roots is left untouched until it escalates to a point where the government is forced to act. At an escalated stage the issue demands more time, energy and resources and is unable to seek the results that could have been achieved if it was to be nipped in the bud.
- The ideal manner in tackling any of these conflicts is to indigenize and localize them with least use of outside forces. Currently, instead of privileging the strengthening of the state police forces, the central police forces have been strengthened to treat the LWE affected areas.
- A people-sensitive approach is inevitable to resolve this conflict. This fundamentally requires political willingness at the level of state governments with the knowledge of local politics to take initiatives to recognize this people's problem with resources from the central government.
- A strategy to cease this conflict indubitably needs to recognize the problems of the people who resorted to using arms.
- It is impossible to deal with the issue in a short period of time. A long-term vision in this direction is demanded for successful implementation of the counter-LWE strategies.
- Key to the success of the state of Andhra Pradesh in countering LWE crisis has not been only in the construction of roads to remote areas of the state alone, but also in developing local production centres.
- The capacity building programme is primarily based on the reverse application of revolutionary field tactics.
- The proactive approach from the police forces as well as from the state administration has been able to gain the trust of the masses, especially

through community development programmes. This technique needs to be popularized.

- The new media could to be utilized with a conscious effort to mould or influence the opinions of those who can avail the luxury of new media.
- Additional aspects of the problem such as ideology, development and outreach of the government are yet to be addressed and till present this has not been engaged with sufficiently as there is no uniformed battle plan.
- If we discuss the LWE causative factors, they revolved around abysmal poverty, under development and a lack of infrastructure.
- The problem needs to be understood and women need to be gainfully recruited otherwise.
- Innovative measures need to take precedence over traditional methods. The strategy needs to be looked from three different perspectives, the local, national and international perspectives.
- When one says that the situation is improving, other indicators are easily missed – the organizational network may have improved but if one is to base it on the number of incidents, the problem is actually long term.
- The government needs to balance its response but more importantly it needs to focus on a third aspect of the problem; the ideology in the minds of people.
- The LWE problem cannot be curbed until the government makes significant changes in its policies. The difference between the law made and law enforced has to disappear.
- Proper measures should be taken by the government to run the schools and not give it as a shelter to the army and the police personnel. Using localized democratic, development units is the answer.
- Political vacuum exists because a dialogue with political leadership is not sustained. Tribal should be included and involved in a big way in development process, policies under consideration to make the tribes the stakeholders.
- The killing of the extremists is not the solution to solve the problems of LWE. The government should find out the root cause of the problem at the grass-roots level.

Conclusion

The current year has seen a decline in violence perpetrated by the CPI (Maoists). This is a continuation of the trend witnessed last year. The situation in the states of uttar Pradesh and Madhya Pradesh has remained by and large peaceful. The states of Andhra Pradesh and West Bengal have witnessed complete turnaround. In the states of Bihar and Odisha, the security environment has also improved. However, Chhattisgarh and

Jharkhand remain the core areas of LWE insurgency. The Government of India in partnership with the states concerned has articulated a 'clear, hold and develop' approach through security and development related schemes. In many LWE affected areas, these steps are reaching criticality. However, the CPI (Maoist) continues to attack development infrastructure to keep the population in their areas of influence marginalized and outside the purview of mainstream development process. But in significantly large swathes of area previously affected by the LWE problem, local communities are beginning to realize the hollowness of the Maoist ideology. There is a growing belief that the ideological paradigm offered by the CPI (Maoist) is completely out of sync with the inspirational matrix of present day Indian society and the world. In addition, the violence and brutality perpetrated by the CPI (Maoist) in states like Chhattisgarh and Jharkhand is resulting in widespread revulsion against them. Also, the propaganda machinery of the CPI (Maoist) led by their Front Organizations and cheerleaders stands discredited and exposed. The peace can be conciliated through democratic way; the insurgents were brought into the mainstream through their participation in the electoral process (Gill, 1997; Bhaumik, 2007: 12–13).

The tribal people in Schedule Five areas today are living through great hardship, conflict, dispossession, and cultural turmoil. The social oppression, discrimination, extreme poverty and neglect experienced by the tribals is inexpressible due to LWE and militarization of the PESA area. The tribal society is deeply implicated in this. If PESA is implemented strictly, we can reduce the Left-wing extremism to some extent and it might help us as a democracy, to begin rewriting this tragic story. Incidentally, this may be the last opportunity that the state may have to retrieve PESA.

References

Acharya, Arabinda (2006), 'Terrorism and Regional Security: Deconstructing the Global War on Terror in Asia', in Arabinda Acharya (ed.), *Global Terrorism: Genesis, Implications, Remedial and Counter Measures*, Islamabad: Institute of Regional Studies, p. 320.

Bharti, I. (1990), 'Bihar: Dalit Gain New IZZAT', *Economic and Political Weekly*, Vol. 25, No. 18–19, May 5–12, pp. 980–81.

Bhaumik, Subir (2007), 'Insurgencies in India's Northeast: Conflict, Co-option and Change', Working Paper, Washington, D.C.: East-West Center.

Christensen, Tom and Per Lægreid (2007), 'The Whole-of-Government Approach to Public Sector Reform', *Public Administration Review*, Vol. 67, No. 6, November–December, pp. 1059–66.

Gill, Kanwar Pal Singh (1997), *The Knights of Falsehood*, New Delhi: South Asia Terrorism Portal.

Iyer, Lakshmi (2009), 'The Bloody Millennium: Internal Conflict in South Asia', Working Paper 09-086, Cambridge, MA: Harvard Business School.

Mehta, A.K. and A. Shah (2001), 'Chronic Poverty in India: Overview Study', CPRC-IIPA Working Paper 7, New Delhi: Chronic Poverty Research Centre, University of Manchester and Indian Institute of Public Administration.

MHA (Ministry of Home Affairs) (2010). *Annual Report 2009–2010*, New Delhi: MHA.

Nai Azadi Udghosh (2010), 'Vedanta Flagrantly Flouted Laws Meant to Protect Tribals and Forest', August–September.

13

Struggles for Survival and Tribal Assertions in South-West Odisha

TAPAS KUMAR DALAPATI

Tribes are the most marginalized section of the society in India. They have been victim of modernization of the mainstream society, spanning from fifteenth century to the current phase of development. Ethnocide and destruction of life chances of tribal communities started long back with colonization of indigenous people's hinterland and today this trend has aggravated by radical restructuring of capitalism for globalization of new economic order (Havemann, 2000). In this trajectory of alien path of development ushered by the so-called mainstream society, tribals have been burdened with degradation of life chances through systematic exclusion from socio-cultural, political and economic sphere of their life. They have been systematically alienated from their native land since pre-colonial days and their plight reached at zenith under aegis of present insensitive neo-liberal state that has repeatedly been negating and violating basic principles of governance for the tribals enshrined in our Constitution. Against this marginalization tribals have asserted their discontent and raised voice against the marginalizing forces since the pre-colonial period and are continuously resisting against oppression even today.

The present paper strives to use political economy framework with a view to understand the structure of marginalization in tribal areas operating at the socio-cultural, economic and political level. This framework revolves around insight from history, economics and governance in the society of

South-Western Odisha to understand the root cause of various tribal movements. The paper analyses the involvement of Kondh tribe in the major tribal movements starting from pre-colonial days to the undergoing neo-liberal phase of development in South-Western Odisha. The political economy perspective examine social relations evolving between people in the process of production, distribution, exchange and consumption of the material resources across pre-colonial, colonial, post-Independence and post-liberalization development in the most underdeveloped region of Odisha. In all the above mentioned period of development, 'state' has been the salient source of discontentment among tribals. In all these periods, the political system strives to introduce new structure and organization designed to penetrate into the society to regulate behaviour in it and draw larger volume resources from its governed territory and invited wrath of the tribal communities.

Tribal movements in India have been analysed by various scholars and their perspectives have been moulded over the time, according to the changing regime, socio-economic and political scenario of the tribal dominated areas of India. Sociologist T.K Oommen analyses relation of state and social movements in India and identified four major phases (Oommen, 1990). First is the pre-political or stateless phase, in this phase spontaneous mobilization occurred in limited geographical area accounting primitive rebellion, tribal outbreaks and slave riots. The second was the phase of dominant imperial colonial state when the notion of nation-state assumed currency and severally collectivities – religious, linguistic, regional groups – began to claim nation-states. The movement during this phase saw anti-imperialist and anti-colonial mobilization. The third phase saw the spread of science and technology followed by industrial revolution and development of modern capitalism. It brought about a new class of political power holders who identified them with poor, disadvantaged and the oppressed and, thus, tried to actualize the socialist and welfare states, respectively. The fourth phase saw the consolidation of capitalist and socialist states on one side and limited number of post industrial societies on the other. It caused a global division of nation-states based on types of economy and the level of economic development. Besides the development of 'state' and social movement relationship several scholars working on tribal movement have evolved different typologies of tribal movement in India. Surajit Sinha (1968) classified tribal movement into: (i) ethnic rebellion; (ii) reform movements; (iii) political autonomy movements within Indian union; (iv) secessionist movements; and (v) agrarian unrest. L.K. Mahapatra (1972) identified three types of tribal movements (i) reactionary; (ii) conservative; (iii) revisionary or revolutionary. According to him, reactionary movement tries to launch a movement to bring back 'the good old days', where as the conservative movement tries to maintain the status quo. The revisionary or revolutionary movements are those movements which are organized for 'improvement' or 'purification' of the cultural and social order by eliminating 'evil' or 'low' customs, beliefs or institutions within tribal communities. However, there is no significant difference among different scholars about nature of tribal movements, but they excluded recent movements around forest rights, environment and displacement of tribals due to 'state' and private company sponsored development projects. Inculcating all the typologies, Ghanashyam Shah (2004) reformulated the typologies into (i) ethnic movement which include culture region/identity; (ii) agrarian and forest rights movements; (iii) environmental movement; (iv) involuntary displacement and rehabilitation movement and political movement for separate state. This paper strives to classify the tribal movements typified by different eminent scholars according to the nature of tribal assertions in South-West Odisha.

Land and livelihood base issues have the salient factor behind tribal assertions in Central India over the ages. An analysis of the land alienation process in the tribal hinterland of South-West Odisha depicts that the non-tribal rulers started the state formation process in the pre-colonial period. The process was further accentuated by surplus maximization policy of British colonizers in the later stage. In the post-Independence period, tribals became the victims of 'internal colonialism' and sacrificed their land in the name of 'national interest' for various development projects to accelerate the process of national development. After the 1990s globalization process opened up the economy and resource rich tribal areas of India to the global capital. Now the resource rich tribal areas are targeted by multinational mining and industrial houses for establishing industries and mines to garner huge profits with less investment. The new process of land acquisitions involved gross violation of tribal rights over land and forest resources, undermining the cultural ethos and environment of these areas. In this context, the paper throws light upon ethnocidal experiences of tribals of south west region of Odisha over the period of historical regimes from pre-colonial to present day neo-colonial era of globalization and nature of tribal assertions to counter the process of land alienation in this tribal dominated area.

Tribal dominated South-Western Odisha witnessed several tribal uprisings since the pre-colonial period. In this paper, analysis is confined to the tribal assertions that occurred in the tribal dominated area of erstwhile Kalahandi state which now corresponds with the Kondh dominated areas of Kalahandi district.

Kondh Rebellion (1881–1883)

The forested tract of Kalahandi inhabited largely by the Kondh tribes was called *Kandhan or Karonde* in the pre-colonial period. The territory was structured on the basis of the *desh* system. The Kondh tradition says 'Seven hundred years ago, 'we (the kondhs) came to *Karonde* or Kalahandi and cleared the forest (*rengal*) and settled the villages, hamlets (padar). Kondhs were originally twelve brothers and gradually from them sprang to thirty two clans' (Deo, 2009). The above Kondh tradition suggests that 'Kondh' were the first settlers who cleared the *rengal* or forest. A group of families took possession of a certain area, which later became their lineage or clan area and came to be known as *desh.* With the increase of population, segments or branches of the patrilineal clans set up new villages and hamlets. The heads of this patrilineal clan were the *Majhis*, *Umrao* and *Jhankars. Majhi* or *Umrao* were secular chiefs of the village and *desh,* respectively. The *Jhankers* were their spiritual head. The Kondh in general owed their allegiance to their *Majhi* or village head and the *Majhi* owed it to the *Umrao.*

In the pre-colonial period, land was plenty in the inaccessible tribal area of Western Odisha. In the pre-sixteenth century, in Kalahandi, the Kondh territory was regulated through traditional chiefs Umaro and Majhi. The tribals also never paid any land revenue on a regular basis; they used to present gifts to the king during *Dusehhra* or life cycle festivals of the royal family. In the later phase of the sixteenth century, the ruling *Nagavanshi* family of Kalahandi expanded and the younger branches allocated small territories as ruler along with fiscal and administrative rights to maintain themselves (i.e. Asurgarh,Thuamul, Mahulpatna, Karlapat, Lanjigarh). Gradually, this political fragmentation entrenched the rulers as independent kings. These independent kings tried to augment their resources and the estate, and needed agricultural surplus to maintain the state machinery. To meet the administrative and estate expanses, they accelerated clearing of forests and invited non-tribal peasants to settle in their territory (Deo, 2009). During this period, the new system of Gountia[1] and Zamindari came into existence and Western Odisha witnessed widespread deforestation and construction of embankments and irrigation tanks.

In the beginning, the *Majhi* or *Umrao* were general cultivators and the right to land for all members of the family was alienable. Gradually the office of the Majhi, the Umrao and the Jhankar became hereditary. The Kondh peasant had to present an offer to the Umrao on special occasions. In addition, the Umaro also started enjoying some land exclusively for their own maintenance; this would generally be the best lands of the desh. Their counterpart, the Majhi at the village level also enjoyed some land for their maintenance subsequently and these arrangements empowered Umraos and Majhis in the pre-colonial period during the initial phase of Nagavanshi reign in Kalahnadi. In the subsequent phase, some Kondh Umraos and Majhis also turned into Zamindars and Gountias in new land revenue arrangements.

The Kondh rebellion was primarily the assertion of the Kondh tribals against the emerging socio-political system introduced by Nagavansi ruler under the aegis of colonial administrative reform in the tribal hinterland of South-West Odisha in the last quarter of nineteenth century. In the pre-colonial set-up in the western Odisha, the non-tribal *Nagavansi* rulers of Kalahandi established a symbiotic relationship with the Kondh tribals. The non-tribal *Nagavansi* rulers to legitimize their status patronized tribal deities to gain confidence among the tribal. They also adopted various traits of tribal way of life in their various social processes through tribalization. In this process, every king of the Kalahandi took a Kondh woman as his first wife. In the coronation ceremony of every king, the Pat Maghi (Kondh patrimonial head) had a special role.

The importance of Kondhs in the Kalahandi kingdom declined due to the state formation process in Kalahandi. In Kalahandi kingdom, king Fateh Narayan Deo invited skilled cultivators from Sambalpur region and settled them in 1840s in the tribal villages to augment agricultural production and collection of land revenue. His successors also continued this policy after him. Fateh Narayan Deo discontinued the Kondh *'Desh'* system and abolished the post of *Umrao* in 1844. Each village was then assessed separately for new form of revenue collection. Villages were auctioned for a term of three years. Heavy *Nazrana*[2] was demanded at the time of auction from the *Gountias* or the leaseholders. The old system of 'One *Umrao*, One *Desh'* or single patriarch for a circle of villages was abandoned. The new land revenue policy had an adverse effect on the Kondh *Umraos* and *Majhis*. The tribal leaseholders who were unaccustomed to the regular system of revenue payment became liable to pay for the villages. The traditional clan heads failed to collect excessive revenue required from their own clansmen. As a result, they could not compete in the triennial auction with the outsider .ulta, .undhi and Mali caste people who were financially better than the Kondh *Gountias, Majhis* or *Umraos*. Gradually a sizable section of tribal *Gountias, Majhis*, and *Umraos* lost their position, power and prestige in the social structure of Kalahandi due to ejection from the traditional function of regulating land relations (Deo, 2009).

In the same period establishment of royal court and maintenance of records needed experienced persons in royal court of Kalahandi. For these functions, Brahmins and Karans (writer caste of Odisha) were invited from coastal Odisha. Malis or gardeners were brought from Nagpur; Muslim horse traders from north India were invited for various royal services and granted rent-free lands and villages to these service providers. Construction of new royal palace and new temples needed more revenue and the burden of the revenue fell upon the peasants. The new non-tribal leaseholders of Kulta, Sundhi, Mali caste had knowledge of cultivation and they exploited the peasants through the *'Da Bheti'* (gift labour) practices and became powerful in the local social structure. On the other hand, traditional tribal Kondh Gountias could not develop such a system of exploitation of their own people. Therefore, the king preferred the non-tribal *Gountias* to Kondh *Gountias*. Under the new land revenue policy majority of tribal *Gountias* borrowed money from the Kultas by mortgaging their land. The Kondh in general also suffered under the new system, mortgaged their land to money-lenders and failed to recover this. In the due process, they became bonded servants of the non-tribals. Their women folk became menial servants and the Kondh became labourers on what had been their own land. When the people in general and Kondhs in particular were suffering, the king went on increasing the revenue burden to meet extravagant expanses. When Udit Pratap Deo became the king in 1853, the assessment of Kondh villages was ₹ 22,000, it was raised to ₹ 1,27,500 by 1881. Due to this revenue enhancement, the Kondhs were ousted from their villages and leased out to Kulta money lender and the Kondh *Gountias* became impoverished in this process. Their impoverishment as well as their downfall in the local socio-political structure endangered a sense of resentment among the Kondhs and forced them to revolt against the exploitation.

The first phase of Kondh rebellion of tribal movements of Western Odisha led by the tribal aristocracies of Kondh *Zamindar* who suffered from ejection from *Zamindaris* and *Gountiaship* due to introduction of the profit maximization policy and concurrent changes in land revenue policy. In this period, the traditional *'Desh'* system was abolished and the office of tribal *Umrao* and *Majhi* was not recognized under the new land revenue policy in Kalahandi. The tribal aristocracies felt that they were losing grip over their environment and land. While the first phase of tribal movement culminated in dissatisfaction among tribal aristocracies, the violent phase of Kondh rebellions' immediate cause was widespread encroachment of tribal land by the *Kulta* cultivators who were brought in by the king of Kalahandi from the Sambalpur region.

In June 1881, some Kondh delegates went to Sambalpur to complain before the Deputy Commissioner against the atrocities of the non-tribal *Gountias* and the ruler of Kalahandi. The Kondh *Gountias* and peasants refused to pay revenue. Again, 24 Kondh headmen representing 121 villages went to Raipur to present a petition to the chief commissioner against enhancement of assessment and the exaction of *Nazrana*. Mr Ismay was deputed by the commissioner to look into the matter; he arrived in capital Kalahandi Bhawanipatna on 30 January 1882 and large gathering of Kondhs gave him 96 petitions relating to 749 villages. In the petition, tribals complained against alleged loss of old rights and privileges, their ejection from the villages, and enhancement of the revenue charges. On 31 January, the Kondhs plundered 85 villages in day light, while police, Paik and other officials became silent spectators of the looting process. Immediately, Kalahandi was taken over by direct management of Court of Wards by the British Government. The police force was reinforced from Sambalpur,

Raipur and Ganjam. The administration approached Kondh through the Majhis and assured reduction in revenue assessment. The Kondh leaders of the movement Khandu Majhi, Rajigaon Majhi and Dungi Pradhani and nearby 100 Kondh Majhis were called upon by the commissioner, issued proclamation order for restoration of plundered property, and promised enquiry into their grievances. Mr Ismay visited some places of Kalahandi and found Kondh grievances genuine. After discussion with the Kondh chiefs, the Kondhs surrendered ₹ 51,037 plundered by them to the non-tribal Kultas. The commissioner appointed Mr Berry, a British officer to manage Kalahandi state after the initial rising by the Kondh. Mr Berry undertook spot inquiry and found excessive coercion by the Kalahandi ruler and ordered surrender of the looted property from the Kondhs. To restore looted property, Mr Berry arrested Magho Kondh and Jagat Gaud who participated in the plunder of Iswar *Gountia* of Asirgarh. The Kondh demanded release of Jagat Gaud. When Mr Berry refused to do the same, the Kondhs killed Iswar *Gountia* and his head, flesh and liver circulated through out the Kalahandi as a beginning symbol of an armed uprising. The uprising spread to other areas of Kalahandi, 400 Kultas were killed and 142 villages plundered. On 5 May 1882 nearly 600 Kondh proceeded to Bhawanipatna to attack treasury but were stopped by the Tahsildar. Mr Berry took suppressive measures to stop the rising. British forces burnt down Kondh villages, several Kondh leaders mere arrested and publicly flogged, and seven leaders were instantly hanged. Subsequently, the Kondh uprising was ruthlessly suppressed by the British administration. An important feature of violent phase of Kondh uprising of 1882–1883 was that the non-tribal service performing castes like Gauds, Doms, and Ghansi also joined with the Kondh tribal against the exploiters that includes also Kondh *Gountias*.

Save Indravati Movement (1989–1992)

Save Indravati Movement was a movement of tribals for getting just rehabilitation and resettlement of tribals of Kalahandi and adjoining Rayagada district who were displaced from the Upper Indravati Hydroelectric Project. Upper Indravati Hydroelectric Project was commissioned in 1978 and supported by World Bank aid in 1979. The project, which is located in Kathiguda at the border of Kalahandi and Rayagada districts, is primarily designed to irrigate the drought affected Kalahandi district. In this development project around 40,000 people, mostly from Kondh and Paraja community, were displaced from 99 villages. The very first phase of displacement in 1989 was followed by formation of a frontal organization of the displaced persons to voice the plights of displaced person of the project. However, the leadership of the organization was soon taken over by scrupulous politician who duped and harassed the displaced persons in collaboration with the government officials. This phase of the movement failed to advocate rights of the displaced tribals. The 'Indravati Gana Sanghars Parishad' (IGSP) was formed in 1990. With active support of 'Ganatantrika Adhikar Surakshya Sanghathana' (GASS) it pleaded for the displaced person's rights. In the month of August 1991, sudden flooding under construction tunnel took lives of 200 workers mostly belonging to tribal communities. This event aggravated protest movement against the irrigation project but the tribal movement to oppose displacement without adequate compensation was crushed with *lathi* charges and mass arrests in April 1992. A heartening feature of the Indravati struggle was the active participation of tribals from the dry areas and workers employed in the project. The tribals have sacrificed and lost their homes and hearth for national development but the irony is that most of the displaced are impoverished today and living under poverty and destitution. Electricity produced from this project has been provided to the non-tribal hoseholds in the plains, running industries in Odisha or even of the neighbouring state but the tribals do not have the electricity connection that was promised to them before the displacement. The Kondh and Paraja tribals have lost their land and livelihood in the upland of Kalahandi to irrigate the land occupied by prosperous non-tribal farmers in the Tel and Hatti valley in the plains of Kalahandi.

No Tea Movement in Thuamul – Rampur (1990–1992)

No Tea Movement was an environmental movement against the plantation of tea to save the indigenous forest and common land of Thuamul Rampur area of Kalahandi District. Thuamul Rampur Block is a highly forested area adjoining the Karlapat sanctuary of Kalahandi district of Odisha. Kondh tribals who mostly depend upon hunting and gathering from the forest and shifting cultivation inhabit the area. In the 1990s, government of Odisha planned to establish tea estates considering the geographical advantages of the area and decided to hand over 4,140 hectares of land to Industrial Development Corporation of Odisha. In June 1991, the peace of the valley of Thuamul Rampur Block in Kalahandi district was shattered by united voices of over 5,000 tribals, who demonstrated at the Block Development office (BDO) under the auspices of the 'Giri Anchal Bhumi Adhikar Samiti' (GABAS). They demanded withdrawal of the government decision to hand over more than 4,140 hectares of land to the Industrial Development Corporation for tea plantation, representing 295 tribal villages in the area. They were opposing the felling down of 5,00,000 valuable species of useful flora mostly used by the tribal to tea monoculture, which is totally alien to the tribal culture and local agricultural practices. In the movement, local Kondh tribals became successful to stall decision of the government to establish tea estate in the tribal dominated area. Earlier, several experiments of tea and coffee plantation were undertaken and as many as 2964 acres of common land acquired for the purpose to conserve soil in the area failed which can be now witnessed as abandoned coffee and tea plantation in the nearby area of Thuamul-Rampur.

Save Niyamgiri Movement (2002–)

Save Niyamgiri Movement is also an ongoing tribal movement against bauxite mining by the multinational mining company Vedanta Aluminium Limited (VAL) around the Niyamgiri hill range of Lanjigarh in the Kalahandi district of Odisha. Niyamgiri range of Kalahandi district is the abode of the Kutia Kondh and Dongaria Kondh community who are living with the bounty of nature. Construction of a refinery is in process while evicting tribals from the Kapaguda and Kinari villages affecting thereby the tribals of the 12 villages adjoining the Niyamgiri range. A total of 2242.33 hectares of private land and 1366.99 hectares of government land have been acquired until now. Since 2004, the displaced people received meager compensation for their land. The tribals who are opposing displacement and not receiving compensation are living under the great pressure of private goons of VAL, local contractors and police.

Tribals knew about the proposed aluminum plant when the Kalahandi district collector served notice for acquisition of land on 6 June 2002. In the same notice, people were intimated to give their opinion or register complaints about the proposed project at the office of Revenue Inspector, Lanjigarh by 22 June 2002. Nearly 1000 people assembled there on that day and submitted a memorandum to the Chief Minister with a view to opposing the project. One hundred ninety nine individual petitions were filed before the Revenue Inspector demanding cancellation of the project. On 26 June 2002, the district collector of Kalahandi called gram sabha meetings at the Gram Panchayat of Batelima and Lanjigarh called a gram sabha meeting. At Batelima, people did not allow the gram sabha to take place to discuss the issue of the Alumina project and demanded outright cancellation of the project. At Lanjigarh, though the gram sabha was held but no resolution could be passed in favour of the project.

Most abominable development associated with this mining project was that the people have been displaced from their houses through physical eviction by the district administration. The employees of VAL beat up many persons. The National Rehabilitation and Resettlement Policy require that land for land should be given after due process of consultation, particularly in the case of the tribals. Contrary to this policy, cash compensation was offered to the tribals but that was not acceptable to many of them. The tribal people living on the plant site are mainly Kondhs who are illiterate and depend totally on their agricultural lands and forest for their subsistence. They have deep spiritual and cultural attachment to their ancestral lands and settlements. They opposed the displacement vehemently despite being offered large cash compensation by VAL. In the face of resistance, the District Collector and the company officials collaborated to coerce and threaten them. An atmosphere of fear was created through the hired goons, the police and the administration. Many of the tribals were badly beaten up by the police and the goons. After being forcibly removed, tribals were kept under watch by the armed guards of VAL and no outsider was allowed to meet them. They were effectively being kept as prisoners in the rehabilitation colony Vedanta Nagar built by VAL. Apart from the land acquired by the district administration from the large number of tribals and the Dalits of Bandhagunda and Rengopali villages, land was also illegally taken over by VAL for which neither acquisition notice was served nor compensation was paid. About 64 households of Jaganathpur village, most of whom are Kondh tribals, have been cultivating Khasra No. 186 – a revenue land for generations. Encroachment cases have been filed against many of them. The tribal families evicted from the land by force were cultivating the land for generations but no compensation was paid to them nor was any shelter provided, thereby taking away their main or only source of livelihood. This has taken place even though these cultivators have been officially shown in government records to be in possession of this land. The eviction has taken place without any process of verification and is in violation of the special protection provided to the scheduled tribes. Though they approached the District Collector against the forcible eviction, no action was taken by him to restore the cultivated land to the tribals.

With vehement opposition for this mining project, an enquiry by the CEC (Central Empowered Committee, advisory body to India's Supreme Court) recommended closure of the whole project on environmental grounds has gone unheeded by the Supreme Court, which has repeatedly delayed judgement in the case during the very space of time when the refinery is fast nearing completion. Tribal's opposition under the Niyamgiri Surakshya Samiti (Niyamgiri Protection Society) was at first relatively muted in the face of violent attacks and arrests by police and goons. These culminated in the alleged murder of Sukra Majhi, a Kondh leader run down alone on the evening of 27 March 2005, on the newly metalled road to Lanjigarh (Padel, 2006).

To save the Niyamgiri range from destruction and keep intact the socio-cultural practices, the tribals of affected villages organized themselves through 'Niyamgiri Surakhya Samiti' to voice their discontent to the 'thekedar-sarkar-company' nexus which was trying to oust the tribals from their abode, the 'Niyamgiri'. In the VAL case, Government of Odisha was playing a double standard role. It was blindly supporting the mining project, which were repeatedly violating Indian Forest Protection Act 1980,

OSATIP Act 1956 and the Scheduled Tribe and Scheduled Tribes (Prevention of Atrocities Act), 1989. As the situation now at Lanjigarh is very alarming, the tribals are living under pressure and fear in their own land, the local goons, contractors and politicians blindly supporting the company and treating tribals as their enemy for short term monetary gains involved in this process. Despite opposition from civil society organizations and wide spread campaigning in the media, the progress of the VAL aluminum project is going on rapidly in tandem with the Odisha State that is marginalizing the poor tribals in the region.

A very interesting phenomenon is that the VAL has been tactically excluded those local leaders who are opposing this project and has co-opted those tribal representatives who are in the support of the VAL through the local elites. There are some non-tribal influential families in Lanjigarh, who exert a decisive dominance in the public affairs of the locality. These are supporting Vedanta. There are other elite families in the localities like the Pesnias, the Mahakuds and the Pujaris. These families came to Lanjigarh during the pre-colonial Nagavansi rule. The Mahakud family was looking after the agricultural activity of the Nagavansi family. Gradually, they occupied substantial amount of land in the locality, and emerged as one of the landlord families with ownership of land in nearby several villages. The family was also involved in money lending activity in the region, and in the process legally transferred the land of those tribal families, who failed to repay the loan amount, in turn making the tribal families tenants on their own lands. Most of these lands were unproductive in nature in the absence of any irrigation and due its existencc in hilly areas. When the proposal for VAL came, the Mahakud family gave away these lands to the company and in return received good price for it. The second family, which serves as the elite family of the locality, is that of the Pesnias. In the pre-Independence era, the Pesnias had some petty shops at Lanjigarh and occupied sufficient amount of land. Members of the family have also played active role in local politics and have occupied important positions like sarpanch, vice-chairman of panchayat samiti, etc. Besides, the Pesnias also run a construction company and work as contractors for local developmental works. The Pesnias are actively associated with Vedanta and carry out the construction activities of the company. These two families are the dominant families of the locality and closely associated with the ruling Biju Janata Dal (BJD) – the party which is in power in the state and which has brought the Vedanta into the state. These local elites followed a systematic strategy to give a shape to their action on behalf of Vedanta. These local elites offered proposals to all the active tribal leaders to support the Vedanta and receive some favours in return. Those who agreed to such a proposal were captured and co-opted by the elite with the personal as well as larger capitalist interest of Vedanta, and were sufficiently rewarded for such an act by the elite on behalf of the Vedanta. And those who denied such an offer were selectively excluded, alienated and side-lined from all public affairs of the locality. Besides, they were also subjected to physical assault, humiliation and threats by the allies of the elites. Therefore, the Kondh Adivasis of the Lajigarh areas have been the victims of 'thekedar-sarkar-company' nexus, who are trying to displace Dongaria and Kutia Kondhs from their traditional abode the sacred Niyamgiri hills (Rout, 2012).

Till now the assertions against the VAL is ongoing and it is interesting that apart from Niyamgiri Surakha Samiti, organizations like Green Kalahandi, Sachetan Nagarik Manch and several national and international environmental protection groups are working in the area for the development of tribals and participating in the movement for the protection of Niyamgiri. There are also certain organizations i.e. Lanjigarh Anchalika Bikash Parishad, Nabin Vikash Trust, Lanjigarh Unnayan Anchalika Samiti, Niyamgiri Adivasi Vikash Parishad, Shakti Organisation, Kui Bikash Parishad which are sponsored by Vendanta to create public opinion for the establishment of refinery and mining in the area.

Nature and Consequences of Tribal Movement

Previous discussion on tribal assertions in Kalahandi district shows that various factors are responsible for tribal assertions in this region. In the colonial period, the revenue maximization policy of British administrators in collaboration with princely state was undermining the traditional cultural practices of the Kondh tribals. This collaboration was responsible for violent Kondh uprising in Kalahandi. In the post-colonial period, several development projects viz Indravati Multipurpose Hydro-electric Project, Tea Plantation Project etc; acquired forest, common and tribal land applying the principle of 'eminent domain' undermining the communal land ownership and forest dependent livelihood of the natives. These processes caused protest movements to save their forest, common land and for adequate compensation for the lost land in the land acquisition process. In the post-liberalization phase, South-Western Odisha is witnessing widespread tribal movements against the multinational mining companies that are acquiring forest, common land and tribal land illegally in a round about way by involving government for land acquisition process. Although, the projects carry very meager long-term advantage for the government and illiterate tribals of the area, immediate monetary benefit in the form of mining royalty for a revenue deficit state like Odisha is being given priority by the ruling regimes negating cultural ethos of tribes of the region.

If we look into the tribal assertions in South-Western Odisha from the colonial period to the present era of post-liberalization, the Kondh rebellion of late nineteenth century comes under the category of restorative armed rebellion where Kondh tribals rose against the princely state of Kalahandi. The princely state of Kalahandi, as an agent of British Government, extracted excessive land taxes, *Nazrana* and abolished the traditional position of Kondh *Umrao* and *Majhi* and appointed the new *Gountias,* belonging to the Kulta, Mali or Brahmin caste people. The new land revenue relations were totally alien to the traditional land relation system prevalent in various *'Desh'* of Kalahandi. In this rebellion the Kondhs targeted the newly selected Kulta *Gountias,* who had charged exorbitant rent from Kondh peasants and exploited them through *'Da Bheti'* (gift labour), which made the Kondhs paupers in this process. In this 'Kondh Meli', (assembly of tribals) Kondh tribals along with service castes Dom, Ghasi and Gaud, who were part of the Kondh social environment, attacked Kulta *Gountias* but they also did not spare the Kondh *Gountias* in power who extracted more revenue from the Kondh peasants. The rebellion involved robbing, looting, plundering, and killings of Kulta *Gountias* and people, to whom they believed as root cause of their pauperization. Because of the Kondh rebellion, the administration of Kalahandi was taken over by the British and compelled the ruler to make new rules to curb land alienation of the tribals.

In the post-Independence Kalahandi and its adjoining areas tribals showed their assertions against various development projects undertaken in this area. Indravati Multipurpose Hydroelectric Project and Tea and Coffee Plantation Project were projects undertaken for development of the backward and poverty stricken area of Kalahandi but in these projects during the land acquisition process, tribal's traditional land ownership structure, their dependence over forests, common property resources has not been taken in to account. As a result, tribals resented against the alien perspective of development, which they felt would impoverish them in the end. The tribals, with the support of non-tribals, stalled the tea Plantation Project before the projects became functional. People asserted against loss of livelihood and ancestral land in the Upper Indravati Project but the movement was not organized properly and it was duped by politicians. All these movements that occurred during the post-Independence period can be categorized under environmental movement and movements for just rehabilitation for the tribal oustees. The movement involved *Pradarshan* (demonstrations), *Dharnas* (sit in protest) and petitioning to the officials and blockade of communication routes. Even if the movement against Indravati Project was a failure, it has compelled the rehabilitation authority to make compensation according to the socio-economic needs of the Kondh tribals with the help of civil society organizations.

The ongoing nature of tribal movements against the VAL is totally different from the erstwhile movements that occurred in the area of South-West Odisha. Earlier, the tribals asserted against the state that tried to impose unacceptable land revenue relations and land acquisition procedures undermining the socio-economic structure of tribals. After liberalization, tribal areas of South-West Odisha are now targeted for extracting bauxite and establishing smelter plants by multinational joints like VAL. These multinational companies are acquiring tribal land through the Government of Odisha using the principle of 'eminent domain' and displacing tribals from their centuries old habitat. Though, forests, common and tribal land are acquired through the government with a minimum compensation price, the companies have captured the local elites and hired goon to threaten Kondh tribals to vacate their land and succumb to the company's mercy. As the new forces of capitalism is not conscious enough about the cultural practices and land relation prevalent in the area, therefore the Kondh tribals of this area are protesting against the VAL mining projects since last twelve years.

Peaceful methods like march against mining, petitioning the government, destruction of property of the companies, non-cooperation in rehabilitation and resettlement operation to show their resistance have been undertaken. During this process, government is acting severely against the protestors by arresting the movement leaders, assaulting the women agitators, *lathi* charging, threatening and even firing bullets at the innocent tribals who are not aware about the present perspectives of development and still revering the earth as their bread giver. Several civil society organizations from all over India and abroad are supporting this movement to save the tribal communities from being marginalized. At present several petitioning and Pradarshan are being organized in the mining area as well as in administrative capital of Odisha as well of the country. Global supporters for these movements are also agitating against the financers of these projects in countries like UK that are involved in the repression of tribals who are struggling to save their livelihood and socio-cultural practices. The impact of these widespread movements is significant. On 23 November 2007, Supreme Court of India has stalled the VAL project on environmental ground. Influenced by the prolonged advocacy of civil society groups our parliament has passed the Scheduled Tribes and Other Forest Dwellers (Recognition of Forest Rights) Act 2006 to safeguard the rights of the tribals on their ancestral land and introduced new rehabilitation policy to minimize the impact of displacement on the livelihood of tribals.

However, the perseverant resistance by the Niyamgiri Surakhya Samiti and allied civil society groups, in August 2010, the Ministry of Forests and Environment had stopped VAL from its plans to mine bauxite at the top on the Niyamgiri Hill for processing in the nearby large Lanjigarh factory. After nominating a special committee of enquiry, the Saxena Committee, the Minister had agreed to its findings that Vedanta Ltd had infringed the Forest Right Act-2006 that protect especially the Kondh's forests. In a precedent setting decision in April 2013, the Supreme Court applied the Forest Rights Act for the first time saying that it was up to the local communities to decide whether the project should go forward through public consultations and votes in each of the surrounding villages. Keeping in view the directives of Supreme Court of India, the Government of Odisha was bound to organize Pallisabha in 12 villages, and majority of Pallisabhas have voted against the VAL mining project unanimously in the presence of judicial officers. Now it seems that the 12-year long 'Save Niyamgiri Movement' against bauxite mining in the Niyamgiri Hill will finally be won by the Kondhs of Kalahandi.

In conclusion, it can be said that whenever the rulers/state tried to disturb the existing social relations of the people in the process of production, distribution, exchange and consumption of the material resources in Kondh dominated Kalahnadi, Kondhs have resented incursions of unwanted Exploiters in their territory. But it is unfortunate that after six decades of Independence, affirmative action and legislation to prevent alienation of tribal land the state have been repeatedly transgressing its own laws and Kondhs have been struggling hard for ensuring their livelihood over the ages.

Notes

1. Gountias are the village headmen responsible for revenue collection in the villages of Kalahandi kingdom under new land revenue arrangements initiated by Nagavansi ruler under the aegis of colonial rulers.
2. During the triennial renewal of *gountiahi* tenure, heavy side payment or tribute demanded from the gountias by the rulers to renew their headship in the villages.

References

Deo, Fanindam (2009), *Roots of Poverty: A Social History,* Bhubaneswar: Amadeus Press.

Gadgil, Madhav and Ramachandra Guha (1994), 'Ecological Conflicts and Environmental Movement in India', *Development and Change,* Vol. 25, No. 1, pp. 101–36.

Havemann, P. (2000), 'Enmeshed in the Web? Indigenous People's Rights in the Network Society', in Robin Cohen and Shirin M. Rai (eds), *Global Social Movement,* London: The Ethlone Press, pp. 18–32.

Mahapatra, L.K. (1972), 'Social Movements among Tribes in India', in K.S. Singh (ed.), *Tribal Situation in India,* Simla: Indian Institute of Advanced Studies, pp. 399–409.

Oommen, T.K. (1990), *Protest and Change: Studies in Social Movements,* New Delhi: Sage Publications.

Padel, Felix and Samarendra Das (2006), *Anthropology of a Genocide: Tribal Movements in Central India against Over-industrialisation,* Report for the SAAG, http://www.freewebs.com/epgorissa/FelixPadel-Samarendra Das.pdf

Rout, Satyapriya (2012), 'Capture, Co-option and Exclusion: Local Governance and Neo-liberal Development in the Scheduled Areas of Orissa', Paper presented in National Seminar on Development and Discontent in Contemporary Tribal India at the M.P. Institute of Social Science Research, Ujjain during 28–29 February.

Shah, Ghanshyam (2004), *Social Movements in India: A Review of Literature,* New Delhi: Sage Publications.

Sinha, Surajit (1968), 'Tribal Solidarity and Messianic Movement: A Review Article', *Contributions to Indian Sociology,* Vol. 2, New Series, pp. 112–118.

14

Naxalite Movement and the Involvement of Tribes

West Bengal Situation

SUBHRENDU MAITI

Organized mainly by the Leftist political parties, there has been a number of widespread agrarian unrest in West Bengal as well as in some other states of India during the last three decades, to force the government to fulfil its commitment to effect equitable redistribution of land among the landless peasantry, who had been deprived variously by the land holding classes and wallowing in extreme poverty and misery ever since the introduction of the land tenure system of the 'Permanent Settlement' in 1793 in Bengal and later in some other states of India by the British and as such became extremely restive and had resorted at times to armed conflicts with the land holding classes for acquisition of adequate agricultural lands for their survival. West Bengal has been the safe breeding ground of various movements in the socio-political set-up of India. Due to defective land tenure system and centuries of neglect of the peasantry, agrarian unrests have a common feature, even today. Perpetual poverty of the rural people and some inherent defects in agrarian infrastructure have created growing discontent among tillers of the soil. Gradually, agrarian conflicts spread over a large area and gained considerable momentum.

The adverse economic situation and pervading poverty that still engulf the rural areas, amidst 'oft-repeated' ideology of democracy and socialism propounded by the leaders of the ruling party and the government have created a sense of frustration that envelope the mind of the average villagers, since they have not been benefitted by the national plans. Under such circumstances, village life oscillated in dualism and becomes occasionally surcharged with conflicts and tensions. Sometimes, these break out in a violent form at different places. The different phases of agrarian unrest in India are a pointer to the fact of impractical agrarian and economic planning.

In West Bengal, there have been a series of such major agrarian unrests and clashes of which Naxalite Movement of 1967–71 took almost a revolutionary shape, and by its impact, had compelled both the central and the state government to effect certain basic land reform measures to pacify the agitated peasantry (Sengupta, 1977). It may be noted that the areas where the Naxalite Movement initially erupted are in West Bengal and it spread over in the rural areas like Debra and Gopiballavpur in the district of Midnapur (now West Midnapur). It spreads over like wild fire. The areas of movements are mostly concentrated by large number of tribal communities, and the local leadership in most cases handed over to them who are not only the sons of the soil but also they are culturally and linguistically non-communicable to the outsiders. They have the strong in-group sentiment, i.e. ethnocentrism which offered them an opportunity to build up a strong and powerful base.

In this paper, an attempt has been made to highlight the various stages of successes and drawbacks of the Naxalite Movement and the involvement of the tribes which took a violent turn in the name of 'Armed Agrarian Revolution' in 1967–1971. The depth and magnitude of this movement have induced to study the manifold causes and aspects of this agrarian tension of West Bengal. For this study most of the data had been collected through field survey in the three police stations namely Naxalbari in Darjeeling, Debra and Gopiballavpur of Midnapur districts in West Bengal.

Movement at a Glance

The movement was initiated from the Naxalbari police station. Naxalbari was one of the most volcanic centres of West Bengal where intermittent armed classes occurred in the year 1967 during the regime of the United Front Government, between the land-holding privileged sections and the poor peasantry for possession of land they cultivated. Following this, there had been persistent demands for effecting rational land reforms. Shortly after the uprisings of Naxalbari in the year 1968, Debra and Gopiballavpur – the two almost unknown police stations in the district of Midnapur (undivided) became the strongholds of these movements and, thus, became famous all over the country for resorting to 'Guerrilla Warfare' tactics for effecting forced land reforms. This movement gradually spread to many other places of West Bengal, as well as to different parts of India in the name of 'Naxalite Movement' (as it was started initially from Naxalbari police station), for mobilizing the peasants as well as the rural proletariats and canalized their crave for agricultural land through armed struggle and to grab political power (Maity, 1977a, 1977b).

The significance of the 'Naxalite Movement' was that it was the first 'Maoist' type of movement in this country. Charu Mazumdar, the supreme propagator of this movement, invoked the principles of Mao-Tse-Tung every now and then, and directed the party cadres that it should be conducted strictly on Chinese line. He also referred to Marx, Lenin, Stalin to justify this armed struggle by the peasantry. He always inspired the people to read Mao's 'Red Book'. Three articles and the three main rules of discipline and eight points of unity. By inspiration of the ideology of Mao-Tse-Tung, Charu Mazumdar, the chairman of the new party i.e. CPI(ML), issued the directives for resorting to 'Guerrilla Warfare' for the success of the movement. The first directive was that 'complete secrecy must be observed in forming 'Guerrilla Unit'. No inkling of such conspiracy should be talked between individuals and on a person to person basis and it is necessary to keep every Unit under a 'Commander'. By introducing the 'discipline and training in the malcontents' their main aim was to canalize the agrarian and tribal unrests against the 'bourgeostic' social system. Their main emphasis was 'on arming the peasants, organizing guerrilla bands and consolidating their power in certain areas which can, in the end, serve as secure bases'.

The movement of Naxalbari, Debra-Gopiballavpur and Birbhum represents three stages of actions and their dimensions in West Bengal. In Naxalbari, the idea was given shape by way of a 'model armed struggle' in the year 1967; in Debra-Gopiballavpur the Guerrilla warfare was launched with conventional weapons in 1969 and in Birbhum, it was conducted with firearms and the guerrilla claimed themselves as a 'Liberation Army' in 1971 at the last phase of this revolution.

Naxalbari area is situated along the international boarder comprising approximately 100 sq miles of highly strategic territory and flanked by Bangladesh on the east, Nepal on the west and Sikkim on the north. Tibet and Bhutan are also situated at about 30–40 miles away on the north of Naxalbari. Besides, this area is also connected with the North-Eastern states of India. Debra and Gopiballavpur are located in the southern border district of West Bengal called Midnapur (now West Midnapur) and adjacent to the states of Jharkhand and Odisha. In Birbhum, the area is not difficult to reach like Naxalbari and Debra-Gopiballavpur. Ecology, environment and facility for quick mobilization of striking Guerrilla Units were considered as advantagious for launching the movement at these places. Besides, these areas are mostly hilly and forest clad inhabited by a large number of tribal communities (Banerjee, 1980).

Though the tribals and the peasants, with whom the Naxalite Movement initially erupted had no or very little consciousness of the situations prevalent in the National Polity. The tribal communities in all the areas of Naxalite operations had been gradually exposed to social, economic as well as political forces generated by the larger society, but they had no clear concept (except a few) of the exact motive and causes of this struggle. Naturally, the tribal participation in the leadership structure of the movement was very marginal and segmental though the central leaders of this movement took the opportunity to control and lead their operation in the tribal concentrated areas.

The movement of Naxalbari started from early March 1967. On 2 March 1967, the United Front Ministry was sworn in and on 3 March, just one day after the formation of the Ministry, a good number of forcible occupation of land occurred in the Terai region. The movement took a bad turn when a tribal share-cropper named Bigul Kisan was evicted and beaten up by the arm agent of a local Jotedar. The news spread like a wild fire throughout the region and as a result forcible seizer of land, looting of foodgrains and cases of arson were indulged in, on a large scale by the peasants. In the initial stage Kanu Sanyal organized 25 people, who were mostly tribals. Of these people, Jungle Santal became the most powerful and prominent tribal leader of the region who had a close association not only with the Kanu Sanyal and Charu Mazumdar groups but also with the local landless and poor masses. The situation in Naxalbari became tense in the third week of May 1967, when the Naxalites committed four murders, two of whom were labouers and the third one was jotedar-cum-businessman while the fourth one was a police inspector. After about 259 incidents of forcible occupation of land, arson, looting and 15 deaths had gone on records, the United Front Ministry finally directed the police to take immediate action appropriately. When the police moved in, Kanu Sanyal, Jungle Santal and other extremists went underground and peace was restored in Naxalbari in August. Kanu Sanyal along with many others were arrested late in 1968 (Maity, 1978).

The movement in Debra and Gopiballavpur came to the limelight in the mid-summer of 1969, but the spade work for it had been started towards the end of the previous year. Debra is within 60 miles from Calcutta and is situated on the Calcutta and Mumbai National Highway No. 6. In Gopiballavpur, Santosh Rana and his wife Jayashree and brother Mihir Rana took the lead and in Debra Ashim Chatterjee was in forefront. Lebachand Tudu and Amulya Kalopahar who belong to the tribal community joined hands with the leaders of Gopiballavpur and organized the tribals at a quick pace. Besides, this area was chosen as a centre of armed struggle for its convenient situation and most of the local CPI(M) leaders joined the new party named CPI(ML). The major part of the area is inhabited by Scheduled tribes of whom Santals constitute the majority. The entire movement of Debra-Gopiballavpur was guided by 'Bangla-Bihar-Orissa Border Regional Committee' of which Ashim Chartterjee, an intellectual from the Presidency College was the Secretary. Like Ashim Chartterjee, Ranabir Samaddar, Dilip Sarkar and some other outsiders of Debra organized the local leaders like Bhavadev Mondal, Bijoy Das and Gunadhar Murmu, the most prominent tribal leader for successful launching of annihilation campaign against the class enemies at Debra. Ashok Maiti, a student leader of CPI(M), established a nucleus of this movement.

Gopiballavpur is an inaccessible area situated in a large tract of dense forest. For 'Guerrilla Warfare' the geographical setting of Gopiballavpur offered an ideal 'muktanchal', so-called as 'Liberation Zone' for its strategic advantages. From Gopiballavpur, Baharagora in East Singhbhum district of Jharkhand is only 5 miles to the north, Baripada in Mayurbhanj district of Odisha is situated 12 miles away from Gopiballavpur to the west and the tribal dominated forest region in West Bengal, Jharkhand and Odisha have direct connection with the people of Srikakulam district in Andhra Pradesh through Odisha. Gopiballavpur too has a large number of Santals and other tribes who are landless *bargadars.* After Naxalbari uprisings, Santosh Rana and his brother Mihir Rana, original inhabitants of Gopiballavpur, were attracted to the movement and contacted Ashim Chatterjee.

The Naxalite Movement in Debra was at its peak from 1969 to middle of 1970. In secret or underground movement, it is usual for the activists to suspect each other. In Debra same thing happened between the leaders, and as a result Baladev Mondal was suddenly arrested. Within a weak of his arrest, Gunadhar Murmu was trapped and caught. In Debra, the Naxalites could manage to get only a few fire arms, including one or two pipe guns. Spears, bow and arrows and such other weapons came in handy during the operation. In Gopiballavpur, the Naxalites confined themselves in looting, murder, arson and snatching of arms, and the people who joined them were mostly from the tribal communities.

Government Strategy and Future of Movement

In late 1969, the United Front Government was, however, compelled to change their attitude towards the movement launched by CPI(ML) in Debra and Gopiballavpur areas, as they continued murder and annihilation of the so-called 'class enemies' and created serious law and order problem thereby. By the impact of this movement, the effective control of the government had practically ceased in the tribal areas of about 200 sq miles and so it had been obliged to take some repressive measures to scotch off this violent movement. At first, it deployed a large police contingent and arrested about 100 suspected CPI(ML) extremists. Then the Eastern

Frontier Rifles came in action and the Central Reserve Force were also sent to these disturbed areas who conducted joint mopping-up operations in the whole areas, arrested them enmasse, killing some in the encounters and, thus, crushing the movement quickly with a firm hand. Besides, annihilation campaign through killing, arson, loot, etc. did not lead to the creation of 'liberated areas' and could not destroy the 'bourgeoistic' system in the country. In Gopiballavpur, towards the end of 1970, Santosh Rana and others practically disappointed and lost their faith in the annihilation campaign. Santosh Rana and Mihir Rana fled Gopiballavpur. In April–May 1971, under the leadership of Ashim Chatterjee, the 'Bengal–Bihar–Orissa Border Regional Committee' discarded the ideology of Charu Mazumdar. The cleft widened gradually and the regional committee was practically liquidated by the arrest of Ashim Chatterjee and later, by the arrest of Santosh Rana and Mihir Rana in Kolkata.

The Naxalite Movement in West Bengal with a view to effect land reforms by armed struggle failed for various reasons:

1. An armed revolution needs long preparations and well-knit organization, adequate supplies of arms and ammunition and long skillful training in the use of arms.
2. The weapons procured and used in this movement were more or less rustic and incompatible and inadequate for an armed revolution specially against the army and police of a modern State.
3. Due to extreme poverty and to satisfy their immediate needs, a section of the peasantry, who were mostly tribes, deviated from the main theme of the movement and indulged in loot and forcibly harvested crops not only from the big 'jotedars' and money lenders but also of other marginal farmers who had hardly 2–4 bighas of land. Besides, the Naxalites could not organize the common masses for 'class struggle' and 'class consciousness' which were the main aim of the revolutionaries. They mostly depended on the tribals and other backward classes in their operational centres for launching the movement, who were not fully aware of the ideals and aims of the revolution.
4. By nature, Indian people are averse to bloodshed and murder for whatever cause it is done. They consider this as crime. Naturally bloodshed and indiscriminate murders which were committed by the Naxalites during this movement alienated a large section of the people, who supported the movement some way or other at the initial stages.

Besides, the Naxalite larders adapted 'guerrilla' technique through armed struggle in West Bengal as well as in different parts of India on the Chinese pattern, which was incompatible in the Indian context. Revolution of China was conducted in the 1930s and 1940s in similar conditions which was obtaining in India in 1970s. The Chinese Government and the administration were decentralized then, with a weak government at the Centre.

But in India, the Government was very strong and intensely centralized and the administrative machinery was highly effective in comparison to the corresponding Chinese Government (Dasgupta, 1974; Roy, 1975).

Ideological Differences and the Present Situation

However, due to ideological differences, as well as mode of operations for the 'peoples struggle' in India the CPI(ML) which was formally formed in April 1969, has now been divided in to several groups and sub-groups and they are in a position to maintain their separate identities. The main splinter groups of the Naxalite today are:

1. Pro-Lin-Piao, pro Charu Mazumder Group of CPI(ML)
2. Anti Lin-Piao, pro Charu Mazumder Group of CPI(ML)
3. Central Committee of CPI(ML)
4. Unity Committee of CPI(ML)
5. Central Organizing Committee of CPI(ML)
6. Unity Committee of Communist Revolutionaries of India (Marxist-Leninist)
7. Maoist Communist Centre
8. Organizing Committee for the Co-ordination of Communist Revolutionaries.

Though the Naxalites have been divided into several groups and sub-groups, a section of them want to abolish the name of CPI(ML). According to Ashim Chatterjee, the 'CPI(ML) was a terrorist party and still it is now'. They think it is not necessary to retain the name of CPI(ML), and if they keep it, it will again unleash terrorism in the countryside. In West Bengal, like some other states of India, the Naxalite Movement is mainly concentrated in the southern border districts as in West Midnapur, and the contiguous areas of Bankura, Purulia and some parts of Birbhum which are popularly known as 'Jungle Mahal' region of the state. Very off and on they are confined to armed struggle and annihilation campaign which create a serious law and order problem thereby.

Some Observations

With the change in the government in 1977 in India and later in most of the states, most of the Naxalite prisoners were granted amnesty and released. Some of the front-rank leaders have publicly eschewed the path of violence and murder for any political movement, while some others still cling to it which is now more active in 'Jungle Mahal' area. Some of the leaders have, however, now realized the futility and redundancies of waging an armed conflicts for a cause which can be achieved by constitutional means. One of the leaders made a statement that 'I no longer believe that the rifle is the only source of power. A strong mass organization can be much more powerful'. Commenting on 'armed struggle' he has stated, 'I believe that the seizure of political power by armed forces and settlement of issues by war is the highest form and central task of revolution. This holds good for all countries, India being no exception'.

From the foregoing analysis it can be said that the Naxalite Movement in West Bengal as well as in India was never fore-ordained 'to be Maoism, pure and simple'. The achievements of the Naxalites under the guidance of Charu Mazumdar were a kind of ideological mixture of extracts from Mao-Tse-Tung's thoughts and actions on the one hand, and of Che Guevara, Rigis Debray, Carlos Marighella and to some extent, Herbert Marcuse, on the other. The Naxalism in India in the late 1960s and early 1970s had an extreme political-ideological background of the extremist sections of the CPIM, which was pursued with a 'logical consistency' and in practice it gave a new shape to the innate ideological discordances in the history of Indian Communist Movement.

References

Banerjee, S. (1980), *In the Wake of Naxalbari*, Calcutta: Subarnarekha.

Beteille, A. (1974), *Studied in Agrarian Social Structure*, Delhi: Oxford University Press.

Bose, S. (1975), *West Bengal: The Violent Years*, Calcutta: Firma K.L. Mukhopadhyay.

Dasgupta, B. (1974), *The Naxalite Movement*, Bombay: Allied Publishers.

Ghosh, S. (1975), *Political Ideas and Movements in India*, Calcutta: Firma K.L. Mukhopadhyay.

Maiti, S. (1977a), 'Naxalbari: A Seed Bed of Agrarian Revolution in West Bengal', *Man and Life*, Vol. 3, Nos. 1–2, pp. 91–104.

——(1977b), 'Agrarian Unrest in West Bengal: A Case Study of the Naxalite Movement in Debra', *Man and Life*, Vol. 3, Nos. 3–4, pp. 109–120.

——(1978), 'Agrarian Unrest: A Case Study on the Naxalite Movement in Midnapur, West Bengal', *Man and Life*, Vol. 4, Nos. 1–4, pp. 123–138.

Roy, A. (1975), *The Spring Thunder and After*, Calcutta: Minerva Associates.

Sengupta, S. (1977), '1967–1977: The Violent Decade', *Sunday*, 6 November.

Singh, K.S. (1982), *Tribal Movement in India*, Vols. 1–2, Delhi: Manohar Publications.

15

Adivasi Movement of Chhattisgarh

Some Issues

MITA SARKAR (DAS)

Talking of the Indian context in general and tribal India in particular, we find that the history of social movements is very old but the anthropological insight is yet to grow in the field. Some of the noteworthy studies in social movements have been offered by political scientists and historians but the anthropological works have been few and far between. Leaving aside the monumental works of Singh (1966), Elwin (1945), Roy Burman (1982), and Oommen (1972) we face a scarcity of what can be called as ethnographic accounts of social movements. Some scholars believe that those are of low level economy like those of South Indian or Birhor, Korwa, Kharia of the Central India, etc, do not find it easy to organize movements (Singh, 1983; Mahapatra, 1968; Sinha, 1972). The facts, however, do not support the arrangement.

As a matter of facts, the tribal landscape of India has witnessed various kinds of movements which are classified differently by different scholars. For instance, Mahapatra (1968) puts these movements into (i) reactionary; movement to bring back the 'good old' days (ii) conservative: to maintain the status quo and (iii) revisionary or revolutionary: for improvement/purification of the social order. K.S. Singh has divided the history of tribal movements into three phases: (i) One that coincided with the establishment of British Empire i.e. between 1795 – 1860 (ii) One that saw the intensive colonization and alienation from land and forest, i.e. between 1860–1920. (iii) The last phase of colonial history from 1920 – 1947. These divisions unfortunately turn blind on the movements talking place in post-Independent India though Singh's work on Forest *Satyagrah* brings some details of tribal struggle in post-Independent Central India.

The current movements have always been there, waiting to become visible on the surface anytime. As Rajni Kothari (1984: 218) observes, 'There is a growing awareness of rights, felt politically and expressed politically ... whenever a mechanism of mobilization has become available, this consciousness as found expression.'. Moreover, the frequency, intensity and coverage of the movements have increased with the globalization. As Nash (2005) opines the issues of social justice are more frequently voiced in global arenas today than in decades preceding global integration.

The present paper looks into the history of tribal struggle in the context of Surguja district of Chhattisgarh. The historical information reveals that the tribal movements that have been launched in the region have always revolved around the issue of autonomy specially with regard to the access to natural resources – *jal* (water) *jungle* (forest), *zamin* (land). Before going into the history of the movement in the area, we need to have a look at the history of the region.

History of Surguja

Surguja was the largest five feudatory states known by the name Surguja group of feudatory states. The other four were Jashpur, Udaipur, Koria and Chand Bhakar. Each state had it's chief but all of the five states submitted their revenue through Maharaja of Surguja. Each of the states were ruled by independent tribal chiefs in the remote past till the Raksel Rajputs from Palamau expanded their empire and penetrated their region. The Rajput kings adopted a policy of complete non-interference to the tribal regions and the rule is hailed as a golden period of the history. With the fall of the Rajput dynasty, the local peasantry fell into the oppressive hands of Maratha rulers but the difficult geographical conditions of the dense forest habitat protected the tribal population. It was during the expansion of British rule that the heat was felt by the tribals. It was during 1870s that the forest wealth attracted the attention of the colonial government and it introduced forest acts to wean away the tribals from the forests. The tribals organized themselves into various movements to reclaim their rights over the forest.

The Movements Bogtah Uprising

The earliest mention of the organized uprising from the tribals of the region is the Bogtah, who were inhibiting the tracts of land between Surguja and Palamau. Some 500 Bogtah united during October 1857 under the leadership of two landlords. With a little force, the British Lieutenant managed to disperse the mob which retreated in the thick forest of Surguja. The Raja of Surguja played a major role in curbing the movement. After a short spell of peace the Bogtahs rose again in November 1958, demolishing the police station and stealing away the crops. The official records shows that 16 rebels were killed, 30 wounded and three were imprisoned while only three from the British side were wounded. In the light of this rebellion, the talks were initiated in July 1858 to bring the area comprising of Palamau, Surguja, Udaipur and the sub-division of Burhee under military charge. But before that could happen on 27 December 1858, some 800 rebels sepoys made a strike in Surguja and Mirjapur districts. The military sections were fanned out to control the situation. By March 1859, it was reported that either all principal leaders had surrendered or they have been captured. The movement is seen as local presentation of the great uprising of 1857 launched nation wide to protest the colonial rule.

Tana Bhagat Movement

The Tana Bhagat Movement launched in Ranchi in April 1914 by Jatra Oraon sent ripples in Surguja as well. Jatra Oraon persuaded the fellow Oraon to give up the warship of spirits, to abjure animal sacrifice, abstain from taking meat and liquor and cease ploughing the fields and working as labours for other castes. Jatra Oraon's followers organized themselves as Bhagat's evading rents and taxes and asserting their rights over the lands. As the movements gets spread to the neighboring district, the authority took a serious note of it and arrested Jatra Oraon with his seven followers. The movement, however, survived and gathered steam again in 1818 when the Bhagats killed the magistrate of Surguja along with a couple of his officials. By the time the news reached Maharaja of Surguja, the Bhagat had further looted 14 villages, a police station and murderd 51 persons including nine state officials. The Maharaja, with support of the commissioner of Ranchi, managed to defeat the rebels.

Despite all the odds, the movement continued to breathe and metamorphosed into the non-violent form. Under the influence of Mahatma Gandhi, the Bhagat joined Satyagrah movements and courted arrests. The Tana Bahagat movement was such a powerful force for the colonial government that the DIG Chhotanagpur expressed his concern in a letter to the Government of India emphasizing on the need to wipe out the movement. The Maharaja of Surguja took the message of the rebels and kept himself abreast with the administrative details and made efforts to develop the area. The roads were opened up in almost all the directions which gave better markets to local produce.

Sporadic Events

When the Quit India Movement was covering the entire country, some sporadic instances of resistance and rebellion took place in Surguja. In his report, dated 15 May 1943, the superintendent of police, Palamau, wrote that there were three individuals – One an Ahir of Surguja and two others from Palamau who reportedly misguided the local of tribals – mainly the Kherwas, Panikas and others that the British had left India and people should now start looting the capitals. On 23 April 1943, a large number of tribals assembled at Tonga-Duban at Surguja with bow and arrows prepared by Korwa of Surguja. The expedition was on to loot a market and the house of merchant but the sub-inspector of Ramanujgang made a timely intervention and averted the massacre.

Forest Satyagraha

The All India Congress Committee (AICC) raised the issue of restoration of customary rights of tribals especially those pertaining to forest and its resources. The tribals found it to be a good platform to raise their voice against exploitative forest laws. Although there was a widespread resentment among tribals with regard to forest policies but it was not until 1930 that they could launch an organized movement against it. The movement which was first launched in Chhattisgarh at Raipur district in April 1930, gradually spread to Surguja. Large scale protests and demonstrations were carried out and all the prohibitive rules pertaining to forest were broken. It took one month by the British government to curb the movement. The colonial government was forced to grant certain concessions like the release of some part of forest land for cultivation and grazing, subject to certain safeguards. This, however, failed to please the tribals who wanted full rights over the forest. Hence, the tribals continued their battle and participated in the freedom struggle thinking that *swaraj* would bring back their autonomy in all spheres especially with regard to forest.

For tribals the *azadi* implied unrestricted movement in the forest and undisputed right over its resources. India achieved Independence in 1947, but not the tribals who were not granted autonomy over forests. The jargons of swaraj and *azadi* that were used to rope in the tribals held different meanings for the tribal and non-tribal freedom fighters. By *swaraj* the leader of AICC meant that India will be ruled by the Indian people while the tribals, thought that swaraj will bring back their respective kingdoms as they existed in pre-colonial era. Moreover, while the AICC leaders used the term *azadi* to create a picture of no interference from the British, the tribals took it as their freedom over forest and its resources. When the Independence of India was not found to be in tune with the tribal perception of swaraj and *azadi*, they felt cheated and launched a struggle to realize their vision of swaraj and *azadi*.

The Post-Independence Struggle for Autonomy

The Forest Satyagrah Movement received after Independence when the tribals realized that they were used as instruments to give impetus to the freedom struggle and that no measures were taken for the restoration for their rights. For them swaraj meant their own sovereignty and autonomy which was denied to them by the Indian Government because forest continued to be under state authority. The tribals took recourse to a rigrous agitation against the Government of India. This time the Forest Satyagrah began with the Khraiwar tribe of Surguja and adjoining areas in 1957. The other tribes soon followed the current, and forest rules were frequently flouted and revenues evaded. Again the movement was dealt strictly with coercive force. The dream to enjoy complete rights over forest remained unfulfilled, which torments the tribals till this day. It is said that the tribals of the regions got motivated to join Naxalite Movement with the hope to reclaim complete *azadi* over *jal, jungle* and *zamin* (water, forest and land). A brief account of the manner in which the tribals of Surguja received the Forest Satyagrah soon after Independence of India, is given here to elucidate the contemporary naxalite movement.

A party called Bhagat Party was formed among tribals of Daltonganj in 1950s under the leadership of Khairwar called Fetal Singh. The party called upon the people to stop playing revenues, use timber and forest produce freely. It claimed that the tribals had complete rights in forest and gairmazarua land (government own land). Fetal Singh and other leading persons succeeded in uniting the tribals of the region on this issue. Their speeches recorded in the reports and section papers give an idea of how strongly the tribals were motivated to reclaim their *azadi*. Here is an excerpt of Fetal Singh's fiery speech: (A free English translation).

'We feel that Britishers have not gone yet. We think that Zamindari is as it was before … Gandhiji had told us … tillers will be owners of land. But we are laboring hard and dying and others are making money … Why should they snatch our lands? … . Now we are not allowed to enter into the jungle even … neither the Zamindars nor the government has irrigated the jungles or planted trees. This is ours … . We do not accept this government. We will establish our own Bharat Raj. We won't pay any sort of rent or tax. We should unite and establish our own Bharat Raj, we don't accept the Police or Magistrate'.

These ideas were conveyed in meeting through speeches and songs. It was the best way to propagate and reinforce the idea through songs. Excerpts from one such song are translated as:

> 'Do not sleep brother kisan
> A Bihari wolf enters Chhotonagpur
> Collect stones to drive away …'
> 'The Forest bush
> was taken away,
> The bush, this hills
> were also taken away
> We are cheated'.

The Kharwars of Khobi village of Ambikapur (district Surguja) were first to launch a strike under the leadership of Fetal's friend Chuni who was earlier a follower of Gond preacher Rajmohini but the latter broke with her and led the movement. Chuni stopped people from paying revenue and forest dues, he used to raise slogans – *Jungle Zamin Azadi Hai* (land and fores are free). Chuni associates from various ethnic groups like Gond, Kanwar, Korwa, Kharwar, etc. felled trees in forest, demanded free use of land and forest, assaulted local officers and evaded arrests.

The resolution on the report of C.B. Kekre, District and Session Judge, on the incident at village Khobi, district Surguja, led to police firing on 12 January 1958 and some of Chungi's men attacked a police picket. A crowd consisting of 150 men and women, armed with *lathis*, spears, axes and *gofans* approached the police picket posted close to one Ghasi's house and asked the policemen to go away. When the policemen refused, the crowd started pelting stones at the police who opened fire in self-defence. Three shots were fired, resulting in the death of two persons and causing injuries to a third.

A few weeks later, Fetal also launched the agitation at village Bahahara, a neighbouring village in Daltonganj. There is a description of incidents which followed in quick succession resulting in firing on 1 February 1958 in a confidential report sent by the local authorities to the government:

Before we could reach the house of Fetal Singh, he and his men spotted us and collecting persons by shouting to their associates. When we arrived in front of the house of Fetal Singh, about 200 persons were collected there and had taken position, and were all armed with *lathis*, *bhalas*, swords, catapults, *tangis*, and *dhelwans*. Many of them were carrying stones in bags hanging round their necks, with *dhelwans*. They challenged us not to proceed further than the board. *52 deg ke bhitar police nahin barh sakti hai* (the police can not enter the radius of 52 feet).'

The magistrate warned the mob to disperse immediately, or it would be dispersed by force. The mob was explained that there was a warrant of arrest against Fetal Singh as his resistance was an unlawful act for which they could also be arrested. When this warning had little effect on the mob, the superintendent of police went ahead and explained them. Fetal Singh and his men shouted that they were prepared for all eventualities. The warnings were reiterated. When this had no effect, the Sub-Divisional Officer (SDO) declared the assembly unlawful and ordered them to disperse failing which they would be compelled to use force. On this a man told the officials that they had their own government and that they would not accept the police and Magistrate. Another man started reading out their *kannuns* (laws) that they had passed themselves ... finding that they were determined to resist the arrest, the SDO ordered '*lathi* charge'. A section of *lathi* party moved ahead on which the mob started throwing volleys of stones by means of *dhewans* which resulted in injuries to 19 men and officers including the Magistrate and the Inspector of Police. The situation was found to be very grave and the *lathi* party proved ineffective. There was great danger to the life of the force and the SDO, therefore, ordered the force to open fire. While the lathi aprty was withdrawing, a person from the other flank of the mob made a desperate rush towards the *lathi* party with sword. The first round was fired on him and he felt dead on the ground. Even this had no effect, and the mob continued throwing stones. Again, the Officer Incharge of Ranka Police Station warned the mob to disperse immediately; otherwise they would resort to more firing which might cause heavy casualty. But the mob was not prepared to listen, and advance towards the force, whereupon another round was fired causing injury to one person. After this Fetal Singh who was directing the operation from behind a cover, left and concealed himself in his house. After this the mob started retreating. The force was then rushed for the arrest of warrantees.

Fetal Singh was finally arrested, convicted and jailed only to be released against a bond for good behaviour. The Forest Satyagarh, thus, came to an end but the dream and desire of the tribals to re-establish their unquestioned and unrestricted relationship with forest could not. The tribal unrest and depleting forest resource led the government to constitute several commissions to review the situation and make suitable suggestions. In 1982, B.K. Roy Burman Committee suggests in its report to integrate the forest policy and tribal sub-plans for the benefit of tribal economy. Most of the recommendations of the committee were given due consideration and a new forest policy was formulated that came into force in 1988.

The new forest policy envisaged people's involvement in the development and protection of forests. It recognizes the symbiotic relationship between forest and tribal people. Hence, the new strategy was devised to control shifting cultivation, which involved an integrated programme of reclamation and development of land for the tribals under agriculture, animal husbandry, horticulture and forestry. As per the new policy, all the agencies responsible for Forest Development Corporations are supposed to associate the tribal people closely in the protection, regeneration and development of forests as well as in providing gainful employment to the people living in and around the forests.

However, the tribal interests and expectation could not be reconciled because it still did not grant them the *azadi* and *swaraj* for which they had been struggling for decades. They looked forward to *azadi* in terms of restoration of their full-fledged rights over forests and *swaraj* was understood as the rival of their autonomous control over it. The tribals are not able to re-establish the relationship with forest in a new way. This is primarily because of their ignorance about forest laws and the respective and intensive attitude of the vigilant guards and forest officials who question them for any activity in the forest.

The Naxalite Movement in Chhattisgarh

The Naxalite Movement began from Naxalbari in West Bengal. The day 25 May is observed every year as the Naxalbari Day to commemorate the killing of 11 innocent people (including seven women and two children), who were attending a meeting, by the Assam Frontier Rifles. The killing was in relation for the killing of Sonam Wagdi by a youth's arrow. Wagdi was an enforcement inspector who was raiding the houses of those suspected of looting foodgrains, arms and taking harsh and unlawful measures such as torture, extra judicial execution, to suppress the movement.

In 1980, another movement was started in the impoverished and under developed Telengana region of Andhra Pradesh by the People's War Group (PWG). Killing of class enemies, petty bourgeois, police informer and sentencing through its 'people's court' became the key features of the PWG functioning. The Andhra Pradesh Government also reacted with equal lawlessness. The state police carried out encounter killings with impunity. There has been a little difference between the security forces and the Naxalite in terms of lawlessness and violation of human rights.

The Naxalite Movement from Andhra Pradesh soon spread to neighbouring states of Chhattisgarh, Odisha, Jharkhand and Maharastra. The present 'Commander' Kosa, the chief Naxalite of Chhattisgarh hails from Andhra Pradesh. The Naxals are believed to have made inroads into Chhattisgarh during early 1990s when they had already established their strongholds in most of rural belts of Surguja and Bastar. In May 2005, a state government intelligence report stated that the Maoists had become a dominant force in 9 out of 16 districts of Chhattisgarh, viz., Kanker, Dantewada, Bastar, Surguja, Balarampur, Rajnandgoan, Koriya, Kawardha and Jashpur and they were fast gaining control over other districts of the state. In July 2005, the Director General of Police of Chhattisgarh stated that more than 40,000 sq miles of area spread over 10 out of 16 districts of the state are under the operational sphere of Naxalites.

The official sources estimate that there are over 3000 cadres of Naxals of Chhattisgarh. There are two units of Naxals – *Dalams* associated with armed attacks, and *Sangams* the hardcore over ground cadres. The majority of Naxals are the Adivasis, lending some support because of the abject poverty amongst the dispossessed, deprived and exploited tribals of the region. A certain of Chhattisgarh saw further stronghold of Naxalites who took over the control of administrative machinery. They distributed land records to the villagers. The *patta* given by the Naxalaties have maps of the land with the seal of the local commander. The Naxalite leaders settled land disputes and if their verdicts were violated, the accused were awarded with harsh punishments including execution.

There are several frontline organizations such as, *Chetna Natya Mandal*, *Mahila Mandal*, *Bal Mandal*, etc. The Naxalites have been reportedly abducting Adivasi children, both boys and girls, to training camps. The children, some as young as 14 years old, are sent as frontline combatments and used as shields during operations against personnel.

The Adivasi joined Naxalite Movement out of frustration with government or out of compulsion due to the force exercised by the Naxalities. Soon the people realized that Naxalite movement was not going to fulfil their aspirations of having free access to *jal, jungle and zamin* (water, forest and land). The Adivasis initially came to support Naxalities because they were frustrated with the exploitative policies of the government. There are several reasons such as the followings:

Forest Policies

Forest was to Adivasis what water is to fish. There may be little exaggeration, but it is true that forest was a complete way of life to many of the tribal groups. The first forest policy came up in 1855 with the introduction of a memorandum of forest conservation. The Forest Department came into existence in 1862 while the forest legislation in the form of Indian Forest Act came into force in 1878. The settlement of forest was undertaken around 1880 when the classification was devised into the categories – reserved, protected and village forests. After Independence, the resolution of Indian Forest Policy was issued in 1952. The new policy was nothing more than the extension of the colonial policy. Tribals were seen as the destroyers of forest resources and, hence, strict resolution was imposed to keep them at a distance. These restriction led to the widespread resentment that came to the surface time and again as protest and agitations. The Forest Act of 1927 made trespassers of the Adivasis – the original inhabitants of the forests. This Act remained in force till 1980 and the Adivasis continued to languish in the colonial hangover. Forest Conservation Act of 1980 was introduced to recognize the rights of the Adivasis and other forest dwellers. However, good it may sound but the Act failed to address historical justice meted out of the tribals under 1927 Forest Act. To control the situation, a committee was instituted to look into the matter. The 'B.K. Roy Burman Committee' submitted its report in 1982 which pointed to the need for integration of forest policy with the tribal sub-plans. To quote from the report:

'The tribal communities are not only forest dwellers but also for centuries they have involved a way of life which on the one hand is woven round the forest ecology and forest resources and on the other ensures that the forest is protected against depredation by men and nature' (Roy Burman, 1982: ii).

The suggestions of the committee report were not incorporated in spirit in the new forest policy of 1988. And, the eviction norms of previous Act still continue to remain effective. As the Forest Conservation Act of 1980 treated

25 October 1980 as the cut-off date for recognizing the rights over forest land, many Adivasis suddenly became the encroachers and, therefore, liable for eviction on the night of 24 October 1980. The National Commission on Schedule Casts and Tribes found that due to this Act, 1.48 lakhs of tribals became encroachers. The Supreme Court was asked to intervene but to no avail. The UPA Government introduced the Schedule Tribes (Recognition of Forest Rights) Bill 2005 but it was just the same as was the last Act of 1980. As such, the tribals are often harassed by the pretty forest offences while the timber mafia continues its business with the virtual impunity. The Forest Department officials and timber mafia play a central role to drive the Adivasis towards the Naxalites.

Police Atrocities

The tales of atrocities by the security forces and police personnel can be heard all over the country, especially in rural and tribal regions. There have been several instances in Dantewada, Jagadalpur and Kanker areas where police *lathi* charged indiscriminately injuring and even killing women who were in their advanced stage of pregnancy. The insensitivity and brutality of local police have also forced the tribals to join hands with Naxalites.

Industrial Houses and Development Projects

Often the atrocities by the forest officials or the police personnel have been perpetrated at the behest of either timber mafia and money lenders or at the behest of state or industrial houses of the country to displace the Adivasis for industrial activities. The industrial houses or development projects result in large scale displacement and constant outbursts resentment due to lack of proper and effective rehabilitation package. The Kalinganagar killing of 2 January 2006 gave a fresh case in point. The Chhattisgarh Government has reportedly signed MoUs with TATA and ESSAR Steel plants to be established in Bastar. This may lead to displacement of hundreds of people. The industrial houses have been instrumental in pushing tribals towards Naxalites.

The Naxalites have a long history of killings, abduction and plundering. The people do not know how to solve the problem and when the state itself has been unsuccessful managing it. A movement called *Salwa Judum* has been launched to allegedly fight Naxalites.

The Counter Movement: Salwa Judum

As the Naxalite menace staggered during 2005, a counter movement came up called as *Salwa Judum*. In Gondi dialect, Salwa Judum means 'Purification Hunt'. The Naxalite translate it as group hunting to instigate the tribals that those supporting people's movements are made targets for *Salwa Judum*. There is no authentic record as to when and how and by whom the

Salwa Judum campaign was launched. There are two popular theories. One suggests that the campaign was launched by a little known schoolmaster from Kutru who made his students to take up struggle against Naxalites. The other story suggests that it was launched by Late Mahendra Karma, a member of legislative assembly of Kutru against the atrocities of Naxalites. As per the theory, in June 2005, Karma's supporters reportedly organized the first meeting of the campaign which was christened by Karma himself on 25 June 2005.

Soon, the Chhattisgarh Government lend its support to the *Salwa Judum* campaign led by the leader of the Opposition in the State Legislative Assembly. On 25 August, the state government announced that it had set up a committee headed by chief secretary A.K. Vijayvargiya to provide direct support such as logistics, arms and funding to *Salwa Judum*.

The persons joining the Salwa Judum camps may be broadly recognized as (1) victims and relatives of victims of Naxalite violence, (2) persons who are allured by free ration and money, and (3) persons who want security in the form of recruitment as special police officers and police informers, and against persons who support the Naxalites. While majority of people join the *Salwa Judum* camps by force, many joined because of the incentives provided – recruitment as special police officer fetched a salary of ₹ 1,500 per month plus free ration.

Naxalite Vs Salwa Judum

Though *Salwa Judum* came up to fight against Naxalite violence and the Naxalites are staunchly against *Salwa Judum*, but the two movements operate in the same fashion and are equally damaging to the people. *Salwa Judum* activists unlawfully check the vehicles plying on the road, burn houses, kill innocents on refusal to join or on the basis of mere suspicion, they also force people to lend men and money for the movement. Like Naxalites, they too recruit minor and children in the campaign. Having the state machinery by its side, the *Salwa Judum* has become more of a menace. Most of the Adavasis are neither in favour of Naxalite nor in support of *Salwa Judum* activists. But they do not have an option but to support both. Both the movements have the same policy – each family has forced to lend a member and there are many cases where within a family one member is Naxalite and other is *Salwa Judum* worker. The two movements are dividing the families and the Adivasis on the whole are pitted against each other in the name of Naxalite Movement and *Salwa Judum* campaign.

The Adivasis of the state have become a rope in the tug of war between Naxalite Movement and the *Salwa Judum* campaign. The NGOs and civil societies in the region are making efforts to address the issue of fighting against both the movements. However, it primarily rests on the state to make feasible strategies to bring peace to the heartland of the tribals.

On the part of anthropologists, there is a need to make a holistic approach towards these movements and offer their analytical inputs regarding what leads to such movements, the change in their trajectories, coming up of counter-movements and, eventually, how the situation could be addressed in a more feasible manner.

References

Elwin, Verrier (1945), 'Saora Fituris', *Man in India*, Vol. 25, No. 4, p. 255.

Kothari, Rajni (1984), 'The Non-Party Political Process', *Economic and Political Weekly*, Vol. 19, No. 5, 4 February, pp. 216–224.

——(1986), 'Masses, Classes and the States', *Economic and Political Weekly*, Vol. 21, No. 15, 1 February, pp. 210–216.

Mahapatra, L.K. (1968), 'Social Movements among Tribes in Eastern India with Special Reference to Orissa', *Sociologus*, Vol. 18, No. 1.

Nash, June (2005), *Social Movements: An Anthropological Reader*, United Kingdom: Blackwell Publishing.

Oommen, T.K. (1972), *Charisma, Stability and Change: An Analysis of Bhhodan-Gramdan Movement in India*, New Delhi: Thomson Press.

Roy Burman, B.K. (1982), *Report of the Committee on Forest and Tribals*, New Delhi: Ministry of Home Affairs, Government of India.

Singh, K.S. (1966), *Dust Storm and Changing Mist: Story of Birsha Munda and His Movement in Chhotonagpur*, Calcutta: Firma K.L. Mukhopadhayay.

——(1972), 'Tribal Solidarity Movements in India: A Review', in K.S. Singh (ed.), *Tribal Situation in India*, Simla: Indian Institute of Advanced Study.

——(1982), *Tribal Movements in India*, Vol. I, Delhi: Manohar Publications.

——(1983), *Tribal Movements in India*, Vol. II, Delhi: Manohar Publications.

16

Forest Conflicts in India

Emergence and Impact

JAYA PHOOKAN

Forests in India are mostly state owned and cover an area of 69.79 million hectares, corresponding to 21.23 per cent of the total geographical area of the country (MoEf, 2013). Nearly 100 million people reside in forests and another 275 million live on the periphery and earn their livelihood from forests. The livelihoods of approximately 370 million people who directly or indirectly depend on forest products and services are, therefore, mired in poverty. Centralized operations with a focus on industrial forestry, have led to the neglect of customary livelihood rights and privileges of the forest dwellers. The protection of India's forest tracts has become a difficult task, seeking to reconcile the needs of the communities while conserving the depleting forest resources (Vemuri, 2008).

Forest resources in India have been increasingly subjected to deforestation and degradation. With the Indian Forest Act 1878, Forest Act 1927 and state enactments after Independence in India, the state gradually gained monopoly over forests. Forests were declared to be reserve forests from where tribals were driven out. Cultivating land, collecting Non-Timber Forest Produce and felling of trees became illegal. Forest dependent communities, who occupied these forests earlier, lost their habitat, their land, livelihood and all else that they had. The prevailing idea in the forest bureaucracy over the last 14 decades has been that conservation is the sole prerogative of the state. This notion undermines the concern and the ability of the forest dependent communities to preserve their own natural resource and ecosystem. And the effective alienation of these communities from their life support systems has resulted in widespread forest degradation, at the same time placing the state forest departments in perpetual conflict with them (Hazra, 2002).

Forest related conflict is widespread. More people competing for fewer resources, rapid socio-political changes, decentralization and expanding markets for land and forest products have heightened tensions and intensified conflicting needs and priorities for resources and their management. The colonial rulers had established state property rights over the forests in the 1860s, prior to which there existed unrestricted use rights in them. The forests continue to be under state property rights and, therefore, fall under the control of the Forest Department (FD). Ramachandra Guha (1983) has argued that before 1947, our forests served the strategic interests of British imperialism, and after Independence, they served the needs of the mercantile and industrial bourgeoisie.

The history of forest governance in India is replete with conflicts between traditional rights of forest users and decades of colonial legacy of 'command and control' forestry. Thus, a change from state ownership of forests to increased community access could lead to contradictions with regard to ease of access and entry into the forests. Over the years, socioeconomic and cultural conflicts for forest livelihoods have inflicted a heavy toll on the state's transaction costs and created several extreme social movements that oppose the state. Though the JFM programme is welcomed as a beginning for socioeconomic sustenance of forestry governance in the country, its qualitative and quantitative achievements are highly debated nationally and internationally (Vemuri, 2008). However, many view the present arrangement of Joint Forest Management (JFM) as a historic turnaround in forest policy.

Although this is true to an extent, yet in reality, the present arrangement of JFM is nothing but a share cropping arrangement between the state and local villagers. Still, most Forest Departments continue to perceive JFM as a grudgingly accepted 'benefit' sharing arrangement to buy some peace with the local villagers. Both the content and process by which most state JFM resolutions have been framed reflect the inevitably unequal relationship between powerful state bureaucracies and the forest dependent communities. In fact, the Forest Departments reserve the right to unilaterally cancel the JFM agreement if the latter is perceived as violating any given condition (Sarin, 1996).

Environment based conflicts which revolve around competing claim on forest, land and water have increased in frequency and intensity in India since 1970s. These conflicts generated a movement struggling for rights of the victim of ecological degradation which also challenged the meaning, notion and patterns of development. These popular movement and opposition also forced some notable changes in forest policy and Acts.

Thus, the present paper explores, through secondary sources, the emergence of forest conflicts in India, related movements and impact of these oppositions in bringing about changes in the forest policy. Conflict situations often characterized on the basis of an analysis of the conflicting actors, differences or incompatibilities among conflict actors and the process by which the conflict unfolds. In the present paper, forest related conflict between Forest Department (their policies and acts) and forest dependent communities have been taken into account. Incidence of protest and oppositions will be discussed from different parts of India.

Forest Based Conflicts and Emergence of Movements

During the British period, the sole purpose of forest management was oriented towards the redistribution of economic gains to the Empire (Kant and Cooke, 1999). This was achieved by commercialization of timber, restriction of the rights of local people and resulted in large-scale deforestation (Gadgil and Guha, 1983 as quoted in Vemuri, 2008). The change in ownership rights and the exclusion of local people disrupted the forest based livelihoods, further alienating the people who depended on the forests. This led to violent and non-violent resistance against the state by forest dwellers and dislodged tribal groups. The British Government ultimately conceded to forest-based community forest management for some forest areas in the Himalayas. These took the form of van panchayats (forest villages) in Uttar Pradesh and Forest Cooperatives in Himachal Pradesh (Guha, 1983).

Emergence of forest conflicts of the 1970s had a long lineage as local opposition to commercial forestry dates from the earliest days of state(colonial) intervention. The takeover of large areas of forest by the colonial state whose imperatives were largely commercial led to social conflict between state and people. The takeover of large areas of forest by the colonial state, thus, constituted an important watershed in many ways: a *political* watershed, in that it represented an enormous expansion of the powers of the state, and a corresponding diminution of the rights of village communities; a *social* watershed, in that by curbing local access it radically altered traditional patterns of resource use; and an *ecological* watershed, in so that the emergence of timber as an important commodity was to fundamentally alter forest ecology (Gadgil and Guha, 1992).

Almost everywhere, and for long periods of time, the takeover of the forest was bitterly resisted by local populations for whom it represented an unacceptable infringement of their traditional rights of access and use. Hunter-gatherers, shifting cultivators, peasants, pastoral nomads, artisans – for all these social groups free access to forest produce was vital for economic survival, and they protested in various ways at the imposition of state control. Apart from forest laws, new restrictions on *shikar* for local populations (while allowing freer hunting for sport by the British and the Indian elite) were another contributory factor in fuelling social conflict (Rangarajan, 1992 as quoted in Gadgil and Guha, 1994).

Ironically, in the post-Independence period, the process only accerlated. Economic development implied more intensive resource use which in the prevailing technological and institutional framework, led inevitably to wide spread environmental degradation. Mono culture plantations for commercial use, dams and mines exerted a largely negative influence on the forests. Prior to Independence, conflicts emerged because of the competing claims of state and people over a relatively abundant resource but post-Independence conflicts were because of a rapidly dwindling forest resource base. A newer ecological dimension has been added to the moral/political/economic dimensions of social conflicts over forests. These processes led to further marginalization of poor peasants and tribals, which are most heavily dependent on forest resources for their subsistence and survival.

Thus, the British period created large-scale conflicts among forest managers and the local people, which marked the beginning of the breakdown of a symbiotic relationship between many communities and the forests in which they were situated. After Independence, the central government tried to redefine social-utility and social-welfare functions, but the emphasis of forest management regimes continued to be on commercial timber exploitation and the exclusion of local people. In 1988, state ownership of forests rose by 50 per cent to cover an area of 67 million hectares through blanket notifications of forests by the government (Kant and Cooke, 1999).

The prevailing customary rights of forest dwellers, who were mostly tribal, were sidelined in an endeavour to expand state ownership of the forests. This was seen as a continuation of the existing authoritarian, exclusionary management. Gadgil and Guha (1983 as quoted in Vemuri, 2008) argues that there have been a number of notable similarities between colonial and post-colonial forest policy. This demonstrates that the national forest policy of 1952 upholds the fundamental concepts of its predecessor, the forest policy of 1894, and it reinforces the right of the state for exclusive control over forest protection, production, and management (Hannan, 1999).

Since the 1970s, there has been an awakening and advocacy for thwarting exclusionary forest management and conservation of forests through the involvement of local people. This was primarily due to conflicts in land ownership and rights over forest produce simmering all across the country. The states were also experiencing a resource crunch in meeting the cost of planting and protecting the forest. The 1970s and 1980s also marked deficit budgeting in most of the states and a shift of the Indian economy towards liberalization. This was also the period when most

Indian states were dependent on external funds to support the forestry plantations. This external funding amidst natural resource management conflicts was responsible for shaping 'people's face of forestry', alternatively called 'Social Forestry' (Vemuri, 2008).

In the Indian context, an adversarial relationship between the Forest Department and the people reflected the historical realities of past centuries. This led to the call for reorientation and attitudinal changes not only in the Forest Departments but also in the communities. As Sunder (2000: 256) noted, officials 'worn out by constant conflict between recalcitrant villagers and beleagured forest staff in which both sides had been known to lose lives and limbs … (felt) there was no alternative but to run from coercion to consent, at least in certain areas' (as cited by Castro and Nielsen, 2001 in Vemuri, 2008). The Chipko Movement (1973) in the state of Uttaranchal was testimony to the people's movement to reestablish a relationship between man and nature over the state's exclusionary management perspectives.

Role of Chipko Movement

The origin of the Indian Environmental Movement in an organized form can be ascribed to the forest conflicts involving the Chipko Movement of the Central Himalayas. In the Chipko Movement, a female peasant uprising in which protesters embraced trees, was successful in reclaiming the peasant's forest rights and stalling the felling of trees by contractors of the Forest Department. In April 1973, the peasants of Mandal, an interior village in the Garwhal Himalayas, effectively thwarted commercial felling in a nearby forest threatening to 'hug the tress'. This brought to the fore a simmering but widespread resentment among the hill peasantry directed at state forest policies which had consistently favoured outside commercial interests at the expense of their own subsistence needs for fuel, fodder and small timber. Thus, the 'Chipko' (Hug the Trees) Movement was born. In the following decade, a wave of protests against commercial logging swept the Himalayan foothills, coordinated by Gandhian as well as Left-wing activists. Notably, the region had a long history of peasant protest which Chipko both drew upon and furthered. As a powerful statement against the violation of customary rights by state forestry, Chipko brought into focus a wide range of issues concerning forest policy and the environmental debate as a whole (Guha, 1989).

Chipko Movement was representative of a far wider spectrum of forest based conflicts in India for example in tribal areas of Central India where the economic dependence on the forests is acute. In these areas, the 1970s witnessed escalating conflict between villagers and the forest department/administration in tribal districts of the states of the Bihar, Odisha, Madhya Pradesh, Maharashtra and Andhra Pradesh. In tribal

India, moreover, forest conflicts often have a sharper edge. Thus, in Bihar, they have been an integral element in the popular movement for a tribal homeland, while in four other states mentioned, the question of tribal forest rights has been actively taken up by revolutionary Maoist groups (Calman, 1985; PUDR, 1982; Sengupta, 1982 as quoted in Gadgil and Guha, 1994). Few individual successful efforts made in the states of West Bengal (Arabari Village, 1972), Haryana (Sukhomajri Village, 1976), and Rajasthan (Gopalpura Village, 1986) to develop rural livelihoods and regenerate forests through co-management in 1970s also caught the attention of foresters, India's politicians, as well as, international environmental activists.

Popular movements in defence of customary rights in different parts of India (Karnataka, kerala, Himachal Pradesh, Siwalik Hills of Uttarpradesh, Madhya Pradesh, Maharashtra) have focused on two issues central to the direction of forest management. First, they have contended that control of woodland must revert to communal hands, with the state gradually withdrawing from ownership and management. Second, those opposing forest management have pointed to the contrast between the subsistence orientation of villagers and the commercial orientation of the state (Gadgil and Guha, 1994).

This contrast can be illustrated by two strikingly similar incidents, separated in time by a few months and in space by some 2000 miles. The first took place in Kusnur village in a Dharwad district of the southern state of Karnataka. Protesting against the allotment by the state of village pasture land to a polyfibre industry which intended to grow eucalyptus on it, the peasants of Kusnur and surrounding villages organized a 'pluck-and-plant' *satyagraha* demonstration on 14 November 1987, when symbolically a hundred eucalyptus saplings were plucked and then replaced with useful local species. Less than a year later, and probably without knowledge of the Kusnur precedent, Chipko activists in the northern state of Himachal Pradesh were arrested on charges of causing 'damage to public property'. Their crime had been to lead villagers in uprooting 7000 eucalyptus saplings from a forest nursery in Chamba district, planting indigenous broad-leaved species in there instead. The Dharwad and Chamba episodes vividly illustrate the continuing cleavages between village interests and the commercial bias of state forestry (Kanvalli, 1991; Modi, 1988 as quoted in Gadgil and Guha, 1994).

Impact of Movements and Protests

These popular movements and opposition also forced some notable changes in forest policy and Acts. Local hostility manifested itself in many ways, including non-cooperation, deliberate destruction of forests and violence against officials. Such instances, along with the alarming degradation of India's forests, led to the government becoming increasingly aware that it was not possible to protect millions of hectares of forest without the co-operation of local communities especially tribals. On the other hand, more and more examples have been emerging about communities who have independently taken the initiative to protect vast tracts of forests in order to meet their livelihood needs, with remarkable results.

During the last quarter of the twentieth century, the Government of India observed that the unsustainable removal of forest produces coupled with uncontrolled grazing and illicit removal were the major factor of shrinking forest resources, finally showed concern to arrest and reverse the forest depletion and degradation process involving local communities. In most part of India, forestry was facing similar challenges. The government tried a variety of initiatives to curtail deforestation, but most programmes failed. The paradigm shift in the forest policies and legislations was noticed in the 1970s and 1980s, with the passage of the Forest (Conservation) Act 1980 (Damodaran and Engel, 2003 as quoted in Balooni and Inoue, 2009), which made the central government's approval mandatory for conversion of forest land for non-forest purposes and highlighted the primacy of forest conservation over other requirements.

During 1980s, evidence of success (experience of Arabari in West Bengal, Sukhomajri village in Haryana etc) through participatory approaches of forest management was brought to the government attention. Due to continuous deterioration of the forests, there was increasing realization that forest could only be protected if the people are actively involved in their management paving the way for the National Forest Policy of India 1988 (MoEF, 1988) which outlined the scope for people's participation in Forest management as one of its basic objectives (2.1), which reads as 'meeting the requirements of fuel wood, fodder, minor forest produce and small timber of the rural and tribal population and creating a massive people movement with the involvement of women, for achieving these objectives and to minimize pressure on existing forest'.

It is a tribute to the resilience of Indian democracy that as a response to public protests the government came out with a National Forest Policy in 1988. There is fundamental difference between the forest policy of 1952 and 1988. While the former emphasized on maximum resource use, the latter is an attempt to restore friendly relationship between locals and the forests. Of its nine objectives, most of them emphasized restoration and maintenance of biological diversity, ecological balance and environmental stability. One of its objectives was related to 'increasing substantially the forest/tree cover in the country though massive afforestation scheme especially on all denuded, degraded and unproductive lands (MoEF, 1988).

Thus, the National Forest Policy of 1988 identified the importance of local community especially tribals to a relatively larger extent. It was realized that active engagement of all community members is essential when control and management of forest is devolved to local communities. The 1988 Forest Policy formed the basis of Joint Forest Management (JFM) which is the primary government programme designed to share benefits with local communities in exchange for helping to protect forests near their villages (Government of India, 1990).

JFM agreements legitimated local people's NTFP collection and offered them a share of the revenue from 'final' timber felling in return for help in protection. Wage labour opportunities were sometimes also provided (from donor funds). However, formal rights were not provided and Forest Departments have often used the JFM programmes as instruments to further extend their authority structures through, first, imposing their management plans on village forests (even taking more lands from local people through planting trees on cultivated plots), and secondly, generating funding support from donors to shore up and even expand their staffing and salary structures. Over 100,000 JFM groups have been formed across the country, (likely to include at least 25% pre-existing community forest management and protection institutions), and the total number that are actually active may be less than half of the original figure. It is apparent that there is growing village level disillusionment with JFM, both because of the ad hoc temporary scheme basis, the perceived arrogance of many FD public servants and the general perception of a 'confidence trick' being played with no rights accorded (Baginski et al., 2009).

However, the 1988 Forest Policy marked a radical shift as it changed the focus substantially. It set a target of increasing forest cover to 33 per cent of India's land area and treated forests primarily as an ecological necessity, then as a source of goods for local populations with particular emphasis on NTFPs and, third, as a source of wood and other products for industry. It acknowledged the dependence of local communities on forests for livelihood, and specifically mentioned the need to involve women to meet the policy objectives.

In the light of National Forest Policy in 1988, efforts have been made to develop forests in a sustainable manner. For this purpose emphasis is on afforestation work. Under it, village forest, *panchvan*, development of degraded forests, road side plantation (tree patta scheme) and Joint Forest Management programme have been introduced. New technology has been introduced to meet growing requirements and grazing rights. Concessions to the tribals have been restricted to the carrying capacity of the forests and the market forces. Restrictions have been imposed on massive diversion of forest lands for other purposes, the relationship between tribals and the forests pertaining to collection of NWFPs have been redefined in favour of the forest and the market forces and shifting cultivation has been discouraged. Also, various forestry schemes have been introduced, forest based researches are promoted, women are imparted *van sevika* training at different places and financial and other incentives have also been given to industrial houses and the NGOs (Chaudhary, 1997).

It is claimed that these efforts have been made by the government in order to stop environmental degradation and to improve the socio-economic conditions of the locals by improving the conditions of the existing and the upcoming forests. It acknowledged the dependence of local communities on forests for livelihood, and specifically mentioned the need to involve women to meet the policy objectives.

Despite severe opposition, the Scheduled Tribes and Other Traditional Forest Dwellers (Recognition of Forest Rights) Act (or simply 'Forest Rights Act') was also passed in December 2006 and came into force in 1 January 2008 with notification of the administrative rules.

The FRA provides for the restitution of deprived forest rights across India, including both individual rights to cultivated land in forested landscapes and collective rights to control manage and use forests as common property. The passing of the Forest Rights Act 2006 undoubtedly represents a seminal moment in India's highly contested forest politics. For the first time, an Act has recognized the 'historical injustice' perpetrated by the state: ... the forest rights on ancestral lands and their habitat were not adequately recognized in the consolidation of state forests during the colonial period as well as in Independent India resulting in historical injustice to the forest dwelling Scheduled Tribes and other traditional forest dwellers (FRA, 2006). The Act, therefore, makes provision for the restitution of rights to forest dependent households. Although not covering all rights deprivations, the livelihoods of perhaps 100 million or more of the poorest of the poor stand to improve (Baginski et al., 2009).

As long as the conflict situation continues between the Forest Department and the community, one cannot hope to preserve India's forests. Forests can be protected only by the people with the help of a social fence. The forest dependent communities have to find a vested interest in preserving forests. That is possible only when their basic requirements on which they still depend like – food, medicinal, fuel and fodder requirements are met. And, at the same time, they are also involved in decision-making related to management of the forests. People's livelihood and conservation are the twin objectives of forests and both should be safeguarded. The law has to make provision for these imperatives by delineating property rights in their favour. Property rights determine the allocation of a society's resources to its individuals. In other words, they determine the distribution of wealth. Laws governing property form a bundle of rights. Thus, the key question becomes: not who gets all the rights (person, state or community) but rather who gets what rights, for how long, and under what conditions. So, an examination and analysis of forest legislation is imperative for an understanding of India's forest policy, especially as legislation has significantly contributed to the process of degradation.

It is our contention that as long as the law related to forests remains unchanged, the trend in degradation of India's forests will continue and reversals, if any will be temporary. In other words, JFM is not the panacea to save India's forests, but a positive step in the ultimate process of decentralization of decision-making and building up of the institutional framework for meaningful preservation and efficient use of the forests … . A meaningful conservation can be expected only when a community is given property rights over the forests and, thus, rights on extraction from the ecosystem they conserve. 'Multiple stakeholder negotiations' must be accepted as the way out (Hazra, 2002). More than hundred years of state policy has resulted affecting the life of the people dependent on forests. They have destroyed the symbiotic relationship or whatever they had built over a period of time in relation to the forest without providing effective alternatives. If decisions and institutions related to forest management are to be fully participative and inclusive, community's role is very important.

References

Balooni, K. and M. Inoue (2009), 'Joint Forest Management in India: The Management Change Process', *IIBM Management Review*, March, Vol. 21, No. 1, pp. 1–17.

Chaudhary, S.N. (1997), 'Tribal, Forests and Markets in India: Some Conceptual and Empirical Issues', *Madhya Pradesh Journal of Social Sciences*, Vol. 2, No. 2, pp. 69–91.

Government of India (1990), Government of India Resolution No. 6–21/89-FP, 1 June.

Guha, R. (1983), 'Forestry in British and Post-British India: A Historical Analysis', *Economic and Political Weekly*, Vol. 20, Nos. 45–47, pp. 1882–96.

——(1989), *The Unquiet Woods: Ecological Change and Peasants Resistance in the Himalaya*, New Delhi: Oxford University Press and Berkeley, CA: University of California Press.

Gadgil, Madhav and Ramachandra Guha (1992), *The Fissured Land: An Ecological History of India*, New Delhi: Oxford University Press.

——(1994), 'Ecological Conflict and the Environmental Movement in India', *Development and Change*, Vol. 25, No. 1, pp. 101–36.

Hannan, K. (1999), 'Environmental Management in India: Recent Challenges to the Indian Forest Service', *Journal of Environmental Planning and Management*, Vol. 42, pp. 221–33.

Hazra, Arnab (2002), 'History of Conflict Over Forests in India: A Market Based Resolution', Working Paper Series, New Delhi: Julian L. Simon Centre for Policy Research, Liberty Institute, April.

Kant, S. and R. Cooke (1999), 'Minimizing Conflict in Joint Forest Management, Jabalpur District, Madhya Pradesh, India', in D. Buckles (ed.), *Cultivating Peace: Conflict and Collaboration in Natural Resource Management*, Ottawa, Canada: International Development Research Centre, pp. 81–100.

Ministry of Environment and Forests (1988), *The National Forest Policy*, New Delhi: Government of India.

——(2013), *India State of Forest Report 2013*, New Delhi: Forest Survey of India, Government of India.

Sarin, Madhu (1996), 'Who is Gaining? Who is Losing? Gender and Equity Concerns in Joint Forest Management', Working Paper by the Gender and Equity Sub-group, New Delhi: National Support Group for JFM, Society for Wasteland Development.

Springate-Baginski, O. et al. (2009), 'Redressing "Historical Injustice" through the Indian Forest Right Act 2006: A Historical Institutional Analysis of Contemporary Forest Rights Reform', Discussion Paper Series, IPPG Discussion Paper, www.ippg.org.uk.

Vemuri, Anuradha (2008), 'Joint Forest Management in India: An Unavoidable and Conflicting Common Property Regime in Natural Resource Management', *Journal of Development and Social Transformation*, Vol. 5, pp. 81–90.

Index

OK